CW01081415

GOTHIC REMAINS

SERIES PREFACE

Gothic Literary Studies is dedicated to publishing groundbreaking scholarship on Gothic in literature and film. The Gothic, which has been subjected to a variety of critical and theoretical approaches, is a form which plays an important role in our understanding of literary, intellectual and cultural histories. The series seeks to promote challenging and innovative approaches to Gothic which question any aspect of the Gothic tradition or perceived critical orthodoxy. Volumes in the series explore how issues such as gender, religion, nation and sexuality have shaped our view of the Gothic tradition. Both academically rigorous and informed by the latest developments in critical theory, the series provides an important focus for scholarly developments in Gothic studies, literary studies, cultural studies and critical theory. The series will be of interest to students of all levels and to scholars and teachers of the Gothic and literary and cultural histories.

SERIES EDITORS

Andrew Smith, University of Sheffield
Benjamin F. Fisher, University of Mississippi

EDITORIAL BOARD

Kent Ljungquist, Worcester Polytechnic Institute Massachusetts
Richard Fusco, St Joseph's University, Philadelphia
David Punter, University of Bristol
Chris Baldick, University of London
Angela Wright, University of Sheffield
Jerrold E. Hogle, University of Arizona

For all titles in the Gothic Literary Studies series
visit *www.uwp.co.uk*

Gothic Remains

Corpses, Terror and Anatomical Culture, 1764–1897

by

Laurence Talairach

UNIVERSITY OF WALES PRESS
2019

www.uwp.co.uk

British Library Cataloguing-in-Publication Data
A catalogue record for this book is available from the British Library.

ISBN   978-1-78683-460-7
e-ISBN 978-1-78683-461-4

The right of Laurence Talairach to be identified as author of this work has been asserted by her in accordance with sections 77 and 79 of the Copyright, Designs and Patents Act 1988.

Typeset in Wales by Eira Fenn Gaunt, Pentyrch, Cardiff
Printed by CPI Antony Rowe, Melksham

In memory of my grandmother, Andrée Wiedemann (1916–2009), with love.

CONTENTS

ACKNOWLEDGEMENTS

It was on a Sunday morning that my grandmother died the first time. She was declared dead by the doctor who was on duty that day. Nevertheless, as her family gathered to prepare her funeral, she suddenly resurrected, wondering what people were doing in her bedroom, fumbling about for her personal papers. She died a second, and final, time a few days later.

Her medical misdiagnosis, and the idea that she might have been buried alive, were sources of inspiration during the years it took me to write this book. *Gothic Remains: Corpses, Terror and Anatomical Culture, 1764–1897* was thus spurred, in part, by a terrifying fear of, and a macabre fascination with, live burial, ignited by my grandmother's medical history which was hardly exorcised by the many tales of terror I have feasted on since that 18 October 2009. *Gothic Remains* also results from my unflagging interest in everything 'medical', both as a former medical student and as a literary scholar examining the relationships between literature and medicine in the nineteenth century, as developed in *Wilkie Collins, Medicine and the Gothic* (University of Wales Press, 2009). In addition to encountering inspiring dead-yet-alive relatives, I have been very fortunate in the last eight years to meet and work with many scholars and artists from around the world who shared a taste for anatomical culture, and I would like to acknowledge my debt to them, as this book would have been very different had my path never crossed theirs.

The idea behind *Gothic Remains* started with a series of conferences I organised and co-organised in London, Paris and Toulouse between 2011 and 2013, as part of the larger EXPLORA collaborative research project. This initiative involved the Toulouse Museum of Natural History and was supported by several research centres from the University of Toulouse Jean Jaurès, notably the CAS research centre (EA 801) and FRAMESPA (UMR 5136). One of the first events around anatomical culture was held in December 2011 at the Toulouse Museum of Natural History and the Museum of the History of Medicine, where I presented a paper on Dr Ledoux's '[s]hapeless dead creatures . . . float[ing] in yellow liquid' in Wilkie Collins's *Armadale*. This furthered my previous work on Collins by focusing exclusively on references to anatomy and dissection. This two-day conference was followed by a second, in June 2012, held at the University of Toulouse Jean Jaurès ('L'Anatomiste et son cadavre: Corps, médecine et éthique, XVIe–XXIe siècle'), where I gave a paper on body-snatchers in the nineteenth century ('Le Marché aux cadavres: Résurrectionnistes et littérature britannique au XIXe siècle').

These conferences and reflections on human remains paved the way for an ambitious three-part project co-organised with Rafael Mandressi, and held at the Toulouse Museum of Natural History ('Medical Museums and Anatomical Collections', February 2013), the Academy of Medicine in Paris ('Anatomical Models', April 2013) and the Hunterian Museum (Royal College of Surgeons) in London ('Exhibiting Human Remains', June 2013). My sincerest thanks go to Samuel Alberti, Francis Duranthon and Jérôme van Wijland – then directors respectively of the Hunterian Museum (RSC), the Toulouse Museum of Natural History and the library of the Academy of Medicine – for welcoming and supporting the conferences and providing a stimulating venue where scholars and artists could exchange ideas. Moreover, the one-day conference at the Hunterian Museum would not have been possible without the generous support of the British Society for Literature and Science. I would like to thank the Society for advancing literature and science studies and continually encouraging new scholars in the field. I am also indebted to my co-organiser, Rafael Mandressi, who, as a historian of medicine, introduced me to new methodologies and with whom I later co-wrote an article on the history of anatomical models. Trips to the Dupuytren Museum with Rafael, or to the dermatological wax moulages of the Saint-Louis Hospital in Paris, with Jérôme, were integral to the preparation of these events, nurturing my interest in the (bleak) future of anatomical collections.

Furthermore, the international scholars and artists who were involved in the 'Human Remains' series, and who travelled from across Europe and America to Toulouse, Paris and London, made working on death and corpses a much more cheerful activity than I would have believed. This was highlighted by Joanna Ebenstein's enthusiasm for 'Morbid Anatomy' and Kelley Swain's reading on wax models at King's College London, as well as visits to the Gordon Museum of Pathology at that institution. I am very grateful to them for creating such a vibrant community of scholars and making research on cadavers and death so much fun.

Among the many artists I encountered, I was also lucky to meet Valentina Lari, then working at the Old Operating Theatre in London. We embarked on a short film and exhibition focusing on the anatomical collections of the Toulouse medical school where I had worked as a medical student twenty-five years before. Throughout the making of the film (*Liminality*, 2014), my contact with anatomical collections and my attempts to trace the identity and history of some of the objects on display, slowly falling into oblivion, increased my desire to spread the word about the future of anatomical collections. Valentina Lari's artistic rendering of the beauty of models and remains left to decompose continually haunted me as I explored their voyage into Gothic texts and nineteenth-century culture more generally.

Furthermore, a large part of the research I performed on live burials in Gothic texts would have been impossible without a collaborative research project involving Martin Willis, then Chair of Science, Literature and Communication in the Department of English at the University of Westminster, between 2013 and 2014. 'Cultural Catalepsy' examined representations of catalepsy in the nineteenth century on both sides of the Channel. It was generously funded by the University of Westminster, and sections of Chapter 5 reflect many of the conclusions that Martin and I then drew on seizures, as found in British and French medical literature and literary fiction.

Throughout the years, my reflections on the traffic between literature and science have been informed by the many discussions I had with John Pickstone. I met John in January 2011 during an international conference on the history of cancer from 1750 to

1950, at the University of Toulouse Jean Jaurès. His many encouragements and dry sense of humour are sadly missed. Among the Gothicists who helped me throughout the years, listened to my endless questions and always provided answers, and to whom I owe so much, David Punter, Victor Sage and Andrew Smith stand out; without them this book would certainly never have come to fruition. Mariaconcetta Costantini and Gilles Menegaldo, who both regularly organised conferences and panels and invited me to present papers, are also warmly thanked, alongside Fred Botting, Andrew Mangham, Catherine Spooner and the many other Gothicists who invited me to write papers and generally haunt the International Gothic Association conferences.

Gothic Remains has also benefited from field work performed at the Wellcome Library and British Library regularly funded by my research centre, the Alexandre Koyré Centre for the History of Science and Technology (UMR 8560). I thank the executive committee and administrative staff for enabling the reading of long-forgotten ghastly tales of terror when one lives on the other side of the Channel.

Lastly, my most sincere thanks go to Neil Davie. This book originally comprised so many pieces which refused to be stitched together to form a whole body that I often thought about burying them all for ever. Neil agreed to read the whole manuscript, bit by bit, and helped me throughout. He provided advice on my written English as well as very insightful comments on content and suggestions for additional references. I owe him more than I can say for his kindness and patience, and for his erudite knowledge on the history of prisons, prisoners and prisoner's bodies.

Several chapters of *Gothic Remains* include portions of papers delivered at various conferences, such as at the ESSE Congress, held at Bogazici University in Istanbul, Turkey, in September 2012 ('Deceiving the Anatomist's Gaze: Poisons, Sensations and the Gothic'); at the CUSVE (Centro Universitario di Studi Vittoriani e Edoardiani) conference, 'Victorian and Neo-Victorian Aesthetics: Texts, Theories, and the Paths of Imagination', held at the University G. d'Annunzio di Chieti-Pescara, in Italy ('Wonder and Horror in Victorian Medical Gothic'), in October 2015, and at the second International Conference on Science and Literature, in

Pöllau, Austria, held in September 2016 ('Medical Practice and the Gothic (1790–1820)'). Sections from former papers delivered in French have also been developed, informed by study days organised by French historians of medicine at Aix-Marseille University in September 2012 ('Du cadavre en putréfaction au corps enterré vivant: Le rôle du corps mort chez Wilkie Collins').

Sections of this book draw on the following articles: 'Morbid Taste, Morbid Anatomy and Victorian Popular Literature', in Mariaconcetta Costantini (ed.), 'Victorian Literature and the Aesthetic Impure', *English Literature*, 2/2 (December 2015), 257–74; '"I have bottled babes unborn": The Gothic, Medical Collections and Nineteenth-Century Culture', in Sara Wasson (ed.), 'Gothic and Medical Humanities', special edition of *Gothic Studies*, 17/1 (2015), 28–42; '"In All its Hideous and Appalling Nakedness and Truth": The Reception of Some Anatomical Collections in Georgian and Victorian England', in 'Bodies and Anatomy: The Corpse in the Museum from Ruysch to Von Hagens', *Medicina nei Secoli*, 27/2 (2015), 553–74; 'The "ghastly waxwork at the fair": Charles Dickens's Sleeping Beauty in *Great Expectations*', in Béatrice Laurent (ed.), *Sleeping Beauties in Victorian Britain: Cultural, Literary and Artistic Explorations of a Myth* (Bern and Oxford: Peter Lang, 2014), pp. 53–72; 'Gruesome Models: European Anatomical Culture and Nineteenth-Century Literature', in Andrew Smith and Anna Barton (eds), *Rethinking the Nineteenth Century* (Manchester: Manchester University Press, 2017), pp. 149–66. I am grateful to the editors of these books and journals for permission to use this material.

This book is dedicated to my grandmother, Andrée Wiedemann (21 December 1916–21 October 2009), who might have well found her name in the tales of terror of John Galt, Samuel Warren or Edgar Allan Poe, had she been born a little earlier.

1

Introduction

At the end of Samuel Richardson's *Clarissa; or, the History of a Young Lady* (1747–8), Lovelace, seeing Clarissa escaping him through death, decides to have her body embalmed, while preserving her heart in spirit in order to keep it forever in sight. Lovelace's urge to preserve Clarissa Harlowe's body, if only in parts, recalls many eighteenth- and nineteenth-century representations of the female corpse, stereotypically white and pure, immaculate, denying bodily dissolution.[1] Like Sleeping Beauties evading decomposition, the female dead of the eighteenth and nineteenth centuries offer a striking illustration of the romantic construction of the corpse, crystallised in death. But such petrification could also have a darker side to it, for surgeons like those hired by Lovelace did not limit their activities to cutting up, preserving and exhibiting human body parts for distraught lovers. Inspired by the contemporary reality of the mid-eighteenth century, Richardson's image recalls the era's fascination with and interest in the inside of the body – a fascination and interest which went beyond medical inquiry but was still rooted in developments in the field of medicine throughout the eighteenth and nineteenth centuries.

As *Gothic Remains: Corpses, Terror and Anatomical Culture, 1764– 1897* will argue, the development of the practice of anatomy, and especially the central part it would come to play in medical education in the course of the eighteenth and nineteenth centuries, informed the Gothic texts of the period in myriad ways. Indeed, while Richardson's sentimental fiction reflected changes in the definition and uses of the human body in the eighteenth century, so did the Gothic a few decades later. Both genres highlighted the imaginative impact and growing power of medical science and scientific knowledge in general. More particularly, as this book will aim to demonstrate, a close reading of the Gothic literature of the period reveals the extent to which knowlege about the living was intertwined with, dependent on, and ultimately inseparable from knowledge about death, which included managing, dissecting and, on occasion, preserving corpses. In her insightful study of the Romantic period, Sharon Ruston has shown that, as science was beginning to get more professionalised and institutionalised, science and medicine played a crucial role 'in the creation of what we now, anachronistically, call "Romanticism"'.[2] For Ann Jessie Van Sant, moreover, the notion of sensibility in the eighteenth century stood at the crossroads of physiological and psychological investigations. Van Sant notes that mental and emotional experience were being redefined throughout the period, often blurring in the process 'physical and psychological states, . . . interior experience and interior function'.[3] In this context, Karl Figlio offers the valuable insight that '[p]hysiological investigation focused on the nervous system as the bridge between the physiological/psychological inquiry into the soul and nature of man and animals on the one hand, and the anatomical/physiological study of their structure and function on the other'.[4]

It is easy to understand why the senses played such a significant part in debates around the question of sensibility. Richardson's emphasis on his heroines' feelings, emotions or even suffering in his sentimental novels, just like the feelings, emotions and sufferings of the Gothic heroines of the late eighteenth century, were all literary products of a period which painstakingly explored sensibility and the senses. Thus, if Gothic writers like Ann Radcliffe warned readers about the dangers of excessive sensibility, they also drew very much upon the medical discourses and practices of their time.

G. J. Baker-Benfield's study of the culture of sensibility in eighteenth-century Britain foregrounds the part played by sentimental fiction in the popularisation of sensational psychology. In particular, he illuminates the links between Samuel Richardson and his doctor, George Cheyne (1671–1743), to explain how the physiological dimension of sensibility lay at the heart of Richardson's sentimental fiction. As Edmund Burke had argued in his 1757 treatise *The Philosophical Origins of the Sublime and the Beautiful*, pain and fear were to be measured according to the tension they produced on the nerves, and this concept was reflected in the fiction of the period. The 'nerves', 'fibres', 'sensations' and 'impressions' of patients and characters alike testified to their sensibility – and therefore to their humanity. Similarly, the stress on 'vibrations' or 'thrills', emblematic of 'the nerve paradigm of the culture of sensibility',[5] pervaded the writings of the time, from Burke's essay to later Gothic novels. In Ann Radcliffe's *The Mysteries of Udolpho* (1794), for example, Emily's father 'listen[s] with thrilling delight to the mystic murmuring of the woods'[6] and Valancourt's heart is 'thrill[ed]' by Emily's voice (p. 193), whilst the heroine's nerves are 'thrilled . . . with horror' (p. 250), when she is not overwhelmed by a 'thrilling curiosity' (p. 356) to discover more about the mysteries of the castle.

Incidentally, Barker-Benfield's tracing of the occurrence of such terms in eighteenth-century fiction and their link with sensational physiology highlights important connections with the world of anatomy. As he underlines, terms such as 'string', for example, 'had for centuries meant muscle, acquiring the meaning of nerve only during the previous century (with the rise of dissection)' – a trope which Radcliffe uses to 'describe sounds vibrating on her heroine's heart'.[7] Similarly, in Mrs Carver's *The Old Woman* (1800) the stress is laid on the heroine's feelings, metaphorised by strings and chords vibrating: throughout the novel, '[t]he more [the heroine] trie[s] to suppress her feelings, the more conspicuous they appear [–] . . . touch but the tender string, and the vibration extends to all the soft chords, and beats with fond emotion'.[8]

The Gothic novel, or Gothic romance, which emerged in 1764 with the publication of Horace Walpole's *The Castle of Otranto*, was then but an extreme form of the genre of sentimental fiction, albeit one which wore out the nerves of heroines and readers alike. And, just like the fictional forms which had preceded it, the Gothic partook of the feelings and ethos of sensibility that characterised the eighteenth century. The first encounter with Radcliffe's heroine in *The Romance of the Forest* (1791) is that of a young woman who 'seem[s] to suffer the utmost distress'.[9] In *The Old Woman*, the text plays recurrently upon the heroine's 'suffering',[10] whilst the epistolary form of the novel strengthens its links with Richardson's sentimental novels. Animal welfare is even used to reflect the character's good character or humanity (p. 91) and contrast it with the villainesses who do not hesitate to wish death on those around them (pp. 108, 211). The Radcliffean female characters are also invited to hone their senses to find their way throughout the maze-like and ruined castles in which they are imprisoned, driven by their curiosity and an insatiable desire for knowledge. Through their narratives and (female) characters, therefore, the Gothic writers of the early phase (1764–1824) participated in the 'verbal and visual discourse of emotion, closeness to nature, and humane feeling'[11] that suffused the culture of sensibility. In addition, their overt display of emotion, inviting readers to vicariously experience their characters' suffering, was also much indebted to the physiologists and anatomists of the time. Gazing on suffering could enable men of science to acquire knowledge; hence, numerous experiments were carried out on animals and humans alike with a view to observing the body's sensibility. Titles of treatises like Robert Whytt's *Observations on the Sensibility and Irritability of the Parts of Men and Other Animals* (1768) or Albrecht von Haller's *A Dissertation on the Sensible and Irritable Parts of Animals* (1755) suggest how much the senses and sensations were being explored and tested by natural philosophers, and how sensibility as a whole infused the practice of the sciences in general.

The idea that suffering could be both 'dramatic spectacle and scientific investigation',[12] and that sensibility could simultaneously mean 'sympathetic identification and objective scrutiny',[13] defines eighteenth-century novelists such as Samuel Richardson as scientific investigators of human psychology who used methods not that far from those of the physiologists and anatomists of the time, then exploring the interiority of the human body. In his search for the 'concealed "material" of the heart',[14] Richardson anatomised his characters by exposing them to sustained suffering, exactly as a vivisectionist would do, and researchers have shown how much his writings were influenced by medical writings, as suggested above. As a consequence, the image of Lovelace holding Clarissa's heart in spirit (in both senses of that phrase) encapsulates Richardson's literary project: the sentimental novelist offers the observer or reader access to the inner sanctuary of the female character's heart and places her heart within reach, as if it had been dissected. The literary motif thus collapses the boundaries between the psychological and the physiological or anatomical, and in so doing blurs the distinctions between the novelist and the anatomist.

Following in the footsteps of sentimental literature, the Gothic contributed to the era's attempt at 'visualizing the invisible interior of the body', in Anne Vila's terms, showing thereby that sensibility was not limited to the medical and ethical realms and that 'the physio-philosophy of sensibility was not without a certain aesthetic dimension of its own right'.[15] By emblematising the search for the inner truth to which anatomists claimed to have access, Gothic texts consistently mapped out how '[t]he flesh was brought down to the level of organism'.[16] Like sentimental fiction, the Gothic capitalised upon the 'formation of the modern self',[17] yet offered 'a code for the representation and working out of anxieties regarding the self's nature'[18] which extended far beyond the end of the eighteenth century. In doing so, as will be argued in this book, the Gothic did more than simply disseminate new constructions of the body in light of the development of modern techniques of dissection, initiated by Andreas Vesalius (1514–64) over two hundred years earlier. Through using what Robert Miles terms the 'forms, devices, codes, figurations, for the expression of the "fragmented subject"',[19] Gothic texts articulated fears related to the modern self and the self's nature with the very same tools used by the scientific explorers of the body in the same period. This is why *Gothic Remains* will reveal how the spectacularisation of such anxieties about the nature of the self borrowed heavily from anatomical culture – a 'modern' sub-field of medicine which itself became increasingly, as Caroline McCracken-Flesher argues, 'a spectacle that expressed itself as gothically animated display'.[20] Gothic characters and readers experienced what Roy Porter calls 'the penetrative curiosity of the scalpel' and the idea that '[o]nce within the anatomy theatre, the corpse ceased to be inviolable and taboo, and carnal knowledge was no longer forbidden',[21] thus allowing them to share common practices with the anatomists. Hence, *Gothic Remains* will examine these common practices, tracing intellectual lineages and proposing a genealogy of some of the Gothic texts which marked the eighteenth and nineteenth centuries.[22]

As will be seen, however, the Gothic explored this 'resurrect[ion] of the body in a more secular guise'[23] in very specific ways, investigating the nature of humankind just as much as did eighteenth-century thinkers, philosophers or politicians. In so doing, it contributed to the elaboration of new ways of thinking about, representing and exploring humankind. Following Porter's study of 'the triangle of the moral, the material and the medical in the anglophone Enlightenment',[24] *Gothic Remains* aims to delineate how the Gothic participated from its origins in the debate around this triangle, 'in the light of changing beliefs about man's place in nature and human nature'.[25] This is why this book will analyse the genealogy of one branch of the Gothic – medical Gothic – from the first Gothic novels to late-Victorian Gothic. It will trace anatomical culture in Gothic texts from Walpole to Stoker, ending in the last decades of the nineteenth century, a period which saw the publication of Stevenson's *Strange Case of Dr Jekyll and Mr Hyde* (1886), in which the laboratory replaced the surgical theatre (thus swapping anatomy for chemistry), and H. G. Wells's *The Invisible Man* (1897) – the latter work being visibly influenced by Wilhelm Röntgen's invention of the X-ray in 1895, a technique which dethroned dissection as the unique means of access to knowledge of human anatomy.

This book will explore, then, how, from the mid-eighteenth century to the last decades of the Victorian period, the Gothic developed and evolved alongside the medical profession. The period saw the establishment of the largest medical collections, and in a parallel development anatomy became central in medical education and pivotal to the construction of medical knowledge. A number of highly influential anatomical textbooks were also published in these years, including Henry Gray's *Anatomy, Descriptive and Surgical*, in 1858. The eighteenth and nineteenth centuries witnessed as well an increasing commodification of the human corpse. A number of laws passed in the same period reflected these changes in the medical profession. As Elizabeth T. Hurren has shown, the rise of the medical profession and of medical knowledge was closely bound up with the development of the body trade, a trade which gave rise to numerous ghastly and hair-raising resurrection tales in the same period. Three significant pieces of new legislation were passed in the nineteenth century: the Anatomy Act of 1832, which allowed the dissection of the poorest; the Poor Law Amendment Act of 1834, which decreed that workhouses should hand over unreclaimed corpses for dissection; and finally the Medical Act of 1858, which not only more clearly defined the medical profession,[26] but also 'gave anatomists the official power to buy human material generated by a body trade to teach medical students'.[27] Increasingly, the place occupied by anatomy in medical education and practice made such human material 'a valuable commodity',[28] a fact which explains why the medical world contained all the ingredients needed to thrill, terrify or horrify readers: it dealt with the body – dead, stolen, open, violated – with crime and with death.

It is easy to perceive, through this evolving legislation and the changing structure and role of the medical profession, how anatomy, which had frequently been used since the seventeenth-century as a metaphor, gained, as it were, corporeality. As Richard Sugg has shown, anatomy became part and parcel of British culture towards the end of the sixteenth century; the 'uses of dissective rhetoric appear[ing] not merely fashionable but highly compulsive, sometimes lacking an integral semantic motivation to the extent that the body must be seen as actively invading the English literary imagination'.[29] Robert Burton's *Anatomy of Melancholy* (1621) is a case in point. It illustrates the rise of a 'literary anatomy',[30] and shows how the practice of anatomy had become a cultural phenomenon, reflecting the period's 'ways of knowing', to borrow John Pickstone's phrase.[31] In the second half of the eighteenth century, as Maggie Kilgour has argued, Gothic writers such as William Godwin often compared the novelist to a scholar carrying out scientific analysis: 'All talent may perhaps be affirmed to consist in analysis and dissection'.[32] In Kilgour's view, Godwin's aim in *Caleb William* (1794) is 'to dissect character to expose motives, Caleb becom[ing] a fiendish author, a psychological spy and torturer who, by vivisecting every action and word, aims at a demonic revelation'.[33]

Interestingly, in the literary examples to be examined in *Gothic Remains*, covering the period between 1764 and 1897, Gothic texts play recurrently upon the literal *and* metaphorical meanings of such activities as anatomising. The Gothic thus lays bare and performs autopsies upon its characters and/or society in general – in every sense of those words. Furthermore, the Gothic itself appears as an anatomised genre, a genre made up of parts rather than a whole, of motifs roughly stitched together for the sake of terror or horror, and which appeared – especially from the 1790s, when the Minerva Press in London first brought Gothic romances to a wide audience – to stand on their own in self-reflexive narratives which playfully reproduced clichéd conventions. In addition, from the origins of the Gothic, tales of terror did not simply illuminate the threat represented by medical science. They pinpointed as well how the art of medicine was increasingly based upon a practical knowledge, based largely upon the practitioner's comprehension of, and skills in, anatomy. In other words, physiological and pathological know-ledge became indissociable from the medical practitioner's manual dexterity. A quick glance at seminal Gothic romances of the first Gothic wave, from Walpole's *The Castle of Otranto* and Clara Reeve's *The Old English Baron* (1778) to Ann Radcliffe's *The Romance of the Forest* (1791), shows that medical men feature in the narratives, narratives which frequently provide readers with many different types of medical practitioner and bind medical practice to the creation of narrative tension. Such medical figures often hold the lives and/or deaths of the leading characters in their hands. They advise, heal (or fail to), misdiagnose or even provoke death; some 'resurrect' characters by applying electricity to corpses. All deal with, study and speculate on death, often, in so doing, exploring the issue of the existence and nature of the soul.

As Kilgour has underlined, the emergence of the Gothic in the eighteenth century has often been read 'as a sign of the resurrection of the need for the sacred and transcendent in a modern enlightened secular world which denies the existence of supernatural forces, or as the rebellion of the imagination against the tyranny of reason'.[34] As this book will show, the medical field, notably medical practice and the rising significance of anatomy in the education of the physicians, surgeons and even apothecaries who made up the medical profession, became a favourite subject for writers, who found in Gothic medicine the essence of the modern enlightened – material – world. The Gothic was part of what Kilgour terms 'the reaction against the political, social, scientific, industrial, and epistemological revolutions of the seventeenth and eighteenth centuries',[35] and offered a nightmarish vision of the modern world, one which 'depict[ed] the individual as fragmented, as alienated from others and ultimately from himself'.[36] Thus, *Gothic Remains* will emphasise how much the Gothic, as a product of its time, played with the codes and conventions informing the representation of the modern, 'fragmented', or dissected, self that emerged at the end of the eighteenth century and took shape throughout the following one.

As will be seen, the Gothic, as a product of Romanticism, has always been fascinated with objects carrying with them a sense of horror – the decomposing body, the rigid corpse, the bleeding statue, the spectral skeleton – capable of creating a sublime form of beauty. Thus, *Gothic Remains* will explore those Gothic tropes and conventions which were most thoroughly steeped in the anatomical culture of the period. From skeletons, used to understand human anatomy, to pathological human remains exhibited in medical museums; from body-snatching, aimed at providing dissection subjects, to live burials resulting from medical misdiagnosis and pointing to contemporary research into the signs of death. The web of motifs borrowed from the field of anatomical culture is not always easy to disentangle. Anatomical models, both natural and artificial, just like pathological specimens, could all be found in medical museums, while corpses stolen by body-snatchers were sometimes 'resurrected' on the anatomist's table or not really dead. All these tropes, moreover, emphasise the uses and abuses of bodies and cadavers in a context of the development of the 'modern' medical profession, a profession which placed anatomy at the heart of its education, knowledge and practice. These tropes also cast valuable light on the increasing fragmentation and commodification of the body – and of the self.

An attempt has been made, however, to separate these entangled motifs, albeit artificially on occasion, and to situate each within its context, so as to offer a historicist reading of canonical and less known Gothic texts, explored through the prism of anatomy. When more obscure or less familiar works are studied, plot summaries are provided so as to highlight more effectively the pervasiveness of some objects and their multiple interpretations or uses. In each chapter, moreover, a (generally) chronological structure has been preferred in order to frame what Michael Sappol terms 'an anatomical gothic', thus highlighting how the medical world and the Gothic make use of similar elements and tropes, notably related to life, death and the boundaries of the self.[37] Following the trajectories of the Gothic from its origins to the end of the nineteenth century throughout the chapters, *Gothic Remains* covers therefore almost 150 years of Gothic writing, and seeks to offer new insights into the ways in which medical practice and the medical sciences informed the aesthetics of pain and death typically found in Gothic texts, and the two-way traffic that emerged between medical literature and literary texts.

This study starts with one of the most iconic of Gothic tropes – the skeleton. In the first wave of Gothic romances (1764–1824), the skeleton often partakes of the Gothic quest/plot. As a stereotypically baroque and allegorical representation of Death, the skeleton nonetheless also emblematises the materiality of the human cadaver. To illuminate this issue, chapter 1 examines the various meanings of the skeleton by following the evolution of the skeleton-in-the-trunk motif, as a potent illustration of the Gothic's terrifying 'objects'. Looking at those Gothic romances which reworked Clara Reeve's original use of the skeleton-in-the-trunk motif in *The Old English Baron*, this chapter highlights how the skeleton is used to generate feelings of horror, terror or/and pity, but also how the motif drives the narrative search for identity, thus offering a literal reading of the quest for the *naked* truth. Indeed, we will see that as both allegorical and scientific objects, the skeletons found in Ann Radcliffe's *The Romance of the Forest* (1791), Mrs Carver's *The Horrors of Oakendale Abbey* (1797), and *The Animated Skeleton* (1798) are human remains which borrow from the anatomical culture of their time and hint at modern constructions of the human subject.

Chapter 2 focuses on artificial anatomical models, thereby furthering the exploration of objects typically used to emblematise terror and/or horror. The chapter illuminates how wax, a motif found repeatedly in Gothic texts, stands as a symbol of the Enlightenment quest for knowledge. As a matter of fact, wax was used to fashion models of the human body; models which could be used as teaching aids for future medical professionals or might alternatively be exhibited to a wider audience in medical museums. As this chapter shows, Ann Radcliffe's *The Mysteries of Udolpho* (1794), Mary Shelley's *Frankenstein* (1818), George Brewer's *The Witch of Ravensworth* (1808) and Charles Dickens's *Great Expectations* (1861) all use wax at significant moments, and each illustrates how wax interrogates the relationship between life and death and touches on the representation of the corpse (especially the female corpse) and the fabrication of horror; a reflection on the self which particularly suited the Gothic sensibility.

The commodification of the human self, illustrated by the changing role of the skeleton, as seen in chapter 1, will be analysed further in chapter 3, which looks at the impact of body-snatching both in the making of medical collections and in the development of the tale of terror. Linked to the shortage of corpses for dissection, body-snatching was inseparable from the onset from a more empirical attitude to the practice of medicine. This chapter will seek to demonstrate that despite the passage of legislation regulating the uses of the human body,[38] the Gothic figure of the body-snatcher was not destined to oblivion. On the contrary, resurrectionists would continue to haunt nineteenth-century Gothic texts, from Blackwoodian tales of terror to Robert Louis Stevenson's 'The Body-Snatcher', published in 1884. However, this chapter argues that the figure of the resurrectionist found in mid-Victorian fiction, such as in the urban Gothic of W. M. Reynolds and Charles Dickens, conveys a discourse on the self which is significantly different from both earlier and later examples. In fact, it will be seen that the meanings of the body-snatcher shifted considerably over time, constantly revisiting and reworking the literary cliché.

The development of pathological anatomy, as chapter 4 underlines, marched hand in hand with the establishment of medical collections. The growth of such collections in the course of the eighteenth and nineteenth centuries, as well as the interest in, and display of, monsters, were reflected in the Gothic writing of the period. The Gothic villain certainly 'fitted naturally into the general taste of the period',[39] as Mario Praz has suggested. Yet the medical museum, by exhibiting nameless patients as mere pieces of matter, also raised the issue of medical ethics – spurring fears related to the definition of the human subject. Thus, chapter 4 follows the making and unmaking of medical collections and public anatomical museums in the context of the proliferation of initiatives aimed at controlling sexual behaviour. It examines Gothic texts, from Mary Shelley's *Frankenstein* (1818) to Wilkie Collins's *Armadale* (1864), looking at constructions of the self in the short stories of Samuel Warren and Silas Weir Mitchell as well as in the fiction of Charles Dickens. As will be suggested, the commodification of the corpse and of the human body at large was condemned and often subverted in such texts which used the medical museum to metaphorise 'the horrible vulnerability of the flesh',[40] while at the same time foregrounding how the cutting of flesh yielded no answer.

From the traffic in dead bodies examined in chapter 3, chapter 5 turns to the study of the changing conceptions of the corpse and of death over the course of the eighteenth and nineteenth centuries. The substantial medical literature devoted to distinguishing real from apparent death (and thus defining mortality clinically) was part of a broader enterprise aimed at constructing the corpse as a scientific object. At the same time, however, medical periodicals, popular magazines and literature more generally regularly channelled anxiety about premature interment. Indeed, live-burial metaphors became a staple of the Gothic. Through focusing on the inter-connections between medical literature and Gothic texts, especially through the use of actual medical cases, this chapter looks at represen-tations of death-like states throughout the nineteenth century, from the cataleptic patients depicted in the short stories of John Galt, Samuel Warren and Edgar Allan Poe, to those of Catherine Crowe and G. W. M. Reynolds at mid-century. It explores also the links between abnormal states of consciousness and work on the reflex actions of the brain, showing how figures of cataleptic patients, like other types of automatic behaviours or dual personalities, staged a fragmented subject which suited Gothic representations of the modern self, as Wilkie Collins's late fiction exemplifies. The chapter closes with a study of Bram Stoker's *Dracula* (1897), whose vampire, as Andrew Smith has argued, functions 'as an image of a living corpse',[41] a striking reflection of *fin-de-siècle* epistemological reflections on death.

As *Gothic Remains* argues, therefore, the genre's 'assorted pieces . . . [which] often seem to disintegrate into fragments', its 'tendency towards dismemberment', and its 'series of framed conventions, static moments of extreme emotions . . . which do not form a coherent and continuous whole',[42] make of the Gothic a striking reflection of the anatomical culture of its day. As a ghastly museum of terrifying objects – from the skeleton and other human remains exhibited in medical collections to the vampire's body which refuses to decompose – the Gothic digs up, resurrects and dissects society, probing the nature and construction of the human self and reflecting upon the nature of the soul and the afterlife. Seen through the prism of anatomical culture, the skeletons, statues, body-snatchers and live burials, for all their conventional forms, succeed in capturing the complex trajectory of the Gothic form. Ultimately, *Gothic Remains* demonstrates that although often dismissed as 'a highly wrought, artificial form , . . . extremely self-conscious of its artificiality and creation out of old material and traditions',[43] the Gothic none-theless continues to slice, gouge and chop into the flesh of the present in myriad and often unexpected ways.

material Gothic
'body horror'

1

Rattling Bones: The Skeleton in the Trunk

୶

The last part of William Hogarth's *The Four Stages of Cruelty*, *The Reward of Cruelty* (1751), depicts the tragic demise of Tom Nero, condemned to be hanged and publicly dissected. As the former pupil of a charity school, who tortured a dog as a boy, beat his horse as a coachman and murdered his lover in a churchyard, Tom Nero ends his life on the anatomist's table. Hogarth's engravings, published as individual prints as warnings against immorality and the barbarous treatment of animals, were aimed at furthering the moral instruction of the lower classes. *The Four Stages of Cruelty* appeared a few years after the split of the surgeons from the Barbers' Company in 1745 to form the Company of Surgeons (later to become the Royal College of Surgeons in 1800),[1] and uses the threat of anatomy as a means of edification at the time of the passing of the 1752 Murder Act. The Act was intended to combat crime in London, which was on the rise, by capitalising upon the terror of a public dissection: it denied murderers the right to a burial and added dissection to the sentence.

In *The Reward of Cruelty*, Hogarth's character is shown lying on the anatomist's table in an anatomical theatre, his noose still fastened around his neck. He is in the process of being dissected, his body parts severed, reversing the previous scene which showed the mangled body of his lover, her head and arm almost cut off. Disembowelled, his eyes extracted from their sockets, his heart lying on the ground, about to be eaten by a dog, Tom is ready to be boiled in a cauldron pictured to the left, where the skulls and bones of his predecessors are still visible. The murderer's dissection unravels in the Cutlerian theatre, near Newgate prison, under the gaze of academics seated in the front row and physicians behind (holding canes, a telltale dress accessory, usually designed as a protection from foul odours[2]), and is presided over by a character sitting at the back, probably John Freke, then president of the Royal College of Surgeons. Freke is not the only identifiable individual. The two skeletons shown pointing to each other on either side of the picture are those of two criminals executed respectively in 1750 and 1751: James MacLaine (1724–50) and James Field (1714–51). Their presence anchors the scene in the everyday reality of Hogarth's day so as to ensure more sensationalism.

Stressing the way in which modern anatomy enabled access to the depths of knowledge located inside the human body, as the knife that one of the dissectors plunging into Tom's eye seems to suggest, Hogarth's *Reward of Cruelty* has often been (arguably) regarded as inspired by the frontispiece of Vesalius's *De humani corporis fabrica* (*The Fabric of the Human Body*).[3] Published in 1543, *De humani corporis fabrica* depicted for the first time the human body with scientific accuracy, correcting Galen's anatomical errors (due to the latter's reliance on dissected animals instead of human bodies), thus stressing the superiority of anatomical practice over theoretical reading. From the frontispiece onwards, Vesalius's book underlines the importance of dissection in the formation of medical knowledge. It shows the author dissecting a female corpse – a prostitute guilty of infanticide, sentenced to death and dissected in Padua – in a crowded anatomical theatre. An ape is shown on the left-hand side, pushed to the margins of the picture, signalling forcefully the advent of a new and modern attitude to human anatomy, based on the scientific observation of human bodies. Furthermore, several characters are pointing to the dissected corpse, and Vesalius's finger, attracting the reader's attention and inviting him to look into the open cadaver, seems to be reflected in the assistant's finger, raised as well, as he sharpens blades under the dissection table. Dissection is what the atlas is about – practical knowledge, as the frontispiece emphasises – and Vesalius even detailed his dissection experiences in the text, including some grave-robbing anecdotes.[4]

The frontispiece and plates of Vesalius's *De humani corporis fabrica* represent a radical shift from the portrayal of medieval skeletons, allegorising the universality of death in the Dance of Death. However, at the centre of Vesalius's frontispiece stands a giant skeleton, looking up and grimacing as if in pain. The skeleton, most probably the one that Vesalius used for his lectures and which is reproduced in another of the book's plates, acts here nonetheless as a *vanitas*. While scientifically accurate, it reminds the reader of the transience of life and the inevitability of death, as do other skeletons depicted in the book, some shown, for instance, contemplating a skull. The tension or confrontation between scientific objectivity and allegory in the way skeletons were portrayed in Vesalius's *De humani corporis fabrica* was reinforced in the medical literature of the following centuries. Indeed, the Romantic aesthetic with its allegories of mortality would permeate many illustrations featured in anatomical atlases.

Through its hints at key Renaissance medical books, Hogarth's closure of *The Four Stages of Cruelty* thus uses the threat of dissection as one of most powerful means of edification available to him, enhancing in so doing the authority of anatomical science at mid-century. The engraving also throws light on the fact that from the Renaissance onwards, the study of anatomy by dissection in medical centres, such as in Padua, was accompanied by changes in the legislation concerning human bodies. According to Ruth Richardson, 'dissection received royal recognition and patronage in 1506, when James IV [of Scotland] granted the Edinburgh Guild of Surgeons and Barbers the bodies of certain executed criminals for dissection'.[5] In England, in 1540, Henry VIII granted the companies of Barbers and Surgeons the right to four hanged criminals per year, sealing the links between dissection and exemplary punishment, the 'surgeon-anatomist [becoming] the executioner of the law'.[6] The number was raised to six by Charles II later, until the provisions of the law were further extended by the 1752 Murder Act.

The Gothic novel, heralded by the publication of Horace Walpole's *The Castle of Otranto; A Gothic Story* in 1764, went on to thrive in the 1790s, especially thanks to the development of the Minerva Press in London.[7] The development of this literary form was not unrelated to the same anatomical culture of the second half of the eighteenth century that informed Hogarth's works. If the prohibition of burial and the display of murderers' cadavers rotting on the gibbet seemed a fate much worse than many of the live-burial tales which would establish Edgar Allan Poe's Gothic reputation in the early nineteenth century, dissection and the dismembering of human bodies underlay many a Gothic novel of the second half of the eighteenth century. The Gothic was, indeed, a product of its time. It reflected the fear of dissection as much as artists such as Hogarth, or as the cases reported in *The Newgate Calendar; or, Malefactor's Bloody Register* (published in bound volumes from the mid–1770s until the first decades of the nineteenth century), which never failed to report the dissection of hanged murderers and the public's hunger for a sight of criminal remains. However, references or allusions to medical practice in Gothic literature, notably anatomy and its 'objects', enabled Gothic writers to combine a baroque and allegorical representation of Death whilst remaining realistic – and therefore even more terrifying. Indeed, because anatomists were much more likely to inspire terror than other figures emblematising death, such as executioneers,[8] for instance, they appealed to Gothic novelists almost as soon as Gothic romances became popular in Britain.

'The fleshless jaws and empty sockets of a skeleton'

The Gothic Revival of the late 1740s in England, which gave rise to Walpole's *The Castle of Otranto*, ambiguously poised skeletons between the Dance of Death themes or *vanitas* revived by Romanticism, and scientific exactitude, as illustrated in the medical literature of the times. Hogarth's *The Reward of Cruelty* plays out such tension through its use of skeletons and dissection for edification.[9] Unlike the anatomist in Vesalius's anatomical atlas, who looks at the reader, in Hogarth's engraving a character in the background is pointing to Field's skeleton so as to warn the viewer of the fate that awaits criminals. The two skeletons, also pointing at one another, create a feeling of imprisonment reinforced by the circularity of the room, the dissecting table, the lines of the cauldron and bucket and the bars on the windows in the background. In addition, the president of the Royal College of Surgeons sits on a chair like some high court judge, presenting Tom's dissection as a process of judgement and punishment, which transcends that already inflicted on the scaffold. As a result, the moral discourse which permeates the series of engravings turns the skeletons in the background – just like the skulls and bones in the cauldron in the foreground (even if they also hint at the large volume of dissections), and Tom's eyes, extracted by the anatomist, leaving empty sockets, staring at us – into so many *vanitas* or memento mori. In other words, the human remains simultaneously belong to the anatomy theatre and exist in a realm independently of the anatomist. The latter's gaze is focused clinically on the cadaver; the pair of glasses on his nose strengthens the importance of scientific observation, whilst the lack of attention of parts of the audience further heightens the physicians' and surgeons' lack of empathy – and, perhaps through an ironic reversal, their immorality.

It is tempting to see the ambiguous morality/immorality[10] of anatomical science depicted in Hogarth's *The Four Stages of Cruelty* as an illustration of what Roy Porter termed 'the triangle of the moral, the material and the medical in the anglophone Enlightenment'[11] – a triangle which permeates most Gothic writing of the second half of the eighteenth century. Robert Miles's choice of 1750 as the date marking the beginning of the Gothic is telling. For Miles, this date 'in its very arbitrariness is meant to signify that Gothic has no strictly identifiable beginning: a genealogy, axiomaticaly [*sic*], must begin with the discourses that in some sense precede the "writing"'.[12] Like Hogarth's character, gutted and displayed on the anatomist's table under the gaze of a crowd of medical practitioners, many Gothic characters were penned in ways that were not that far removed from the medical enterprises of the time, attempting as they did to lay bare and understand human nature. Witnessing their suffering as some kind of dramatic spectacle, readers were invited to take part in the scientific exploration of human nature and sometimes even that of human bodies. As argued in the intro-duction, the recurring scenes of suffering in eighteenth-century literature typified the age of sensibility; they also reflected the antithetical meanings of sensibility itself, as Van Sant posits, with suffering both leading to sympathetic identification and inviting curiosity.[13] As Van Sant adds, Tyburn,[14] where criminals were hanged until 1783, was 'an especially good place to experience drama and conduct an experiment' – an idea which Hogarth's engraving certainly hinges upon.[15] Significantly, the combination of emotions spurred by an object, such as a human skeleton, and its simultaneous intellectual exploration may be traceable in the Gothic novels of the last decades of the eighteenth century, more especially so when sensible heroines encounter naked bones and try to uncover their identity. Indeed, many of the skeletons found in the Gothic romances of the first phase (1764–1824), used to inspire feelings of horror, terror or/and pity, also drive the search for identity which underlies most narratives. As the ultimate secret to unveil in the novels' explorations of haunted abbeys or ruined castles, the skeletons point powerfully to the naked truth, whilst the trunks in which they are generally concealed emblematise secrecy. Most especially, the motif of the skeleton in the trunk, which recurrently punctuates the Gothic novels of the late decades of the eighteenth century, often symbolises death while at the same time introducing a more realistic image of the decaying body. This motif illuminates therefore the ways in which medical knowledge and anatomical culture informed early Gothic writing.

In the Preface to the first edition of *The Castle of Otranto*, the narrator claims that the work has been found in the library of an ancient Catholic family in the north of England and printed in Naples in 1529. The novel relates the story of Manfred, Prince of Otranto, whose son Conrad is 'dashed to pieces'[16] by a giant helmet on his wedding day, at the opening of the narrative. The supernatural accident threatens Manfred's ownership of Otranto since it marks the end of his bloodline and the realisation of a prophecy which warned that '*the castle and lordship of Otranto should pass from the present family, whenever the real owner should be grown too large to inhabit it*' (p. 51). Manfred thus decides to marry his son's wife-to-be, Isabella, and divorce his wife, now too old to bear him a new heir. Isabella escapes, launching a quest through the maze-like castle. The story, which initiated the enduring popular genre, introduced the conventions which came to define the Gothic novel. Among Walpole's supernatural paraphernalia can be found enchanted objects, animated portraits and uncanny resemblances to ancestors; prescient dreams; locked, haunted or uninhabited rooms; a spectre with 'the fleshless jaws and empty sockets of a skeleton' (p. 139); and a bleeding statue. Just as the reader must try to reunite the pieces of the puzzle in order to solve the mystery of the haunted castle, identifying resemblances between the giant helmet in the courtyard and that of Alfonso the Good, or tracing Theodore's resemblance to the portrait of Alfonso, so the body of the spectre that haunts the premises to reclaim his vengeance appears as dislocated as 'the bleeding mangled remains' of Conrad at the beginning (p. 53). Indeed, the giant helmet which crushes Manfred's son to death is soon followed by the appearance of a gigantic leg and foot or a hand – body parts which terrify the inhabitants of Otranto. Although Walpole's images of bodily dismemberment are not directly related to the anatomical culture of his day (surgeons do appear several times in the narrative to examine wounds but the medical field does not particularly inform his Gothic plot), later rewritings of Gothic motifs involving human remains, such as skeletons, increasingly pointed to the links between (human) identity (through orphans or usurpers) and medical practice. In so doing, they patently brought to the fore the seeds Walpole had first sowed in his original Gothic story, and emphasised how much the Gothic owed to the anatomical culture of its time. As will be seen in the following discussion, the reconstruction of identity on which depends the closure of many a Gothic novel of the time was increasingly associated with dislocated bodies, with anatomised bodies standing as a powerful image of the loss of, and search for, identity.

Indeed, in the Gothic romances published by the Minerva Press in the late 1780s and 1790s, the skeleton became an enduring Gothic motif, especially when concealed in a trunk. In Clara Reeve's *The Old English Baron*, first published anonymously in 1777 as *The Champion of Virtue, a Gothic Story*, the skeleton discovered in a trunk marked the first in a series of other trunk-bound skeletons. These include: Ann Radcliffe's *The Romance of the Forest* (1791); Stephen Cullen's *The Haunted Priory* (1794) and *The Castle of Inchvally* (1796); *Mort Castle* (1798); John Palmer's *The Haunted Cavern* (1796); *The Phantom of the Cloister; or the Mysterious Manuscript* (1795); *The Spirit of Turretville; or the Mysterious Resemblance* (1800);[17] William Charles Proby's *The Spirit of the Castle* (1800); and T. J. Horsley Curties's *Ancient Records; Or, the Abbey of Saint Oswythe. A Romance, etc.*

(1801).[18] The sheer number of Gothic romances using the motif of the skeleton in the trunk testifies to the popularity of the convention. In addition, the frequency of the motif, which placed a naked, fleshless body at the heart of the narrative quest,[19] reflects the Gothic's interest in, and obsessive discourse on, the self. If the formation of the modern self was more and more indissociable from the development of anatomical investigation and knowledge of the human body, looking at the Gothic writing of the late eighteenth century through the lens of anatomical culture throws valuable light on the history of the 'subject' which Robert Miles believes is central to the Gothic project.[20] From this it follows that the 'coherent code' which the Gothic uses, as Miles contends, 'for the representation of fragmented subjectivity'[21] draws heavily on contemporary anatomical culture and the practices involved in the construction of medical knowledge. This 'code', it could be argued, is particulary explicit when we look at the evolution of the skeleton-in-the-trunk motif as a potent illustration of the Gothic's terrifying 'objects', in the years that followed the publication of Reeve's *The Old English Baron*.

In her preface to this work, Reeve explains that her plan was to follow in the footsteps of Walpole: '[t]he Story is the literary offspring of the Castle of Otranto, written upon the same plan, with a design to unite the most attractive and interesting circumstances of the ancient Romance and modern Novel'.[22] However, Reeve's intention was to tone down Walpole's supernatural machinery so as to propose, instead, a 'probable' ghost story:[23] '[t]o attain this end, there is required a sufficient degree of the marvellous to excite attention; enough of the manners of real life to give an air of probability to the work; and enough of the pathetic to engage the heart in its behalf' (p. 13). Her attempt at 'engag[ing] the heart' showed Reeve's indebtedness to Richardson's sentimental fiction. Reeve praised Richardson's novels and believed in the edifying potential of romance. As she argued, '[t]he business of Romance is, first, to excite the attention; and secondly, to direct it to some useful, or at least innocent, end' (p. v). As a result, *The Old English Baron* rewrites conventional Gothic motifs in a more probable plot permeated with morality, turning Richardson's sentimental novels into a Gothic romance suitable for a bourgeois readership.

The stress on the story's credibility is important, as Reeve's Gothic paved the way for Gothic romances which toned down the super-natural and marvellous elements, preferring instead more gruesome plots which often involved a human corpse. Following Walpole's example, Reeve reuses the old manuscript to convey an effect of reality. This allows her to offer the reader only fragments of the story, since some parts of the narrative have been effaced by time and damp. The first part of *The Old English Baron* relates the adven-tures of Sir Philip Harclay, who returns from abroad and decides to visit his old friend, Arthur Lord Lovel, only to find him dead. He learns from John Wyatt, a cottager who offers to put him up for the night, that Arthur died fifteen years before, leaving a wife pregnant with their child and who is believed to have died of grief. Lord Lovel's cousin, Sir Walter Lovel, has inherited the estate and sold the castle to Baron Fitz-Owen. Fitz-Owen's two sons, William and Robert, along with his daughter, Emma, live there with a kinsman, Richard Wenlock, and Edmund Twyford, a peasant's son to whom Sir Philip takes an immediate liking because of his uncanny resemblance to his lost friend. But while sleeping at John Wyatt's cottage, Sir Philip dreams about the late Lord Lovel. The latter takes him through several rooms of the castle where he discovers a suit of armour stained with blood belonging to Lord Lovel. The manuscript ends after Sir Philip has offered to take Edmund with him and adopt him. The latter refuses to stay with the Baron, but is told that he can rely upon Sir Philip's protection should he need it.

Four years later, the manuscript is resumed by another hand. The second part takes place after Edmund has distinguished himself in battle. The young man is denied a knighthood because of his peasant origins, but he nonetheless excites the jealously of Wenlock, who is, like Edmund, in love with Emma. As a trial, Edmund must sleep for three nights in the east apartment, formerly occupied by Arthur Lord Lovel and which has remained shut up ever since his widow claimed to have seen her husband's ghost. Lady Lovel had reputedly been driven to insanity and death after being confined in the same apartment, and is believed also to haunt the place. To prove his courage and combat the superstitions attached to the place, Edmund enters the east apartment. The description teems with Gothic clichés, offering readers a pre-Victorian Satis House, left to decay:

He then took a survey of his chamber; the furniture, by long neglect, was decayed and dropping to pieces; the bed was devoured by the moths, and occupied by the rats, who had built their nests there with impunity for many generations. The bedding was very damp, for the rain had forced its way through the ceiling[.] (p. 23)

Nature has reasserted itself throughout the castle. As Edmund falls asleep in the apartment, he dreams that the man in armour and the lady who appear to him are in reality his unknown parents. He is then told by one of the servants that Lord Lovel was probably murdered, and that his wife mysteriously disappeared when she claimed her husband's ghost had visited her. While Edmund and the servant explore the apartment, they come across a picture of Arthur Lord Lovel – who bears a striking resemblance to Edmund – and find a suit of armour stained with blood. From under a loose board on the floor of the closet they suddenly hear a groan and start praying.

In order to elucidate the mystery of Edmund's origins, they next ask Edmund's mother, Margery Twyford, to relate the circumstances of his birth. It transpires that Edmund was found in a bundle trimmed with gold lace, while the dead body of his mother – Lady Lovel – floated upon the water nearby. Margery and her husband buried the body of Lady Lovel, in order not to be accused of murder.[24] Once his identity as the true heir has been revealed, Edmund visits Sir Philip to implore his protection. Sir Philip summons Sir Walter Lovel (now Lord Lovel) and challenges him to a duel. The latter is wounded, but his life is spared on condition that he confesses to the murder. This he does, and proceeds to surrender his title and estate to Edmund. Once back at the castle, Edmund discovers the place where his father's skeleton has been concealed, behind a tapestried door. When some debris behind the door is removed, the trunk is found with Lord Lovel's skeleton inside, still bearing the signs of where he was bound at the throat and ankles. The remains of both parents are subsequently buried in consecrated ground. As for the coffin of Lady Lovel interred in the church, it is revealed to contain nothing but stones and earth. Edmund finally marries Emma and their daughter is married to Robert Fitz-William's son, thus ensuring the continuation of the family line.

Conventional Gothic motifs accumulate thoughout the story. The stereotypical figure of the usurper, the old manuscript (some of whose details have been effaced by time and damp, thus concealing from view a part of the story), the haunted and shut-up apartment, locked rooms, draughts and blown-out candles, dreams, portraits and uncanny resemblances feature among the Gothic topoi. However, the supernatural machinery so central to Walpole's Gothic story has been attenuated: statues do not bleed, nor do giant legs or hands appear to the characters. Instead, haunting results from bones concealed in a trunk and which have not been buried in consecrated ground. The trunk emblematises the secret that needs to be discovered just as it symbolises the denial of burial which traps the victim's soul.[25] The ghost which haunts the premises and whose groans can be heard by the novel's characters recalls popular beliefs about the corpse. Ruth Richardson's examination of the importance of the human corpse in popular beliefs surrounding death in the early nineteenth century[26] is significant to this discussion. As she explains, the corpse played a central role in popular culture in this period, but folklore often tempered the physical processes of death, such as putrefaction, by stressing 'the corpse's metaphysical attributes'[27] instead. The notion of a period between death and burial when the human being hovered between life and death, for instance, suggests 'a widely held conviction that the human corpse possessed both sentience and some sort of spiritual power'.[28] The soul was thought to remain in the body until all the flesh had decayed, but the corpse's spiritual status was also related to uncertainties about the signs of death.[29] This explains the presence of customs, such as the importance of burial in consecrated ground, which feature systematically in Gothic novels following Reeve's ghost story in order to provide a more 'probable' explanation for apparitions.[30] Moreover, as Richard Sugg contends, beliefs linked to the process of death itself varied throughout Europe, which may explain why the Gothic novel emerged more forcefully in Britain than elsewhere. Indeed, Sugg explains, '[w]hile the Italians understood death as a clean and absolute extinction of life, the British, among others, believed that a dwindling but quite stubborn degree of life persisted in the corpse for up to a year'.[31]

What is most significant in the case of *The Old English Baron* is the stress on the physicality of the human corpse. Reference is made to the dead bodies of Edmund's mother (stripped before being buried) and father (bound and placed in a trunk), and the sight of the corpse is used to trigger feelings, such as guilt or moral sense. For instance, during Sir Walter Lovel's confession, the sight of Arthur Lovel's corpse brings forth 'pangs of remorse':

> I sent them back to fetch the dead body, which they brought privately into the castle: they tied it neck and heels, and put it into a trunk, which they buried under the floor in the closet you mentioned. The sight of the body stung me to the heart; I then felt the pangs of remorse, but it was too late. (p. 151)

The body and its treatment lie, therefore, at the heart of the Gothic story. Not only does the sight of a cadaver forced into a trunk with its neck and ankles tied together[32] give psychological depth to the Gothic villain, but the latter, when wounded after the trial, also asks for 'a surgeon and a confessor' (p. 144). By aligning the priest and the medical practitioner, Lord Lovel (Sir Walter Lovel) fore-shadows the surgeon's own part in the dispensation of justice: as a matter of fact, the latter makes Lord Lovel fear for his death until he has restored his title and estate to its rightful owner, and is thus instrumental in the re-establishment of order and the closure of the narrative. While strongly linked with emotion, therefore, the corpse in *The Old English Baron* is never to be read as allegorical. On the contrary, once the flesh is decayed, the remaining skeleton functions as material evidence to resolve the mystery of the ghost and put an end to the haunting of the apartment. Once he has recovered the bones of his parents, indeed, Edmund waits for the Baron before burying the bones: 'I waited for your arrival, that you might be certified of the reality, and that no doubt might remain' (p. 214). Reeve's rewriting of Walpole's original story, therefore, enhances the materiality of the 'fleshless jaws and empty sockets' of Walpole's spectre the better to weave the human remains into the plot.

Launching as she did the motif of the skeleton concealed in a trunk, Reeve marked the first stage in a series of Gothic narratives which capitalised upon the materiality of the human cadaver and increasingly bound the skeleton in the trunk to contemporary anatomical knowledge and practice. A few years later, Ann Radcliffe used the very same motif in *The Romance of the Forest* (1791), a novel which overtly revisited Reeve's *The Old English Baron*. Radcliffe was born the same year as Horace Walpole's *The Castle of Otranto* was published. *The Romance of the Forest*, published twenty-five years later, was significant in launching Radcliffe's career as a writer of romance and was hugely popular. It relates the story of Adeline, who is cared for by Pierre de la Motte and his wife, who flee Paris in order to escape creditors. Adeline has been raised harshly by a stranger whom she believes has been following her father's orders. They all find shelter in a ruined abbey, hiding beneath a trapdoor. While exploring the abbey, La Motte discovers a skeleton in a chest but decides to keep his discovery from his wife and Adeline. Adeline later encounters a stranger in the forest around the abbey whom she realises is La Motte's son, Louis, who is looking for his parents. Meanwhile, Adeline arouses Madame La Motte's jealousy, since the latter is convinced that Adeline is having an affair with her husband. The Marquis de Montalt, the owner of the abbey, and one of his attendants, Theodore, appear near the abbey. Theodore tries to warn Adeline of the danger that lies in store for her but is sent back to his regiment before he is able to communicate with her. Frightened that her father may find her again, Adeline soon understands that the Marquis wants her to be his mistress, pretending a fake marriage. Three supernatural dreams, showing her a man dying in one of the abbey's chambers, lead her to discover the manuscript of a man – in fact, her father – kept prisoner in the abbey in 1642. As she tries to escape from the abbey, she is made prisoner and taken to the Marquis's residence but is quickly rescued by Theodore. The couple are later discovered by the Marquis; Theodore wounds him and is then imprisoned and sentenced to death, whilst Adeline, sent back to the abbey, escapes to Leloncourt with the help of La Motte. She is nursed there by Clara La Luc and adopted by her father, Arnaud La Luc, who happens to be Theodore's father as well. They all travel to Paris, where Theodore is to be executed but is released once the truth is revealed about the Marquis's murder of Adeline's father and his theft of the latter's title and inheritance. The Marquis poisons himself but has time to confess all his sins; Adeline inherits her title and legacy.

The motifs used by Radcliffe – notably, the skeleton in the trunk, the manuscript, the supernatural dreams – are highly reminiscent of Reeve's *Old English Baron*. But Radcliffe presents here some of the elements which later made her fame and which came to define Radcliffean Gothic. The quest for knowledge, epitomised by the characters' 'curiosity' when they investigate unknown dwellings, are typical of Enlightenment-inspired explorations of the physical world and resonate throughout the narrative. When La Motte discovers the chest in which he finds 'the remains of a human skeleton', Radcliffe uses the skeleton as both an object of 'horror' and 'curiosity', conveying emotion as well as prompting an intellectual exploration:

> Upon the ground within it, stood a large chest, which he went forward to examine, and, lifting the lid, he saw the remains of a human skeleton. Horror struck upon his heart, and he involuntarily stepped back. During a pause of some moments, his first emotions subsided. That thrilling curiosity, which objects of terror often excite in the human mind, impelled him to take a second view of this dismal spectacle.[33]

The character's nerves, perceptible through words such as 'thrilling',[34] which evoke sensational physiology, as mentioned in the introduction, testify to La Motte's sensibility just as much as they reveal his thirst for knowledge: La Motte's 'thrilling curiosity' combines the 'heart' and the 'mind', thus blurring the physical and the psychological and foregrounding the importance of the senses in the acquisition of knowledge.

The collapse of the boundaries between the psychological and the physiological, or anatomical, pregnant in terms such as 'thrill' or sometimes 'strings', whose meaning changed with the rise of dissection, as Barker-Benfield argues,[35] typifies Radcliffe's adherence to the eighteenth-century ethos of sensibility. Moreover, the most significant change that Radcliffe makes to Reeve's narrative is that she shifts the focus on to her heroine, who embodies the ideals of sensibility. Indeed, the narrator tells readers that distress embellishes Adeline's features ('Her features, which were delicately beautiful, had gained from distress an expression of captivating sweetness' (p. 6)), and her sensibility 'deserves to be reverenced' (p. 347). Adeline's sufferings, dramatised from her first appearance in the text,[36] 'almost beyond her power of enduring it' (p. 216), are described at length throughout the novel – Adeline is even encouraged to weep by La Luc (p. 304). Her thoughts often '[fill] her heart with anguish and her eyes with tears' (p. 229), and the 'swelling anguish of her heart' is indissociable from the tears that 'bath[e] her' (p. 229). The parallel between the heart[37] and the eyes, which metaphorises the anxiety flowing through her heart, endows the heart therefore with a physiological dimension that transcends the symbolic one.

Hence, the central function of the hidden manuscript, which the heroine must discover and which records Adeline's father's sufferings, and is used to reveal her capacity for pity. The latter asks the reader to weep for him: 'O! ye, who may hereafter read what I now write, give a tear to my sufferings: I have wept often for the distresses of my fellow creatures!' (p. 132). Moreover, the similarities between the manuscript – an embedded story, recording a man's suffering – and the skeleton, hidden in a chest, are noteworthy. Both relate the secrets of the body. The naked bones, without any flesh once the corpse has decayed, reflect the written chronicling of the man's suffering, which also provides access to the interiority of the human body, demanding both 'sympathetic identification' (Adeline's pity) and 'objective scrutiny' (Adeline's search for the victim's identity).[38] The link between the manuscript and the skeleton in the trunk is further strengthened by the Marquis's confession at the end of the novel. The Marquis reveals 'where the remains were concealed', whilst Adeline decides to preserve the manuscript 'with the pious enthusiasm so sacred a relique deserved' (p. 355), as if the text possessed the physicality of corporeal remains. This parallel therefore fuses the text and the body and aligns the tale of suffering with the naked bones.

Such a physiological exploration of suffering, implicit throughout the novel, is also hinted at by Radcliffe's use of medical professionals in the plot, an aspect of the novel which it is necessary to develop here to fully grasp Radcliffe's treatment of human remains. As a matter of fact, characters recurrently fall ill, are wounded or injured throughout the novel. As in *The Old English Baron*, this leads medical professionals to play an active part in the Gothic romance, since fear and anxiety are related to the characters' health. Adeline's safety thus depends upon Theodore's well-being. The physical danger that threatens him is also used to reveal the heroine's heightened sensibility – and ultimately her love. After escaping with Adeline, Theodore is struck on the head and falls dangerously ill. He is first examined by a man 'who acted as physician, apothecary, and surgeon to the village' (p. 177). If the readers are spared some of the medical details, as the dashes suggest in the following quote, underlining the medical practitioner's lack of knowledge, the surgeon nonetheless provides some anatomical details concerning the wound, and his words betray his general lack of affect, increasing thereby the heroine's potential danger and isolation:

> 'It is possible that the wound may not have reached the—', he stammered; 'in that case the—', stammering again, 'is not affected; and if so, the interior membranes of the brain are not touched: in this case the wound may, perhaps, escape inflammation, and the patient may possibly recover'. (p. 179)

Furthermore, although the surgeon walks away 'with an air of chagrin and displeasure' (p. 179), his attitude when he claims his patient is sure to die, presenting a snuffbox to Adeline as sole comfort, anticipates the following confrontation between the surgeon and a physician. Unconvinced by the surgeon's prognosis and having taken a dislike to him (p. 182), Adeline seeks out another medical professional. Her sensibility once again informs her intuition. It is manifest in her seemingly irrational lack of trust in the surgeon ('she had hitherto given little faith in his judgement' (p. 188)) and in his 'conceited manners' (p. 186), whilst her search for a physican reveals her capacity to interpret symptoms and form her own opinion regarding Theodore's actual condition.[39] She later challenges the surgeon's refusal to give liquid to the patient: '[y]ou do not approve, then, of the method, which I have somewhere heard of', said Adeline, 'of attending to nature in these cases' (p. 185). Unsurprisingly, Adeline's independence of mind is not welcomed by the surgeon, who tells her about a recent confrontation with a physican, bent upon prescribing 'remedies' (p. 183) to a patient whose case he also believed to be hopeless. Comparing himself several times to his 'brother physician' (pp. 183, 184) – hence denying any social difference between the two – the surgeon then relates how he altered the treatment in line with the physician's prescription, becoming – ironically – the one who administered the medicine which would kill his patient. Irony is further developed when the medical practitioner discusses the 'Art' of medicine (p. 186), increasing all the more the heroine's helplessness: the more the surgeon stresses his own distress ('It distressed me so much', 'It affected me a good deal' (p. 184)), the more his speech underlines his lack of empathy for his patients.

This idea is confirmed once Adeline has succeeded in discovering the address of the physician that had been kept 'secret' (p. 186) from her. The physican 'proceed[s] upon contrary principles' (p. 213), allowing liquids to be freely consumed (p. 188) (thereby confirming Adeline's own knowledge of medical treatments), a treatment which saves Theodore's life. More significantly perhaps, the physician is shown to have much more empathy for his patients. He listens to Theodore 'with attention and compassion', and attends 'to his narrative with deep concern', his countenance 'express[ing] strong agitation' (p. 202). His 'sympathy' and empathy ('having endeavoured to attain a degree of composure, which he found difficult to assume' (p. 202)), the 'violence of his distress' (p. 204), and his inability to speak (p. 205) because of emotion construct the physician as the antithesis of the surgeon, who merely foretells the death of his patients or administers fatal medicines. The physician, in contrast, is driven by his '[h]umanity' (p. 213) alone.[40] Once again, sensibility is inseparable from medical investigation, enabling simultaneously 'sympathetic identification and objective scrutiny'.[41]

The way in which medical knowledge permeates the narrative and informs the secrets at the heart of the Gothic romance (be it through debates around (mis-)interpretations of the body's symptoms or, more literally, through concealing a physician's name and address from the heroine) helps us to better understand Radcliffe's reworking of Reeve's romance. Here, moreover, Radcliffe's contrasting of a physician and a surgeon makes medical practitioners pivotal to the Gothic plot, revisiting Walpole's surgeons (who merely served a realistic function) and suggesting thereby new ways of reading and interpreting the skeleton in the text in line with the anatomical culture of the day. Adeline reads the manuscript and its record of suffering, agreeing to 'weep for [his] sufferings' (p. 132), in the same way as the physician who rescues Theodore is shown to be able to listen to his patient's narrative. The parallel between Adeline and the physician, together with her ability to interpret symptoms noted above, highlights Radcliffe's highly intellectual construction of the corpse/skeleton in the trunk. After all, Adeline is allowed to read the story of the skeleton, yet not to visualise the 'dismal spectacle' (p. 56) of the concealed bones. As soon as he discovers the trunk, La Motte is, indeed, 'anxious that his family should not perceive the skeleton; an object, which would, probably, excite a degree of horror not to be overcome during their stay' (p. 56). The skeleton in the trunk remains therefore hidden until the Marquis's final confession, which reveals the location of the human remains.

In the years that followed the publication of *The Romance of the Forest*, Radcliffe's euphemisation of the human remains at the heart of her narrative was widely subverted, notably in the many Gothic romances published by the sensational Minerva Press. These highly popular novels played upon much more graphic depictions of the body, making increasing use of the anatomical culture of the period to revisit Reeve's or Radcliffe's plots. A significant case in point is *The Horrors of Oakendale Abbey*, published in 1797 by the Minerva Press. This work rewrites the motif of the skeleton in the trunk, dramatically playing upon corporeal horror and using fears of medical practitioners – in particular anatomists – as figures of horror.

The Horrors of Oakendale Abbey was published anonymously, but attributed to 'Mrs Carver' in the 1814 catalogue, although it is now believed to have been penned by Sir Anthony Carlisle (1768–1840), an English surgeon, to whom several other Minerva Gothic romances have since also been attributed.[42] The novel relates the story of Laura, whose identity is unknown to her, but who is the daughter of Captain William Carleton and a Greek woman, Zelima – a captive who was used to pay for her brother's ransom, and with whom William Carleton fell in love while heading for the West Indies. At the death of her parents, the orphan girl is brought to Paris and raised by the Parisian surgeon Du Frene, a Protestant of English extraction 'in high repute in that profession, and which he now followed from motives of humanity rather than from lucrative ones' (p. 88).[43] In Paris, she meets Eugene. We discover subsequently that the latter is the illegitimate son of Lord Oakendale's wife, Miss Rainsford, and her first love, Vincent, later to succeed to a title and estate and become Edward Lord Vincent of Vincent Castle. Eugene has been sent to France by Du Frene's brother, also a surgeon, in order to improve his knowledge of the French language. Having formed an attachment to Laura, a young woman unsuitably inferior to Eugene's actual social rank, the young man is recalled to England by Mr F. (Du Frene's brother), who believes it is now time to introduce him to his real mother. But Eugene soon vanishes after a trip to the Lake District. The suspicions that Eugene's mother has secreted him for fear her past might be made public are strong and later confirmed by her deathbed confession.

Meanwhile, Laura's protector, 'too much attached to his king' (p. 96), ends with his head 'stuck upon a pike, reeking and clotted with blood' (p. 97) in revolutionary Paris. Laura then escapes to Britain where she settles in Wales. Ironically, the French Terror is used here only to underline the even more horrifying deeds which take place in Britain (a contrast which Dickens explores at length in *A Tale of Two Cities* (1859), as will be seen in chapter 3). For Laura soon charms Lord Oakendale, a married man who happens to be William Carleton's brother (and therefore her uncle). Eager to possess the young woman, Lord Oakendale invites Laura to accompany him to London. Laura refuses her suitor's advances, and as result finds herself confined in a haunted abbey. Her imprisonment has a view to 'enervate[ing]' (p. 55) her mind so that she might 'gladly fly to [Lord Oakendale] . . . rather than be condemned to a hateful solitude, like that of Oakendale Abbey'. As Laura explores the place, she discovers a human skeleton in a chest, as well as the gift she had given Eugene before the lovers were separated. Convinced that Eugene has been murdered in the abbey, she pursues her examination of the place, regularly returning to the room where the skeleton is kept. Instead of encountering spectres, however, Laura finds herself locked up with cadavers and even sees a dead man walking out of the room and escaping from the abbey. The young woman nonetheless manages to escape, her disappearance leading Lord Oakendale to search the abbey where both Eugene and Laura have been held captive. The truth about the identity of the 'ghosts' which appear to be haunting the abbey is ultimately revealed to consist of a group of body-snatchers using the building as a base for their traffic in human cadavers. The lovers are finally reunited, their true identity restored and Lord Oakendale saved from committing incest with his niece.

As in other contemporary Gothic romances, the abbey is purportedly haunted by the ghost of someone believed to have been murdered in one of the rooms:

> It was currently reported, that various figures had been seen flitting about after twilights; ghastly visions had appeared, smeared with blood; and the ghost of a lady, who was supposed to have been murdered in one of the rooms, was usually seen after it was dark looking through the windows, with streams of blood running from her throat. Tales of this nature had filled the minds of the simple villagers with dreadful apprehensions; but what had given more reasonable colour and strength to these fears were, two circumstances, which had happened within only a twelve-month of each other; one was, that of a young gentleman's never being heard of after going to explore the Abbey; the other, of another gentleman's endeavouring to sleep there, who was so extremely terrified by noises, howlings and phantoms, that, although a determined and resolute man, he was obliged to relinquish the design, and to pass the remainder of the night with one of the villagers in a cottage. (pp. 36–7)

Yet from the beginning, the immaterial ghosts 'flitting about' are 'colour[ed]' with much more ghastly and corporeal details: the spectral victim is 'smeared with blood', 'streams of blood running from her throat'. In addition, popular beliefs in supernatural beings are sharply contrasted with the two gentlemen who try to elucidate the mystery of the haunted abbey. But unlike Reeve's Edmund or Radcliffe's Adeline, the gentlemen are unsuccessful; the plot twists characterising his work thus enable Carlisle to propose a much more realistic form of Gothic rewriting. Indeed, reports mentioning 'men and women being seen carrying their heads in their hands, and of monstrous eyes looking through the windows flaming with fire' (p. 108) illustrate Carlisle's graphic horror, with the Gothic emphasising physical dismemberment and foreshadowing the series of revelations at the end of the novel. As in Radcliffean Gothic, moreover, the heroine is systematically measured against her maid, Mary. The latter's nights are punctuated by the sound of doors opening and shutting, voices whispering and footsteps, all of which her mistress, Laura, believes are 'idle chimeras of a fearful apprehension' (p. 41). Throughout the novel, Laura remains a highly rational being, such as when she believes that the oblique reflection of the moon has led her to be deluded by a shadow which appeared larger than that of a man (p. 58). The reference to optical illusions[44] is significant, for the main leitmotiv of the narrative is a giant skeleton kept in a trunk but which does not result, as we may be led to suppose, from any optical trick.

Thus, although *The Horrors of Oakendale Abbey* conjures up much of the familiar Gothic paraphernalia (ghosts, an ancient abbey descending with the Earldom of Oakendale, whose 'low crumbling walls, long passages, or cloisters' conceal 'vaults and subterraneous passages' (p. 29), and whose medieval objects (such as a rusty helmet and a large sword) are reminiscent of Walpole's *Castle of Otranto*), Carlisle's Gothic romance remains a realistic story, albeit a horrifying one, which capitalises on the fear of anatomy. The threat of illicit sexuality (such as incest), stereotypically associated with the Gothic genre from its origins, is transformed here into a threat of illicit anatomy, in the form of body-snatching. The shift from illicit sexuality to illicit anatomy places the naked body at the heart of the narrative. This is particularly visible in the way in which the skeleton in the trunk is used as a leitmotiv throughout the narrative. The first time Laura discovers the trunk, the skeleton concealed within it is barely mentioned:

> a large trunk, or coffer, which stood in one corner of the room, attracted her notice, and she instantly accounted for the rustling, by supposing that a rat or mouse might be withinside of it; and, as this idea dispelled her fears, and renewed her courage, she advanced to the place where it stood, determined to lift up the lift, and see what it contained. She did so; but how was she struck with horror and astonishment, when the skeleton of a human body presented itself to her affrighted view! (pp. 46–7)

Unlike in previous Gothic romances, Laura's initial interpretation of the trunk offers a symbol of the denial of burial: 'What was there to fear in seeing the bones of a fellow creature, whose peaceful ashes were as quietly deposited there as in the mouldering earth?' (p. 48). The fact that the cloister communicates with the churchyard leads her to believe that the corpse has been stored in the trunk while awaiting burial, thus anchoring death in the everyday reality of churchyard management: 'it was easy to suppose a skeleton might well be conveyed to a place so near it, for want of room, or for some other reasons' (p. 50). It is only when she comes across the parting gift she had given Eugene that the skeleton starts becoming an object of terror. Interestingly, Laura's discovery of the skeleton bears no resemblance to Adeline's hyper-sensibility in Radcliffe's *Romance of the Forest*, which supernaturally guides her to the manu-script recording her relative's fate.[45] Here, the skeleton in the chest functions as a structural trigger, ratcheting up the suspense as Laura tries repeatedly to visit the room in which it is concealed: 'although she made several attempts to visit the room, which contained the skeleton, she never found her courage quite equal to the enterprise' (p. 55); 'she again resumed her intention of looking at the room which contained the skeleton' (p. 61). The skeleton also serves to reactivate Laura's own knowledge of Gothic romances, such as when she imagines what may have happened to Eugene:

> In those moments she supposed a gang of banditti concealed in a subterraneous vault, who rushing upon Eugene at the moment he was exploring their secret haunts, having robbed and murdered him, had put his body in the trunk, had carelessly dropped the letter-case in the room where she found it. (p. 57)

The imagined story is overtly borrowed from Radcliffe's second novel, *A Sicilian Romance* (1790), which stages banditti in a ruined monastery – a scene inspired by the paintings of Salvator Rosa. This intertextual vignette, however, lays bare Carver's modern rewriting. While in the room, Laura perceives some light through boards forming a partition, and looks through the cracks. She first notices a length of white linen, then a large rolling eyeball looking at her through the cracks. She then, ironically, collapses on the trunk

(p. 63), her heart throbbing and tears flooding from her eyes. The constant return to the trunk (in the narrative, for the sake of suspense, or literally when the female character sits upon it) liberates the symbolic meaning of the Gothic trope. Laura, like Bluebeard's wife, has entered the forbidden chamber, realising the fleshly horror of sexuality, as in Charles Perrault's fairy tale: 'she now blamed herself for having attempted to make an investigation which had led her to encounter so much terror' (p. 64).[46] This blurring of sexuality and anatomy is a recurrent feature of Carlisle's romance, as already suggested, and the female character's constant analysis of the gruesome objects she encounters during her exploration of the abbey underlines this parallel repeatedly. Laura surmises, for instance, that '[t]he skeleton, the shadow, and the eye-ball, might be managed by his Lordship's contrivance' (p. 67). In doing so, she constructs them as a collection, making sense of individually terrifying objects by imagining Oakendale as a puppetmaster in order to rationalise her fear: 'consequently, they lost their terror, and she looked upon all that was past as an artful delusion' (p. 67). However, her reasoning serves to emphasise their very materiality – or corporeality. That human remains might be employed by Oakendale merely as terrifying props exposes the artificiality of the Gothic tale just as it commodifies the corpse, foreshadowing the body-snatching plot.

The fleshly materiality of the human body is reinforced in the following scene, when one afternoon, Laura walks out of the abbey to explore the surroundings only to find herself, she believes, back in the abbey. She opens one of the doors leading to an apartment and

> a sight more horrible than imagination can form, presented itself to her. The dead body of a woman hung against the wall opposite to the door she had entered, with a coarse cloth pinned over all but the face; the ghastly and putrefied appearance of which bespoke her to have been some time dead. (p. 73)

No sooner has she seen the corpse than she encounters a figure staggering towards her: 'The face was almost black; the eyes seemed starting from the head; the mouth was widely extended, and made a kind of hallow guttural sound in attempting to articulate' (p. 74).

The dead–alive creature – an executed criminal not thoroughly dead – escapes through the door that Laura has left open, locking the young woman in the room with the other cadavers. The reversal deflates the romance once again: although Laura is terrified by the man, the latter quickly vanishes from the scene, and in any case his horror at the sight of the surrounding corpses is much greater than hers. This is confirmed later in the novel, when the resurrected criminal, Patrick O'Dennis, protects Laura from an impertinent suitor. We learn that O'Dennis was terrified before his execution both by the fate that awaited him (dissection) and by his own knowledge of the traffic in dead bodies taking place in the abbey, having formerly assisted the resurrectionists working there. The character's description of his physical sensations and the medical details informing O'Dennis's physical powerlessness when coming back to life is one of the first examples of the use of the fear of being buried alive, which would be a prominent feature of Edgar Allan Poe's later tales of terror:[47]

> His mind was all in a state of confusion; and, if any thoughts did occur, they were only on the wretched state to which his body would be subjected after he was dead; nor could the clergyman, who attended him, impress any ideas of that more and more toll and immaterial part of him, which could not suffer by the hand of man.
>
> The first idea of recollection he experienced (after the noise of the crowd and the mob that tended him to the gallows had ceased) was of extreme pain in his head and neck, and a violent oppression upon his lungs. He struggled for a few seconds, and gained respiration; a mist before his eyes seemed to vanish, and he recovered sufficient sight to perceive he was in a room with a dead body, upon one side of it. It instantly occurred to him that he was in the Abbey. He was horribly frightened, and he tried to articulate; but found his throat so swelled that he could only utter a guggling kind of sound[.] (p. 180)

One of the resurrectionists of Carlisle's novel thus ironically escapes punishment, giving a twist to the romance's moralising discourse. This idea climaxes when Carlisle provides a telltale clue to enable readers to read the skeleton in the trunk at the end of the novel. Although the corpses stored in the abbey remain nameless to the end, Lord Oakendale's description of the skeleton resonates with hints at Carlisle's own contemporary reality:

> They approached the trunk wherein the skeleton was deposited. Lord Oakendale ordered his servants to lift up the lid; and the light had no sooner glanced upon the ghastly figure, when the man, dropping the lid from his hand, exclaimed, 'God preserve us! here is a dead man, bigger than a giant, with saucer eyes, and huge limbs!' (p. 112)

As Don Shelton has argued,[48] Carlisle's giant might have been inspired by the eight-foot-tall Irish giant Charles Byrne (1761–83), exhibited in London freak-shows and known to have been terrified by anatomists and dissection, who arranged for his body to be protected after his death. Byrne was to be sealed in a lead coffin, watched for four days and buried at sea so as to escape the clutches of the anatomists, in particular the famous London surgeon John Hunter (1728–93), whose extensive anatomical collection reflected both his surgical dexterity and his thirst for medical knowledge. After the announcement of Byrne's death, surgeons battled for possession of his corpse. While undertakers were offered bribes, news of his burial at sea was circulated. The latter, however, was intended to mislead, for in reality Hunter had paid off the undertaker soon after the giant's death. The surgeon had then taken the dead body to his house in Earls Court, hurriedly chopped the giant to pieces and boiled his body parts in a vat so as to avoid being found out by Byrne's friends. The skeleton, once reassembled, remained hidden from the public for four years, and thus Hunter evaded suspicion.[49]

The connections between Carlisle's skeleton in the trunk and John Hunter's concealed giant skeleton can be linked to the giant who haunts Walpole's castle of Otranto. Yet, in *The Horrors of Oakendale Abbey*, in contrast, the human remains are merely gruesome and never actually threaten the living. On the contrary, Lord Oakendale's ultimate description of the resurrectionists' abode, where body parts have been scattered here and there,[50] serves above all to magnify the anonymity of the dead, their lack of identity recalling Laura's and Eugene's own namelessness at the opening of the novel:

Lord Oakendale was convinced it was the very same apartment he had been in before; but everything now bore a different aspect! Nothing appeared in the room but a large table, and some loose boards. There are were [*sic*] evident marks of blood upon many parts of the floor, and in one corner lay a human scull! Lord Oakendale shuddered! . . .

'The scull cannot be Laura's' said Mr. F.— ; 'it would not have been in this state from the time of she has been missing'; yet it might be Eugene and the thought rested upon his imagination with a sickening horror!

Lord Oakendale, having searched every part of the room to no purpose, ordered the floor to be taken up; when, as the men were beginning to execute his orders, they discovered a trap-door, which was instantly opened, and they descended down several winding steps into a huge vault, which seemed to extend under the church. They lighted more candles, and left no part unsearched. No object presented itself; but they picked up bones and sculls in various parts of the vault. (p. 152)

Thus, the narrator's final conclusion on the ghosts of Oakendale Abbey and his denunciation of body-snatching are jarring, hardly reconciling Carlisle's depiction of the profession as evading justice:

Thus was that this great mystery at once explained, and the ghosts of Oakendale Abbey were indeed the dead; but brought thither by those unfeeling monsters of society, who make a practice of stealing our friends, and relations from the peaceful grave where their ashes, as we suppose, are deposited in rest. (p. 159)

The symmetrical construction of the plot – two orphans, both imprisoned in the abbey and related through Lord Oakendale's marriage to Eugene's mother – illuminates a carefully structured narrative which functions as a frame, releasing horror the better to contain it. The medical field which permeates Carlisle's Gothic romance only marginally points to the moralising uses of dissection in the second half of the eighteenth century. Anatomy serves to remove fears of illicit sexuality from the narrative, as suggested, but Carlisle's use of human remains as props and his commodification of the human body ultimately illustrate late eighteenth-century Gothic's search for sheer horror. This stress on fear, deprived of much of the moralising undercurrent which defined the first Gothic romances, would be further developed in the following century as the Gothic became increasingly anchored in everyday reality, dismissing dusty skeletons and feathered helmets to favour instead actual anatomical theatres and ambitious surgeons. The eighteenth-century Gothic rewritings which followed Reeve's *Old English Baron* illuminate therefore the secularisation of British culture and the loss of the customary belief in the marvellous.

A jack-out-of-the-box: The Animated Skeleton

Carlisle's use of the medical reality of his day to dismiss the supernatural and revisit the Gothic romances of Clara Reeve or Ann Radcliffe presents the Gothic as an artificial assemblage of conventional motifs. In other words, the motifs which had assured the growing popularity of the Gothic novel at the turn of the nineteenth century were now coming to be seen as clichés – mere stage props. In addition, the narratives increasingly highlighted ghastly and gory references to the dead body, playfully using human corpses. Titles such as *The Animated Skeleton* (1798), for instance, exemplify the overt construction of the Gothic as a set of (sometimes loose) terrifying/horrifying objects. Thus, in this work the reader knows even before starting to read the story that the mystery will revolve around an 'animated skeleton', that is, articulated bones set in motion by a fraudster in order to terrify (potentially female) readers.[51] Illusion and delusion, which lie at the heart of the Gothic novels of Radcliffe or Lewis, are here laid bare, exhibited and exposed to the reader, with the Gothic skeleton and its motifs, conventions and stock characters, literally represented in the text as so many accessories.

As in earlier Gothic romances, *The Animated Skeleton* features a haunted wing, a usurper and an uncle who intends to marry his niece. Ludovicus, married to a perfect woman, falls under the charm of the villainess Gunilda. Little by little, Ludovicus becomes suspicious and unfeeling, and his wife suffers from a fatal bout of melancholy. She eventually dies in childbirth, leaving a daughter (Emma) and an infant son. Ludovicus is now free to marry Gunilda, with whom he has two children, Brunchilda and Hubert. Ludovicus's first child (supposedly) dies of natural causes (he is in fact murdered by Gunilda's accomplices), but the dead body of the infant has a black mark around his throat, which raises Ludovicus's suspicions. The post-mortem 'examination'[52] (also carried out by some of Gunilda's accomplices) indicates a natural death by convulsion and the reader is led to believe that the body is buried. Gunilda also gets rid of the rightful owner of the castle, Count Richard, his wife and servants, by spreading false reports about the Count. The guilty villainess, meanwhile, poisons her criminal accomplices and also decides to get rid of Ludovicus's first daughter, Emma, along with her husband, Etheburt. The latter is quickly dispatched, but Emma manages to escape, and takes the veil in a distant convent.

When Count Richard comes back to the castle, Gunilda murders him in the northern apartments, spreading the news that he has gone away. Her son Hubert then assumes Count Richard's title and name, whilst the apartment becomes haunted and is closed up. Hubert tries to marry his niece, the beautiful Hildergarde. The latter, the offspring of Brunchilda and Duke Albert, has secretly borne two sons by Edgar, the son of Grodern, a peasant. When Hildergarde's father hears the news, he becomes furiously violent but Hildergarde is rescued by Count Richard – who is in fact still alive. As it happens, Grodern is Count Richard in disguise; the Count never drank the fatal poison given to him by Gunilda and Hubert. Moreover, on the night of his supposed murder, Count Richard kept the corpse of his servant, stabbed by Gunilda and Hubert, and put it in a chest, before escaping from the castle through a sliding panel. Having access to all the rooms of the castle, he could easily terrify Gunilda, making people believe that the wing was haunted. Changing his identity and living the life of a peasant, Count Richard, however, regularly punished Brunchilda by terrifying her, using the skeleton of his servant as a puppet ('By cords and springs I brought it to act as was seen' (p. 113)) or even using a mask to mimic the ghost of Brunchilda, after the latter has killed herself by dashing her brains out on the floor. We learn at the end, moreover, that the abbess of the convent which shelters some of the characters from the evil Brunchilda or Count Richard (Hubert) at the beginning of the story, was none other than Princess Emma, Ludovicus's first daughter. Similar to Brunchilda in stature, she wore a mask to make people believe in Brunchilda's ghost. As for Edgar, Ludovicus's son, his life has also been preserved, the black marks around his neck being nothing but stains.

From the beginning of the Gothic romance, the narrative stresses the materiality of the body/corpse. The novel opens with the assaulted body of Dunisleda, Jacquemar's wife, a peasant who has gone to sell her cheese to the villages around the castle and who first finds refuge in Grodern's cottage with her husband and children before fleeing to the convent, convinced that Duke Albert or Count Richard prey upon every beautiful woman. Dunisleda's face is bloody; she has been captured by two men who attempted to sell her body to the Count. Terrified by the assault, Dunisleda gives birth to a stillborn child and eventually dies herself: 'Life, no longer willing to animate her body, departed rudely, and in the shock caused her jaw-bone to descend. The starting of her eyes taught her Jacquemar his fate!' (p. 16). Around the same time, Grodern and Jacquemar (Dunisleda's husband) stab Conrad, one of Brunchilda's partners in crime, burying the body for fear the blood may betray them. The corpse is soon discovered, however, and pulled out of its grave, its clothes stolen:

> Passing over the way we came by, one of her household saw a dead body lying on the ground: it appeared to have been torn up from a hole which was fresh and near it. It was wounded in the bosom, and appeared to have been murdered: it had no covering whatever; and already the birds of prey were hovering over it. The body appeared to have been many days deprived of life; but the extreme coldness of the weather had prevented it from becoming putrid. (p. 18)

Stripped naked, Conrad's cadaver, like Dunisleda's, is graphically depicted. The focus on Dunisleda's jawbone, which descends mechanically once life has departed the body, just like the deciphering of potential signs of death in Dunisleda's eyes or in Conrad's decomposing corpse, participates in the construction of horror. Likewise, the reference to the marks around the neck of Ludovicus's son and the post-mortem examination of the corpse suggest a forensic investigation of the body/crime.

The realism of the description of corpses is in keeping with the discourse on ghosts developed early on when a mysterious knight, going by the name of 'Grimoald the Avenger', arrives at the castle with Sir Raymond Fitz-Henry, an English knight. He asks permission to sleep in the apartments of the northern wing so as to dismiss all supernatural tales, believing that ghosts are mere rats and owls. The intention to disclose 'knavery' and tricks of all sorts leads the characters to investigate the mystery of the 'she-devil locked in a box in the northern wing' (p. 25). Similarly, the decayed apartments they discover foreground the physical decomposition of the discarded food, whilst mildew has pervaded the premises. The stress on the smell of putrefaction, just like the emphasis on worms, describes the apartments as though they were a corpse. Likewise, the image of the 'winding cloisters' shaped by the work of the worms or the maze created by spiders metaphorise imprisonment. But in doing so, they also play upon scale, shaping a miniature Gothic castle made up by living creatures with organic matter:

> Damp, musty, and unwholesome vapours issued from every room; in most of which they found the furniture remained as if people had but a minute before ceased to use them: some placed by the ashes of fires which seemed just decayed; some placed at tables on which the vessels yet remained; but all covered with the accumulated dust of distant times. In some rooms the ravages of time, added to the weakening of neglect, had brought the roofing to decay; the rains had entered, and the damp had clothed the walls with its verdant mantle; whilst all the moveables were covered with the grey spotting mildew; and any thing which arose from the labours of the loom, fell to pieces on removal. Here the worm worked its winding cloisters, and there the spider spread her mazy dwelling; devastation and decay had passed through each apartment. They continued to go through all the lower suite of rooms without meeting ghost or goblin, or any thing worth further notice, until coming to a large room, they beheld a table surrounded by seats, and spread with viands all dusty, and of ancient date. Some were decayed in the dishes, and others dried and mouldy: as to their nature and sort, time had made that impossible to guess; but it appeared as if people had arisen from a splendid feast,

where the rites of Bacchus had not been neglected; or rather let me say, were meant to be celebrated; for the vessel remained wherein the liquor had dried up, or become unfit for use. (pp. 40–1)

Moreover, as the characters are investigating the haunted apartments, a voice warns them not to '[d]isturb . . . the ashes of the departed' or 'the repose of the dead'. They next encounter 'the hollow skull and dry bones of a skeleton' (p. 43). As they attempt to escape, 'the hand of a skeleton fasten[s] upon [Grimoald's] arm' (p. 44) before 'unfasten[ing] from something, and fall[ing] upon the ground' (p. 44). Just like previous images of physical decomposition, the terrifying animation and sudden dismemberment and lifelessness of the skeleton stresses the significance of corporeality in the construction of horror. Yet the anticlimactic manner in which the hand falls to the ground also emphasises the role of the skeleton as mere anatomical remains, subsequently confirmed when Hubert (alias Count Richard) is chained in the haunted apartment and encounters the animated skeleton:

From one of his slumbers he was awakened by a noise in his room; when turning his head to from whence it proceeded, he beheld the iron pan drawn to a distance from him, and a skeleton sitting by it. The appearance had a double portion of horror, because the light which was caused by the embers was too feeble to strike to advantage upon any but near objects: the chamber, in consequence, seemed almost entirely dark, except in the spot on which sat the skeleton. The Count, in amazement and horror, started up, and attempted to rush forwards, to dash in pieces the phantom which awaked him, but a sudden pull backwards robbed him of the power; at the same time the skeleton moved further from him, and as it went backwards drew along with it, by grasping it with its long and uncased fingers, the iron-pan. Sinking again upon his rushes in an agony of terror, he hid his face in his hands, unable to bear the strangeness of the spectacle; but he found, on their noise having restored him partly from his fright, that it was nothing but his chains which had caused the sudden pull: they were fastened to an iron in the wall, and by their not giving way, caused the resistance. For a while he continued hiding his face with his hands; but a noise like raking the ashes in the pan, made him again start up; but he only did so again to sink, overwhelmed with horror at a sight far more surprising and perplexing than what he had last beheld. (p. 84)

Both Hubert and the skeleton are fastened by chains which shape them as puppets, the term 'spectacle' emphasising even more the idea of a show. Count Richard appears at this moment to accuse Hubert of murder and of being a usurper before taking the skeleton by one hand and vanishing.

In the several scenes in which the 'animated skeleton' appears, therefore, the human remains appear recurrently as reified and inanimate, albeit mechanically animated by a third party – movement is due to chains or to Count Richard's agency. Tellingly, the more the reader understands the meaning of the skeleton's 'animation' suggested by the title, the more the narrative stresses the character's fear, evolving here from 'terror' to 'horror'. The jarring contrast, while increasingly ridiculing or belittling the power of the villains, also connects fear with the manipulation of human remains. The animated skeleton, just like the corpse of Brunchilda later on, from which her spirit seems to speak (in fact due to Princess Emma wearing a mask and mimicking the corpse), aims at frightening the villains and leading them to confess their crimes. One can but recall here Hogarth's Tom Nero, mentioned at the opening of this chapter, whose untimely end on the anatomist's table has a similar edifying purpose.

This unromantic use of skeletons, which constructs the self, when dead, as mere commodity, is revealing of a changing history of the subject in the last decades of the eighteenth century. The recycling of Gothic motifs and conventions, climaxing here with the skeleton in the chest used as a puppet to terrify villains, shows how Gothic texts, through repetition, raised ideologically charged issues, such as the question of the use of human remains as anatomical material. Walpole's giant skeleton, with its fleshless jaws, empty sockets and dislocated body parts in the first Gothic story thus reverberated, retrospectively, with the anatomical culture of the period, which his contemporaries capitalised on in their reworking of the original Gothic motifs. Interestingly, the increasing realism of the skeleton in the Gothic novels we have examined mirrors in fact the changing status of the skeleton in the medical literature of the time. As

Benjamin A. Rifkin et al. argue, books such as Bernard Siegfried Albinus's (1697–1770) *Tabulae Ossium Humanorum*, published in 1747 (which appeared in London in 1759 as *Tables of the Skeleton and Muscles of the Human Body*), with illustrations by the engraver Jan Wandelaar (1690–1759), 'marked the end of a line' in the contemporary representation of human remains:

> The flayed Apollos lost their tormented wildernesses, elegiac parks, vistas, and hillocks to the divorce of science from the romanticised world of the dead. From here on the science of subject would show the dead as just that, dead, while the art of setting would never again conjure up the cadaver in environments of moral, poetic, and theological imagery.[53]

Anita Guerrini, in contrast, sees the skeleton as a much more ambivalent object throughout the romantic period and beyond – a point which is reflected in the literature and the arts of the time. As she points out, until the seventeenth century, the skeleton 'continued to be symbolic and emotional – a religious object – at the same time as it was anatomical and rational – a scientific object'.[54] In the eighteenth century, skeletons would become sought-after scientific objects, but they also 'served as the decoration (for lack of a better word) of the places where dissection took place, retaining their strong symbolic and emotional resonance'.[55] Thus, for Guerrini, between the sixteenth and the nineteenth centuries, 'medical and scientific uses [of skeletons] never entirely displaced the long-held symbolic and emotional connotations of the human skeleton'.[56] Through their spectres and haunted apartments, Gothic writers repeatedly confronted contemporary scientific constructions of the skeleton or cadaver with popular beliefs about the corpse, the soul and death. The 'phantoms' the characters saw, like Hubert in the above-mentioned example, even when seen as assembled skeletons animated by chains or hands, retained their spectral immateriality for the onlooker, thus confronting the reader with powerfully contradictory images of human remains and constructions of the human subject.

2

The Chamber of Horrors: Anatomical Models and the Gothic

When I was shewn these human petrifications, I shrunk back with disgust and horror. 'Ashes to ashes!' thought I – 'Dust to dust!' – If this be not dissolution, it is something worse than natural decay. It is treason against humanity, thus to lift up the awful veil which would fain hide its weakness. The grandeur of the active principles is never more strongly felt than at such a sight; for nothing is so ugly as the human form when deprived of life, and thus dried into stone, merely to preserve the most disgusting image of death.[1]

Waxen artefacts, even when removed from the practical ground of their origin and their legal and medical uses are no longer apparent, retain their challenge to the stuff of life, their antithetical connection with bodies and embodiment . . . At the same time, however, wax gives rise to thoughts of mortality: it melts, it burns down, it suggests the vanity of the world, . . . the deliquescence of flesh. The material implies organic change. Like many symbols, it packs and binds opposite meanings within its range . . . Wax cheats death; it stimulates life; it proves true and false.[2]

Marina Warner's definition of the ambivalent meanings of wax, unlike Mary Wollstonecraft's 'disgust and horror' at the sight of embalmed corpses, reveals wax's capacity to evoke both wonder and terror and encapsulate the kind of contradictory emotions eagerly seized upon by novelists in search of new ways to thrill their readers. As a material long used in preserving the dead and creating the illusion of life, wax was central to the Gothic, as this chapter will demonstrate, especially because, as Warner underlines, it 'belongs in the embalmer's pharmacopeia; working with wax is a forensic skill'.[3] Life casts of bodies or body parts made of wax were particularly common in Catholic Europe, and from the late seventeenth and early eighteenth century onwards they became closely linked to medical education and epitomised the Enlightenment search for knowledge. That being said, anatomical wax models took many forms, from the eighteenth-century Florentine anatomical models of the Specola museum, which opened in 1775, to the ghastly reproductions of corpses by Joseph Towne (1806–79), displayed at Guy's Hospital in nineteenth-century London. On the one hand, the peaceful Italian sleeping beauties of the eighteenth century, adorned in jewellery, seemed to invite the beholder to gaze lasciviously into their entrails; on the other, hospital cadavers with grey faces and mouths open, as if screaming in agony, gave the appearance of having been abandoned on the anatomist's table after being cut up and disembowelled.

For John Pickstone, the natural and artificial anatomies which were produced and circulated from the seventeenth century onwards were 'part of the new natural history':[4] the human body was conceived 'as a land to be explored'; the practice of this new anatomy thus paralleled 'the voyages of exploration then revealing the contents of new continents and shipping them back to the old'.[5] The Gothic emerged at precisely this time, when natural philosophers were trying to systematise and classify nature and bring order to the natural world. Imperial expansion and global exploration revealed ever more new species and specimens to be brought back to Britain, discoveries which confounded previous systems of knowledge and increasingly shattered long-held definitions of what it was to be human. Eighteenth-century collectors participated actively in this quest for knowledge. Among their number were literary figures such as Horace Walpole, whose collecting and writings illuminated his attempt at defining the human, as part of the Enlightenment project.[6] The Gothic, as originally imagined by Walpole, with its villains, its cruelty and its violence, explored over and over again the divide between the human and the savage, the civilised and the exotic or the unknown. From its origins, in fact, the genre dealt with the human–animal boundary, at a time when the idea was gaining ground that humans might not be that far removed from the apes then being exhibited in Britain's menageries and fairs. Mary Shelley's *Frankenstein* (1818) offers what is certainly the most striking illustration of this way of seeing both the world and the body in terms of exploration. But Radcliffean heroines can also be seen in this light, as they travel through Europe, explore castles and examine mysterious bodies or corpses. Moreover, in ways very similar to Clara Reeve's *Old English Baron* (1778) or Ann Radcliffe's *Romance of the Forest* (1791), both Radcliffe's *The Mysteries of Udolpho* (1794) and Shelley's *Frankenstein* revolve around corpses which function as a form of narrative tease. In each case, however, the corpses are reproductions, fake imitations of human cadavers or artificial reconstructions of human beings, all powerfully informed by European anatomical culture.

Wax effigies, as in Radcliffe's *Mysteries of Udolpho*, emblematise the threatening and terrifying Catholic culture which underlies many a Gothic plot. In Italy, Catholic saints were often found exhibited in glass coffins, their bodies a mix of wax and embalmed body parts. Yet the veiled statue at the end of *The Mysteries of Udolpho* is also symptomatic of the hermeneutic quest that permeates Gothic novels. The statue oscillates between two ways of reading the world: it is meant first as a harbinger of death, and thus can be read symbolically or allegorically. However, as Emily mistakenly deciphers the body of her deceased aunt in the putrefied features of the (artificial) corpse, the effigy can also be read in a more 'scientific way', as a 'natural object' – an idea which is sustained by the guidebook from which the object has been inspired, as will be seen. The statue is thus located at a crossroads, poised between two different readings in ways that are very similar to the cabinets of natural history which in the eighteenth century still combined natural historical objects, human artefacts and 'wonders'. The Gothic atmosphere – the hesitation at the root of the fantastic – results from this tension between reading the statue as a corpse (it is the model of a corpse) or as an omen (metaphorising monkish superstition). Yet if both readings are potentially as terrifying, the medical (or realistic) one is ultimately the most horrifying to the female character, thus intimating that the medical reading is the 'dominant paradigm', emblematic of the 'knowledge systems' of the time.[7]

As will be seen in the first part of this chapter, some of the objects which evoke terror and horror 'appropriat[e] from contemporary travel writing an equation between the foreign and the forbidden'.[8] By proposing a thrilling, terrifying or even macabre version of the Grand Tour,[9] they also reflected changing trends in medical education and practice, and were closely related to the rise of anatomy in medical education.

'I'll have you all modelled in wax and clay'[10]

In eighteenth-century England, anatomy was taught mostly through private lectures which were illustrated with imported anatomical models, such as those by French surgeon, Guillaume Desnoues (d.1735). Exiled in Italy, Desnoues started working in 1699 with the Sicilian modeller Gaetano Giulio Zummo (1656–1701), famous for such macabre artworks as *The Plague* and *The Tomb*, which featured decomposing corpses. Zummo's waxworks were well-known to European travellers, above all because they were exhibited in the Specola museum in Florence, which attracted many visitors, whose experiences of the museum were frequently related in travel guides and narratives. The Marquis de Sade, famous for his erotic novels, recorded for instance his visit to the collections in 1775 in his *Voyage d'Italie*, just before the opening of the Florentine museum.[11] The morbid wax models he discovered on display in the Medici gallery (before their transfer to the cabinet of natural history) were those of the Sicilian modeller:

> One of these vitrines reveals a sepulchre containing numerous corpses which enable the visitor to observe the various stages of decay, from the day-old corpse to the completely worm-eaten cadaver. This bizarre idea is the work of a Sicilian named Zummo. Everything is made of wax and coloured with natural tints. The impression is so intense that the senses seem to mutually warn one another. You

naturally and inadvertently bring your hand to your nose when you look at the horrible details, and you can hardly examine them without remembering sinister ideas of destruction and consequently the more consoling thought of the Creator. Close to this vitrine is another similar one, representing a sepulchre in a church rectory where the same stages of putrefaction may likewise be observed. Particularly striking is the presence of a wretch, stark naked, carrying a corpse which he throws over the others. Suffocated by the smell and the spectacle, he falls on his back and also dies. The realism of the group is frightening.[12]

The corporeality of the human bodies represented here in different stages of decay mirrors the type of corporeal horror found in the Gothic literary tradition of the turn of the nineteenth century. A particularly good example of this are the tales of terror inspired by German ballads, penned by such authors as Matthew Lewis.[13] Many early modellers, such as Ercole Lelli in Bologna, 'cast directly from bodies and from body parts, and built the results on to actual skeletons',[14] reproducing the different stages of medical dissection to display the inner workings of the body.

Interestingly, the scene depicted by Sade at the Florentine museum later appeared in *Juliette; or Vice Amply Rewarded* (1801), a narrative which accompanied *Justine; or Good Conduct Well-Chastized* (1791). In *Justine*, regarded as the prequel of *Juliette*, the female character notices the very same details:

We can see a sepulchre full of cadavers, in diverse stages of dissolution, from the moment of death to the complete destruction of man. This grim work is made of wax, coloured so naturally that nature could not be more expressive nor truthful. The impression is so intense, when one looks at this masterpiece, that the senses seem to mutually warn one another: you inadvertently bring your hand to your nose. My cruel imagination delighted in this spectacle. How many creatures have suffered from these horrible stages because of my wickedness? . . . Not far from there is another sepulchre full of plague victims where the same degrees of putrefaction may be observed: a wretch, stark naked, may be seen carrying a corpse to throw it with the others and who, suffocated by the stench falls on his back and dies. The realism of the group is frightening.[15]

These examples point to the pervasive presence of waxworks representing the dead body and the way in which they both symbolised knowledge and touched upon tabooed (female) sexuality. The connections between dissection and sexual promiscuity (or even pornography) will be further developed in chapter 4, but the passage here highlights the way in which waxworks were related to the foreign and the forbidden – an idea which is better understood when looked at from the perspective of the history of wax collections and their circulation throughout Europe.

Zummo's wax models are a case in point. The partnership between the French surgeon and the wax modeller aimed initially at providing Desnoues with enough models and preparations for his lectures. However, the two men quickly started exhibiting and selling their models. Although the association of Desnoues with Zummo did not last long, both men continued to make, exhibit and sell anatomical models in the following years, this time in Paris. Desnoues formed a partnership with another artist, François de La Croix, presenting his models for the first time in Paris in 1711 and creating the very first museum of anatomical wax models.[16] The models did not stay in Paris; they were soon exhibited all over Europe, in particular in England, where many anatomists giving lectures for professional and lay audiences were in need of models to illustrate their talks. The rarity of modellers in England (apart from the aforementioned Joseph Towne, active in Guy's Hospital in the mid-nineteenth century) explains why English anatomists imported many models for their private lessons.

The circulation of Desnoues's anatomical models from continental Europe to Britain also exemplifies how eighteenth-century culture delighted in 'curiosities' of all sorts, beyond the medical sphere. The exhibition of his models was advertised in magazines such as the *Daily Courant*, as in March 1719, when the journal announced that four new models were then on view near Southampton Street in the Strand 'to the Curious of both Sexes'.[17] The advertisements also indicate that Desnoues's wax models were used by British surgeons, like John Sargent in Charles Street, Covent Garden, in 1728.[18] It is interesting to note that the advertisements which circulated from 1718 to 1728 all implied that the wax models could be seen by men and women alike.[19] The association of anatomical models with the development of the discourse and knowledge about sexual reproduction in the course of the eighteenth century is highly significant. The emergence of gynaecology and obstetrics was accompanied by debates around the appropriateness of anatomical collections for female audiences,[20] and anatomical knowledge more generally raised suspicions because of its frequent focus on sexuality.[21] Tellingly, the debate frequently crystallised around waxworks, which may explain why wax models appear now and again in the Gothic romances of the 1790s.[22]

From Radcliffe's statue to Frankenstein's models

Ann Radcliffe was familiar with a wide range of authors, from Shakespeare to Milton and Spencer. However, scholars have also highlighted her knowledge of the many travel guides of her time. The publication of *The Mysteries of Udolpho* in 1794 was followed by that of *A Journey Made in the Summer of 1794, through Holland and the Western Frontier of Germany, with a Return down the Rhine: To which are added Observations during a Tour of the Lakes of Lancashire, Westmoreland and Cumberland.* Her travel narrative owed much to works such as Samuel Johnson's *A Journey to the Western Islands of Scotland* (1775).[23] The narrative recorded her unique experience on the Continent, even though most of her famous descriptions of picturesque scenery were the product of her imagination and reading, rather than first-hand experience. Radcliffe's use of travel books did not pass unnoticed by her contemporaries. In *Diary of a Lover of Literature* (1810), Thomas Green traced her borrowings from Mrs Piozzi's *Observations and Reflections Made in the Course of a Journey through France, Italy and Germany* for some of her descriptions in *The Mysteries of Udolpho*.[24] Examined by critics such as Clara Frances McIntyre or J. M. S. Tompkins, in the 1920s, Radcliffe's debts to the travel literature of her time indicate the extent to which her novels combined fact and fiction, thereby adhering, as Tompkins points out, to Walpole's definition of the Gothic as the blending of 'two kinds of romance'.[25] Indeed, the way in which Radcliffe set her objects of terror in a realistic setting may well help to account for their success with readers. A case in point might be the piece of wax concealed behind the black veil in *The Mysteries of Udolpho*. The motif drives the suspense of the narrative until the very last pages as the reader longs to know what Emily St Aubert saw behind the black veil. Tompkins's analysis of Radcliffe's borrowing from Ramond de Carbonnières's *Observations faites dans les Pyrénées* (1789) and P. J. Grosley's *New Observations on Italy and its Inhabitants* (1769) for *The Mysteries of Udolpho* reveals that Grosley's travel guide may have been the inspiration for Radcliffe's object of terror. In the Benedictine church of St Vital in Ravenna, Grosley came upon a curiosity – a piece of waxwork representing the decomposing body of a young man's fiancée:

> A young man, passionately in love with a very beautiful woman, went for a few days to his relations, to settle matters on the occasion. In the meantime, this beauty fell sick, died, and, at the young man's return, had been buried three days. Fancying the sight of his mistress might somewhat alleviate his despair, he got the vault to be opened, and there she was seen in reality, as we saw her represented in wax. Extremely beautiful, among the damp regions of the dead; a lizard is sucking her mouth; a worm is creeping out of her cheeks, a mouse is gnawing one of her ears, and a huge swollen toad on her forehead is preying on one of her eyes. I own, at first sight, I took this to be no more than a pious contrivance for mortifying pride, and alienating the heart from too violent a love of sublunary inticements [*sic*]; but I have still been convinced of its possibility.[26]

The similarities between the representation of the decomposing corpse in this travel book and in Radcliffe's Gothic romance are striking. Radcliffe revisits the Italian curiosity, building on Grosley's descriptions to blend horror with anti-Catholicism:

> It may be remembered that in a chamber of Udolpho hung a black veil, whose singular situation had excited Emily's curiosity, and which afterwards disclosed an object that had overwhelmed her with horror; for, on lifting it, there appeared, instead of the picture she had expected, within a recess of the wall, a human figure, of ghastly paleness, stretched at its length, and dressed in the habiliments of the grave. What added to the horror of the spectacle, was that the face appeared

partly decayed and disfigured by worms, which were visible on the features and hands . . . Had she dared to look again, her delusion and her fears would have vanished together, and she would have perceived, that the figure before her was not human, but formed of wax. The history of it is somewhat extraordinary, though not without example in the records of that fierce severity, which monkish superstition has sometimes inflicted on mankind. A member of the house of Udolpho, having committed some offence against the prerogative of the church, had been condemned to the penance of contemplating, during certain hours of the day, a waxen image, made to resemble a human body in the state, to which it is reduced after death.[27]

Furthermore, although Grosley's narrative does not contain the type of gruesome details generally found in the popular Gothic tales of the last decades of the eighteenth century, his narrative is replete with descriptions of Italian funeral practices, from burying to embalming, references to the dead body which informed the Gothic novel from its origins. If Radcliffe's cadavers and skeletons bear little resemblance to the corporeal horror found in collections of Gothic tales such as Lewis's *Tales of Wonder* (1801) or the anonymous *Tales of Terror* (1887), edited by Henry Morley (many of them, as we have noted, adaptations of German ballads), the intertextual allusions to the travel narrative construct *The Mysteries of Udolpho*, to some extent, as an alternative Grand Tour experience. Thus, Emily grows in curiosity, knowledge and education through exposure to new places and new sensations – a view in keeping with the latest thinking among the educational reformers of the period. Interestingly, Grosley's travel narrative also contains descriptions of places such as the Institute of Bologna, a museum which contained the wax anatomical models made by Ercole Lelli (1702–66) and his wife Anna Morandi Manzolini (1716–74),[28] exhibited from 1776.[29]

The influence of travel and travel narratives is very similar in Mary Shelley's *Frankenstein* (1818). Journeys of all sorts punctuate Shelley's Gothic novel, from Captain Robert Walton's scientific expedition to the North Pole, to Victor Frankenstein's numerous voyages between England and Switzerland, throughout Europe and finally to the North Pole in search of his creature. Victor Frankenstein in particular never fails to take the longest route possible in order to discover new regions or places, eager as he is to take in new sights and acquire new knowledge along the way. During his 'voyages of discovery', moreover, he happens upon various 'objects' or curiosities which feature prominently in contemporary accounts of nineteenth-century tourism. Indeed, the many places seen or visited by the characters shape the novel to some extent as a travel narrative, more especially so as it was published after 1815, when continental travel was resumed at the end of the Napoleonic Wars (1803–15).[30] In addition, the novel provides regular echoes of Mary Shelley's own travels through Europe in 1814 and 1816, recorded in her *History of Six Weeks' Tour through a part of France, Switzerland, Germany, and Holland; with Letters Descriptive of a Sail Round the Lake of Geneva and of the Glaciers of Chamouni* (1817). Written with Percy Bysshe Shelley, the journal describes two journeys: one through Europe (France, Switzerland, Germany, the Netherlands) in 1814, as the unmarried couple eloped from England with Mary's stepsister, Claire Clairmont, and a second, to Lake Geneva in 1816, which inspired Mary Shelley's story of *Frankenstein*. Four letters and a poem by Percy Shelley were added to the travel narrative. Both *Frankenstein* and the *History of Six Weeks' Tour* were thus written in 1817, and the links between the two narratives invite readers to examine the significance of these texts' shared motifs.

The connections between Shelley's travel narrative and her novel can be clearly observed in the use made in both texts of objects seen, noticed or examined by the characters, objects which are particularly emblematic of European travel. In each narrative, Shelley mentions cabinets of natural history. The cabinets visited by the Shelleys at Servoz and Chamonix, which they compare with those in Matlock, Keswick, Clifton and Bethgelert (*sic*), are mirror images of those which Victor Frankenstein visits in 'Matlock', 'Chamounix' and 'Servox'.[31] Some late eighteenth-century cabinets of natural history continued to resemble closely the cabinets of curiosities prized by early modern collectors. Others, however, grouping together several private collections, paved the way for the natural history and medical museums which would open their doors to the public in the course of the nineteenth century.[32] Whether displaying 'curiosities', the most fantastic forms of nature, or collections of minerals, shells or fossils, they frequently brought objects from around the world under one roof, thus associating travel with erudite investigation. In her *History of Six Weeks' Tour,* Mary Shelley relates the purchase of specimens of minerals and plants, such as crystal seals, and of seeds which she hopes will 'colonize in [her] garden in England'.[33] This example illustrates how such collections facilitated exchanges of various sorts through the circulation of travellers and their purchases. In their travel narrative, the Shelleys also condemn some of the cabinet-owners, like the proprietor at Chamonix, a 'quack' who 'subsist[s] on the weakness and credulity of travellers as leaches [*sic*] subsist on the sick',[34] a remark which recalls to some extent Shelley's anatomist, trained by his father not to believe in superstitions. The comparisons of Mary Shelley's travel narrative with *Frankenstein* are telling, for the echoes between the two narratives highlight the traffic between two different literary genres: Shelley's 'mad scientist' – to use an anachronistic term – is depicted as a Romantic traveller following in the footsteps of the Shelleys, whilst the Romantic couple demonstrate a taste for scientific enquiry throughout their journey.

Indeed, while the travel narrative is peppered with references to picturesque scenery and ruined castles, the Shelleys also pay attention to animals, minerals and plants, describing for example the horns of the chamois and the bouquetin. In this way, the narrative deals recurrently with the acquisition and dissemination of knowledge.[35] Moving away from Grand Tour narratives, however, Shelley's travel writing constantly merges Romantic descriptions with references to natural history. Likewise, Victor Frankenstein's journey is punctuated by sublime descriptions of the Swiss mountains. Moreover, Frankenstein also visits cabinets of natural history, paying attention to the way in which the objects are arranged:

> We passed a considerable period at Oxford, rambling among its environs and endeavouring to identify every spot which might relate to the most animating epoch of English history. Our little voyages of discovery were often prolonged by the successive objects that presented themselves . . .
>
> We left Oxford with regret and proceeded to Matlock, which was our next place of rest . . . We visited the wondrous cave and the little cabinets of natural history, where the curiosities are disposed in the

same manner as in the collections at Servox and Chamounix. The latter name made me tremble when pronounced by Henry, and I hastened to quit Matlock, with which that terrible scene was thus associated.[36]

The arrangement of the natural history cabinet he observes at Matlock revives his memory of the collections at 'Servox' and 'Chamounix', thereby connecting England to mainland Europe. Significantly, the echo between the collections in Matlock, 'Servox' and 'Chamounix' provokes a surge of horror in Frankenstein, reminding him of his creature. This comes at a significant point in the novel, since Frankenstein is on his way to Scotland to create a mate for the creature, having collected his 'materials' (p. 428) in London with the intention of touring England and reaching Scotland six months later. Although Frankenstein remains insensitive to his task in the first part of the novel, blind to 'every object the most insupportable to the delicacy of the human feelings' (p. 312), unemotionally observing 'the natural decay and corruption of the human body' (p. 311), the sight of the collection, through a series of associations, shakes him profoundly, thereby drawing attention to the issue of sensitivity that is so central to the novel and to the understanding of Frankenstein's tragic lack of feeling. While the 'curiosities' are not described as such, it is nonetheless significant that the cabinets of natural history mentioned in the novel reveal Frankenstein as a flawed Romantic traveller, doomed by his lack of sensibility.

The exchanges between the material cultures of natural history and medicine on the one hand, and literature on the other, throughout the nineteenth century, illuminate how the literature of the period reflected the evolution of scientific knowledge and the role played by museum collections in its construction and dissemination. As mentioned above, the striking similarities between Sade's travel narrative, *Voyage d'Italie*, and his novel *Juliette; or Vice Amply Rewarded*, like the echoes between Mary Shelley's *History of Six Weeks' Tour* and *Frankenstein*, highlight the permeable boundaries between genres just as much as they point to the influence of such representations of the body on contemporary culture.[37] In both cases, moreover, the sight of the models spurs a reflection on villainy in the characters (which Sade's character delights in, however). For Ann Williams, the links between the two writers – who were near contemporaries – is not solely to be found in the choice of the name 'Justine' by Mary Shelley for one of the creature's victims. As she argues, both Shelley and Sade 'lived in a period of revolutionary upheaval, and . . . both deployed Gothic conventions in the service of philosophical romance'.[38] Furthermore, she adds that although Sade never appeared on the Shelleys' list of reading matter, Byron was known to own a copy of *Justine* in 1816 before he left England. Whether or not a connection may be traced between Shelley and Sade, the similarities between their travel narratives and novels remain significant, especially as they both revolve around collections exhibited in cabinets of natural history and their impact on late eighteenth-century travellers. The difference between Shelley's *Frankenstein* and Sade's *Juliette*, however, is that no details are given concerning the 'curiosities' seen by Shelley's villain, apart from mentioning their layout in the cabinet. This stress on the arrangement of the collection is typical of the evolution of cabinets of natural history, which aimed increasingly to diffuse knowledge rather than simply provide a frame for displaying freaks of nature. Indeed, the morbid aesthetics typified by artists such as Zummo gradually fell out of fashion. Thus, when the Florentine museum came to display new objects designed to reveal the secrets and mysteries of the human body to the general public, instead of decay and decomposition, the anatomical models presented in the cabinet of natural history were characterised by the orderly fashion in which they were arranged. The French sculptor Charles Dupaty (1775–1825) noted the change in his *Lettres sur l'Italie* (*Letters on Italy*) (1785):

> I would like to describe the cabinet of natural history that the Grand Duke has been enlarging and Mr Fontana arranging . . . It is hard to do justice to the refinement of the apartments, the order and the organisation; . . . the vitrines of this cabinet represent so many compartments in Mr Fontana's memory, filled with natural history.[39]

Similarly, the French writer Stendhal, travelling through Italy, visited the Florentine museum on 27 September 1811:

Museum of Natural History. – How pleasurable it must be for an anatomist to step into this Museum! Nothing is cleaner, more comprehensible nor more instructive. Everything is arranged in order to present intelligible ideas effortlessly. The room devoted to childbirth seems to me notably superior to those in Bologna and Vienna. I remember with delight when I visited the Josephinum in Vienna and saw the childbirth room with Lady A.

I behold, with the pleasure of the ignorant, the muscles and the nerves, all meticulously represented . . . I saw there for the first time a skeleton that looked beautiful. It is easy to see how beautiful a skeleton can be . . . It is situated on the left when you enter the rooms with the wax models, in a beautiful glass cage.[40]

Instead of disease and decay, the collection was now characterised by beauty, order and cleanliness. Stendhal's praise reflects the changing status of the skeleton in the medical literature of the time, as seen in chapter 1. Likewise, the wax models are no longer designed for connoisseurs of morbid aesthetics but are aimed at 'the anatomist', most likely to appreciate the beauty of the (scientific) exhibits. Stendhal's comparisons between the different collections accessible to the European traveller are compelling, pinpointing as they do how seeing such collections prompted travellers to develop their own systems of classification – their own natural history of natural history cabinets, so to speak. This move away from a focus on 'curiosities' as emblems of sixteenth- or seventeenth-century wonder to a more scientific and comprehensive view of the natural world is illustrative of a move away from emotions and passions. Exhibited in a glass case, the skeleton is observed from a distance and the writer's 'feel[ing]' appears all the more detached. Stendhal's remarks were echoed in England by the board of curators of the Royal College of Surgeons, which noted in July 1813 that 'the utmost order and decorum prevailed' among its collections.[41] According to Samuel Alberti, such remarks on order typified new modern ways of displaying and viewing throughout Europe, especially in the last decades of the century. He argues that '[i]n the expanding public museum sector in the late Victorian period, the emphasis shifted to transparent, ordered display and clear labelling', thus placing the displayed objects 'within taxonomic schemes' and 'remov[ing] them from the realm of the curious'.[42]

As Shelley's novel exemplifies, Gothic literature charted the same gradual changes in natural history and anatomical displays, following the evolution of museum display throughout Europe. In addition, inspired by the recorded impressions of those actually visiting the Continent's collections, the literature of the period represented the characters' reactions to the displays, as in the case of Victor Frankenstein. As suggested above, Shelley constructs the scene in which the villain looks at the collection as a pivotal moment in his moral awakening: Frankenstein's clinical detachment when he looks at the collection is followed by a painful memory of the creature. It is tempting to conjecture that Shelley had in mind visitors' responses to such collections. In 1813, Joseph Forsyth mentioned in his travel book the impressive size of the Florentine collection.[43] Forsyth had visited the museum in 1803 and discussed it in an 1813 review which, according to Feldman and Scott-Kilvert, Shelley would not read until April 1819, while she was making preparations for her own journey.[44] In January 1820, Shelley recorded her visit to the Italian museum in her diary in the following terms: 'The Gabinetto Fisico was a museum of natural history, chiefly celebrated for its collection of wax models of the human anatomy, some of which were extremely gruesome.'[45] If Shelley had not read the Forsyth review when she wrote *Frankenstein*, it is highly likely that she had heard about the collection, especially as many nineteenth-century writers mentioned it in their own diaries. Moreover, Forsyth's description of the museum focused on the anatomical collection, emphasising the evolution from Zummo's morbid aesthetics to Fontana's experiments with wax. The following quotation maps out the aesthetic changes in the displays and is worth quoting at length:

> This, being originally an assemblage of several scattered collections in natural history, is rather full than complete. It is richest in fossils, corals, shells, and insects; but celebrated only for the anatomical imitations.
>
> Wax was first used in imitating anatomy by Zumbo, a Sicilian of a melancholy, mysterious cast, some of whose works are preserved

here. Three of these bear the gloomy character of the artist, who has exhibited the horrible details of the plague and the charnel-house, including the decomposition of bodies through every stage of putre-faction – the blackening, the swelling, the bursting of the trunk – the worm, the rat and the tarantula at work – and the mushroom springing fresh in the midst of corruption.

I was struck by the immensity of this collection, which occupies fourteen rooms; yet, considered as a system, anatomists find it both defective and redundant. Sig. Fabbroni told me that many articles should be melted down as useless; that others were inaccurate; that all, from the yielding nature of the wax, wanted frequent retouching; and that, beginning anew, he could make the system more complete in half the compass. But such is ever the course of experiment. Every new step in science is the correction of an old one. Science may be considered as the art of remedies which originate in defect and end in it . . .

This museum is under the direction of Felice Fontana . . . Fontana readily entered into the history of imitative anatomy, 'an art invented by Zumbo, and revived', he said 'by me . . . I stood alone in a new art, without guide or assistants . . . Thus obliged to form workmen for myself, I selected some mechanical drudges, who would execute my orders without intruding into my design . . .'

This active Prometheus is creating a decomposable statue, which will consist of ten thousand separable pieces, and three millions of distinct parts, both visible and tangible.[46]

Whether Shelley had read the review before 1819 or not, Franken-stein appears as an uncanny double of the Florentine modeller, a latter-day Prometheus selecting workers to achieve his art and collect the pieces to create a composite model.[47] Furthermore, as in *Franken-stein*, the making of wax anatomical models implied the use of up to 1,000 cadavers, as some travellers noted,[48] whilst models which could be disassembled promised to reveal the secret inner workings of the human body. If Feldman and Scott-Kilvert are correct in their assertion that Shelley only read Forsyth's review in 1819, the echoes suggest that recreations of artificial models of the human body from cadavers, especially in Italy (Bologna, Florence) and France, were popularised through many travel narratives, which in turn influenced the literary scene of the Romantic period. In the case of *Frankenstein*, the interest lies in the dual nature of Frankenstein's reaction to the 'curiosities' he sees – both in terms of distance and in the emotional reaction generated in him by a series of associations. According to Alberti, the development of literary genres or modes was closely related to the evolution of collections of natural history and anatomy:

> The roots of Gothic literature were in the fascination with an imagined and terrible past, and visitors' engagement (with fossils in particular) may reflect this interest. By the late nineteenth century, medicoscientific discourses contributed to the somatic emphasis of Gothic fiction, which privileged racial degeneration, atavism, deviant sexualities, and monstrosity – examples of which would all be found in anatomical museums.[49]

Alberti refers here to late-Victorian medical Gothic, but the example of *Frankenstein* as a nineteenth-century novel poised between the tradition of the Gothic novel and the later Victorian Gothic is illuminating: the Gothic villain that is Frankenstein experiences contradictory reactions (indifference/horror) when he looks at the objects exhibited in the cabinet of natural history. The oscillation between detachment and empathy mirrors the evolution of aesthetics which marked nineteenth-century representations of human remains and human anatomy more generally. In addition, as Alberti suggests, many of the specimens exhibited played more and more upon the tension between normality and pathology as well as contrasting the civilised and the wild – Britishness and foreign otherness/exotic degeneracy – far beyond Europe's frontiers. Shelley's *Frankenstein*, as an early nineteenth-century example, may, indeed, record how the various forms of nature collected, recreated and exhibited in natural history cabinets impacted contemporary fiction. Frankenstein's creature is compared to a mummy at the opening and the end of the novel: 'A mummy again endued with animation could not be hideous as that wretch (p. 319); 'one vast hand was extended, in colour and apparent texture like that of a mummy' (p. 492). The comparison brings to mind early nineteenth-century Egyptomania and evokes debates around race and national identity. Moreover, the focus on the texture of the skin might even be read as a reference to desiccated specimens, with the mummy subtly constructed as a museum exhibit. This is further suggested by the anatomist's fight against the appearance of death, as manifest in the creature's watery eyes (which signal the onset of putrefaction), the colour of the lips and the texture of the flesh. Frankenstein is a typical anatomist who 'collect[s] [his] materials' (p. 164), preserves them and exhibits them through his 'monster' – as a living representation of the Latin term *monstrare* (to show), as I have argued elsewhere.[50] In addition, as Stefani Englestein has pointed out, Frankenstein's activities are very close to those of wax modellers: Frankenstein starts with 'bones from the charnel house', and the coloured wax models were 'sometimes constructed on the foundations of real human skeletons'.[51]

Examining *Frankenstein* through its connections with European travel literature and Shelley's own travel narrative enables us therefore to see the links between Frankenstein's creature and the many naturalistic forms that were displayed in museums throughout Europe and/or which tapped into global travel and its impact upon the construction of British imperial science. Through the creature or through the ways in which Frankenstein reads the displays in the natural history cabinets he visits, the novel also mirrors changing contemporary aesthetics by portraying the eponymous anatomist as the double of artists such as Fontana in Florence. Increasingly associated with a lack of human sympathy or sensitivity, the anatomical collections which appeared in Gothic narratives actively participated in characterisation, particularly, perhaps, when the objects were imported from Europe or the British colonies. Their association with pathology and monstrosity, moreover, explains why they resurfaced recurrently on the literary scene, especially during the Victorian period, as objects epitomising fear.

Waxing and waning: morbid Sleeping Beauties

– All moveables, of wonder from all parts,
Are here, Albinos, painted Indians, Dwarfs,
The Horse of knowledge and the Learned Pig,

The Stone-eater, the man that swallows fire,
Giants, Ventriloquists, the Invisible Girl,
The Bust that speaks and moves its goggling eyes,
The Wax-work, Clock-work, all the marvellous craft
Of modern Merlins, Wild Beasts, Puppet shows
All out-o'-the-way, far-fetched, perverted things,
All freaks of Nature, all Promethean thoughts,
All jumbled up together to make up
This Parliament of Monsters. Tents and Booths
Meanwhile, as if the whole were one vast Mill,
Are vomiting, receiving, on all sides,
Men, Women, three-years' Children, Babes in arms.[52]

William Wordsworth's depiction of Bartholomew Fair, with fleshly freaks and artificial waxworks 'all jumbled together', seems poles apart from specimens exhibited in medical museums clinically displayed along shelves. Wax models were among the chief attractions on display in fairs in the 1830s, alongside the menageries, the 'living skeletons', the pig-faced ladies and the Scottish giants;[53] all potentially evoking both wonder and horror. As a carnivalesque version of the medical museum, exhibiting its anatomical models, preparations and monsters,[54] Wordsworth's 'Parliament of Monsters' nevertheless blurs the boundaries between the world of entertainment and that of medicine.

Gothic romances published by the Minerva Press, which foregrounded in particular the artificiality of the genre, also used wax to attract readers, employing it as a significant plot device, at the crossroads of the world of the fair and that of the medical museum. This is notably the case with George Brewer's *The Witch of Ravensworth* (1808), a Gothic romance which places a female corpse at the heart of the narrative. The cadaver, however, remains suspended between life and death, mirroring through its resistance to decay the pure, chaste, gentle and courteous Lady Bertha, whose husband, the Baron de la Braunch, has married out of base desire only to quickly shift his attentions towards another – Lady Alwena. The Baron in fact falls victim to optical illusions made with 'horrid images of wax',[55] orchestrated by the witch (or 'Hag'), alias Lady Gertrude, assisted by the monk Velaschi:

The night arrived; he found the Hag ready to receive him, and to conduct him to the chamber of horrors.

The witch led the baron, covered with his mantle, in the way she had before done, to the palace of Askar.

It was empty of its dreadful inhabitants.

There was not any thing to be seen, but the altar, and throne, with a bier, placed in the middle of the room. On the bier was laid the body of lady Bertha.

The Hag led the baron to the altar.

She required from him an horrid injunction; his hair stood on end, as she pronounced the sentence: he was to plunge his dagger in the bosom. (pp. 65–6)

The Baron's desire, merging with the image of his hair standing on end, his symbolic rape, metaphorised by the phallic dagger,[56] and the narrative's suggestion of necrophilia, forcefully highlight the strong connection between wax models and female sexuality. Indeed, while wax anatomical models were praised as icons of eighteenth-century Enlightened science, they were also condemned for revealing the (female) body's most private secrets. The wax motif, therefore, serves the Gothic plot by hinting both at female sexuality (women's periodical cycles, identical to the waxing and waning of the moon) and anatomy (anatomical wax Venuses). In other words, the wax motif sexualises the female corpse even further, eroticising the cadaver, which epitomises female passivity. Furthermore, while the Baron is hidden from view by his cloak, the female body is offered to the reader's gaze, since Lady Bertha is displayed in the middle of the room.

The Gothic narrative, which hinges upon optical illusions and tricks of all sorts, connects the world of Gothic phantasmagoria with that of waxworks, demonstrating how anatomical wax models, exhibited both in medical museums and fairs, carried powerful associations of sexual promiscuity. Lady Blessington, for example, described the Gabinetto Fisico waxworks collection in Florence as a revolting place, one which men and women should not be allowed to visit simultaneously:

I entered the Gabinetto Fisico today, and though I only remained a few minutes . . . I carried away a sense of loathing that has not yet left me. Surely some restriction should exist to preclude men and women from examining these models together! . . . It is meet that we should know that we are fearfully and wonderfully created; but not that we should witness the disgusting and appalling details of the animal economy in all its hideous and appalling nakedness and truth. What a lesson for personal vanity does this exhibition convey!

I told that its fearful images will recur to my memory when I behold some creature, in the zenith of youth and beauty, who almost believes that she is not formed of the perilous stuff so shockingly delineated in the *Gabinetto Fisico*.[57]

Blessington's depiction of the place, echoing that contained in Forsyth's travel book, establishes a close connection between the mysteries of the human body on display and sexual reproduction:

I was struck by the immensity of this collection, which occupies fourteen rooms . . .

This awful region, which should be sacred to men of science, is open to all. Nay, the very apartment where the gravid uterus and its processes lie unveiled, is a favourite lounge of the ladies, who criticise aloud all the mysteries of sex.[58]

The fact that the Florentine anatomical models could provide sexual information to the 'gentler sex' permeated many reviews, whether written by men or women. The fainting of many women during the guided tour of the Specola anatomical collection is another indication of the impact that the models had on the 'weaker sex',[59] and visitors frequently regarded the visit as 'a sort of pre-deflowering [that] was sometimes even planned'.[60] Moreover, while little remains known of the reactions of visitors other than the upper- and middle-class travellers quoted above, Anna Maerker suggests that the administrators' decision to put locks on the showcases displaying the genitals was probably symptomatic of many visitors' visceral responses to the Italian anatomical collection.[61]

These reviews of the Specola anatomical waxes provide a good illustration of the mixed responses prompted by anatomical collections. Even though the Italian anatomical Venuses looked as if they were merely asleep rather than dead, their nakedness and the open bodies they offered to the audience's gaze were more often than not deemed inappropriate for the 'gentler sex'. The many wax shows which opened in London throughout the eighteenth century, aimed both at instruction and entertainment, provide a good illustration of this point. One such case, Rackstrow's museum at 197 Fleet Street, promoted sexual reproduction as the central point of the exhibition in the 1780s. Significantly, however, the museum's owner, Benjamin Rackstrow, chose to collaborate with a midwife, Catherine Clarke, who attended female visitors and provided midwifery education.[62]

Brewer's *Witch of Ravensworth* similarly uses wax artefacts which evoke both the entertaining world of the fair and the representations of the female body found in natural history or medical museums. The novel has all the ingredients of the fanciful Gothic novel, taking its readers into a world of wonders and magic which recurrently flirts with the world of the fairy tale. As the title suggests, the main character is a witch. The 'Hag' lives completely isolated on a wild heath, Ravensworth-Moor, in a miserable hut, 'covered with soot, and curiously embossed with cobwebs' (p. 3). Her description matches to perfection the portrait of the witch in classical fairy tales:

> She was little, thin, bent almost double, and very aged; her flesh was of a dark brown, and so lean and skinny, that it hung in a variety of folds from her arms; her face was wrinkled all over; her eyes small, and the sockets red, as if inflamed by disease, or anger; her head was long, and sunk between her shoulders; her nose was prominent and crooked, besides that it was constantly smeared with snuff; her lips were pale, and her single tooth, for she appeared to have but one, stood projecting its black arc over the front of her wide mouth: in short, she was so horribly ugly, that no one would come within two yards of her, when she approached. (p. 3)

Accompanied by a half-starved cat and a one-winged raven, the Hag is believed to possess all the powers of witchcraft, to whip and torture babies to death and feed on their flesh, and to turn men, women and children into 'loathsome reptiles, such as bats, or efts, or lizards' (p. 5).

Two additional villains are introduced into the narrative in the second chapter: the monk Velaschi, whose actions are 'enwrapped in a dark veil of mystery, that seemed to conceal some malignant design, or mischief' (p. 7), and Baron de La Braunch – 'mistrustful, suspicious, and cruel, delighting in the combats of animals, insensible to pity, and regardless of the complaints and sufferings of the poor' (p. 8). Rumours concerning his past 'infidelity' towards a lady named Gertrude are mentioned at the beginning of the story, but no one knows 'how the matter had terminated' (p. 8), and the narrative soon focuses on his attempt to seduce the newly widowed Lady Bertha, who becomes the victim of the evil Baron. Baron de la Braunch marries Lady Bertha. However, on their wedding night, the Hag invites herself to the nuptial dinner and curses the bride. The Gothic rewriting of *Sleeping Beauty* is telling, for at the heart of the fairy tale lies a female body 'stuck in limbo, neither fully in the world of the living nor entirely in the world of the dead',[63] – a preserved corpse likely to both fascinate and horrify.

Indeed, the narrative uses a ghastly Sleeping Beauty in ways very similar to that of anatomical Venuses by medical museums, placing them at the heart of the exhibition the better to draw the public's attention to the mysteries of the human body, which they promised to reveal by taking away the removable parts of the wax statue. This idea that the Gothic rewriting of *Sleeping Beauty* will draw upon the horrors and tantalising secrets of the female body is furthered throughout Brewer's novel. Soon after his wife has given birth to a son, Hugo, Baron de la Braunch seeks to learn about the secret powers of the Hag, who has invited herself again, this time to the christening of the baby. The witch is believed to be insane, but the Baron, 'superstitious enough to believe in the power of the spirits of darkness' (pp. 17–18), hopes that the Hag, who can 'divine everything that can happen in the future' (p. 24), can teach him about the evil spirits which haunt the castle in the wood, 'choked up by the growth of brushwood and under-wood' (p. 28). He thus visits her and finds her 'stooping over a large kettle, or cauldron [which] seems to contain large pieces of human flesh' (p. 27).

At these words the Hag stamped with her foot; a thick smoke filled the hut.

She stamped a second time. The baron fixed his eyes attentively upon her.

The Hag stamped a third time. The space of the cabin was filled with flame: it encircled the witch. (p. 34)

His body covered entirely with a cloak so that he may not see where he is taken, the baron opens his eyes to reveal a dark vaulted chamber:

In exploring every avenue and recess of this dreary place, the baron beheld only gloom and darkness.

The Hag placed the lamp on the ground.

The baron's eyes were fixed upon a dark recess in the chamber, from whence he had heard proceed a dismal moan. He beheld a stupendous object arise! It was misshapen, but had something of the appearance of a human being. It was huge in form, its body black, and its face jaundiced, and smeared with blood. It roared, as it arose, like a lion which is roused from its den.

The baron started at this object of terror; but how was his horror increased, when he saw that the monster held in one hand a javelin imbrued in human gore, and in the other a cup full of blood, and which it hugged close to its bosom.

A distant scream now reverberated through the chamber, at which the spectre started into a recess of the vault, and was seen no more. 'What was this?' cried the baron, the hair of his head standing on end. (p. 35)

The whole scene stages terror through playing upon sight (and visual deception, as we discover at the end). The Hag then introduces another element: a figure that 'seemed formed only of transparent ether' (p. 36), terrifying the Baron, who asks to be 'hid[den] from that horrid sight' (p. 36). The power of the Hag's 'art' (p. 36) revolves, therefore, in her handling of the powers of delusion. But the Baron has nonetheless been struck by what he has seen and is now haunted by frightening images ('his imagination presented before him the foul spectre, with the javelin, and the bowl of blood' (p. 40)), and he agrees to give his wife's son to the witch so as to inherit his wife's fortune. The young Edward is from that moment on believed to have been 'taken away by fairies' (p. 47), an explanation which strengthens the fairy-tale dimension of the story.

Eleven years later, his own son Hugo now dead, the Baron falls for a woman whose unchaste desires are in inverse proportion to her perfectly moulded features:

> The lady Alwena was of uncommon stature; she was six feet four inches in height, and formed with an exquisite proportion, her limbs were in perfect symmetry, and she trod the ground with the grace and dignity of a princess; her countenance was as open and beautiful as the rich and luxuriant face of autumn; her eyes resembled sparkling gems; her cheeks were as the lily flower, tinged with the red rose; her lips were of a rich crimson, and her fine turned neck and bosom, were finished with the most exquisite workmanship of the hand of Nature, and outvied, in colour, the whiteness of the breast of the swan: her whole form was luxuriant, and teemed with the full ripeness of womanhood. (p. 51)

In order to be able to possess her, the Baron visits the Hag a second time. The price he has to pay is to 'see the demon' himself 'in all his horrors' (p. 57) in the illuminated castle. Once again, the stage is set for horrors to appear. The scene is composed of a 'fantastically drest' figure wearing a crown, the head and arms of a skeleton lying at his feet and a bowl 'filled with a liquid that resembled human blood' (p. 60) placed on a small altar. The Baron sees the same female spectre appear and vanish. Then the Hag appears, to the sound of a trumpet blast:

> She dragged at her heels a loathsome carcase.
> It was the same female form that had just appeared.
> It was no longer a spirit; it was a body, but without life.
> The baron shuddered. (p. 61)

As mentioned above, the Baron's ordeal consists this time in plunging a dagger into the breast of the corpse that has just materialised in front of him – a 'chamber of horrors' (p. 65) where he can gaze, in fact, upon the body of his wife laid on a bier. The murder of his wife leaves him free to marry Lady Alwena. Yet, the Baron soon realises the uninhibited appetites of his new bride and increasingly feels the weight of his crimes. While his castle is turned into a 'mansion of pleasure' (p. 83), the Baron retreats into an apartment in the western turret in order to meditate. The female corpse, suspended between life and death, erotic yet macabre, evoking both wonder and horror, functions as a gateway to the Gothic. A series of crimes and murderous deeds follow, increasingly binding sexuality and death: Lady Alwena, who now wants to seduce a young knight, tries to poison the Baron. He stabs her before dying, and on his deathbed bequeaths all his possessions to a woodcutter and his wife, who live in the forest with a child they have found. The condition for the bequest is that the woodcutter go alone at midnight on the seventh day after the Baron's death to the western turret to recover the title-deeds of his estates. The woodcutter discovers there the figure of a woman, lying on a bier, and that of an infant, placed in a cradle next to her. He also finds out that the deeds containing the Baron's titles are not kept in a chest, as expected, but written on a parchment scroll and suspended from one end of the bier. The scroll contains a written confession from the Baron to the murder of Lady Gertrude, whom he had seduced before marrying Bertha, with the help of Velaschi. The scene prepares, in fact, the final revelation. The Hag next appears with Edward – who had, as it appears, not been killed – and his mother, Lady Bertha. The witch reveals her own identity: hidden under the ugly mask is Lady Gertrude ('her deformity was only in her mask, her gloves, and mantle' (p. 102)). As she explains, the demonic apparitions and the corpses that punctuate the narrative were but illusions contrived by the monk Velaschi with the help of the brotherhood, while the corpses were merely 'horrid images of wax' (p. 102). The tale closes on Lady Gertrude retiring to a convent 'after the wonders she had performed', whilst the Baron, who had not in reality been poisoned, withdraws to a life of pious reflection in order to seek redemption for his intended crimes.

Brewer's Gothic story thus merges horror and wonders through revealing the whole plot as entirely stage-managed and giving wax figures a central part to ensure corporeal horror. The story illustrates, to borrow Marina Warner's terms, how much 'spirits and science were deeply interwoven' in early popular Gothic horror shows, such as in Etienne-Gaspar Robertson's show 'Phantasmagoria', exhibited in Paris in the 1790s, where the 'images flickered and fluttered, and so created an illusion of possessing that quality of conscious life: animation. As Robertson boasted, he could "raise the dead"'.[64] Moreover, 'the devil's power lay in conjuring phenomena that were delusions',[65] binding even more the scientific world with a Gothic world of demons and spectres. Hence the use of wax corpses shifts the story from the realm of Catholic effigies to that of mechanical illusions and medical science.

The subtle way the narrative hovers between Gothic story and fairy tale – a macabre fairy tale – and the play with literary conventions and clichés enable Brewer to lay bare the artificiality of the story. The rewriting of the fairy tale mirrors the reproduction of the body cast in wax which the reader must discover. Far from simply being an extravagant Gothic story, *The Witch of Ravensworth* uses the fairy-tale intertext throughout the narrative as a clue for the reader to anticipate the deception. However, the twist in the (fairy) tale enhances the reality effect and therefore the horror. As argued above, the female corpse at the heart of the narrative, suspended between life and death, enables Brewer to suggest necrophilia as the Baron plunges his phallic dagger into the female form. In doing so, the wax corpses in the story remind the readers how much anatomical Venuses were suffused with eroticism and embodied mystery – the mysteries of (female) sexuality as well as the secrets of life and death. As an object in the text related to medical knowledge and education, they thus function as potent symbols and hermeneutic motifs to drive the narrative towards its conclusion/closure on the one hand, and to metaphorise the secrets of the body's inner workings, on the other.

The 'ghastly waxwork at the fair'

As the novels of the first Gothic wave highlight, waxworks and crime often worked in tandem. Such a connection may be situated as early as at the beginning of the eighteenth century, exemplified by enterprises such as that of the above-mentioned surgeon Guillaume

Desnoues (1650–1735), who opened the first anatomical wax museum in Paris in 1717. Desnoues added a wax model of the renowned thief Cartouche (Louis-Dominique Bourgignon) in 1721. His model was an early example of the interest in criminals' physiognomical (or phrenological) features, laying the foundations for late nineteenth-century collections of criminal anthropology.[66] At the end of the eighteenth century, Madame Tussaud's 'uncle', Philippe Curtius (1737–94), a physician who had abandoned a medical career to set up a wax exhibition, ran two exhibitions in Paris. The first, the 'Salon de Cire', opened at the Palais Royal in 1776; the other, the 'Caverne des Grands Voleurs', opened on the Boulevard du Temple in 1782 – 'a prototype of the Chamber of Horrors, with re-creations of scenes of the crime and portraits of famous villains'.[67] These two exhibitions clearly separated respectable and fashionable figures dressed in court robes and rich garments from criminals. The interest in crime highlighted by Curtius's salon was also exploited by Madame Tussaud in England. In the early nineteenth century, the number of executions declined, due to changes in the criminal law, reducing the number of entertainments for people eager to look at the writhing bodies of murderers choking to death. Still, the popularity of public executions[68] remained reflected in that of Madame Tussaud's 'Chamber of Horrors', as *Punch* would call the room in 1846, which offered portraits of British murderers whose models were sometimes fashioned from death masks made by surgeons.[69]

Dickens's Victorian Gothic has generated much literary criticism. So has his use of, and interest in, waxes, as John Carey has highlighted.[70] *Great Expectations* (1861) was published just as Tussaud's Chamber of Horrors was expanded in 1860, including a 'Chamber of Comparative Physiognomy'.[71] At the time, criminals sentenced to death even gave their clothes to Tussaud's before their executions, and Tussaud's bought the contents of rooms linked to famous murders for their tableaux. Casts of criminals' faces and heads were often made after their execution, with wax modellers like Curtius and Tussaud competing with surgeons and anatomists to reproduce, preserve and display criminals. The relevance of Dickens's Gothic, as an heir to the first wave of Gothic fiction, is undeniable. As seen in chapter 1, the description of the decayed premises where the skeletons are found in both *The Old English Baron* and *The Animated Skeleton*, 'devoured by the moths, and occupied by the rats',[72] the worm and spiders, tables 'spread with viands all dusty, and of ancient date',[73] pave the way for Dickens's Satis House, where time has been stopped at twenty minutes to nine.

Moreover, Dickens's fascination with waxes was foregrounded in several of his articles published in *Household Words* and *All the Year Round*,[74] as well as in many of his novels, which refer to contemporary wax exhibitions. In *The Old Curiosity Shop* (1840–1), for example, the character of Mrs Jarley resembles many women wax modellers who ran wax exhibitions at the end of the eighteenth and the beginning of the nineteenth centuries (such as Mrs Mills, Mrs Goldsmith, Mrs Sylvester, Mrs Patience Wright, Mrs Salmon, Mrs Clark[75] or Mrs Bullock),[76] and who proposed models based on characters ranging from royalty and natural wonders like Patrick O'Brien (1760–1806), a famous Irish giant, to celebrated criminals like Abraham Thornton, tried for the murder of Mary Ashford in 1817, and even stock characters, such as Othello. The models, like those of Mrs Jarley, merged the glamorous and the sensational or displayed the normal and the pathological, as exemplified by the twin infants united at the breast which appeared in the 1820s and 1830s.[77] Mrs Jarley's collection as a whole, therefore, pays homage to the world of the fair and its wax exhibits; criminals are exhibited alongside models of royalty, while tall men are contrasted with short and thin ones. Indeed, Little Nell, as the epitome of the feminine ideal, is presented to the reader in the following terms: 'so small, so compact, so beautifully modelled, so fair, with such blue veins and such transparent skin, and such little feet'.[78] Sometimes believed to be 'a cunning device in wax', Little Nell is also described as 'an important item of the curiosities' (p. 179), offered by Mrs Jarley's waxworks exhibition. The novel, written at the time when Bartholomew Fair was threatened with closure,[79] constantly plays with curiosities, from the giants[80] and dwarfs who surround Jarley's caravan, to the waxworks, with the villain Quilp – 'an uglier dwarf than could be seen anywhere for a penny' (p. 64) – appearing as both freak and waxwork in Little Nell's dreams ('[he] was somewhat connected with the wax-work, or was wax-work himself' (pp. 177–8)), an emblem of both the wonder and horror exhibited at fairs.

Dickens's Mrs Jarley may in fact also have been inspired by an even more popular wax modeller: Madame Tussaud. For like Madame Tussaud, who moved away from the world of the fair and settled in Baker Street in 1835, Jarley dreams of appealing to a middle-class and respectable audience. The novel's association of waxes with women, the feminine ideal, the Victorian bourgeoisie, freaks and criminals, and even with death, as when the doll-like little Nell looks eternally frozen in death at the end of the novel,[81] is of particular relevance in this context, for it paves the way for one of Dickens's much more Gothic narratives: *Great Expectations*. Published two decades later, *Great Expectations* reactivates these connections between waxworks, femininity, death and the Gothic. In the novel, Miss Havisham, the witch-like lady who has stopped all the clocks on her aborted wedding day, is also compared to a waxwork from the fair. Dressed in her bridal gown, with only one shoe on, Havisham looks like a macabre Cinderella. However, her connection with the waxworks at the fair also shapes her as a morbid Sleeping Beauty, eternally waiting for her bridegroom to return, as the novel links the aestheticisation of women to the medical world, using hints at anatomical practice to construct secrecy.

Although published in 1861, *Great Expectations* opens in the 1830s, for Pip starts his story at a time 'long before the days of photographs',[82] that is, before the invention of photographic prints by Fox Talbot and Daguerre in 1839. The novel thus takes place before mid-century, which explains why Pip borrows from the world of fairs and popular entertainments to shape his experience when he discovers a mysterious character – Miss Havisham – who lives secluded in a Gothic mansion, having stopped watches and clocks at twenty minutes to nine on the day when she was jilted by her fiancé as she was getting dressed for her wedding. Significantly, Pip's first meeting with Miss Havisham is depicted in terms reminiscent of the world of the theatre – a realm where acting – or shamming – reigns supreme. As he waits to enter Miss Havisham's room, a disembodied voice tells Pip to step in. The voice is the first spectral image Pip encounters, soon followed by a network of allusions to the ghostly and ghastly body of Miss Havisham. As in a phantasmagoria, the room on the other side of the door, artificially lit by wax candles, suggests how deceptive reality can be, as Pip mistakes tatters

for rich materials and a corpse-like woman for a rich and beautiful
lady:

> [P]rominent in [the room] was a draped table with a gilded looking-
> glass, and that I made out at first sight to be a fine lady's dressing-table.
> Whether I should have made out this object so soon, if there had
> been no fine lady sitting at it, I cannot say. In an armchair, with an
> elbow resting on the table and her head leaning on that hand, sat the
> strangest lady I have ever seen, or shall ever see.
>
> She was dressed in rich materials – satins, and lace, and silks – all of
> white. Her shoes were white. And she had a long white veil dependent
> from her hair, and she had bridal flowers in her hair, but her hair was
> white. Some bright jewels sparkled on her neck, and on her hands,
> and some other jewels lay sparkling on the table. Dresses, less splendid
> than the dress she wore, and half-packed trunks, were scattered about.
>
> It was not in the first moments that I saw all these things, though I
> saw more of them in the first moments than might be supposed. But,
> I saw that everything within my view which ought to be white, had
> been white long ago, and had lost its lustre, and was faded and yellow.
> I saw that the bride within the bridal dress had withered like the
> dress, and like the flowers, and had no brightness left but the brightness
> of her sunken eyes. I saw that the dress had been put upon the rounded
> figure of a young woman, and that the figure upon which it now
> hung loose, had shrunk to skin and bone. Once, I had been taken
> to see some ghastly wax-work at the Fair, representing I know not
> what impossible personage lying in state. Once, I had been taken to
> one of our old marsh churches to see a skeleton in the ashes of a rich
> dress, that had been dug out of a vault under the church pavement.
> Now, wax-work and skeleton seemed to have dark eyes that moved
> and looked at me. (pp. 56–7)

Miss Havisham's pose, her head leaning on her hand, and the
scattered dresses all around her, suggestive of costumes, construct
the character as an actress. Pip's perceptual delusion, as he suddenly
realises he has been dazzled by the profusion of wealth, is presented
as an anamorphosis. The play on perspective, recalling baroque
memento mori, just like the looking glass, suggestive of a *vanitas*,
foreshadows the comparison of Miss Havisham with a skeleton and

a waxwork representing a corpse.[83] However, the images soon become much more modern and typically anchored in Victorian visual culture. The importance of sight, underlined by the repetitions of 'I saw', enhances Pip's scopic drive, staging the scene as a show. As the eyes become animated, they turn the skeleton and waxwork into mechanical contrivances, such as automata, developing further the numerous allusions to phantasmagorias and other Victorian optical gadgetry that permeate the narrative.

Moreover, as a 'personage lying in state', Miss Havisham recalls many popular figures of the time. The wax effigy Pip has in mind may be one of the models of royalty which appeared in many a wax exhibition both in fairs and in museums, such as Tussaud's, like that of George IV, which fascinated Dickens. Many coronation displays were exhibited at Tussaud's, an institution which very much promoted and popularised the monarchy, as with the coronation of George IV in 1821, or the model of Queen Victoria, which participated in maintaining the queen's visibility even after her retreat following Prince Albert's death in 1861.[84] The link with the monarchy strengthens Pip's vision of Miss Havisham's social class as different from his own, the image encapsulating inaccessibility. But wax models also played a 'democratic' function, annihilating social boundaries between viewers and the represented celebrities – and even sometimes enabling the public to touch them. The waxwork in the narrative thus captures the tension between social distance and social proximity which pervades Dickens's novel.

In addition, the waxwork betokens Pip's refusal to acknowledge the reality of Miss Havisham's corpse-like appearance, her body shrunk to skin and bone ('It was not in the first moments that I saw all these things, though I saw more of them in the first moments than might be supposed'). Wax displaces and replaces the gruesome body. Wax models of royal characters had been used since the fifteenth century to display kings and queens without fearing decomposition. Similarly, dressed in bridal attire, Miss Havisham's wax-like and virginal corpse highlights her attempt at arresting physical decomposition and counteracting time and death. The wax model thus typifies the narrative's interplay of anxieties related to time and bodily decay, especially when Miss Havisham expresses her wish to be laid upon the table when dead, with people coming to look at her – 'the complete realisation of the ghastly waxwork at the fair' (p. 83).

Laid upon the table, as both female corpse and artwork, Miss Havisham's body is very much redolent of the wax anatomical models that were popular in the mid-eighteenth century and throughout the Victorian period, as exemplified by the anatomical Venuses discussed earlier, displayed both in medical museums and at fairs. However, such anatomical waxes, though modelled from cadavers, represented female bodies much more than corpses. Hardly any trace of bodily decomposition ever appeared on the Florentine waxes; the waxworks looked rather like women asleep, an impression reinforced by the use of rich accessories. In fact, the anatomical models, blending art and science, were conceived as objects of the gaze: ideal bodies revealing their secrets to medical professionals. These anatomical Venuses also circulated in fairs and anatomical museums open to the public (although frequently for men only), especially in the second half of the nineteenth century. In 1839, Antonio Sarti, a Florentine, ran an exhibition at 27 Margaret Street in London, showing a Venus that could be taken apart, like those of Dr Joseph Kahn, whose Venus was made up of eighty-five pieces, or J. W. Reimer, whose Anatomical and Ethnological Museum opened in the city in 1853.[85] When separated from the world of medical education, however, anatomical Venuses fed the public's appetite for the macabre and the erotic. The normative and idealised female body was offered to the gaze of (often male) viewers, its internal organs gradually revealed in a morbid striptease.

Introducing herself as a woman with a broken heart, Miss Havisham defines her body in mechanical terms, the play on the broken heart suggesting parallels between the state of her house, with clocks stopped at twenty minutes to nine, and her physiology, which seems to have gone wrong. The metaphor thus constructs her as an anatomical Venus, made up of multiple pieces likely to be disassembled. But Miss Havisham also recalls one of the most famous mechanical automata displayed in the nineteenth century: Madame Tussaud's Sleeping Beauty – Madame du Barry's wax model – which again connects Dickens's female character with the world of waxworks exhibitions.[86] Du Barry's 'breathing' wax model had a mechanical beating heart, and her chest could be seen rising as she lay asleep on a sofa, disturbingly disrupting the boundaries between the real and the artificial as between the animate and the inanimate.[87]

Throughout *Great Expectations*, the multiple associations of Miss Havisham with contemporary models of Sleeping Beauties demonstrate how both anatomical Venuses and automata linked death and wax, and framed the body in representation, with women more often than not 'subjects to this imaging', in Giuliana Bruno's terms.[88] In fact, as Bruno contends, just like anatomical Venuses, the 'fascination for automata, which extended from the eighteenth through the nineteenth centuries was embedded in the struggle against decay', as 'movement transformed the inorganic into organic matter'.[89] Like an automaton, Miss Havisham repeats identical words ('Play! Play! Play') and movements, walking 'round and round the room' (p. 83). Her movements are also suddenly arrested, as when Pip describes the stopping of her body parts one after another as if she were made of independent pieces:

[Miss Havisham's] face had dropped into a watchful and brooding expression – most likely when all the things about her had become transfixed – and it looked as if nothing could ever lift it up again. Her chest had dropped, so that she stooped; and her voice had dropped, so that she spoke low, and with a dead lull upon her; altogether, she had the appearance of having dropped, body and soul, within and without, under the weight of a crushing blow. (p. 60)

The construction of Miss Havisham as a character out of Madame Tussaud's museum is further emphasised when Pip relates his visit to his sister, Joe and Pumblechook. Pip believes that 'if [he] described Miss Havisham's as [his] eyes had seen it, [he] should not be understood' (p. 64). Worse, Miss Havisham herself would not be understood. The story he then makes up, as he faces an eager audience, with Pumblechook 'preyed upon by a devouring curiosity' and 'gaping over in his chaise-cart' (p. 65), reinforces the connections between Miss Havisham and the world of waxworks. Indeed, Pip portrays her sitting in her room in a black velvet coach eating cake on a gold plate while dogs fight for veal cutlets out of a silver basket. The flags, swords and pistols Pip plays with, alongside the other 'marvels' (p. 68) of the room are, moreover, reminiscent of some of the exhibits at Tussaud's, notably the tableaux, or Napoleon's Waterloo carriage, which was exhibited in 1843. The latter could be used as a kitchen, a dining-room, a study, a bathroom or even a bedroom. All the kitchen utensils were gold and silver, and visitors could even climb aboard the carriage.[90]

Interestingly, Dickens's Miss Havisham brings to light the extent to which the relationship between automata, female physiology and the feminine ideal embodied by Tussaud's Sleeping Beauty were representative of mid-Victorian definitions of femininity. The figure of the automaton offered a potent symbol of woman's subjection to the forces of her body, as defined by contemporary medical discourse. The passivity of Sleeping Beauty, furthermore, strengthened woman's helplessness, both biological and cultural. The construction of woman as a passive automaton permeated exhibitions, Tussaud's Sleeping Beauty being a case in point. Even dolls were based on anatomical models; both underlined ideals of normality and both framed the female body the better to control it. A significant example may be found in an article entitled 'Dolls', published in *Household Words* in 1853. In the article, the reviewer explains that dolls are like 'watch[es]',[91] thus drawing a parallel between the toys and contemporary mechanical conceptions of human physiology. The dolls are devised as doubles of the little girls who will play with them, their 'humanized' eyes 'made by the same persons as those who manufacture eyes for human creatures' so as to 'bear a resemblance to nature'. Similarly, the hair used was often human hair.[92] The result was an object of 'life-like truthfulness'.[93] Inevitably, the comparison also shapes little girls as dolls, with female physiology consequently likened to a watch mechanism. More significantly still, the article shifts from the manufacturing of dolls to wax dolls – such as Madame Napoleon Montanari's wax dolls, exhibited at the 1851 Great Exhibition, which displayed the different stages of femininity. In addition, the parallel between dolls and girls growing into women is reinforced when the reviewer proceeds to explain the links between wax modelling and anatomical models. He explains that Dr Auzoux's life-sized papier-mâché anatomical models, showing the workings of the human body in all its minute details,[94] are very similar to automata. Thus, by connecting dolls, girls, waxworks, anatomical models and automata, the article reveals the ways in which medical discourse – in particular physiology – informed mid-Victorian definitions of women. Throughout the Victorian period, the development of medical science gave rise to an increasingly mechanistic vision of female physiology which constantly underlined the necessity for medical professionals to control the forces to which women seemed subjected. [95] The anatomical Venuses and other waxwork models of ideal women therefore both conveyed and reinforced contemporary associations between woman and the body.

Although anatomical Venuses and other sleeping beauties embodied the Victorian ideal of feminine weakness, passivity and vulnerability – images of ideal womanhood heavily influenced by contemporary medical discourses – Dickens's Miss Havisham is far from being a passive virgin awaiting her prince or a female corpse submitting to the anatomist's blade and compliantly awaiting dissection. The 'sleep–death equation',[96] which enabled nineteenth-century artists to portray passive sensuality and avoid morbidity, is undermined by Dickens's Gothic. Indeed, the narrative highlights tensions regarding Miss Havisham's body, particularly in the way it uses Gothic paraphernalia to metaphorise the villainess's corporeality. As noted above, one of the motifs which connects Miss Havisham to Sleeping Beauty may be her wish to be laid on the table after her death and remain for ever accessible to the gaze of her friends, who may 'feast upon [her]' (p. 86). In Charles Perrault's *Sleeping Beauty*, Sleeping Beauty's stepmother is an ogress who wishes to eat Sleeping Beauty and her children with 'sauce Robert'. Similarly, in *Great Expectations* the play on the term 'feast' blends the issue of the female body accessible to the (male) gaze with that of food, Miss Havisham's body replacing the wedding cake. Moreover, the scavenging 'crawling things' (p. 83) Pip notices on the table, the 'speckled-legged spiders with blotchy bodies', beetles and mice, hint at the bodily dissolution of Dickens's Sleeping Beauty, turning the sight of eternal youth into a macabre spectacle of decomposition.

Inevitably, such allusions to Miss Havisham's Gothic corporeality shatter the reassuring image of wholeness represented by Sleeping Beauty's body eternally frozen in youth and evading death. Miss Havisham, who has locked herself up in Satis House, is a morbid Sleeping Beauty, her 'corpse-like' appearance (p. 59) giving a macabre twist to stereotypical representations of ideal femininity locked in virginity. Furthermore, the spectral bride is also seen as a mummy threatened to be reduced to dust if taken into the natural light (p. 59), a death-in-life figure signalling instability, her body likely to crumble and disappear. Thus, while the image of Sleeping Beauty's crystallised body promises eternal life, Dickens's Gothic dooms the female body to decomposition. As 'yellow skin and bone' (p. 84), Miss Havisham's body is an envelope hosting a skeleton, her lack of fleshliness pointing even more powerfully to her material body, like a corpse urging anatomists to investigate it before putrefaction sets in.

As Elisabeth Bronfen has argued, the dead woman was a topos in eighteenth- and nineteenth-century culture.[97] Whether dead or in a trance, corpse-like women haunted the period. Often portrayed as on the boundary between life and death, dead women were stereotypically white and pure – immaculate – in their eternal sleep. However, they were also seen as mysterious and unfathomable, especially in scenes of dissection featuring anatomists dealing with dead female bodies. These Sleeping Beauties hovered uncannily between stereotypes of virginal femininity (safely protected from temptation by death) and corpses hosting mysteries likely to escape the anatomist once decomposition started. In J. H. Hasselhorst's *The Dissection of a Young, Beautiful Woman by J. CH. G. Lucas (1814–1885) in order to Determine the Ideal Female Proportions* (1864), Gabriel von Max's *Der Anatom* (1869) or even Enrique Simonet y Lombardo's *Anatomy of the Heart* (1899) at the end of the century, the white virgins lying on the anatomists' tables look like so many Sleeping Beauties, locked in eternal slumber. Yet their skin, like a sheet or shroud covering the mysteries of the female body, lures the anatomists, inviting them to lift it. As Bronfen argues, even as the painted female corpse 'signifies an immaculate, immobile form, [this form of beauty] potentially contains its own destruction, its division into parts'.[98] The corpse, as representation, is thus stuck in limbo – seemingly stopping time and denying bodily dissolution while simultaneously pointing to its inevitable decomposition.

In *Great Expectations*, the body of Miss Havisham magnifies such tensions. As Sleeping Beauty, the character promises revelation, matching Pip's fairy-tale ideals and his belief that he is meant to restore the desolate house, admit the sunshine into the dark rooms, set the clocks a going and the cold hearths a blazing, tear down the cobwebs, destroy the vermin – in short, do all the shining deeds of the young Knight of romance, and marry the Princess. (p. 229)

As corpse, she threatens to deny access to the truth, concealing secrets locked away forever. Both self-constructed as a passive body and as a plot-maker or puppetmaster directing Pip and Estella's romance, Miss Havisham brings to light the contradictions inherent in the image of Victorian Sleeping Beauties. In doing so, Dickens's Sleeping Beauty, likely to break into pieces and disintegrate, reflects the narrative mechanisms of the novel, as Pip tries to reassemble the pieces of the puzzle and unveil the secrets of Estella's and his benefactor's identity. Indeed, the failed romance of Dickens's Sleeping Beauty introduces the issues of femininity, sexuality and death into the narrative, constructing the female body as a site of mystery the better to metaphorise the secrets of the text. It is a path away from the fairy tale and the glamorous world of the theatre, of exhibitions and artificiality that Pip must find, learning that being a gentleman does not simply mean wearing fine clothes and having an education. The world of wax exhibitions – with their artificiality, their costumes and their Sleeping Beauties – thus paves the way for Pip's apprenticeship, especially as its macabre atmosphere takes the hero to London, where wax signifies crime and its punishment.

It is thus no coincidence that in *Great Expectations* wax should be linked to punishment[99] and that the world of wax exhibitions courts that of crime. Throughout the novel, the motifs which associate waxworks exhibitions with the realm of death are in fact the same as those which are used to define crime. The dust and the mould which cover the room where the wedding table has been laid in Satis House, as evidence of Sleeping Beauty's decomposition, recur in London, this time associated with Newgate, as when Pip feels 'contaminated' by the dust on his feet and in his lungs (p. 261). The disease metaphor, together with the way in which the dust is related to Pip's body, penetrating his organism, strengthens the parallel between the two places. In addition, the motif of the scaffold, which Pip had associated with Magwitch in the opening chapter, appears as well when Pip leaves Satis House after his first visit. The sight of

Miss Havisham hanging on a great wooden beam by the neck connects the two characters, giving ominous tinges to the fairy godmother very early in the narrative. Furthermore, the candles, which encapsulate artificiality and the make-believe world of Satis House, reappear in Jaggers's office, this time 'decorated with dirty winding-sheets, as if in remembrance of a host of hanged clients' (p. 384).

Even more significant perhaps are the casts of hanged criminals in Jaggers's office, offering as they do a much more macabre vision of the world of waxworks exhibitions. Mr Jaggers is Pip's guardian, whom Pip had first met at Miss Havisham's (hence his belief that Havisham is his benefactress). His office is another Gothic realm. It is a dismal place with the skylight 'patched like a broken head' (p. 162), where Jaggers's chair resembles a coffin and where two casts of hanged criminals with swollen faces are exhibited on a shelf. Like Miss Havisham's body, which is either compared to a waxwork resisting bodily decomposition or to an embalmed corpse likely to crumble into dust, the casts are unstable motifs. Though made of wax, the artificial reproductions of the criminals' heads are surrounded by flies which settle on them as they might on decomposing bodies and appear animated every time Pip notices them. Tellingly, Jaggers, whose hands smell of scented soap, reminding Pip of doctors (p. 81), washes 'his clients off, as if he were a surgeon' (p. 208). Penknife in hand, he reads people's bodies like an anatomist, as when he reads power in Molly's hands, 'coolly tracing out the sinews with his forefinger' (p. 212). This network of motifs evokes the world of anatomy, recalling how murderers' bodies were handed to surgeons and anatomists after their execution in order to be dissected. The casts, therefore, unite the legal and medical fields.

Moreover, crime, the casts suggest, can be exhibited. When Pip later travels with two convicts, their guard is compared to a curator, the prisoners making 'an interesting Exhibition not formally open at the moment' (p. 224). This 'most disagreeable and degraded spectacle' (p. 225) is found again in Wemmick's 'museum', as he keeps in a 'chamber of the Castle' a 'collection of curiosities' (p. 207). The latter are items that previously belonged to executed criminals, including human remains, such as locks of hair. This echoes the image of Miss Havisham as anatomical model,[100] the wax metaphor blurring the boundary between the medical world and that of exhibitions, all the more so as Newgate is a place of entertainment very similar to wax exhibitions. Indeed, as Pip is waiting for Jaggers, he walks out of the office and takes a look at Newgate. A drunk minister of justice invites him to step in and hear a trial: for half a crown, Pip should 'command a full view of the Lord Chief Justice in his wig and robes – mentioning that awful personage like waxwork, and presently offering him at the reduced price of eighteen pence' (p. 164).

In fact, the relationship between waxworks and crime which is developed throughout the narrative gradually guides the reader towards the truth, suggesting that the motif of wax works in tandem with secrets which Pip must discover. Jaggers is the man who is 'more in the secrets of [Newgate] than any man in London' (p. 265), and his casts function as landmarks in the novel, appearing every time Pip is about to discover something. Pip notices them on the shelf each time he enters Jaggers's office; they also become animated each time the narrative refuses to lift the veil on a character's identity. Pip remarks their swollen faces when he meets Jaggers's mysterious housekeeper, Molly (p. 198); they seem to eavesdrop on the conversation or to be about to sneeze on the day when Pip comes of age, when Jaggers refuses to reveal the identity of Pip's benefactor (p. 282); they try to open their eyelids when Jaggers asks Pip under what name Magwitch has written to him (p. 333); they seem to play bo-peep when Pip tries to connect Estella and Molly; and finally they look as if they have smelt fire when Pip conceals his identity to send nine hundred pounds to Herbert (p. 404).

As a result, the casts pave the way for Pip's discovery of the truth and for his self-discovery, playing a significant part in the *Bildungsroman*. As already noted, the hero's maturation depends on his relinquishing the fairy-tale scenario with its macabre Sleeping Beauties and Cinderellas. The motif of wax, as malleable material, thus aptly mirrors the way the hero is moulded into an adult, especially since it is associated with forms of visual education and amusement like waxworks. As suggested, wax, as a form of representation, epitomised particularly the desire to freeze the body in order to 'harness the emotion of the body and its temporal history'.[101] Consequently, as Pip and the reader discover, the comparison of

Miss Havisham to a waxwork, just like the hints at female physiology associated with anatomical Venuses, encapsulates the mechanisation of her feelings, eventually highlighting the character's heartlessness. Dickens's Sleeping Beauty is ultimately but an automaton, a stereotype which illuminates the reification of individuals in mid-Victorian England. As an animated doll unable to feel, Miss Havisham threatens to contaminate Pip and shape him into another 'model with a mechanical heart to practise on' (p. 319). From the beginning, indeed, Pip is a 'young parcel of bones' (p. 75), his 'anatomy' noticed by Herbert 'as if he were minutely choosing his bone' (p. 90) the first time he meets him, or by Miss Havisham, who seems to 'pry into [his] heart and probe its wounds' (p. 298). The physical description of the hero as a mere collection of bones or a body capable of being opened hints again at the world of anatomy and its anatomical models, the better to show how Dickens's characters all flirt with mechanisation. However, as Pip gradually realises, becoming a gentleman does not simply mean wearing fine clothes as so many costumes and exhibiting one's 'mechanical appearance' (p. 170), like Wemmick. On the contrary, it means empathising with others, regardless of their social class, and experiencing feelings and emotions. The motif of the waxwork, which, as we have seen, is closely related to secrecy throughout the novel, therefore eventually represents repression, more especially so, perhaps, because of its connections with death.

Thus, while wax was used throughout the eighteenth and nineteenth centuries to mask death and master emotions related to the body, by the end of *Great Expectations* it becomes obvious that the network of motifs in the novel referring to wax in manifold guises is being used to signal the reification and mechanisation of feelings, as if this was the ultimate secret Pip needed to unveil. Because, the novel shows, repression works in tandem with crime and death, Dickens's characters – crushed by blows, turned into automata, grotesquely disguised until they look like corpses (like Magwitch, whose dressing up has the 'effect of rouge upon the dead', p. 334) must therefore learn to open up their hearts and shed tears, even if Dickens's prince is finally denied marriage to his princess and his Sleeping Beauty eventually crumbles into dust.

As seen with Dickens's Victorian Gothic, the hermeneutic function of the waxwork motifs is to guide hero and readers towards the discovery of the truth. As they take the body of the text to pieces, as one might disassemble an anatomical Venus, what is revealed is the influence of anatomical culture on the literary stage. As both stage props pointing to the Gothic's paraphernalia and icons of knowledge, mapping out the secrets of female sexuality and the mysteries of human anatomy, wax models partook of the Gothic throughout the long nineteenth century. Such connections between waxworks, femininity, crime and the Gothic were still to be found at the very end of the century, as in Wilkie Collins's *The Legacy of Cain* (1888), where a murderess worries that her face may be swollen after her execution, resembling the waxworks of criminals she has seen. Increasingly associated with the development of criminal anthropology, phrenology and craniology, the waxwork captured the evolution of Victorian mental science, as indicated by the numerous casts of the heads of criminal and racial 'types' realised in the last decades of the century. In contrast, anatomical wax models would be gradually marginalised in medical museums and more and more linked to fringe medicine, as will be explored further in chapter 4.

3

Body-snatching

The corpse was cold now, but not still, and when the murderers tossed it roughly upon a dark table, it lay there like a reclining marble statue, beautifully faultless in all its proportions, which the long tresses of hair, which had once been the pride of the wearer and the admiration and envy of friends and acquaintances, lay coiled upon the snowy neck, and trailed half way along the table.

One of the assistants came forward, and at the first glance could not suppress an exclamation. This caught the attention of Knox, and he too came forward.

'There's a purty wun, sur', said Burke, who was always spokesman on these occasions.

Knox said nothing, but ran his eye slowly over the form.

'She has been a *very* pretty girl that', he remarked, after several moments of silent inspection. 'Upon my soul, I never saw a more beautiful body'.

. . . So pleased was Dr Knox with the 'thing', that he told his cashier to give fourteen pounds for it – the largest sum that these men had yet received for the articles in which they trafficked.[1]

We saw in chapter 2 that the popularity of anatomical wax models, especially in the eighteenth and early nineteenth centuries, was closely related to the rise of anatomy in medical education and the shortage of dead bodies for dissection. Waxes might be used as substitutes for the latter, but once transposed into the literary genre, the human cadaver could take on a new life, so to speak, as a suggestive motif, intimating notably the secrets of female sexuality. Yet, if anatomical wax models had a flavour of otherness, or exoticism, and hinted at the Grand Tour and travel literature, the shortage of corpses for dissection, and the numerous murder cases linked to them, were, above all, rooted in the realities of late Georgian and early Victorian Britain, and associated with such cities as London and Edinburgh.

Body-snatching and body-snatchers are key themes and figures of Gothic literature, resurrectionists standing out as iconic villains throughout the long nineteenth century. However, the way in which the rise of body-snatching, closely related to changes in medical education, knowledge and practice, impacted the trajectory of the Gothic from the 1790s to the 1830s has seldom been examined, in particular when analysed through the numerous forms of cross-fertilisation between medical culture and the tale of terror, with each constantly informing the other and blurring the boundaries between fiction and reality. As Megan Coyer has shown, the public outcry which greeted the savage Burke and Hare murders of the late 1820s, with the victims' cadavers sold to Edinburgh anatomist Dr Robert Knox (1791–1862), went hand in glove with changes in the literary construction of the figure of the medical practitioner. The transformation of the latter into an increasingly humane medical professional, Coyer argues, drew upon eighteenth-century Scottish medical culture and reflected 'the empirical project of post-Enlightenment medicine'.[2] This change was most strikingly visible in periodicals known for popularising ultra-realistic tales of terror, generally based upon medical realism and practice. *Blackwood's Edinburgh Magazine* is a case in point, advocating as it did a conception of the advancement of medical knowledge grounded firmly in morality, and promoting a new and idealised figure of the literary medical man. Whether body-snatching fictional narratives denounced or, on the contrary, promoted the uses of anatomical material for dissection, they did not confine themselves to attempting to thrill readers with modern and realistic tales of terror. They also drew inspiration from contemporary debates about medical practice and ethics and the construction of the medical professional. With physicians now required to train in anatomy and practise dissection, and surgeons no longer contenting themselves to hew off limbs as quickly as possible, previously clear-cut professional categories were increasingly breaking down. This change was even more evident as many of the authors of such tales of terror were themselves medical practitioners. As this chapter will highlight, focusing on the complex traffic between literature and medicine in the period under study offers new readings the figure of the body-snatcher, especially when the staple Gothic character is traced throughout the eighteenth and nineteenth centuries, remaining active on the literary stage even once the villain has become redundant in the medical field.

The rise of 'modern' medicine and body-snatching

Burke an' Hare
Fell doun the stair,
Wi' a body in a box
Gaun to Doctor Knox.

Charge against a surgeon for the removal of a dead body for anatomical purposes.—At the last Surrey Sessions, the Grand Jury Returned a true Bill against Robert Henry Hodson Parrott, Surgeon, of Walworth, for removing a dead body for anatomical purposes without the authority required by law. The case was adjourned until next sessions, Nov. 5th.[3]

In a satirical etching by the Scottish artist Isaac Cruikshank (1764–1811) entitled *Resurection [sic] Men Disturbed or a Guilty Conscience Needs no Accuser* (c.1794), six men are shown digging up corpses in a churchyard. Naked corpses are being bundled into sacks and carried to a nearby cart where several cadavers have already been loaded. The body-snatcher in the centre, with a wig and a tricorn hat, is undoubtedly a (Scottish) doctor, while his terrified accomplices, their hair standing on end, implore angels to protect them. On the left of the picture, a bellowing mule makes one of the grave-robbers start with fear, while one of his accomplices is seen to be carrying his own father on his back. William Austen's *The Anatomist Overtaken by the Watch . . . Carrying off Miss W— in a Hamper* (1773) is another example of the eighteenth-century caricature of medical men in search of anatomical material. Hinting at William Hunter's lectures (a copy of which lies on the ground), the engraving features a gentleman, similarly wearing a tricorn hat and carrying a physician's stick, who is running away, denounced by a body-snatcher who has just been arrested with his bounty. In a final example, a water-colour by Thomas Rowlandson entitled *Resurrection Men* (n.d.), the anatomist is caught in the act, not, this time by the watch, but by an animated skeleton. The word 'Resurgam' ('I will rise again') on the coffin lid in the foreground humorously blurs the boundaries between the fictional and supernatural world of the Gothic and that of medical practice, ultra-realistic in its treatment of human corpses.

These three graphic examples linking the medical field with the body trade reflect widely held popular views about medical professionals in the second half of the eighteenth century.[4] Indeed, if modern anatomy dates back to the early modern period and the work of the anatomist Andreas Vesalius (1514–64), the creation of anatomy as a discipline in the long eighteenth century was closely related to the broader Enlightenment project, and the discipline flourished in that period as never before or since.[5] Key events in the history of medicine illustrate the rise of anatomy and anatomical science more generally, such as the dissolution of the College of Surgeons, founded in 1745 after the separation from the College of Barbers in 1796, and the establishment of the Royal College of Surgeons in 1800 by a new Royal Charter. The last decades of the eighteenth century also witnessed the foundation of the great museum collections of anatomy and comparative anatomy, such as that of the Scottish anatomist John Hunter (1728–93), purchased by the government in 1799, and which constituted the basis of the Hunterian Museum at the Royal College of Surgeons in London. The rapid development of anatomy in the eighteenth century was due to several factors, principally an increased interest in human anatomy and physiology and the growth of medical schools, both public and private. The result was a sharp rise in the demand for human bodies: unlike the teaching hospitals, private anatomy schools taught anatomy by dissection, but were not legally entitled to have access to corpses.[6]

As Andrew Cunningham has argued, the shortage of bodies for dissection was more marked in Britain than elsewhere in Europe, at a time when the Continent's 'greatest density of anatomical teachers'[7] was to be found in London and Edinburgh. As a consequence, in London, 'practical anatomical teaching could not have been possible without a regular trade of grave-robbers'.[8] Indeed, until the passage of the 1832 Anatomy Act radically reformed anatomy, in England, just like in Scotland, Ireland and North America (but in contrast to the situation in much of the rest of Europe), the bodies of executed criminals could be used for medical purposes only in very specific circumstances, and those of paupers not at all.

As indicated in chapter 1, the earliest anatomy legislation in Britain dates back to 1540, when Henry VIII allowed anatomists the use of the bodies of four hanged felons per year. This quota was extended to six by Charles II, until the 1752 Murder Act granted anatomists the use of all the criminals hanged at Tyburn, and from 1783 at Newgate. Even after the 1752 Murder Act, scenes of rioting were a frequent occurrence at the gallows as anatomists and surgeons struggled to take possession of criminals' bodies. In some cases, the corpse of an executed criminal might be acquired before even it had been handed over to its 'rightful' owner, and an anatomist might therefore see 'his' bounty being spirited away by one of his fellow practitioners.[9] Body-snatching of a more conventional kind flourished, particularly in the first decades of the nineteenth century, to make up for the shortage in cadavers for medical education. Among the best known cases are those of Joshua Naples, the leader of a gang of resurrectionists in London,[10] of William Burke (1792–1829) and William Hare (1792?–1858?), convicted of throttling sixteen victims in 1828 to provide anatomical material for Dr Knox,[11] and of John Bishop and Thomas Williams, sentenced to death in 1831 for the murder of a young Italian boy who had been exhibiting white mice in the streets of London.

Although cases of body-snatching had been reported in Britain as early as in the seventeenth century,[12] in the last decades of the eighteenth century and early nineteenth century grave-robbery led to a public outcry, and details of cases were widely circulated in broadsides[13] and newspapers.[14] Near-riot situations were a regular occurrence, with resurrectionists sometimes even asking to be put in jail in order to escape from an angry mob.[15] William Hunter warned his students, for instance, that:

> [i]n a country where liberty disposes the people to licentiousness and outrage, and where anatomists are not legally supplied with dead bodies . . . it is to be hoped that you will be on your guard and, out of doors, speak with caution of what may be passing here, especially with respect to dead bodies.[16]

The burking (smothering a victim so as to sell the corpse for anatomy) cases and their trials took place against the backdrop of a change in the law that would grant anatomists access to the unclaimed bodies of the workhouse: the 1832 Anatomy Act. As Ruth Richardson notes, a select committee was appointed by the House of Commons in the spring of 1828 to 'inquire into the manner of obtaining Subjects of Dissection in the Schools of Anatomy'. This was before the discovery of the Burke and Hare murders and was thus more a response to the shortage of bodies for dissection than an attempt to deal with the issue of grave-robbing itself.[17] The increase in the availability of anatomical material after the Act would reduce the exodus of medical students to Paris, where opportunities to work on corpses for dissection purposes had been much more plentiful. The Act would also lead to a rise in the numbers of medical students enrolled in the hospital schools and a corresponding fall in those attending private and provincial anatomical schools, since, as a result of bye-laws passed in 1823 and 1824, only anatomical certificates issued by schools and universities recognised by the Royal College of Surgeons were considered legally valid.[18]

It was especially in the 1820s that anatomists such as John Abernethy (1764–1831) and Thomas Southwood Smith (1788–1861) pressed for anatomy reform, highlighting the centrality of anatomical knowledge in medical science and the potential for therapeutic applications of dissection.[19] In 1819, as Richardson explains, Abernethy 'had raised the idea of using paupers' bodies' in his *Hunterian Oration*.[20] In his view, '[o]pportunities of dissection should . . . be afforded [to medical practitioners]', '[a]natomical knowledge [being] the only foundation on which the structure of medical science can be built'.

'Without this', he claimed, 'we should but increase the sufferings of those afflicted with diseases, and endanger their lives'.[21] A few years later, in an article published in the *Westminster Review*, Thomas Southwood Smith also stressed the extent to which 'anatomical knowledge [was] the means of saving human life'.[22] The significance of anatomical knowledge and practice within the medical field illustrates the shift to a much more empirical attitude to the practice of medicine and underlines the rise of pathological anatomy. That body-snatching was closely related to changes in definitions of the body and in the understanding of disease cannot be gainsaid; in the eighteenth and nineteenth centuries, dissection became increasingly synonymous with medical knowledge, as the Scot George Mac Gregor made explicit in 1884:

> This practice of violating sepulchres, which must ever be regarded as one of the foulest blots on Scottish civilization, may be said to have had several contributing causes. The principal of these is admitted on all hands to have been the discovery on the part of the medical faculty that the knowledge they possessed of the human frame was founded rather upon uncertain tradition than upon empirical science; that they were practically ignorant of anatomy; and that if they hoped to make any advance in the art of healing human diseases they must devote more attention to a minute study of the dead subject.[23]

The fashion for Gothic romances, launched with the publication of Horace Walpole's *The Castle of Otranto*, and continuing throughout the Romantic period, coincided thus with a period in which corpses were·in constant need in the medical field. Gothic romances, especially those published by the Minerva Press, regularly mediated such uses and abuses of human bodies. As seen in chapter 1, in *The Horrors of Oakendale Abbey* (1797) Mrs Carver placed body-snatchers at the heart of her Gothic plot, with graphic horror and the corporeality of the cadaver replacing the supernatural.[24] As a result, if fears of body violation are undeniable Gothic topoi, fears of having one's body stolen, manipulated, cut up, sold and dissected did not belong solely to the province of Gothic literature, but were a reality of everyday life during the period from the end of the eighteenth century to the first decades of the nineteenth century, especially (but not exclusively) in the years before the passage of the 1832 Anatomy Act.

Romantic grave-diggers

Throughout the Romantic period, artists and writers alike followed developments in medical practice, using art to voice the uses and abuses of the human body. Robert Southey's 'A Surgeon's Warning' (1796) is a humorous case in point, echoing the caricatures of George Cruikshank, William Austen or Thomas Rowlandson, mentioned at the beginning of this chapter. The poem describes a surgeon begging for his coffin to be looked after so that his corpse may not fall into the hands of body-snatchers:

> All kinds of carcasses I have cut up,
> And the judgment now must be –
> But brothers I took care of you,
> So pray take care of me!
> I have made candles of infants' fat
> The Sextons have been my slaves,
> I have bottled babes unborn, and dried
> Hearts and livers from rifled graves.
> And my Prentices now will surely come
> And carve me bone from bone,
> And I who have rifled the dead man's grave
> Shall never have rest in my own.
> Bury me in lead when I am dead,
> My brethren I intreat,
> And see the coffin weigh'd I beg
> Lest the Plumber should be a cheat . . .
> And let it be solder'd closely down
> Strong as strong can be I implore,
> And put it in a patent coffin,
> That I may rise no more[.][25]

More seriously, poetry like this illuminates how Romantic poets were influenced by the 'knowledge systems'[26] developed by medical professionals – and anatomists especially – during the course of the eighteenth century. In Percy Bysshe Shelley's 'Alastor; or the Spirit of Solitude' (1815) knowledge is buried in the depths of the earth, in charnels and coffins, places where corpses putrefy and crumble into dust:

> I have made my bed
> In charnels and on coffins, where black death
> Keeps record of the trophies won from thee,
> Hoping to still these obstinate questionings
> Of thee and thine, by forcing some lone ghost,
> Thy messenger, to render up the tale
> Of what we are[.][27]

The wandering of the lonely poet among corpses links to some extent the Romantic poet with the anatomist: the poem places the body at the heart of the poet's quest for knowledge, implying that the material body holds the keys to the secrets of nature. The poem highlights, indeed, the ways in which the culture of the period was informed by new ways of looking at, and defining, the material body. In Shelley's poem, the corpse leads the Romantic quest. The corpse itself is never described; we are only allowed to see the burial site and the coffin, as if the body had already vanished, thus dooming the poet's search for knowledge. The human remains are never visualised, and endlessly evade the poet's grasp.

The mention of Percy Bysshe Shelley here is no coincidence, as one of the most famous body-snatchers of British literature is undoubtedly his wife's Victor Frankenstein. In Mary Shelley's *Frankenstein* (1818), Frankenstein's search for 'the physical secrets of the world'[28] can be compared to the anatomist who plunders graveyards in order to further his experimental knowledge. Like Percy Shelley's poet, Frankenstein 'dabble[s] among the unhallowed damps of the grave' and collects bones from charnel-houses (p. 55). Knowledge is constantly associated with death and depths, and the Gothic motifs and stereotypes which permeate the narrative point to anatomical science as a significant subtext throughout the novel.

As someone who haunts cemeteries and dissection rooms for his body parts, Victor Frankenstein matches the portrait of the early nineteenth-century anatomist to perfection. Although there is no material evidence that Mary Shelley knew about Abernethy's calls for reform,[29] *Frankenstein*'s 'slippage between the surgeon, the dissector, the murderer'[30] indicates that Shelley was aware of contemporary debates about the figure of the anatomist and of anxieties relating to anatomical practice. The Gothic plot draws overtly on fears linked to medical practice at a time when the legislation regulating the uses of the human body was beginning to be debated in the public sphere.[31] As his creature becomes a serial killer, Frankenstein, revealingly, feels guilt for the crimes the creature has committed[32] ('the crimes which had their source in me'; 'they all died by my hands' (p. 189); 'I am the assassin of those most innocent victims; they died of my machinations' (p. 190)). He is also eventually accused of the murder of his friend, Henry Clerval, before being released without charge, like several anatomists of the time suspected of participating in the body trade. In addition, Frankenstein's experiment seems to have been directly inspired by research on human corpses conducted by Giovani Aldini (1762–1834). Of particular significance in this context is the occasion on 17 January 1803 when Aldini experimented publicly upon the fresh cadaver of murderer Thomas Forster at the Royal College of Surgeons in London. He applied electrodes to various parts of Forster's body and made the jaw quiver and one eye open.[33]

Although some of the details concerning Frankenstein's body-snatching lack realism (such as when Frankenstein collects his anatomical material over a few months in London before travelling to Scotland without taking the effects of putrefaction into account), Frankenstein's traffic in bodies is usually presented indirectly, as when he appears as a body-snatcher in one of his dreams – or rather, a nightmare – just after the creature's birth:

> I thought I saw Elizabeth, in the bloom of health, walking in the streets of Ingolstadt. Delighted and surprised, I embraced her, but as I imprinted the first kiss on her lips, they became livid with the hue of death; her features appeared to change, and I thought that I held the corpse of my dead mother in my arms; a shroud enveloped her form, and I saw the grave-worms crawling in the folds of the flannel. (p. 59)

The corpse of the mother, wrapped up in the shroud and already infested with worms, functions here as an unconscious confession, suggesting that his theft of corpses may be what the narrative tries to repress.

Following in the footsteps of Shelley's villain, several tales of terror published in *Blackwood's Edinburgh Magazine* in the 1820s and 1830s capitalised upon body-snatching and the underbelly of Georgian medicine. Tales such as John Galt's 'The Buried Alive' (1821) highlighted the relationship between medical practice and body-snatching,[34] establishing in so doing the clichés of the literature of terror which would later mark Victorian popular fiction. In Galt's tale, the narrator, who suffers from catalepsy, is buried alive because of an incorrect medical diagnosis. Yet, ironically, the protagonist is rescued by resurrection men, who take his body to an anatomist's for a demonstration. However, before dissecting the subject, the anatomist practises a galvanic experiment on the narrator's body, prompting his eyes to open, whilst the knife piercing his chest brings him out of his trance. As will be seen in chapter 5, cases of patients waking up on the anatomist's table, found in both fictional and real-life narratives,[35] became a staple of the nineteenth-century tale of terror.

Megan Coyer's study of the relationship between medical culture and the periodical press in the early nineteenth century demonstrates how some titles regularly published literary pieces penned by authors from a medical background. *Blackwood's Edinburgh Magazine* is a case in point, particularly during the period between the founding of the periodical in 1817 and the death of William Blackwood in 1834. The tale of terror, Coyer argues, may be considered as 'a form of hybrid "medico-popular" writing',[36] blurring boundaries between literature and medicine. She highlights, moreover, the way in which the tale of terror provided a new perspective on the medical case histories that were appearing in periodicals such as the *Edinburgh Magazine*, offering in particular the patient's viewpoint on trauma rather than that of an authoritative observer. The emphasis on the Gothic in such first-person narratives and the focus on the patient 'marks', she observes, 'a significant shift in the treatment of medical subject matter' and also 'represents a significant innovation in Gothic form'.[37] By using a Gothic aesthetic (in particular through portraits of human suffering), these tales may thus be viewed as 'a subversion of the developmental trajectory of the medical case history of the nineteenth century'.[38] Coyer suggests, in addition, that the increasing tendency to highlight the moral integrity of physicians in such tales of terror paved the way for the medical man of the highest ideals which would become a commonplace of Victorian literature.[39] Such tales thus bridged the gap between the Georgian satire of the medical profession and the Victorian idealisation of its practitioners.

That being said, short stories published in the periodical press of the period that focus on body-snatching do not by any means offer a monolithic image of medical education and practice. In 'On the Pleasures of Body-Snatching',[40] for instance, which appeared in the *Monthly Magazine* in April 1827, the cold and clinical view of a student of anatomy on body-snatching is counterbalanced by that of one of his accomplices, a stranger to the medical profession. From the title on, the story promotes the therapeutic uses of dissection. The narrator (a student of anatomy) refers to the ethical arguments against body-snatching, but only to explain how he has chosen to discard them, arguing that all considerations should be subordinated to the necessity for medical professionals to master surgical technique:

> When a man has made up his mind to the alternative of having his leg cut off, or of being lithotomised, instead of losing his life, he does not bother himself as to the means by which the surgeon acquired his dexterity; he does not care a straw for the morality of the question. (p. 355)

The characters set up a society of resurrectionists, made up of young surgeons and students of anatomy, and the narrator gradually becomes acquainted with body-snatching and used to encountering the corpses of people he knows on the anatomist's table:

> I forced myself to advance to the table, and, willing to give him a good opinion of my courage, uncovered the face, I cannot help laughing at it now; but, at that time, it was an awful moment. I had forgotten that the man was an acquaintance of my own. Ever since

the moment of resurrection, my mind had been absorbed by the one single abstract idea of an anatomical subject; all thought of individuality was lost; I made no personal reflections. But here was the strong, heavy, corpulent man, I had seen alive and kicking a few days ago, lying on his back, naked and helpless, – straight, stiff, and motionless – waiting to be cut up! (p. 359)

This passage prepares the ground for the climax of the narrative, which contrasts the reaction of the narrator (who pours scorn on his former moral scruples) with that of a sailor who has been persuaded to help steal more bodies:

By the time we had got the coffin open, however, and its contents deposited in the sack, his spirit seemed to desert him altogether; and while we were filling up the grave, and putting matters *in statu quo*, he leant in silence against a tomb-stone. When we were preparing to depart, I went up and shook him violently, to rouse him from the trance in which he seemed to have fallen. '*It is a woman!*' said he, at length, in a whisper, so deep and horror-struck, that I instinctively let him go. I could hear P— chuckle at the idea. I endeavoured to explain to him that a dead body was of no sex; but, notwithstanding, it was as much by compulsion as any thing else, that we got him to assist in removing the spoils. (p. 364)

Unsurprisingly, the sailor, engaged to a young girl, Susan, soon realises that the corpse he has helped steal is that of his beloved:

At this moment, R— awoke, and turning down the mouth of the sack, held the candle to examine our prize; and, still under the *gineal* influence, began to rhodomontade like a mad player. 'A woman, by G—!', cried he; 'aye, and a fair one, too – beautiful even in death! Her auburn ringlets hanging, in love-like languishment, over her neck of snow – her pencilled eyebrows – her dimpled chin – her modest lips, cold even as chastity!' At every disjointed sentence, the stranger advanced a step nearer: till, at length, when the fair and dead face came completely under his view, his hands met with a sound like the report of a pistol – and, in something between a shriek and a convulsive groan, he exclaimed, 'It is *Susan!*' – and fell senseless on the floor. (p. 365)

It would appear then that this short story highlights the crucial part played by body-snatching in medical education and progress with the principal aim of focusing on the feelings of the bereaved sailor and the callousness of body-snatchers – who are here all medical students eager to practise dissection. The contrast between these two points of view enables the author to evoke sadism and necrophilia, forcefully galvanising in so doing the Gothic character of the narrative. Although the narrator tells the sailor that 'a dead body [is] of no sex', the horror-struck man is 'rouse[d]' from his trance when faced with the figure of his chaste sweetheart. The latter's body is painstakingly detailed, the dashes in the narrative constructing a blason[41] which fetishises even more the parts of the female body, as if anatomising it. This idea is further stressed by the mention of the sailor's 'disjointed sentence(s)', hinting as it does at the process of fragmentation. The focus on the hair and face of the woman's corpse, moreover, recalls eighteenth-century Italian wax anatomical models (similarly constructed as 'languish[ing]' sleeping princesses with pencilled eyebrows and seemingly denying death,[42] as seen in chapter 2) as well as letting the reader imagine the rest of the naked body on the table, as the sailor's gaze gradually sweeps down the corpse. The scene climaxes with the sailor's 'convulsive groan', after which he faints, a sequence of events that hints at sexual orgasm followed by *petite mort*. Blurring pain and pleasure from the title on, this short story plays with the eroticism of the 'fair and dead face'. The female corpse epitomises therefore both virginal femininity (safely protected from temptation by death as 'cold even as chastity' suggests) and eroticisation.

A similar play on contrasting views regarding the practice of anatomy and body-snatching can be observed in a later short story, also published in *Blackwood's Edinburgh Magazine*. In 'A Recent Confession of an Opium-Eater' (1856), it is the narrator this time, intoxicated with laudanum, who falls victim to body-snatchers. He is taken to the resurrectionists' den and sees another victim about to be burked:

> The room they entered was small, and its only furniture was a bed and a sack. The bed was peculiar, consisting of two thick mattresses, without bedclothes, and a complication of ropes, pulleys, and weights.

Presently Bill and the woman, each seizing a rope, began pulling, and the upper mattress slowly rose. Heaven and earth! what a thought flashed across my mind! I had heard of such things before – the unhappy being, stupefied by opium, was placed between two mattresses, and smothered so as to produce the appearance of natural death, and his body sold to the surgeons! The *sack* was irresistible evidence – it must be so! I was in the company of body-snatchers, and about to be BURKED!!!![43]

Although the system of ropes, pulleys and weights is only meant for smothering here, it also evokes anatomical theatres and demonstrations, anticipating therefore the victim's dissection. However, the narrator soon reflects on how his own body, as that of an opium-eater, might provide a potentially interesting case for medical science:

The thrill of horror which now naturally passed through my heart, did not prevent me from seeing the case in all its philosophic bearings. My natural impulse was, of course, self-preservation; but still, as a philosopher, I was bound to consider also the interests of the public. I had every reason to believe that my organs and functions had become so vitiated by the use of opium, as to insure, to him who should lay bare, with scientific knife and anxious inquiry, this earthly tabernacle, the disclosure of the most remarkable phenomena. Had I then, as a citizen, the right to withhold this perishable frame, which would inevitably be dissolved in a few years, and perhaps under far less important conditions (for I might leave off opium, and, thus restoring my body to a healthy condition, render it comparatively valueless), when I might, by submitting to the fate designed for me, remain for ages, in spirits of wine, a monument of opium-eating? (p. 636)

Informed by anatomical tropes (clearly visible in the 'thrill' of horror, recalling the nervous system, or in images of penetration ('passed through')), this passage defines the body as the locus of secret knowledge ('lay bare', 'disclosure'). The narrator's 'philosophical' view of his own situation is significant in the way in which it promotes dissection and the practice of body-snatching by constructing the victim of medical practice as a valuable medical case to be preserved and displayed for all time as a wet specimen. The irony which pervades the passage reaches a peak at the end of the short story. Having managed to stupefy the resurrectionists with laudanum, the narrator effects his escape, but takes time beforehand to indulge in an opium trance. The final part of the story reworks Thomas De Quincey's *Confessions of an English Opium-Eater* (1821), as the narrator offers his body for anatomical dissection as an interesting medical case.[44] The narrator imagines, indeed, that Aesculapius, Galen, Hippocrates, Agrippa, Garth, Harvey, Hunter and Astley Cooper are all about to dissect his brain, thereby liberating his genius. Through the pleasure of the opium-eater in visualising his own dissection, as well as its discourse on the benefits of dissection, this short story, narrated from the viewpoint of the victim, thus seemingly offers a defence of anatomical experimentation on the human body the better to play on the grotesque. Yet with its transformation of the narrator from terrified victim to elated megalomaniac, this work also illuminates the evolution of medical Gothic texts in the first decades of the nineteenth century. The blurring of clear-cut categories and the complexification of the roles of victim and/or villain are telling here, for they increasingly marked the figure of the Victorian body-snatcher.

Also significant in this context is a series of short stories penned by Samuel Warren. Written around the time when the second edition of *Frankenstein* was published, the tales appeared in *Blackwood's Edinburgh Magazine* between August 1830 and October 1837, and would subsequently be republished in 1838 as a three-volume set entitled *Passages from the Diary of a Late Physician*.[45] The collection contains a series of medical cases purportedly involving the narrator, a physician. The stated aim of Warren's tales was to open the 'sealed book' (I, p. ix) of the medical world: 'those pregnant scenes of interest and instruction which fall under the constant observation of the medical profession' (I, p. vi) – that is, the mysteries of life, or rather, death.

Among the medical cases and situations with which the physician finds himself confronted, one relates to an episode of body-snatching. His medical studies completed, the narrator is now 'walking the hospitals' in order to gain practical experience. The tale bears the punning title 'Grave Doings',[46] as if to play upon the physician's

sense of responsibility, but nonetheless brings home the pivotal role
of grave-robbing in medical research, education and practice. It
records the 'first and last exploit' of the narrator 'in the way of
body-stealing' (I, p. 321), but makes explicit once again the therapeutic role of dissection in medical research:

> My gentle reader – start not at learning that I have been, in my time,
> a resurrectionist. Let not this appalling word, this humiliating con-
> fession, conjure up in your fancy a throng of vampire-like images
> and associations, or earn your 'Physician's' dismissal from your hearts
> and hearths. It is your own groundless fears, my fair trembler – your
> own superstitious prejudices – that have driven me, and will drive
> many others of my brethen, to such dreadful doings as those hereafter
> detailed. Come, come – let us have one word of reason between us
> on the abstract question – and then for my tale. You expect us to
> cure you of disease, and yet deny us the only means of learning *how*!
> You would have us bring you the ore of skill and experience, yet
> forbid us to break the soil or sink a shaft! Is this fair, *fair* reader? Is
> this reasonable? (I, p. 321)

The emphasis in the story on the significance of autopsy for medical
progress highlights the influence of new theories emerging in that
period regarding pathology and the localisation of seats of disease.
The study of organs and tissues was increasingly seen as providing
the key to medical understanding, while constituents of the body
such as blood and urine were considered of lesser interest. Far from
being a Gothic villain or vampire, the body-snatcher of this story
is presented as neither heartless nor cruel, and should not, as the
physician begs, be 'dismiss[ed] from [his clients'] hearts and hearths'.
This insight into the reality of the difficulties of medical practice
aims to challenge readers' assumptions about medical practice
(illuminated here by the Gothic paraphernalia, clearly visible in
terms like 'confession', 'fears', 'trembler', 'superstitious' or 'vampire'),
and present true-to-life medical conundrums, such as a case of heart
disease that defies diagnosis, as the kind of mysteries that ought to
pique people's interest instead:

> A young and rather interesting female was admitted a patient at the
> hospital I attended; her case baffled all our skill, and her symptoms

even defied diagnosis. *Now*, it seemed an enlargement of the heart –
now, an ossification – then this, that, and the other; and at last it was
plain we knew nothing at all about the matter – no, not even whether
her disorder was organic or functional, primary or symptomatic – or
whether it *was* really the heart that was at fault. She received no
benefit at all under the fluctuating schemes of treatment we pursued,
and at length fell into dying circumstances. (I, p. 322)

The slippery quality of the external signs of disease in this case
makes the search for internal symptoms compulsory, thereby rendering the post-mortem examination essential. The patient's family,
understanding that the surgeons wish to keep the patient in hospital
until she dies in order to dissect her, ask for the patient to be carried
home. The story, first published in June 1831, certainly references
contemporary debates on dissection and the calls from medical
professionals for anatomy reform. The passage of the Anatomy Act
in July 1832 enabled anatomists to use unclaimed and donated
bodies for dissection, including the corpses of patients who had died
in hospital and whose relatives were unable to cover the costs of a
burial. However, although published some months before the passage
of the Act, it is significant that the hospital is presented here as a
place where dissections do in fact take place, even on the illegally
claimed patients' bodies. Indeed, the physician explains to the
patient's brothers that they will be able to get hold of their sister's
body whether she dies in hospital or at home ('we can get hold of
her . . . as easily if she die with [her family] as with us' (I, p. 322)).
Thus, the patient's inescapable fate constructs her as a typical Gothic
victim, whilst the hospital is portrayed as a site of torture, run by
unscrupulous medical practitioners, transformed into body-snatchers
to exhume the body and secure their pathological specimen.

The scene is hence set for the story's body-snatching episode, as
the doctor, failing to find a professional resurrectionist (all being on
'*professional tours*' (I, p. 323)), hires an Irish porter instead and makes
for the churchyard three days after the burial of the patient. They
start at sudden noises (an ass,[47] a human voice), but eventually
manage to raise the coffin and find 'the shrouded inmate – all white
and damp'. The narrator is in the process of 'remov[ing] the face-
cloth, and unpin[ning] the cap, while M— [is] loos[ing] the sleeves

from the wrists' (I, p. 332), when the group suddenly see a human figure approaching and they decide to flee. The thrilling midnight adventure turns – once again – into farce, as the characters, believing they have been discovered, all run away in different directions, with the porter even falling into a newly opened grave. Ironically, the apparently threatening figure turns out to be only the coachman, who had come to rescue them, believing they had fallen into an ambush. The story ends with the narrator swearing never to practise body-snatching again. The collection thus promotes a more sensitive and responsible image of the medical practitioner/body-snatcher, as Coyer suggests.[48]

Warren's short story, like the short stories published in *Blackwood's Edinburgh Magazine* and the *Monthly Magazine* in the first half of the nineteenth century, published in the months that preceded or followed the passing of the 1832 Anatomy Act, reverberated with pervasive fears of body-snatching as much as they capitalised upon an iconic Gothic motif. In fact, despite the closure of the private anatomy schools and the establishment of the teaching hospitals, body-snatching would not be relegated to the status of a historical curiosity in the subsequent period, as that 'stuff of the old medicine'.[49] On the contrary, as a topos of the literature of terror emblematising fears related to the violation of the body and the fragmentation of the self, it continually resurfaced in mid-century Gothic. However, in that later period body-snatching would be used more to purvey a social discourse than to emphasise the medical reality of the day, as the novels of G. W. M. Reynolds and Charles Dickens illustrate.

G. W. M. Reynolds's and Charles Dickens's body-snatchers

Famous for his supernatural novels, such as *Faust* (1845–6), *Wagner, the Wehr-Wolf* (1846–7) and *The Necromancer* (1852), G. W. M. Reynolds (1814–79) was also known for his urban Gothic series, *The Mysteries of London* (1844–8) and *The Mysteries of the Court of London* (1848–56), which located horror in contemporary London. As a political activist much involved with Chartism, Reynolds gave shape to the form of urban Gothic that would later feature heavily in the novels of Charles Dickens, offering a bleak and terrifying picture of London squalor and the living conditions of the working classes. In Reynolds's urban Gothic, the London underworld is a site of dirt, disease and death where body-snatchers prosper. Anatomical culture informs, indeed, *The Mysteries of London*, which pivots around the figure of Anthony Tidkins, a resurrection man, who persecutes the main male character, Richard Markham, throughout the first volume. Interestingly, the body-snatcher's trafficking in cadavers highlights Reynolds's discourse on British commodity culture and political economy more generally. The British capital is depicted in the first chapters of the novel as a 'labyrinth of narrow and dirty streets',[50] where subterranean sewers running below the houses carry corpses and materialise horror. Trapdoors conceal the dens of criminals, whilst prostitution, gambling and forgery abound. Putrid smells permeate the air, frequently resulting from the decomposition of human remains. Corpses (or 'stiff 'uns') proliferate throughout the narrative: they are stolen, exchanged, measured, examined by surgeons (or 'Sawbones') whose forensic expertise allows the causes of death to be identified. Human bodies are also portayed as valuable commodities[51] and dangerous decomposing matter.[52] Crude anatomical details are commonplace. In the resurrectionists' den, for instance, the stress is laid on the colour of the corpse: 'Stretched upon a shutter, which three chairs supported, was a corpse – naked, and of that blueish or livid colour which denotes the beginning of decomposition!' (I, p. 338). The reference to the nakedness of the corpse and the graphic depiction of the cadaver (its colour and later smell) draw attention to the connections betwen anatomy and pornography. The corpse of a sixteen-year old girl is later depicted, similarly stripped naked, aestheticised as a statue, as the 'polished marble limbs' suggest, the better to be 'rudely grasped' by the body-snatchers:

> 'This is the right one', said the surgeon, casting a hasty glance upon the face of the dead body, which was that of a young girl of about sixteen.
>
> The Resurrection Man extinguished the light; and he and his companions proceeded to lift the corpse out of the coffin.
>
> The polished marble limbs of the deceased were rudely grasped by the sacrilegious hands of the body-snatchers; and, having stripped the

corpse stark naked, they tied its neck and heels together by means of a strong cord. They then thrust it into a large sack made for the purpose. (I, p. 350)

The figure of the callous body-snatcher enables the sensational author to rewrite desire as a search for a (female) corpse. 'Death, like sexual desire', in Sappol's terms, is here 'what bourgeois morality and aesthetics cannot contain'.[53] Likewise, in the surgeon's out-house, the description of the system of levers and pulleys emphasises the physical materiality (the weight) of the corpse, while the focus on the fluids pouring out of the subjects for dissection constructs horror through elements which ooze out of the body:

> The Resurrection Man and the Buffer conveyed the body into a species of out-house, which the surgeon, who was passionately attached to anatomical studies, devoted to purposes of dissection and physiological experiment.
>
> In the middle of this room, which was about ten feet long and six broad, stood a strong deal table, forming a slightly inclined plane. The stone pavement of the out-house was perforated with holes in the immediate vicinity of the table, so that the fluid which poured from subjects for dissection might escape into a drain communicating with the common sewer. To the ceiling, immediately above the head of the table, was attached a pulley with a strong cord, by means of which a body might be supported in any position that was most convenient to the anatomist. (I, p. 925)

Like the colours and the fluids of the cadavers, the smell of putrid corpses contributes to the construction of a realistic and scientifically accurate scene of horror. This paves the way for the abject sight of decomposing bodies, such as when the Resurrection Man's mother – the 'Mummy' (her name ironically hinting at preserved bodies) – is described treating corpses like so many commodities:

> What a lurking hole of enormity – what a haunt of infamy – what a scene of desperate crime – was this in which he now found himself! A feculent smell of the decomposing corpse in the next room reached

his nostrils, and produced a nauseating sensation in his stomach. And
that corpse – was it the remains of one who had died a natural death,
or who had been most foully murdered? . . .

The revolting spectacle of a corpse putrid with decomposition produced no more impression upon [the Mummy] than the pale and
beautiful remains of any lovely girl whom death had called early to
the tomb, and whose form was snatched from its silent couch beneath
the sod ere the finger of decay had begun its ravages. That hideous
old woman considered corpses an article of commerce, and handled
her wares as a trader does his merchandise. (I, pp. 341–3)

Reynolds's series as a whole abounds with references to sensational
cases of body-snatching, such as the previously mentioned 1831
case of the Italian boy murdered by Bishop and Williams (I, p. 126),
and the term 'burking' is used now and then (I, p. 838). Body-
snatching enables Reynolds to combine graphic horror and sensational realism, as when the murderer William Bolter, condemned
to be 'hanged, drawn, and quartered, and his dissected corpse
disposed of according to the will of our Sovereign Lady the Queen'
(I, p. 275), imagines the pain of being hanged and is later visualised
in convulsions on the gibbet.[54] Reynolds hints repeatedly at contemporary sensational cases of murderers awaking in anatomical
theatres by including several instances of corpses coming back to
life after being hanged up (p. 352). The narrative also reflects
contemporary medical practitioners' difficulty in gaining access to
corpses,[55] and includes a number of surgeons who feel guilty about
their involvement in body-snatching activities.

But if the medical practitioners do not feature principally in *The
Mysteries of London* as accomplices in crime, the 'Resurrection Man',
although in many respects a clichéd Gothic villain, is nonetheless
delineated in sometimes intriguing ways. The 'cadaverous-looking',
shaggy-browed body-snatcher is presented from the beginning as
'a villain stained with every crime – a murderer of the blackest dye –
a wretch whose chief pursuit [is] the violation of the tomb' (I,
p. 915). Yet, Reynolds's characterisation also features some telling
allusions to Mary Shelley's iconic Gothic villain. The body-snatcher's
story, located at the heart of the first volume, shapes Anthony
Tidkins as a double of Frankenstein's creature. Complexifying as

it does the roles of victim and victimiser – or mixing the figures of the resurrected creature with that of the resurrectionist – the embedded first-person narrative casts the Gothic villain in a new light, for the narrative contains the record of Tidkins's struggle against poverty and alienation, shaping the body-snatcher as a victim of capitalist society forced into crime – a product of a society that 'persecute[s]' (p. 545) the poor for fear they might rise up against the rich. As a result, as Tidkins seeks vengeance against those responsible for his hardship, the figure of the body-snatcher undermines the construction of the Gothic villain and villainy more generally. As in *Frankenstein*, moreover, the network of Gothic motifs shapes Tidkins's quest for identity. The field of anatomy and its use of nameless or stolen dead bodies and body parts become pivotal to the plot, since Reynolds locates the melodramatic recognition scene in an anatomy theatre, where the body-snatcher realises that his own beloved lies on the dissecting table:

> We carried the corpse into the surgery, and laid it upon a table. 'You are sure it is the right one?' said the surgeon. – 'It is the body from the grave that you pointed out', answered my father. – 'The fact is', resumed the surgeon, 'that this is a very peculiar case. Six days ago, a young female rose in the morning in perfect health; that evening she was a corpse. I opened her, and found no traces of poison; but her family would not permit me to carry the examination any further. They did not wish her to be hacked about. Since her death some love-letters have been found in her drawer; but there is no name attached to any of them . . . I am therefore anxious to make another and more searching investigation than on the former occasion, into the cause of death. But I will soon satisfy myself that this is indeed the corpse I mean'. – With these words the surgeon tore away the shroud from the face of the corpse. I cast an anxious glance upon the pale, cold, marble countenance. My blood ran cold – my legs trembled – my strength seemed to have failed me. Was I mistaken? could it be the beloved of my heart – 'Yes; that is Miss Price', said the surgeon, coolly. All doubt on my part was now removed. I had exhumed the body of her whom a thousand times I had pressed to my sorrowful breast – whom I had clasped to my aching heart. I felt as if I had committed some horrible crime – a murder, or other deadly deed! (p. 540)

By displaying the 'nameless' body-snatcher's feelings and emotions (manifest in terms such as 'anxious', 'trembled', 'sorrowful breast' and 'aching heart'), the scene provides a radical reworking of the Gothic archvillain. The embedded narrative, climaxing as it does with the recognition scene (when the identity of the corpse – not that of the body-snatcher/lover – is revealed), shifts the positions of Victor Frankenstein and his creature on to the anatomist's table, with Tidkins's feelings of guilt providing further evidence of his links with Frankenstein. Reynolds's play with the clichés of the literature of terror and his ironic and constant reversals literally anatomise his portrait of modern society. The figure of the body-snatcher is informed by iconic Gothic texts, figures and conventions in order to subvert them all the more effectively. This figure functions thus within the text as a conspicuous cliché emblematising fear – an empty trope, or mere signifier, which appears repeatedly in the text (Tidkins constantly pops up throughout the episodes) to emphasise its artificiality, but whose meaning lies elsewhere. By the end of the first volume, the 'Resurrection Man' appears, indeed, as a thing of the past – an 'abomination' – of which society is now rid thanks to the passage of the 1832 Anatomy Act. If made redundant by the new legislation on the uses of the human body, the body-snatcher nevertheless continually haunts Reynolds's narrative, but as symbol of the widespread and legal forms of violence against the bodies of the weakest:

> 'But do you think there are such people as resurrection men now-a-days?'
> 'Resurrection men!' ejaculated the reverend visitor, bursting out into a laugh; 'no, my dear madam – society has got rid of those abominations'.
> 'Then where do surgeons get corpses from, sir?'
> 'From the hulks, the prisons, and the workhouses', was the answer.
> 'What! Poor creatures which goes to the workus!' cried Mrs. Smith, revolting at the idea.
> 'Yes – ma'am; but the surgeons don't like them as subjects, because they're nothing but skin and bone'. (I, p. 883)

Throughout *The Mysteries of London*, then, the traffic in bodies functions as a sensational means to merge medical and social realism.

Both persecuted by the (enduring) body-snatcher and discriminated against by legislation, the novel's 'poor creatures' and their appalling conditions of life and death lie at the heart of Reynolds's popular fiction.

Like Reynolds's *Mysteries of London*, Dickens's most famous body-snatcher, Jeremiah Cruncher, who features in *A Tale of Two Cities* (1859), owes a great deal to *Frankenstein*. Both novels refer to the medical culture of their time and point to the shortage of corpses for medical education and practice. Both novels are set moreover against a revolutionary backdrop; the French Revolution and the Reign of Terror inform both Shelley's[56] and Dickens's plots. Tellingly, in both novels, social revolution is metaphorised through images borrowed from the field of anatomy. Indeed, like other Gothic novels of the period, *Frankenstein* plays with anxieties related to persecution, imprisonment and arbitrary justice which are rooted in revolutionary fears. Throughout the Romantic period, the motif of the 'monster' frequently served to represent fears related to the French Revolution. In *Reflections on the Revolution in France* (1790) and *Letters on the Proposals for Peace with the Regicide Directory of France* (1796–7), Edmund Burke makes explicit how unnatural political regimes generate monsters. Burke's writings denounce the Enlightenment and the development of a form of experimental science, cut adrift from moral values. Defining French revolutionaries mostly through their scientific activities, Burke posits that scientific materialism will lead to the destruction of the human race.[57] Yet, surprisingly, the cruelty of the 'revolutionary' science he condemns echoes the state of popular opinion regarding the gangs of body-snatchers then active in Britain:

France, such as it is, is indeed highly formidable: not formidable, however, as a great republic; but as the most dreadful gang of robbers and murderers that ever was embodied. But this distempered strength of France will be the cause of proportionable weakness on its recovery. Never was a country so completely ruined; and they who calculate the resurrection of her power by former examples have not sufficiently considered what is the present state of things. Without detailing the inventory of what organs of government have been destroyed, together with the very materials of which alone they can be recomposed, I wish it to be considered what an operose affair the whole system of taxation is in the old states of Europe.[58]

The term 'resurrection' is associated with a description of the body politic (the 'organs of government'), while the idea of the 're-compos[ition]' of 'materials' evokes dismemberment and anatomical culture. Moreover, as gangs of thieves and murderers led by physiologists, revolutionaries track down the 'priviledged orders' to their graves, Burke argues. The grave becomes therefore the ultimate site of crime:

That revolution seems to have extended even to the constitution of the mind of man. It has this of wonderful in it, that it resembles what Lord Verulam says of the operations of Nature: It was perfect, not only in its elements and principles, but in all its members and its organs, from the very beginning. The moral scheme of France furnishes the only pattern ever known which they who admire will *instantly* resemble. It is, indeed, an inexhaustible repertory of one kind of examples. In my wretched condition, though hardly to be classed with the living, I am not safe from them. They have tigers to fall upon animated strength; they have hyenas to prey upon carcasses. The national menagerie is collected by the first physiologists of the time; and it is defective in no description of savage nature. They pursue even such as me into the obscurest retreats, and haul them before their revolutionary tribunals. Neither sex, nor age, nor the sanctuary of the tomb, is sacred to them. They have so determined a hatred to all privileged orders, that they deny even to the departed the sad immunities of the grave. They are not wholly without an object. Their turpitude purveys to their malice; and they unplumb the dead for bullets to assassinate the living. If all revolutionists were not proof against all caution, I should recommend it to their consideration, that no persons were ever known in history, either sacred or profane, to vex the sepulchre, and by their sorceries to call up the prophetic dead, with any other event than the prediction of their own disastrous fate.—'Leave me, oh, leave me to repose!'[59]

Burke's visual and anatomical rhetoric permeates *Frankenstein*. Victor Frankenstein's creature is the product of scientific materialism; it also threatens the social order by seeking to exact vengeance on its creator. This may explain Shelley's choice of Ingoldstadt as the setting for the novel, for the Bavarian town was linked to the Illuminati, a secret society which embodied faith in the Enlightenment and rejection of superstition and obscurantism, as explained by the work of anti-Jacobin writer Augustin de Barruel, familiar to Percy Shelley.[60]

Although published a few decades later, Dickens's *A Tale of Two Cities* similarly foregrounds the links between revolution and (medical) science. Dickens's historical novel relates an episode from the French Revolution during the Reign of Terror, drawing parallels between France and Britain. France is characterised in the novel by the number of guillotined heads falling on the scaffold, while Britain is a country where dissection flourishes and body-snatchers haunt churchyards in search of fresh material. The system of parallels and echoes between France and Britain is sustained throughout the novel and underpins Dickens's social discourse. Dickens was known for his denunciation of the appalling living conditions of the lower classes in the industrial cities, but many of his novels also drew public attention to how the poor fell victim to the development of medical science and scientific progress more generally. In his 1836 short story 'The Black Veil', for instance, a mother has her hanged son's body stolen by body-snatchers and brought to a surgeon for reanimation. The motif of the criminal body sentenced to death is also found in Dickens's later novels, such as *Barnaby Rudge* (1841) and *Great Expectations* (1861),[61] whilst *The Pickwick Papers* (1836–7) shows medical students talking about dissecting corpses.

In both his fictional and non-fictional works, Dickens condemned the use of dissection in medical education as a necessary tool for obtaining knowledge. In 'A Great Day for the Doctors', published in *Household Words* in November 1850, he traces the rise of 'a race of resurrection men' whose trade provided the raw materials for the development of anatomical schools in Britain:

> Every living being every man, woman, and child endures a certain ascertained amount of sickness during life, for the alleviation of which, medical knowledge and skill is required. But medical efficiency in the treatment of disease cannot be gained unless the young doctor bases all his subsequent studies upon a thorough knowledge of the

structure of the human body. This information can only be had by the use of the scalpel upon the dead. The very notion is apt to send a thrill through every nerve of those unaccustomed to regard the subject in a philosophical light. But the terms are absolute: no dissection no knowledge. For generations, such means of information were forbidden to the student; and being denied by law, and abhorrent to popular feeling, the unlucky doctors had to run all sorts of risks, and to resort to all kinds of improper and disagreeable expedients to procure the means of teaching the art of the anatomist. Hence sprang up a race of 'resurrection men', as they were called, men who stole the bodies of the dead, to sell them to anatomical schools for dissection. Their robberies of the grave were carried on at great risks. The public detestation of the crime was so great, that when a clumsy or unlucky follower of it was detected, he had to fight for his life, or submit to be kicked and beaten, and trampled to death.[62]

However, as he further explains, by mid-century corpses were no longer robbed from churchyards but obtained from workhouses, with the bodies of the poor now constituting a legal source of anatomical material for dissection:

But the first of October is no longer preceded by the forays of the 'resurrectionist'; no longer clouded by the lack of means for pursuing the branch of study on which the superstructure of medical knowledge must be raised. A population of two millions has ever some members dropping from the ranks solitary and unknown the waifs and strays of society without friends to know or to mourn their fate. Almost always paupers, often criminals, though their lives may have been useless, or worse, they seem to make, when the fitful struggle is over, some atonement after death. The wreck of their former selves is offered at the shrine of science for a while, and when thereafter they are gathered to the kindred dust of the graveyard, they may sleep none the less calmly for having contributed no mean help to the advancement of that branch of human knowledge which has its annual ovation on the first of October – the great day for the doctors.[63]

Dickens's plea for a more ethical regard for the bodies of the poor and his attack on a society which placed the body of the murderer and that of the pauper on the same level – equating therefore crime and poverty – also permeates 'Use and Abuse of the Dead', an article published in *Household Words* on 3 April 1858. As he observes in this article, the masters of workhouses regularly provided anatomical material to the London hospitals:

> One does not forget in a month or two the scandalous details recently made public as to the manner in which masters of workhouses and petty undertakers may, by the disregard of honesty, decency, and common human feeling, increase the supply to the London hospitals of subjects for dissection.[64]

Dickens's article relates the history of anatomical science from Vesalius's work to his own day.[65] But he also points out that body-snatching activities developed because of the absence of legislation regarding the uses of the human cadaver:

> Thirty years ago, in England, it is hardly exaggeration to say, that there no more existed honest means of studying the Divine handiwork in our own frame than in the days of Vesalius, three hundred years ago. The necessity of dissection was indeed admitted, but the power to dissect, except by encouragement of desecration, was denied. Churchyards were robbed, sick chambers were robbed; the high price that anatomists were compelled to pay for means of study tempted wretched men to commit murder . . . In those days the calling of the resurrectionist was followed as an independent business by men who took pride in it, scorned the clumsiness of amateurs, and even resented all intrusion on the churchyards over which they had established claims. The professional resurrectionist chose for himself a well-filled city graveyard, and then worked it, with a miner's industry, in the most systematic manner. The vast majority of the bodies taken in this way were those of paupers, who, being buried near the surface, were accessible, and upon whose undistinguished graves a skilful robbery could be made with little or no chance of detection. The practice was to remove carefully the soil at the head of the grave and expose one end of the coffin, open that, and with an instrument contrived for the purpose, draw out the body by the head. The coffin was then closed again, and the grave also closed again, so neatly that no sign of its desecration could be easily perceived. The value to the

resurrectionists of each body so stolen was ten, twelve, and, sometimes even fifteen pounds.[66]

Whilst 'Use and Abuse of the Dead' illuminates changes in the uses and legal status of human bodies up to his own day, Dickens's *A Tale of Two Cities*, published a few months later, is situated decades before the passage of the 1832 Anatomy Act. Jerry Cruncher, the body-snatcher, whose very name suggests dismemberment, haunts Old Bailey, waiting for the corpses of hanged criminals. His 'spiky' hair, as sharp as blades ('his spiky hair looking as if it must tear the sheets to ribbons'[67]), much like the 'spiked wall' (p. 60) of Newgate, binds the character both to the world of punishment and to that of dissection, suggesting therefore the links between the legal and the anatomical realms. Cruncher's hair, indeed, '[b]ecom[es] more and more spiky as the law terms bristled it' (p. 61), as if already dissecting the criminal's body ('The accused . . . was . . . being mentally hanged, beheaded, and quartered, by everybody there' (p. 61)). Punishment is also described in terms reminiscent of the public dissection ('The form that was to be doomed to be so shamefully mangled, was the sight; the immortal creature that was to be so butchered and torn asunder, yielded the sensation' (p. 60)), binding the world of justice even more closely to that of the anatomical theatre:

[H]e'll be drawn on a hurdle to be half hanged, and then he'll be taken down and sliced before his own face, and then his inside will be taken out and burnt while he looks on, and then his head will be chopped off, and he'll be cut into quarters. That's the sentence. (p. 59)

Likewise, trials are depicted through images of clothes turned inside out and outside in, strengthening even more the connections between the court and the dissection of the criminal's body:

Mr Attorney-general turned the whole suit of clothes Mr Stryver had fitted on the jury, inside out . . . Lastly, came my Lord himself, turning the suit of clothes, now inside out, outside in, but on the whole decidedly trimming and shaping them into grave-clothes for the prisoner. (p. 72)

The frequent use of metaphors which materialise the corpse and its dismemberment are all the more important as Cruncher's night-time activities are described indirectly, through a change of point of view: the body-snatcher is followed by his son, who is trying to understand his father's actions. Ironically, as the repetition of the appellation 'honoured parent' intimates, the profanation of the tombstone metaphorises the desacralisation of the father's image:

> They fished with a spade, at first. Presently the honoured parent appeared to be adjusting some instrument like a great corkscrew. Whatever tools they worked with, they worked hard, until the awful striking of the church clock so terrified young Jerry, that he made off, with his hair as stiff as his father's.

> But, his long-cherished desire to know more about these matters, not only stopped him in his running away, but lured him back again. They were still fishing perseveringly, when he peeped in at the gate for the second time; but, now they seemed to have got a bite. There was a screwing and complaining sound down below, and their bent figures were strained, as if by a weight. By slow degree the weight broke away the earth upon it, and came to the surface. Young Jerry very well knew what it would be; but, when he saw it, and saw his honoured parent about to wrench it open, he was so frightened, being new to the sight, that he made off again, and never stopped until he had run a mile or more. (pp. 154–5)

The striking of the church clock represents the moral order, terrifying the young boy who has become contaminated with his father's sin: his stiff hair is now similar to his father's, evoking simultaneously dissection and terror. However, the scene ends before the body-snatchers open the coffin: the corpse remains invisible despite the stress on vision ('when he saw it . . . and saw his honoured parent . . . being new to the sight'), and is only alluded to or visualised indirectly throughout the novel. Terror emerges thus through a lack of vision, the latter mirroring the body-snatcher's dispassionate view of his activity. Likewise, the many ironical comments the narrator makes on Cruncher's 'meditations on mortality' (p. 151) creates a distanced perspective which forcefully conveys

Dickens's satire on the uses and abuses of corpses.[68] Cruncher's trade is related to 'a branch of Scientific goods' (p. 157), and his reluctance to tell his son if he is dealing with 'Persons' bodies' (p. 157) stresses the connections between anatomy and secrecy. These connections become pivotal to the dual structure of the novel, as the narrative compares and/or contrasts guillotined French bodies with dissected British ones.

Dickens's novel was originally entitled *Buried Alive*. As we shall see, the motif of live burial encapsulates several different meanings which increasingly place the body and its uses at the heart of the narrative. *A Tale of Two Cities* opens with the release of Dr Manette after eighteen years' incarceration in the Bastille. The physician's imprisonment is likened to a live burial, as the reflections of Jarvis Lorry (a bank manager) illustrate. Lorry compares Manette's release with being dug out from the earth:

> After such imaginary discourse, the passenger in his fancy would dig, and dig, dig – now, with a spade, now with a great key, now with his hands – to dig his wretched creature out. Got out at last, with earth hanging about his face and hair, he would suddenly fall away to dust. (pp. 18–19)

Similarly, the prisoner's cadaverous face ('varieties of sunken cheeks, cadaverous colours, emaciated hands and figures' (p. 18)) and his mysterious disappearance eighteen years earlier, 'as if he had been spirited away' (p. 27), portray the physician as a corpse, such as might be robbed by body-snatchers. It is ironic, therefore, that Cruncher is present to witnesses the 'digging out' of Manette, as Mr Lorry emphasises: 'What a night it has been! Almost a night, Jerry', said Mr Lorry, 'to bring the dead out of their graves' (p. 99). The comparison between Manette's imprisonment and the theft of his body is repeated throughout the novel. His 'haggard eyes' (p. 41) and 'transparent' (p. 42) bones suggest that Manette is a living corpse ('recalling some very weak person . . . the spirit of a fast-dying man' (p. 43)); or rather, a body hosting secrets which only dissection can reveal. Indeed, Manette suffers from monomania; the physician mechanically makes shoes, and his mental condition resurfaces whenever an event recalls his buried past, such as when the Frenchman Charles Darnay, about to marry Manette's daughter, reveals that he is Monseigneur St Evrémonde's nephew – the cruel aristocrat who had had Manette arrested. Hence, the secret at the core of the novel is both psychological (Manette's monomania) and political. The parallels between the physiologial and the political plots are sustained throughout the novel, as when the shoe-maker's equipment is buried in the garden to suppress all traces of Manette's activities, as one might get rid of a human body:

> The burning of the body (previously reduced to pieces convenient for the purpose) was commenced without delay in the kitchen fire; and the tools, shoes, and leather, were buried in the garden. So wicked do destruction and secrecy appear to honest minds, that Mr Lorry and Miss Pross, while engaged in the commission of their deed and in the removal of its traces, almost felt, and almost looked, like accomplices in a horrible crime. (p. 197)

The connections between Manette's monomania and anatomical culture (suggested here by images of burial) are no coincidence. In fact, Manette's secret has been repressed/buried in his brain; the surgeon's brain thus functions as a double of the tower in which he was imprisoned and where he buried the missing piece of evidence: the letter which reveals the Marquis's crime and which leads to Darnay's second imprisonment. Thus, the novel continually plays upon images of burial and digging out – the burial and digging of the truth or of bodies:

> In making some alterations, the workmen came upon an old dungeon, which had been, for many years, built up and forgotten. Every stone of its inner wall was covered by inscriptions which had been carved by prisoners – dates, names, complaints, and prayers. Upon a corner stone in an angle of the wall, one prisoner, who seemed to have gone to execution, had cut as his last work, three letters. They were done with some very poor instrument, and hurriedly, with an unsteady hand. At first, they were read as D. I. C.; but, on being more carefully examined, the last letter was found to be G. There was no record or legend of any prisoner with those initials, and many fruitless guesses

were made what the name could have been. At length, it was suggested that the letters were not initials, but the complete word, DIG. The floor was examined very carefully under the inscription, and, in the earth beneath a stone, or tile, or some fragment of paving, were found the ashes of a paper, mingled with the ashes of a small leathern case or bag. (pp. 96–7)

Buildings, like bodies, host secrets. The Gothic topoi of the prisoner buried alive in the tower and of the buried letter invite us to read the body as a double of the mysterious tower in the Bastille, as the narrator suggests from the beginning of the novel. In the following passage, buildings enclose secrets, like human creatures, and their impenetrability is compared to death:

A wonderful fact to reflect upon, that every human creature is constituted to be that profound secret and mystery to every other. A solemn consideration, when I enter a great city at night, that every one of those darkly clustered houses encloses its own secret; that every room in every one of them encloses its own secret; that every beating heart in the hundreds of thousands of breasts there, is, in some of its imaginings, a secret to the heart nearest it! Something of the awfulness, even of Death itself, is referable to this . . . My friend is dead, my neighbour is dead, my love, the darling of my soul, is dead; it is the inexorable consolidation and perpetuation of the secret that was always in that individuality, and which I shall carry in mine to my life's end. In any of the burial-places of this city through which I pass, is there a sleeper more inscrutable than its busy inhabitants are, in their innermost personality, to me, or than I am to them? (p. 17)

Once again, the parallel between buildings and the construction of the dead body, both as an image of knowledge and of its inaccessibility, reflects the anatomical culture of the time. The embedded structures (the prisoner burying a letter in the tower in which he is himself buried; the secret buried in the prisoner's mind) define the mind as the ultimate space to explore – the unassailable tower. Manette is therefore buried alive twice: he is imprisoned in the Bastille but also made prisoner of a body which refuses to give away its secrets. The character consequently embodies both secrecy and the quest for the truth; the secrets of his imprisonment and of his sealed body become indissociable.

Unsurprisingly, the Marquis is the villain of the piece. He has the power to seal at will the fate of men like Manette, and his castle provides a material reflection of his crimes:

> For three heavy hours, the stone faces of the château, lion and human, stared blindly at the night. Dead darkness lay on all the landscape, dead darkness added its own hush to the hushing dust on all the roads. The burial place had got to the pass that its little heaps of poor grass were indistinguishable from one another . . . Lighter and lighter, until at last the sun touched the tops of the still trees, and poured its radiance over the hill. In the glow, the water of the château seemed to turn to blood, and the stone faces crimsoned. (p. 121)

The Gothic rhetoric of violence and death is intermingled here with the historical narrative and, more particularly, Dickens's social discourse. The buried bodies ('little heaps of poor grass') are those of the 'poor' starved by the Marquis, their corpses bearing witness to the politital regime before the Revolution. The use of indirect representation pinpoints the way in which meaning must be systematically decoded: the poor appear through the adjective in 'poor grass' or even 'little', simultaneously signalling their insignificance and their merging with the earth. Crime is represented through the metaphor of blood, while the castle is personified. Identical metaphors thus build a network of associations which connect the two parts of the novel and the two countries/cities. Indeed, at the beginning of the novel, France and Britain are compared through the image of two kings with large jaws ('There were a king with a large jaw and a queen with a plain face, on the throne of England; there were a king with a large jaw and a queen with a fair face, on the throne of France' (p. 7)) 'carr[ying] their divine rights with a high hand' (p. 9). The jaw (or mouth) able to eat metaphorises power, while on the other hand, the citizens are starved ('starved fingers and toes' (p. 32)), as if already dead ('cadaverous faces' (p. 32)), placed naked on a dissecting table ('bare arms' (p. 32)) and dismembered, as suggested by the synecdoche of the 'starved fingers and toes'. As '[h]unger rattle[s] its dry bones' (p. 33), the metaphor of the corpse circulates throughout the narrative, foreshadowing the moment when the French people rise up, as if resurrected from the earth, to claim vengeance:

> A tremendous roar arose from the throat of Saint Antoine, and a forest of naked arms struggled in the air like shrivelled branches of trees in a winter wind: all the fingers convulsively clutching at every weapon of semblance that was thrown up from the depths below, no matter how far off. (p. 206)

The Marquis's sword-like fingers ('as though his finger were the fine point of a sword' (p. 118)), echo Cruncher's stiff hair, hinting at the anatomist's knife or lancet, while his mysterious face seems to conceal as many crimes as a medical practitioner trafficking in cadavers.

Thus, the narrative draws parallels between France, where the king possesses 'the right of life and death over the surrounding vulgar' (p. 116), and Britain, where people seem about to dislocate ('as if they were falling to pieces at the larger joints' (p. 10)), and where medical practitioners use the bodies of the poor for research and education. This is the reason why the pauper's corpse, dissected on the anatomist's table, is never described, or is stolen but never visualised in the narrative. Instead, it is evoked indirectly, through Dickens's system of parallels between the two countries. Both monarchy in France and medical practitioners in Britain use the bodies of the poor, dismembering them or 'resurrecting' them.

Through this system of correspondences, the French people's vengeance in Paris mirrors the pauper's fantasised revenge in Britain, as when Madame Defarge makes knots as if she were strangling her enemies (p. 172), her knots recalling the public executions of Tyburn. Guillotined or hanged, the bodies of those sentenced to death end up dismembered in both countries. Like anatomists, revolutionaries observe their enemies' corpses, such as that of the Marquis, 'scattered far and wide' (p. 224), or long for their body parts ('Give us the blood of Foulon, Give us the head of Foulon, Give us the heart of Foulon, Give us the body and soul of Foulon, Rend Foulon to pieces, and dig him into the ground, that grass may grow from him' (p. 215)). Dickens's echoes between France and England thus create corpses that only appear analogically. Just like young Cruncher, who sees only the coffin his father is digging out, the cadaver materialises only through the discourse of its representation. Dickens's use of Gothic topoi to express fears related to capitalism and the transformation of human material into profitable goods shows how the field of anatomy informed cultural representations and participated in shaping discourses about the body and the self. Yet paradoxically, Dickens's medical realism – his use of body-snatchers and hints at anatomical dissection – remains purely rhetorical and artificial. His network of correspondences strongly echoes Edmund Burke's anti-revolutionary rhetoric, as reworked by Thomas Carlyle[69] in *The French Revolution* (1837). Like Burke, Carlyle defines the Enlightenment in terms of scientific experimentation and materialism. Once again, the dissecting room informs Carlyle's vision of Enlightened science, whilst galvanism conjures up the making of Victor Frankenstein's creature:

> For if Government is, so to speak, the outward SKIN of the Body Politic, holding the whole together and protecting it; and all your Craft-Guilds, and Associations for Industry, of hand or of head, are the Fleshly Clothes, the muscular and osseous Tissues (lying *under* such SKIN), whereby Society stands and works; – then is Religion the inmost Pericardial and Nervous Tissue, which ministers Life and warm Circulation to the whole. Without which Pericardial Tissue the Bones and Muscles (or Industry) were inert, or animated only by a Galvanic vitality; the SKIN would become a shrivelled pelt, or fast-rotting raw-hide; and Society itself a dead carcass, – deserving to be buried.[70]

As Chris Baldick has argued, Dickens frequently associated dissection with galvanism.[71] But the parallels he draws between France and England in *A Tale of Two Cities* construct the Revolution as a monster created by society, yet one which threatens to escape its creator. As in Mary Shelley's novel, Burke's anti-revolutionary discourse pervades the narrative whilst nonetheless defending the poor and the unprivileged. In both novels, therefore, the references to anatomical science convey their authors' sociopolitical discourse, a point which would later be sensationalised in Victorian popular fiction, which played upon the melodramatic potential of the body of the poor as anatomical material.

The example of David Pae's *Mary Paterson; or, The Fatal Error. A Story of the Burke and Hare Murders* (1866) is significant in this context, for it draws on the same ingredients which were ensuring the fame of sensation novels around the same period, namely violent and brutal murders, stolen, concealed and recovered wills, illegitimate children and forged documents. Moreover, the novel places the Burke and Hare case at its heart, thus forcefully blurring boundaries between truth and fiction and foregrounding the very elements for which sensation fiction was denounced and dismissed as low literature by contemporary literary critics.

The novel relates the story of Mary Paterson, a young woman seduced by Duncan Grahame, a young medical student. When she becomes pregnant with their child, her lover asks her to leave her father's house in secret and stay away until the birth. Left in the care of Helen M'Dougal and her partner, William Burke, the forlorn woman soon hears that Duncan has married another woman. Mary Paterson falls into poverty and Duncan Grahame is only reunited with her again when the young woman's cadaver is lying upon the table of Dr Knox, about to be dissected, having fallen victim to Burke and Hare. The novel then relates the murders committed by Burke and Hare and their subsequent trials and punishment before focusing again on the case of Mary Paterson. As Mary's identity as one of the Burke and Hare victims is revealed, Leech, the lawyer who has managed Mary's father's property while forging a series of documents to make his client's money his own, gnawed by remorse, gives everything back to Mary's cousin, Dick. Meanwhile, Mary's illegitimate child, Duncan, raised by her nurse, remains penniless. However, James Crawford, Mary's first wooer, reveals Mary Paterson's will, which acknowledges her son and thus establishes the true heir to Mary's father's fortune. Mary Paterson's will is promptly stolen by Dick but his former mistress, Bet (a woman he has cast out, refusing to marry her as he had promised), manages to get hold of the document, which had been concealed in 'the old useless clock standing like a skeleton against the wall'.[72] Bet believes she can force Dick to marry her, instead of the heiress he intends to wed. James Crawford then happens upon the will, concealed this time in a tombstone, and prevents Dick's marriage to heiress Kate Sutherland. The end of the novel jumps forward twenty years. James's daughter, named Mary, is now married to Mary's son, Duncan. Hare is dead and Duncan Grahame, cast off by his wife and now a drunkard, has left for Ireland.

Mary Paterson's melodramatic story, as the innocent victim of Burke and Hare, thus frames the sensational narrative. But Pae's emphasis on bodies – real corpses – whose materiality is foregrounded throughout the novel, blurs the boundaries between fiction and sensational journalism, overtly constructing the narrative as an opinion column and inviting readers to participate in the legal debates surrounding the trial:

> Who can forbear remarking the fatal facility for the disposal of human bodies with the history of this transaction discloses? We designedly and deliberately say a *fatal* facility. Here was a man, a perfect stranger to these doctors, offering a dead body for sale, and it was bought and no questions asked – not one simple interrogation as to how the body had been procured; and not only so, but an invitation was given to bring more. Was this not, *at the least*, presenting a very strong temptation? Was it possible that the idea never occurred to the doctors that the subjects which they bought so freely, and paid for with a comparatively large sum, *might* have been got in a criminal way? Was their faith in the men who engaged in such traffic so great that they considered them incapable of doing anything *worse* than robbing a churchyard or purchasing unburied bodies from needy relatives? We cannot think so. We are forced to believe that with them the exigencies of science were made paramount, and that they made it a point to ask no questions, lest they should be put in possession of dangerous knowledge. But the fact is, the principle of their procedure was immoral. They based the claims of their humane science on a practice not only at variance with honesty, but abhorrent to all human feeling, that it was impossible that a system, illicit in every sense, should not lead to crimes of the worst description; and of these crimes we must consider the doctors *presumptively* guilty, inasmuch as they carefully abstained from satisfying themselves that they were not committed. When the fearful truth did come to light, the doctors tried to clear themselves by protesting their ignorance. In our opinion, it was this ignorance which constituted their greatest guilt. (pp. 57–8)

Stressing as he does the ethics of science, the narrator's advocacy incriminates the medical professionals. This is characteristic of mid-Victorian constructions of medical science, the term 'science' having subsumed 'anatomy' in this passage. Throughout the second half of the nineteenth century, indeed, if body-snatching still reflected popular fear of the medical world, it often hinted far more at medical research than at medical education, with the 'poor, miserable bod[ies] [being] sold for a sacrifice to the Moloch of science' (p. 81). In Victorian realist novels, such as Harriet Martineau's *Deerbrook* (1839) or George Eliot's *Middlemarch* (1871), the various physicians suspected of body-snatching are all deeply involved in medical research. As a late-century example, Robert Louis Stevenson's 'The Body-Snatcher' (1884) is a good instance of the ways in which tales of body-snatching were used to encapsulate a variety of types of discourse on medical research and a popular distrust of the medical profession. The horror tale was written in June 1881 for the *Cornhill Magazine* but was refused by that periodical and later published in the *Pall Mall Journal*'s Christmas issue of 1884. This was a time when physiologists were experimenting on the live bodies of animals, culminating at the International Medical Congress in August 1881 when the pioneering Scottish physiologist/neurologist David Ferrier took part in the cerebral dissection of a living monkey. The physiologist's 1881 trial for his animal experiments – and his subsequent acquittal – had been preceded by a significant rise in the number of the applications for licences and certificates to perform vivisection.

Stevenson's tale rewrites in part the 1828 Burke and Hare case which, as we have seen, had involved another Scottish anatomist – Dr Knox. It relates the medical experience of Fettes, as a sub-assistant in Dr Knox's class, and of the young Doctor Wolfe MacFarlane. Fettes receives 'subjects'[73] ready for dissection, the 'unfriendly relics of humanity' (p. 249) or 'the raw material of the anatomists' (p. 250), brought in (illegally) every night. Fettes and MacFarlane also regularly practise body-snatching themselves. The class is large and the students are eager to dissect parts they have not practised on. One such student is Richardson, who longs to be let loose on one of the subjects' heads – perhaps echoing here contemporary research in cerebral localisation. Hence some of the subjects are killed on purpose, like a woman whose face Fettes recognises, while another – Gray –

becomes anatomical material after a row with Fettes's medical colleague, MacFarlane.

At the end of the short story, however, as Fettes and MacFarlane believe they are transporting the body of a woman they have just 'resurrected', the 'thing' (p. 273) bumping between them turns out to be the body of Gray, whom they had dissected and whose head had been given to Richardson for dissection. The twist in the plot turns the Gothic tale of terror into a ghost story: the corpse which refuses to disappear ironically reappears as the materialisation of the guilty conscience of the two body-snatchers.

Like his predecessors, Stevenson's Gothic constructs the medical world as a criminal realm, but rewrites the issue of guilt through a corpse which refuses to crumble into dust and decompose. The characters' psychological obsession with Gray's corpse, which climaxes when Gray's head seems to appear on the female corpse recently dug up by the two body-snatchers, does not result from any optical trick, as in many of the Gothic romances of the first phase (1764–1824), discussed earlier.[74] Stevenson's ghost story illustrates rather the '"somatic" aspect of late-Victorian Gothic fiction',[75] as Robert Mighall terms it, showing how threat is increasingly located inside the individual by the end of the nineteenth century, paving the way for the psychiatric discourse later found in *The Strange Case of Dr Jekyll and Mr Hyde* (1886) and in Bram Stoker's *Dracula* (1897). Indeed, Stevenson's late-Victorian Gothic posed questions related to medical ethics, yet his rewriting of clichés borrowed from early nineteenth-century tales of terror constructed horror first and foremost in physiological or biological terms, as 'embodied . . . monstrous bodies',[76] such as Mr Hyde, rather than as the monstrous bodies earlier laid out on the dissecting table, like Victor Frankenstein's creature. By the last decades of the nineteenth century, therefore, the Gothic enabled writers to turn the world of medical experimentation upside down and let readers dissect the very brains of the body-snatchers typically found in Blackwoodian tales of terror so as to visualise (and vicariously experience) the physiology of guilt. As we will see in the next chapter, the victims, once dissected, were sometimes exhibited in medical museums, places where preserved human remains reflected the period's fascination with the study of death. Significantly, medical museums were also sites where the dissected subject appeared most fragmented – and thus most likely to be of Gothic interest.

4

The Pandemonium of Chimeras: The Medical Museum

O William dear! O William dear!
My rest eternal ceases;
Alas! my everlasting peace
Is broken into pieces.
. . .
The body-snatchers they have come,
And made a snatch at me;
. . .
They've come and boned your Mary.

The arm that used to take your arm
Is took to Dr. Vyse;
And both my legs are gone to walk
The hospital at Guy's.

I vowed that you should have my hand,
But fate gives us denial;
You'll find it there, at Dr. Bell's,
In spirits and a phial.

As for my feet, the little feet
You used to call so pretty,
There's one, I know, in Bedford Row,
The t'other's in the City.

I can't tell where my head is gone,
But Doctor Carpue can;
As for my trunk, it's all packed up
To go by Pickford's van.

. . .

But I'll be yours in death, altho'
Sir Astley has my heart.

Don't go to weep upon my grave,
And think that there I be;
They haven't left an atom there
Of my anatomie.[1]

Robert Southey's poem, 'A Surgeon's Warning' (1796), discussed in chapter 3, and Thomas Hood's 'Mary's Ghost: A Pathetic Ballad' (1827), quoted here, both illustrate how the fear of falling into the hands of body-snatchers was indissociable from that of being dissected, dismembered, dried or preserved in spirits for subsequent exhibition in a medical museum. In Southey's poem, the narrator's preserved specimens, whether dry, wet or mounted skeletons, represent the surgeon's skill as an anatomist as much as his use and abuse of cadavers. As for Hood's Mary, the fragmentation of her body, whose parts are sent to various medical men to be preserved, dried or bottled and displayed, provides an example of what Samuel Alberti has termed the *dividual* body.[2] Indeed, throughout the eighteenth and nineteenth centuries, the human body, dismembered, sold or exchanged and put on display in the growing medical collections, reflected the objectification of nature: to 'anatomize was to atomize', as Alberti puts it.[3] In addition, medical museums were anchored just as much, if not more, in British industrial culture. Morbid specimens provided by hospital wards, as exchangeable goods, were equivalent to manufactured goods for consumption: the patient's identity was more often than not erased and subsumed under that of the anatomist or collector. The examples from Southey's and Hood's poems thus illustrate fears typically associated with anatomical practice around the turn of the nineteenth century, and the pieces constitute significant examples of the ways in which the Romantic period as a whole played upon anxieties related to the construction of medical collections.

It has already been seen in chapter 1 that Mrs Carver's *The Horrors of Oakendale Abbey* (1797) reworked Ann Radcliffe's *The Mysteries of Udolpho* (1794) by suggesting that skeletons were more likely to be kept in surgeons' cupboards than anywhere else, since the plot climaxes with a giant skeleton, inspired by the case of Charles Byrne (1761–83). Byrne, it will be recalled, was the Irish giant whose corpse had been secretly bought by London surgeon John Hunter (1728–93), and then hidden away for four years before being exhibited in his museum. As underlined in chapter 2, furthermore, the anatomical collections which appeared in Gothic fiction were increasingly associated with a lack of human sympathy or sensitivity, a feature which became pivotal to characterisation. We saw that when Mary Shelley's prototypical Romantic villain Victor Franken-stein instils life into his creature, the anatomist's anxiety during the creation scene not only underlines the extent to which his creature is made up of various body parts stolen in cemeteries, dissecting rooms and slaughterhouses, but also points to his concerns for size, colour or texture, through words which recall the endeavours by anatomists and conservators to capture or retain qualities their specimens had possessed in life:

> His limbs were in proportion, and I had selected his features as beautiful. Beautiful! – Great God! His yellow skin scarcely covered the work of muscles and arteries beneath; his hair was of a lustrous black, and flowing; his teeth of a pearly whiteness; but these luxuriances only formed a more horrid contrast with his watery eyes, that seemed almost of the same colour as the dun-white sockets in which they were set, his shrivelled complexion and straight black lips.[4]

As in Carlisle's Gothic romance, the creature recalls the exhibition of famous giants at the same period, from Charles Byrne to the Patagonian giants whose legend had been revived a few decades earlier by the expedition of *HMS Dolphin* (1764–6).[5] According to Paul Youngquist, Frankenstein's quest for 'a physiologically functional human being' leads him to 'create[–] a pathological specimen'; the specimen in turn 'tests functional norms against singular bodies, producing a bounty of corpses to verify the principle of life', thereby 'aveng[ing] the bones of Charles Byrne'.[6]

Youngquist's study shows how the emphasis placed by Mary Shelley (and her contemporaries) on the material culture of medicine lies at the root of the Gothic. The cultural appeal of remains, like ruins, which characterises the Gothic as a whole, explains the interest in, and the legitimisation of, collections and exhibitions of human remains during the Romantic period. From its origins, the Gothic was informed by a scientific culture bent upon collecting, compiling, registering and classifying. As an obsessive collector trying to artificially reconstruct past worlds, Horace Walpole himself created a genre teeming with stock characters, motifs and conventions, with wild and eccentric characters who resembled many of the wonders of nature displayed in cabinets of curiosities, studied by natural philosophers or dissected. The Gothic emerged when medical professionals and anatomists attempted 'to display the underlying laws of abnormal growth'.[7] Anatomists such as John Hunter, with his collection of abnormal bodies (the most famous being certainly Charles Byrne and the Sicilian dwarf Caroline Crachami), helped 'medical authorities to manage and control monstrosity',[8] in order to 'bring it under the institutional control of medicine'.[9] Youngquist's analysis offers valuable insights into the ways in which Hunter's work contributed to the cultural construction of the 'proper' body (and 'the full normative force of proper embodiment'[10]). Gothic 'monsters', from the giant Byrne-like skeleton in *The Horrors of Oakendale Abbey* to Frankenstein's giant creature – 'aveng[ing] the bones of Charles Byrne' – take on new significance when placed in this context of developments in anatomy and physiology in the late eighteenth century. Such fictional monsters often functioned to counteract or subvert contemporary discourses linked to the management of the body.

The material construction and display of disease in the nineteenth century was directly related to the development of pathological anatomy (especially in the first half of the eighteenth century), as exemplified by the work of William (1718–83) and John Hunter in Britain and Marie François Xavier Bichat (1771–1802) and Théophile Laënnec (1781–1826) in France. The emergence of pathological anatomy was itself linked to the development of dissection (much more than other disciplines, such as practical chemistry, for instance, as Russell C. Maulitz underlines[11]), which entered the medical curriculum around the 1830s, gradually collapsing 'the tripartite division of surgeons, physicians, and apothecaries'.[12] In addition, as Alberti has shown, the rise of pathological anatomy also needs to be linked to the development of material culture which increasingly dehumanised the human body. Anatomists such as the Hunter brothers 'render[ed] an intangible disease concept into a physical thing, to be studied, analysed, displayed, and compared with other objects'.[13] Disease was thus materialised and could be looked at in the medical museums of the period. The many 'curious' specimens on display in medical collections typified Enlightenment science, with the idea of the 'curious' serving to define what Richard Sugg terms 'a new community of inquirers by sensibility and object'.[14]

Incidentally, curiosity also defines Gothic characters, especially when they wander through maze-like buildings in search of knowledge in order to ultimately lift the veil. The 'pain of suspense' and 'the irresistible desire of satisfying curiosity'[15] are, indeed, staple ingredients of the popular Gothic romances of the eighteenth century, as Anna Laetitia Barbauld and John Aikin pointed out in their essay 'On the Pleasure Derived from Objects of Terror' (1773). Their work highlights the links between terror and 'curiosity', 'the excitement of surprise from new and wonderful objects' and 'the apparent delight with which we dwell upon objects of pure terror'.[16] Barbauld and Aikin's essay also clearly demonstrates the extent to which the Gothic, with its 'new objects' likely to arouse curiosity, wonder and awe, was a product of the eighteenth-century Enlightenment. When faced with the unknown or the fantastic, the monstrous or the spectral, readers of Gothic romances and eighteenth-century researchers into human nature had much in common.

These links can be seen particularly clearly in texts dealing with medical collections. In such cases, the medical museum crystallises ideas relating to normality and becomes therefore a significant locus to test the shapes and meaning(s) of monstrosity. Furthermore, medical collections aroused feelings of wonder, terror and horror, positioning readers like viewers peering into a cabinet of curiosities, or *Wunderkammer*, whilst the characters, often described by literary critics as monsters or curiosities, were – literally or metaphorically – dissected and put on display. In this way, horror was merged with pleasure, and wonder with terror, a reflection of public demand for the morbid and the macabre.

We shall see that by epitomising the manipulative aspects of medicine, medical collections became significant Gothic tropes of the violation of the body, even if references to them are frequently buried in the margins of texts and as such have tended to be over-looked by literary scholars. Indeed, nineteenth-century literature, especially during the Victorian period, often stresses characters looking at bodies on display. True, the bodies in question are not necessarily exhibited in medical collections, but illuminating examples, such as Lucy Snowe's viewing of *Cleopatra* in the picture gallery in Charlotte Brontë's *Villette* (1853), reveal the part played by the exhibition of corporeality. Peter Brooks has argued that bodily exhibition of this kind functions to undermine the 'aesthetics of realism', since the latter is based on eschewing 'the more graphic and detailed report of the naked body'.[17] In Brooks's view, realistic fiction focuses rather on the accessories that 'adorn and mask the body',[18] so as to avoid being read as pornographic. The Gothic, on the other hand, regularly borrowed from the museum culture of its day in order to foreground the issue of the representation of the proper/improper body in the public sphere. The result was to lay bare the meanings of human remains on display in medical collections.

The medical museum and the management of the corpse/body

ANATOMICAL STUDIES – MRS. SEXTON, the Popular Lecturer to Ladies at Dr. Kahn's Museum, encouraged by the great success her lectures have met with, begs to inform her patronesses in general, and strong-minded ladies in particular, that it is her intention to open a summer class of anatomy at the sea-side. The great advantage of this new course will be, that the truths will be demonstrated, not by wax models, but by living figures. The first lecture will take place in the open air on the sands at Ramsgate, and will be carried on during such time as the gentlemen remain in the sea, bathing. The second lecture will be at Margate during the same hours. The terms of subscription may be ascertained at the Marine Library, the Hospital, and the principal Chemists' shops, in each place.[19]

Medical museums and public anatomical museums alike were generally praised by the medical profession in the nineteenth century. In *The Anatomist's Instructor, and Museum Companion* (1836), John Frederick Knox aimed to 'make the student *really* fond of visiting museums', insisting, however, on the fact that 'there can indeed be nothing in an anatomical museum calculated to amuse any one'.[20] The need for both medical lecturers and students to make use of anatomical museums is stressed throughout Knox's essay, a point which recalls not only the central role of anatomy in medical education at the time but also the part played by anatomical collections. Indeed, while public anatomical museums opened their doors both to professional and lay audiences, medical collections became a pivotal tool in medical education.[21] In Victorian London, the collections of Antonio Sarti (1839–50), J. W. Reimer (1852–3) and Dr Kahn (1851–72) were amongst the most famous to be visited by men and women alike.[22] Some, however, such as Madame Caplin's, were reserved exclusively for women.[23]

As suggested in chapter 2, many of the objects exhibited in medical museums were anatomical specimens, models and preparations, comprised of artificial (mainly wax) models, body parts in jars, and articulated skeletons. After the 1832 Anatomy Act allowed the supply of unclaimed corpses to licensed schools, artificial anatomical models met with a less enthusiastic reception from medical professionals. Knox argued that the practice of dissection was of much greater value to the medical profession than the use of models, many of which, he considered, provided 'erroneous views' of anatomy:

> Casts and wax-models, &c. form at present a large part of these collections, but I rather think that they are not exactly so invaluable as they were considered some years ago; I am of opinion, indeed, that the museum of most teachers of midwifery are at present made up with erroneous views; and, at all events, there are many preparations which can be of little real utility to the teaching of the sound principles of that branch of our profession. Thus it seems to me that the series of fœtuses, put up without dissection, and forming so large a part of these museums, are mere store for the anatomist. The gravid uterus, as seen in most cases, I consider as so much *treasure* locked up, for the present locked up, in fact, in a double sense: first, by means of

the key of the museum; and, secondly, by the walls of the uterus being entire. All specific aberrations in Nature's productions un-examined and undissected, are mere objects of curiosity; and *amusement* should never form a feature in an *anatomical* museum. I remember, in assisting to draw up a catalogue of the Barclayan Museum, I was forcibly struck with the vast number of objects of curiosity contained in the collection.[24]

The growth of medical collections in Britain, destined principally for medical education, in particular the growing reliance on the preservation and display of dry and wet specimens, along with the waning interest in wax models, may help explain changing attitudes to public collections. In addition, as Francesco de Ceglia argues, shifting responses to anatomical collections and the representation of corpses during the eighteenth and nineteenth centuries need to be seen in the context of changes in aesthetics. The morbid aesthetics of the late eighteenth century linked the corpse, 'especially if decomposed and disarticulated' with 'the dominance of the wild, [and] thereby opened the floodgates of an uncontrolled sexuality', while in the nineteenth century, death would flirt with pornography 'so "other" as to be unmentionable and unrepresentable'.[25] This point is also underlined by Pamela Pilbeam, who notes that wax exhibitions were often promoted in almanacs that included porno-graphic images,[26] while the recumbent anatomical Venuses, especially those of the late-eighteenth-century Florentine school with their flowing hair, certainly functioned on one level as not free of sexual titillation. A good example of this is the *Punch* caricature cited above, proposing as it does a summer anatomy class with living female bodies in place of wax models. However, the story of the reception of Kahn's anatomical museum also reveals other reasons why most public anatomy museums closed down in the second half of the nineteenth century.

Dr Kahn's Anatomical Museum opened in London in 1851. It was owned by Joseph Kahn, a self-styled German 'medical doctor', and comprised natural and artificial anatomies of both the normal and morbid kind. The following review published in the *Medical Times* shortly after the museum opened its doors had nothing but praise for Kahn's collection:

Dr. Kahn's Anatomical Museum.—We have this week paid a visit
to the museum, Oxford-street, and were much gratified by its numerous
and varied contents. The collection consists of about 350 preparations
well arranged; useful for the medical student, and interesting to the
public. The progress of the embryo, from its deposition in the uterus
to the time of birth, is clearly shown by a number of preparations of
each successive week of development, as is also the gradual progress
of ossification, by a series of foetal skeletons, commencing from the
second month after conception. Preparations in leather and in wax,
exhibit very correctly the course of the arteries, veins, and nerves of
the trunk and extremities, also the vessels and nerves of the cranium
and face. These are well worthy of notice from their extreme delicacy
and minuteness. We have then a gradative representation of the
progress of deglutition. A number of sections of the human brain as
compared with those of lower animals now follow, a, [*sic*] also, models
of the eye, ear, tongue, heart, &c. Considerable space is also devoted
to preparations illustrating various positions of the foetus at the period
of parturition; and there are some very curious specimens of jeux de
nature, arising generally from arrested foetal development. The most
beautiful and interesting part of this museum is a series of 103 figures,
representing the microscopic appearances of the embryo from the
moment of conception. The correctness of this series may be inferred
from the fact, that Dr. Kahn has received an order to remodel a
portion for the use of St. Bartholomew's Hospital. It commences
with magnificent views of the spermatozoa, female ovum, and the
female generative organs, and progresses through every stage of
development until the period of the birth of the child. Another series
illustrates the incubation of the hen's egg. The progress of gonorrhoea
and syphilis is beautifully exhibited in a series of excellent models,
taken from cases in the Hôpital des Vénériens and Val de Grace. Two
full length figures show the fatal effects of tight lacing, and the mode
in which the Caesarian section is performed; and a third takes entirely
to pieces, exhibiting the relative position of each organ. The Museum
is decidedly the best ever exhibited in London, and we recommend
our readers to pay Dr. Kahn a visit.[27]

A very similar review was published in the *Lancet* in 1851, sing-
ling out the Anatomical Venus for particular praise. The article
mentions, however, that the room in which the ravages of syphilis

and gonorrhoea are exhibited is set apart and admittance is reserved exclusively to members of the medical profession.[28] Interestingly, the question of who might visit Kahn's collection was at the root of a heated debate in the 'Answers to Correspondents' section of the *Lancet* in the years that followed the opening of the museum. Kahn was accused of allowing women access to all the rooms in the museum, in particular the one containing models representing the effects of venereal disease. In June 1854, Kahn replied to the editor of the *Lancet* that 'not only is "the room for medical men" in the museum closed on the days that ladies are admitted, but all the models in the other room which could offend the most prudish taste are removed'.[29] The following week, a response to Kahn's answer appeared. The correspondent – 'J. Leach, M. D.' – a former lecturer at the museum, argued that despite Dr Kahn's assurances, females had indeed been 'permitted to inspect the syphilitic models, without distinction of age'.[30] The following week, Kahn sent another letter to the medical journal:

> It is perfectly true that I have at one period admitted ladies, who expressed a particular interest to see the midwifery models, to visit the 'room for medical men', but, finding that some objections were made to my so doing, I discontinued that procedure, and that before Dr. Leach left me. At the present time my course is this: to allow the ladies, on certain days set apart for that purpose, to visit the large room in my exhibition, closing the 'room for medical men' at that time, except under the following circumstances, which occasionally occur – viz., the visit of nurses, midwives, and other persons professionally interested in these matters, and who bring with them a recommendation from a medical man. If anything, even in the large room, be considered by any professional gentleman who may visit the museum as unfit to be viewed by ladies, I shall at all times be happy to receive a suggestion from him, and will remove such preparation or model accordingly.[31]

A week later, a new notice in the journal asserted that Dr Kahn had been true to his word and had followed some recommendations regarding the removal of certain models or preparations. The *Lancet* expressed the hope that the museum 'might be made the means of advancing the studies and researches of the junior members of the profession'.[32]

The issue of female visitors having access to anatomical material deemed improper for their sex would, however, later be over-shadowed by another debate which would ultimately cause the museum's demise. In 1857, complaints about Kahn's Museum resurfaced in the pages of the *Lancet*. This time, the museum was described as a 'den of obscenity . . . [s]o disgusting and immoral, so determinedly arranged for the purposes of depraving the minds of the ignorant and unwary', that it should be closed, in order 'to guard public moral and to respect public decency'.[33] If the language used by the author may suggest a concern that the collections might shock the uninitiated, it was not the question of female visitors which was at issue this time. In fact, the article's denunciation of the 'filthy wax models'[34] sprang above all from disquiet concerning Dr Kahn's involvement (along with manufacturer Perry and Co.) in the sale of quack remedies claiming to treat venereal disease.[35]

The debates and controversies surrounding the opening and closing of public anatomical collections such as Dr Kahn's in the middle of the nineteenth century, or their dispersal and demise in the following decades, highlights the ways in which the medical field became more and more dominated by medical professionals in the years preceding the creation of the Medical Register in 1858.[36] As we have seen, anatomical collections evidenced the increasingly central part played by anatomy in medical knowledge and education. However, anatomical models, which had been particularly associated with women, – be they midwives, as shown by the example of Catherine Clarke,[37] or wax modellers (such as Angélique Marguerite Le Boursier du Coudray (1712–98), Marie-Catherine Biheron (1719–86), or even the celebrated Anna Morandi Manzolini (1714–74)) – would later be dismissed as mere quackery. In fact, after the passage of the 1832 Anatomy Act, the supply of corpses benefited exclusively licensed schools.[38] In this new context, anatomical models came to be seen as suitable teaching tools only for fringe medical professionals and quacks. In 1857, moreover, the passage of the Obscene Publications Act offered a legal means of closing down Dr Kahn's Museum, as the Act condemned 'conduct inconsistent with public morals',[39] thereby providing a way to 'regulate popular anatomy selectively'.[40] The Act also enabled the prosecution of authors and publishers selling pornographic material.

The Obscene Publications Act provides a striking example of the expanding role of the state in the control of sexual behaviour. As Alison Smith explains, the 1850s saw a growing concern for public morality.[41] Representations of the body, especially the female body, were increasingly regarded with suspicion, and artistic displays of nudity were likely to be considered as obscene.[42] The influence of the evangelical campaigners on definitions of art in the 1850s was not unrelated to this phenomenon. Artistic forms, shows or displays of sorts considered likely to corrupt or deprave the most emotionally susceptible – particularly women and children – came under close scrutiny. The boundary between art and pornography was hotly debated. This was particularly the case with 'non-art shows', which, Smith notes, 'played provocatively with the language of high art through tactics of innuendo and arousal'.[43] Anatomical waxworks and preparations frequently occupied centre stage in this respect, for many focused overtly on sexuality, showing for example the ravages of syphilis or the various stages of pregnancy. Many combined the use of a medical discourse with highly ornamented anatomical models (often wearing necklaces, for instance), both to instruct medical professionals and to entertain the lay public. The contents of Kahn's museum were ultimately confiscated by the police in February 1873. Significantly, the first objects to be destroyed were the anatomical waxes.

This history of Dr Kahn's museum is of interest for it highlights the connections between medical collections, medical knowledge and power, illuminating how anatomical museums could be used in Gothic writing to map out anxieties related to the self. Indeed, medical collections would inform the Gothic throughout the nineteenth century. However, from iconic venues emblematising modern medicine and anatomical culture in the early decades of the nineteenth century they became increasingly associated with fringe medicine, sexuality and licenciousness in Victorian Gothic, just like Kahn's museum.

The 'world of spirits'

In Thomas Hood's 'Mary Ghost: A Pathetic Ballad' in 1827, Mary becomes the pathetic victim of material medicine, her spectre not simply representing a modern rewriting of the helpless Gothic heroine but embodying above all the denial of her identity as a human being. Hood's ballad illustrates forcefully the ghastly corporeality of medical collections and medical activity at the turn of the century, a sensational quality missing in earlier Radcliffean ghosts. Tellingly, Hood's ballad echoes strongly older ballads which also dealt with the establishment of medical collections, as in the following early eighteenth-century broadside denouncing body-snatching:

> Methink I hear the latter trumpet sound,
> When emptie graves into this place is found,
> Of young and old, which is most strange to me,
> What kind of resurrection this may be.
> I thought God had reserved this power alone
> Unto himself [*sic*], till he erect'd his throne
> Into the clouds, with his attendance by,
> That he might judge the world in equity.
> But now I see the contrar in our land,
> Since men do raise the dead at their own hand;
> And for to please their curiosities
> They them dissect and make anatomies.
> Such monsters of mankind was never known,
> As in this place is daily to be shown;
> Who, for to gain some worldly vanities,
> Are guilty of such immoralities
> . . .
> These monsters of mankind, who made the graves,
> To the chirurgeons became hyred slaves;
> They rais'd the dead again out of the dust,
> And sold them to satisfy their lust.
> As I'm informed, the chirurgeons did give
> Fourty shillings for each one they receive:
> And they their flesh and bones asunder part,
> Which wounds their living friends unto the heart[.][44]

As the ballad suggests, curiosity, dissection and the making of 'anatomies' marched hand in hand. Yet, the poem makes it hard for readers to decide whether the body-snatchers or the 'chirurgeons' best deserve the epithet 'monsters of mankind'. Indeed, both appear in the same sentence, the pronoun 'they' blurring the distinction between the two figures – those who raise the dead and those who make anatomies: 'Since men do raise the dead at their own hand;/ And for to please their curiosities/They them dissect and make anatomies'.

As seen in chapter 3, this intermingling of the two figures lies at the core of Samuel Warren's short story 'Grave Doings', reprinted in his collection, *Passages from the Diary of a Late Physician* (1838). The body-snatcher is a medical practitioner who needs to practise his skills upon cadavers. Warren's 'Grave Doings' emphasises, as we saw, the figure of the repentant practitioner, since the narrator swears never to practise body-snatching again. The narrative seems thus thoroughly in line with the periodical's promotion of an increasingly more sensitive figure of the medical practitioner, as Megan Coyer contends. However, this analysis of the short story fails to take into consideration the footnote added at the end of the short story, which turns on its head the good practitioner's discourse:

> ★ On examining the body, we found that Sir —'s suspicions were fully verified. It was disease of the heart – but of too complicated a nature to be made intelligible to general readers. I never heard that the girl's friends discovered our doings; and, for all they know, she is now mouldering away in — churchyard; whereas, in point of fact, her bleached skeleton adorns —'s surgery; and a preparation of her heart enriches —'s museum![45]

As Meegan Kennedy has argued, the case history was seen throughout the nineteenth century as 'the public face of medicine' and 'became a crucial site in which to construct an ideal of clinical medicine'. This implied the consistent use of a scientific and objective discourse in order to bring out the 'seriousness of the medical knowledge production at work in the text'.[46] This is the case to a certain extent in the *Diary*: the editor's regular intrusions aim at strengthening verisimilitude, claiming that the medical details are 'founded upon truth' (p. xi), '*facts* witnessed by the author' (xi), 'coloured and veiled by a fictional dress' (pp. xi–xii). The footnote positioned at the end of 'Grave Doings' certainly attempts to heighten the realism of the clinical case history. Yet, turned into anatomical material and exhibited in a surgery and a museum, the medical patient is now a nameless skeleton and preparation. The metaphor of the heart, which illustrated the physician–patient relationship at the beginning of the tale,[47] has now taken on material form; the physician has, very ironically, secured his patient's heart. As a consequence, the metatextual piece of clinical discourse gives a twist to the Romantic discourse of the repentant practioner. The patient's missing identity, once her body has been stolen, dissected, bottled, dispersed and exhibited in two different places, comes to reflect the inhumanity of the medical student depicted as a body-snatcher. Up to that point, in contrast, the narrative had been presented as a farce and seemingly offered the remorseful medical professional's viewpoint. Thus, the bottled heart becomes the most significant element here through the tension between its position in the margin of the text (a footnote) and its status as a museum exhibit, permanently accessible to the public gaze. The contrast, therefore, places the preserved organ – appropriately – at the heart of the narrative, just as it was at the centre of the medical diagnosis, superseding the tale of body-snatching and underlining how preparations of this type are used to stress the implications of medical research and education.

In fact, the erasure of the patient's identity (like the names of all the other patients which have been suppressed throughout the collection of short stories) constructs the bottled heart as a purloined letter – an emblem of the perfect Gothic crime. This idea is confirmed by Victorian historian James Blake Bailey, who argues that the story was probably based on fact and aimed at 'obtain[ing] a valuable pathological specimen [rather] than a body for dissection'.[48] The objective clinical prose of the added footnote functions therefore as the antithesis of the patient's history: the superimposition of the two 'stories' at the end of the short story enables Warren to play with his readers' emotions. The tension between the Gothic tale of body-snatching and the objective record of the securing of the pathological specimen illuminates therefore the widening gap throughout the nineteenth century between medical professionals and their patients. Indeed, this growing rift is palpable from the title on, since in an early American edition of 1831–2 the collection of cases was published under the title, *Affecting Scenes: Being Passages from the Diary of a Physician*,[49] which suggests the collection was aimed at emphasising the links between emotion and medical practice.

Warren's collection of short stories is significant because it is situated at the cusp of the Romantic and Victorian periods. His narrative reveals how pathology was coming to replace the super-natural, and stresses the increasing medical realism of Gothic texts. The dismemberment of the human body and the sensational display of the fragmentation of the human subject, both characteristic of medical collections, explains why the Gothic seized upon their imaginative potential. Moreover, medical practice did not merely imply the manipulation of bodies and corpses, for the places where medicine was practised were also suffused with the aura of criminality. Indeed, medical museums were the places where criminals might end their lives on display, as exemplified in *Oliver Twist* (1839), where Sikes believes Fagin is 'fit for nothing but keeping as a curiosity of ugliness in a glass bottle'.[50] The bottled specimen could thus easily function as a modern ghost, a spectral genie locked up in a bottle.

As a matter of fact, the world of 'spirits' was part and parcel of the medical world, as the 1866 American short story 'The Case of George Dedlow' illustrates. In July 1866, the American physician Silas Weir Mitchell (1829–1914), famous for his discovery of causalgia (complex regional pain syndrome) and also known as a psychiatrist and the father of neurology (as well as the inventor of the rest cure), published his short story in the *Atlantic Monthly*. The story relates the experience of a Unionist doctor and was written in the form of case notes, in the manner of Samuel Warren's stories, leading many readers to believe it to be a real medical case. After suffering the amputation of both arms and legs, George Dedlow discovers, 'to [his] horror',[51] that he now looks 'more like some strange larval creature than anything of human shape'. The tale records his feelings and sensations (the latter reduced by half after his amputation), 'half of [him] [being] absent or functionally dead'. His reflections on human individuality and consciousness, while 'leading an almost vegetative existence' and on the relations between the soul and matter, which 'merely changes form', lead him to take part in a spiritualist seance and communicate with 'the world of spirits'. Ironically, the spirits with whom he enters into contact are those of his legs, preserved in alcohol in an army medical museum. He then becomes suddenly filled with '[a] strange wonder' and is able to walk across the room on invisible limbs for a few seconds before '[a]ll that is left of [him] faint[s] and roll[s] over senseless'.

The short story is typical of Victorian Gothic, often marked by ghost stories which regularly tapped into new ideas circulating in the fields of mental science and psychical research.[52] The Gothic texts of the period also foregrounded anxieties related to the human subject. Seen as half-human, half-beast, especially in the last decades of the nineteenth century, the human subject appeared increasingly 'abhuman', in Kelly Hurley's terms, 'bodily ambiguated or otherwise discontinuous in identity'.[53] Mitchell's short story does indeed show how Victorian Gothic dealt with fears related to human identity, but it does more than this, revealing the part played by the medical context and anatomical culture of the time in changing views of the human body and human identity. The story also explores how scientific or medical experiments with, or on, the (human) body unsettled the definition of the human. The 'world of spirits' with which George Dedlow communicates is made up of pieces of matter floating in alcohol, the play on the word 'spirit' shockingly revealing the impact of anatomical science and the making of medical knowledge on definitions of the human. The 'strange wonder' experienced by George Dedlow as he walks for a few seconds on phantom limbs has become inseparable from the horror at seeing the human being dismembered, his body parts separated and exhibited in a medical museum.

Even before the Enlightenment, the culture of wonder was closely related to the making of natural history and medical collections. Lorraine Daston and Katharine Park's study of the definition and role of wonder and wonders in the period between 1150 and 1750 is illuminating in this context. The authors argue that the part played by sensibility in the making of scientific knowledge was particularly manifest in the evolution of the perceptions of wonder and wonders, for as 'a cognitive passion', the latter were 'as much about knowing as about feeling'.[54] The concepts of wonder and wonders entered natural philosophical writing between 1370 and 1590, particularly because Renaissance physicians underlined the marvellous aspects of medical practice. These included medical peculiarities such as physical abnormalities, or mysterious phenomena such as that of hanged thieves miraculously escaping death.[55] Studies of remarkable medical cases like these proliferated in the sixteenth century, illustrating, according to Daston and Park, 'the ramification of medical writing on the marvelous over the course of the sixteenth century, not only in Italy but also in the rest of Europe'.[56] Likewise, exotica and rarities, such as unicorn horns, were often used for pharmaceutical purposes, which explains why in sixteenth- and seventeenth-century Europe 'physicians and apothecaries dominated the collecting of naturalia'.[57] The same period also saw the growth of medical and natural history collections, either in medical faculties or learned societies.[58] Naturalia or exotic objects thus epitomised the link between wonder and scientific inquiry, for these unusual objects, steeped in mystery, triggered intense curiosity. Interestingly, as the authors underline, the multiplication of these works reflected the emergence of a sizeable lay and professional audience fascinated by such accounts of natural wonders. Books of marvels continued to develop in Europe in the second half of the sixteenth and early seventeenth centuries. It is a period rightly known as the 'age of wonder', for the concept became 'a nexus of cultural symbols – not only in the natural philosophy and medicine of the age, but also in its literature and art'.[59]

That the connection between the emergence of a discourse on wonder and wonders and medical professionals should have a long history is interesting in the context of the development of the Gothic at the close of the period of the first wave of Gothic novels (1764–1824). Gothic novels during these years both exemplified the age of reason and challenged Enlightenment thinkers' emphasis on rationality. Whilst Enlightenment science increasingly warned against wonder in scientific inquiry, marvels persisted in eighteenth-century Europe:

Fairs and coffeehouses still showed monsters; cabinets still displayed curiosities; the almanacs and gazettes reported bizarre weather, talking dogs, and balloon flights; savants demonstrated the wonders of electricity and luminescence; provincial academies pursued preternatural history; and the popular French series of volumes in the Bibliothèque Bleue entertained their readers with wondrous stories.[60]

The increasing popularity and exhibition of rarities, freaks and monsters thus coexisted with the waning of the marvellous and the fantastic. Indeed, the continuing force of those forms of public entertainment and literature served only to intensify the anxiety felt by Enlightenment thinkers with regard to popular fear and wonder. The rise of the Gothic novel, with its tales of giant helmets and supernatural horror, magnified therefore a popular reaction against Enlightened rationalism, competing with the development of marvellous technology, as illustrated by automata, for instance, or even contemporary constructions of the body as a marvellous machine, the mysteries of which only physicans could access. Furthermore, if the Gothic was linked with a barbaric medieval past – a wild and superstitious age – it was nevertheless firmly rooted in its times. According to Daston and Park, the fantastic and the marvellous – 'the products of imagination, the invention of folklore and fairy tales, fabulous beasts of legend, freaks of sideshows and the popular press, and, more recently, the uncanny in all its forms'[61] – were thus inextricably linked to a particular view of wonders created by Enlightenment thinkers. In their search for understanding the natural order, those thinkers 'marginalized both the passion of wonder and wonders as objects, in favor of a view that emphasized both the regularity of nature and the completeness of the philosopher's knowledge, marred by no unseemly gaps'.[62] The 'wonderful' objects were those that stood outside the natural world. In other words, wonder and horror became encapsulated in the 'monster' – a staple figure of the Gothic, a frighteningly unnatural object to be shown (*monstrare*) and yet which also functions as a harbinger, as in Shelley's *Frankenstein*, both objectified as a medical curiosity and retaining a whiff of mystery and of the supernatural.

George Dedlow's phantom limbs and experience of 'strange wonder', while firmly anchored in the medical reality of his day – as a spectacle of modern medicine expressed in the form of 'gothically animated display',[63] as argued in the introduction – also reflect a sense of wonder directly borrowed from the eighteenth-century culture of the 'curious', but which continued to permeate the nineteenth century. The reader's sense of horror, on the other hand, is linked to the gross corporeality of Dedlow's legs, preserved in spirit. Horror flows from the clash between the spectral and the medical realism of the bottled legs. Whilst Victorian medical doctors collected and displayed body parts, and spiritualists attempted to materialise the soul, nineteenth-century writers used the very objects that embodied the medical culture and knowledge of the time to play with fear and/or to suggest, on the contrary, that humankind could not be known. Consequently, as scientists and medical professionals attempted to classify and contain deviancy, the Gothic increasingly foregrounded the malleability of the human body and spirit and the impossibility of bottling it up. In other words, by recurrently locating the villain in the surgery and the monster on the shelves of the medical museum, the Victorian Gothic challenged the very places where knowledge about humanity was constructed, defined and mastered, and from where anatomical science had supposedly cast out wonder and terror.

Silas Weir Mitchell's 1866 short story recalls the case of Silas Wegg in Charles Dickens's *Our Mutual Friend* (1865), or that of Mrs Gamp's deceased husband in his *Martin Chuzzlewit* (1844). Dickens's novels frequently denounced cultures of collecting and the commodification of the human body in Victorian society, as did many sensation novelists writing in the same period. Dickens's attacks on medical professionals and their 'use and abuse of the dead' permeates both his fictional and non-fictional works, as we saw in chapter 3. In his fiction, sollicitors keep wax effigies of their clients in their offices, as Jaggers does in *Great Expectations* (1861). But bodies are also often found preserved in bottles. This is notably the case in *The Lamplighter* (1838), a farcical play never performed, but converted into a narrative ('The Lamplighter's Story') in 1841. Dickens's story relates the tale of Tom Grig and humorously plays upon the supernatural, prophecies and death – even alluding to Matthew Lewis's *The Monk* (1797). It also features references to exhibited human remains.

'The Lamplighter's Story' patently borrows from eighteenth-century culture. It echoes for instance certain of William Hogarth's etchings and engravings, which play on the connections between astrology, magic, alchemy and medicine. In the third part of William Hogarth's *Marriage-à-la-Mode*, *The Inspection*, for example, the married nobleman visits a quack doctor. As Fiona Haslam has shown, the doctor's surroundings offer 'a background to quackery'[64] by stressing their close connection to magic. Indeed, the scene looks very much like a previous illustration by Hogarth which featured in Samuel Butler's *Hudibras* (1725–6). The image depicts Sidrophel, the astrologer and magician, in a room complete with a skeleton in a cupboard and an alligator hanging from the ceiling. As Haslam points out, both rooms look alike, and both bear some resemblance to Dr Samuel Garth's 1699 mock-epic poem *The Dispensary*, read throughout the eighteenth century, which also focuses on the quack's cabinet of curiosities, which comprises mummies, a tortoise and an alligator,[65] alongside dried bladders and drawn teeth. The emphasis on curiosities is aimed at evoking wonder, thereby suggesting the quack's magical powers of healing (or lack thereof). Moreover, the presence of a two-headed figure in one of the pictures on the wall in *The Inspection*, together with a baby in a bottle in the foreground of the engraving *Hudribras Beats Sidrophel and his Man Whacum*, point to an abiding interest in ethnographic monsters and pathological specimens. Haslam reasons that both pictures may have been inspired by specimens from the Royal Society museum,[66] used to connote here the links between monsters and omens.

The case is very similar in Dickens's 'The Lamplighter's Story'. It is not Tom Grig's head, face, legs, arms, hands, feet or chest which are cast (in plaster), but his fate. The play on the word 'cast' not only foreshadows Tom's death, but also the narrative's construction of the body as a material object which is no longer possessed by the person to whom it belongs. Indeed, Tom meets an elderly scientific gentleman with a telescope in his hand who is able to read what is going to happen in the stars. The scientific gentleman takes him to the room of an astronomer (Mr Mooney) at the back of the house, which is full of bottles, globes, books, telescopes, crocodiles, alligators, and other scientific instruments. The 'hallowed ground'[67] (n.p.) foreshadows the sight of a large bottle containing a child with three heads, used as a charm in astrology. There is also a skeleton in a glass case, 'labelled, "Skeleton of a Gentleman – prepared by

Mr. Mooney", – which [makes Tom] hope that Mr. Mooney might not be in the habit of preparing gentlemen that way without their own consent' (n.p.). The nameless gentleman, whose body may not have been lawfully acquired, together with the bottled pathological specimen, link the reading of the stars with the study of the body. In this context, the glass bottle and the glass case suggest access to hidden mysteries, whilst the setting constructs Mr Mooney as a quack – a double of the 'Pox' doctor and charlatan Mr Pillule, in Hogarth's *Marriage-à-la-Mode*. Even more significant is the fact that both the skeleton and the three-headed baby have been objectified, their names erased and their meaning changed, since the bottled freak is now used as a charm.

Such objectification participates in the farcical atmosphere of the narrative, which derides Gothic motifs and the sense of impending doom. This prefigures Dickens's later discourse on Victorian consumer culture, clearly visible in the preserved collectibles – human and animal remains – sold in Mr Venus's shop in *Our Mutual Friend* or the teeth and hair (often stolen from the dead) on display in Mr Krook's shop in *Bleak House* (1853). Human remains – especially, perhaps, when in the hands of quacks – are not simply 'Scientific goods', as the body-snatcher Cruncher tells his wife in *A Tale of Two Cities* (1859), but above all commodities sold behind the counter and exchangeable.

Whether bottled heads metaphorise the character's evil nature, like the image of Fagin's bottled head in Dickens's *Oliver Twist*, or reveal their owner's quackery, like Mr Mooney's three-headed child, such literary pathological specimens highlight the normative discourse that underpinned the establishment of anatomical collections. In both art and literature, the skeletons of criminals were displayed as warnings against immorality. Notable examples include Tom Nero's body in William Hogarth's *The Reward of Cruelty* (1751) and William Burke's skeleton, preserved in the College of Surgeons 'in order that posterity may keep in remembrance [his] atrocious crimes', as mentioned in David Pae's *Mary Paterson; Or, the Fatal Error. A Story of the Burke and Hare Murders* (1866), over a century later.[68]

Catherine Crowe played as well upon bottled specimens to add moralising thrills to her work, as in 'The Poisoners', included in

Light and Darkness; or, Mysteries of Life (1850). Crowe was famous for such supernatural stories as *The Night Side of Nature; or, Ghosts and Ghosts Seers* (1848) – stories which were often retellings of actual reports of supernatural occurrences. Most of the tales included in *Light and Darkness*, referred to as 'Tales of Continental Jurisprudence', were based on real legal or criminal cases, while others were written as Gothic or even sensational narratives. The result is a collection with an intriguing mix of the fictional and non-fictional, which explores the nature of deviance, using recorded cases to reveal the truth about hidden crimes and bring those responsible to justice. This is typical of the nineteenth century, when the popular press capitalised on criminal cases reported by the police or the courts, providing increasingly technical (medical) details in their reports – especially in cases of dissection. It was a type of narrative which would pave the way for the development of sensation fiction and detective fiction, both popular literary genres which borrowed or sought inspiration from contemporary criminal cases.

'The Poisoners' relates the case of murderer Gesche Margarethe Gottfried, from the 1820s. Gottfried poisoned men, women and children alike, and was arrested in Bremen in 1828 and executed three years later. As sensation writers would do a decade later, Crowe emphasises the murderer's vanity. Seemingly pious and loved by those around her, Gottfried is a fascinating double of Mary Elizabeth Braddon's calculating Lady Audley, whose appearance in the seminal 1862 sensation novel bearing her name established Braddon's fame. Gottfried is bewitching and 'etherial',[69] although, as the tale reveals, she is in reality 'nothing but a hideous skeleton. Her fine complexion was artificial – her graceful embonpoint was made up of thirteen pairs of corsets, which she wore one over the other' (p. 97). Crowe plays upon the parallel between the woman's 'physical deformities' and her 'moral obliquity' (p. 97): her body is 'made up of paint and paddings', just as her life was 'a tissue of deceit and hypocrisy' (p. 128). It is significant, however, that the author chooses to close her story with a description of the head of the poisoner preserved in spirits and her skeleton exhibited in the museum in Bremen. Signifying as it does the ultimate stripping away of all of Gottfried's artifices (part of her punishment before she is executed consists in being confronted with a picture of herself stripped of all her 'paint and paddings'), the bottled head symbolises medical professionals' access to the truth, the glass acting as an emblem of control and discipline.

Although Crowe's story places bottled specimens and medical collections in general within a clear moralistic framework, such associations were often undermined in the Victorian period. In fact, the 'bits of things in phials',[70] such as those examined by Dr Lydgate, eager to reform the medical profession in George Eliot's *Middlemarch* (1871), would increasingly be used by authors to challenge what they considered a heartless medical culture, one which reduced patients to the status of mere pathological specimens. The portrayal of exhibited human remains could thus be a powerful tool for subverting medical authority.

From Dr Kahn's Anatomical Museum to Docteur Le Doux's Sanatorium

A vein of obscenity . . . pervades and deforms the whole organization of this novel, which must ever blast, in a moral view, the fair fame that, in point of ability, it would have gained for the author; and which renders the work totally unfit for general circulation.[71]

As Michael Gamer has noted, although the word 'pornography' only appeared in England in 1857, prosecutions involving obscene books had begun there almost two hundred years earlier.[72] The 1797 review of Matthew Lewis's *The Monk* (1797), cited above, emphasises the book's immorality. According to Gamer, such reactions illustrate how a part of Gothic writing, notably what is now termed 'horror gothic' – typified by Lewis's works and also those of Charlotte Dacre and Charles Robert Maturin[73] – was closely associated with sexuality (and knowledge). Likewise, when the sensation novel appeared in Victorian Britain over half a century later, contemporary critics criticised the genre for its obscene exhibition of (female) bodies. The novels, especially Wilkie Collins's, were also largely informed by the medical culture of the time. References to human remains abound, from Count Fosco in *The Woman in White* (1860), a chemist who has found a means of preserving the body after death, to cadavers left to decompose in *Mad Monkton* (1855) and in *The Haunted Hotel: A Mystery of Modern Venice* (1878); cadavers which are examined in the narratives through their colours, smells and ghastly shapes.[74]

Whether obscene like Lewis's *The Monk*, or shocking the 'most prudish taste', like Kahn's museum, the Gothic plots of sensation fiction placed the pleasure of the senses at the heart of the reading experience. As a result, the sensation novel challenged contemporary definitions of art and was frequently condemned for encouraging base forms of taste in its readers. At a time when most art critics, such as John Ruskin, believed in the necessary relationship between art and morality, sensation novelists flouted moral concerns with their unladylike heroines and subverted the Hegelian belief that art should generate moral betterment. As many critics have already highlighted, the female body plays a central part in most sensational plots. Masquerading, displayed on canvases, diseased or disfigured, or even metaphorically unveiled through the investigation, the spectacularised female body of sensation fiction represented a clear challenge to Victorian realism. As Pamela Gilbert argues, '[r]ealism comes to be understood as a genre which constructs itself on the basis of difference from the popular, and thus, as a genre which relies on framing the body in more careful, more nuanced and less spec(tac)ular ways'.[75] Sensation fiction was poles apart from mainstream realistic fiction. Not only did it exhibit the female body, it also explored the genre's boundaries by transgressing the space of its (female) readers, regularly testing their nerves, notably when it chose to violate the bodies of its characters. Significantly, sensation novelists played with representations of the body in ways that were reminiscent of contemporary medical shows and exhibitions. Defined as 'curiosities of literature',[76] sensation novels frequently placed medical curiosities in the margins of the texts, where they functioned as telltale devices, laying bare the mechanisms of the detective narratives and repeatedly suggesting images of the body opened, dissected and exhibited.

Both Charles Dickens and Wilkie Collins were concerned with the challenges represented by the arrival of a new mass reading public, and saw it as their duty to educate readers' taste. Wilkie Collins's essay, 'The Unknown Public', written in 1858 for *Household*

Words and reprinted in 1863 in *My Miscellanies*, deals with the penny-novel journals and reveals how mass consumption was raising concerns among Victorian intellectual elites about the boundaries of taste. Collins's essay strongly echoed Dickens's aesthetic viewpoint, expressed in his account of a journey to the Paris morgue, published around the same period in his collection, *The Uncommercial Traveller* (1863). Dickens's essay stresses the public's lack of education when looking at the 'objects' on display. The scene describes a custodian who advises the crowd to entertain themselves 'with the other curiosities'[77] whilst a newly arrived corpse is being prepared for exhibition. The cadavers are constructed as objects to be looked at and associated with museum exhibits. Furthermore, Dickens compares the visitors' base appetite for sensations with 'looking at waxwork without a catalogue': 'There was a wolfish stare at the object, in which the homicidal white-lead worker shone conspicuous. And there was a much more general, purposeless, vacant staring at it – like looking at waxwork, without a catalogue, and not knowing what to make of it.'[78] Dickens's association of the corpses with artificial wax models is highly significant. Although waxworks could encapsulate – as we have seen – objects as different as characters from royalty, natural wonders, celebrated criminals, and even stock characters typically found in waxworks exhibitions and fairs, the reference to 'waxwork' here alludes rather to the type of wax models found in the teaching cabinets of medical schools and medical museums. The description of the public's untrained gaze directed at the naked body on display suggests that their perception of the corpse is as mere entertainment and therefore potentially vulgar and typical of low mass culture.

These examples show how displays and readings of the body in the Victorian era criss-crossed with aesthetic considerations. If Dr Knox, cited at the beginning of this chapter, stressed that '*amusement* should never form a feature in an *anatomical* museum',[79] here viewers' lack of education prevents them from seeing corpses in any other way. With their inability to see the pedagogical possibilities of the human body, Dickens's morgue visitors are depicted as resembling the compulsive and barely literate readers Collins had denounced in 'The Unknown Public'. Such concerns about exhibitions and readings of the body explain why the sensation novel provoked so much virulent criticism in the 1860s. The narratives displayed female bodies which were passively consumed by their readership whilst the detective elements invited readers to uncover the secrets of the female characters, as in a morbid striptease. Thus, sensation novels appealed to readers in the same way as freak shows or medical collections: they promised to show readers what lay beneath the skirts or skin of their heroines and villainesses, and strongly relied on medical diagnosis to reveal the truth. These highly popular novels were inspired, as reviewers noted, by 'highly-spiced police reports instead of politics'.[80] Thus, critics denounced 'the false taste which made the whole interest of a book turn upon mere horrors of blood and crime and the gallows'[81] and the 'perverted and vitiated taste' of periodical or magazine readers.[82]

Unsurprisingly, the metaphors used in many of the reviews denouncing the sensation novelists' appeal to the public's baser instincts compared literary creativity with the display of diseased specimens, recalling once again Victorian visual culture and the shows which promised to unveil the mysteries of the body. In the following review, the sensation novelist is depicted as revealing the diseases of society:

> We are in a period of diseased invention, and the coming phase of it may be palsy. Mr. Collins belongs to the class of professing satirists who are eager to lay bare the 'blotches and blains' which fester beneath the skin and taint the blood of humanity.[83]

The sensation novelist was regularly compared to an anatomist 'lay[ing] bare' the 'bones' of society, while the reviewer suggests here that the novelist would do better to refrain from treating such unattractive aspects of life: 'one is rather curious about the quality of mind that can produce such wonderfully intricate skeletons of stories without the power of more completely hiding the dry bones with the better-known and more attractive covering that we see in the life about us'.[84] This remark highlights how mainstream Victorian realist fiction veiled human bodies rather than exposing them. Sensation novels, in contrast, invited readers to metaphorically tear away the veil from their characters' bodies, or even strip off their skin. The medical vocabulary which peppers the reviews is illustrated

by the recurrent use of the term 'morbidity'. The 'morbid im-
probability'[85] of novels like *Armadale* or the 'morbid analysation of
mere sensation'[86] turn narratives into so many bodies subjected to
a medical gaze. In 'The Morals of Literature', published in 1864,
Frances Power Cobbe reflects upon the ethics of modes of writing
and the writer's duty when 'expos[ing his characters] to the public'.[87]
As she deals with biographies and the 'violations of the sanctities of
the inner life',[88] corporeal metaphors are present in abundance.
Thus, images of the opening and violation of the 'heart' or of 'the
soul's secrets', 'injur[ies] done by such a literature . . . like a blow
on a woman's face'[89] are considered to define works of sensational
literature. Writers are compared to medical professionals, able with
their 'pen [to] tear open all the wounds, expose all the diseases of
humanity'.[90] What Cobbe's metaphors denounce, above all, is the
realism of this type of literature: 'Men first fall into the delusion
that all that is real is a subject of art, and that nothing is real except
the ugly and the mean'.[91] Cobbe's remark betrays a common view
of her age which sees a close link between morality and aesthetics.
Sensational realism is therefore associated with exposure, exhibition
and opening, terms which are reminiscent of anatomical culture.
The 'ugly and the mean' are, indeed, what literary critics like Cobbe
condemn, drawing censorious attention to characters with 'so much
deformity', like Lady Audley, that 'lovely woman with the fishy
extremities'.[92] Moral deformity is rendered visible and material, as
tangible as a natural curiosity or a medical exhibit, as when Wilkie
Collins's Lydia Gwilt is compared to 'a waxwork figure displayed
from time to time in every conceivable sort of garish light',[93] recalling
the anatomical Venuses whose body parts could be lifted so as to
reveal their internal organs. The medical realism of sensation novels,
it appears, turned sensational characters into medical specimens
exhibited in anatomical collections, their characterisation betraying
the writer's lack of good taste: '[I]n his most horrible moments . . .
[Wilkie Collins] is never otherwise than entertaining, except when
he commits a breach of good-taste . . . Moral deformity is as much
a matter of growth, organisation, and permanence as is physical
deformity.'[94]

The comparison of sensation fiction with the field of medicine,
surgery or anatomy was developed further by many reviewers who

defined sensation novels as 'surgical' or 'medical novel[s]',[95] an
epithet applied for example to *Poor Miss Finch* (1872) or *Heart and
Science* (1883). Reviewers emphasised, in the latter case, that the
novel contained 'a good deal of science', especially in the 'physiological part' of the narrative, 'the manuscript having been submitted
to an eminent London surgeon',[96] and likened the writer to the
physician:

> Most of the writers who find fault with the institutions of their
> country – with its legal, medical and theological doctrines and
> practices – have remedies to propose for all the ills they discover; but
> Wilkie Collins contents himself generally with pointing out the
> evils that exist, leaving to others the work of devising the cure. In
> this respect he presents a marked contrast to Charles Reade, who
> prescribes minutely for everything from tight lacing to the treatment
> of the insane, teaches the doctors how to deal with sprains, and defines
> the changes that should be made in the statutes.[97]

It is significant that although many of the critics denounced the
mechanical construction of the plots and the stereotyped characters,
the issue of taste was more often than not related to the medical
realism of the narratives and to the presentation of characters in a
manner which reviewers considered resembled medical curiosities.
In fact, the links between the medical field and the (female) body
constantly foregrounded in sensation novels constructed a typically
'modern' reading experience which challenged contemporary notions
of bourgeois taste: sensation novels thus lay bare the 'epistemophilic'[98]
urge to know the body of the woman, in Peter Brooks's words,
constructing the female body as the archetypal object of desire.

Lawrence Rothfield has argued that the use of clinical discourse
by novelists emerged with the publication of Gustave Flaubert's
Madame Bovary in 1857, and that Flaubert's novel constructed 'the
relation of self to body as a medical one'.[99] This clinical mode of
representation (in which the appearance of illness becomes an
'integrated aspect of narrative') defines realistic description as 'an
almost microscopic precision about the material conditions of the
body'.[100] With their detective plots and investigations, sensation
novelists thus created narratives that played on the tension between

the visible and the invisible, reading symptoms on the surface of the body and tracing them 'back to the interiority of the body',[101] as in the case of Lady Audley, whose secrets are related to hereditary insanity. In other words, the plots 'dragg[ed] the invisible into the realm of the visible',[102] recalling the anatomists' search for the seats of diseases and truth.

The influence of French fiction on Victorian sensation fiction is evident in the novels of Mary Elizabeth Braddon, and many references to characters reading French novels, as in *Lady Audley's Secret*, or having a French education, as in Collins's *The Moonstone* (1868), gave a taste of licentiousness, immorality and flightiness to the sensational characters.[103] But the characters were also associated with French medicine, as in Collins's *Armadale* (1866), where an abortionist and quack psychiatrist purchases his medical credentials from a French doctor. Dr Le Doux's enterprise may to some extent be reminiscent of that of the 'German doctor', Dr Kahn, in London. Interestingly, the debate around Kahn's quackery was still intense in the 1860s and therefore likely to inspire authors of sensation fiction.[104] Indeed, the murders reported in the newspapers sometimes indicated that the guilty parties educated themselves in the art of killing by learning about human anatomy at Kahn's museum.[105] Set in 1851, *Armadale* draws on many of the motifs typically associated with 'morbid taste' in the years that preceded the passing of the 1857 Obscene Publication Act and is one of the sensation novels which hints most explicitly at medical collections and post-mortem examinations.

When *Armadale* appeared in 1866, an article in the *Westminster Review* compared Collins to the showman John Richardson, whose famous travelling show had exhibited freaks and exotic creatures at the beginning of the century. The review focused on taste and compared the sensation novel to bizarre food and to disease; both the eating metaphor and the trope of the epidemic/endemic disease suggest the contamination and 'violation of the domestic body',[106] to borrow Pamela Gilbert's terms. The review articulates the connection between social and mental poverty, moral corruption resulting from the reader's lack of taste and collapsing thereby social differences between readers:

There is no accounting for tastes, blubber for the Esquimaux, half-hatched eggs for the Chinese, and Sensational novels for the English. Everything must now be sensational. Professor Kingsley sensationalized History, and Mr. Wilkie Collins daily life. One set of writers wear the sensational buskin, another the sensational sock. Just as in the Middle Ages people were afflicted by the Dancing Mania and Lycanthropy, sometimes barking like dogs, and sometimes mewing like cats, so now we have a Sensational Mania. Just, too, as those diseases always occured in seasons of dearth and poverty, and attacked only the poor, so does the Sensational Mania in Literature burst out only in times of mental poverty, and afflict only the most poverty-stricken minds. From an epidemic, however, it has lately changed into an endemic. Its virus is spreading in all directions, from the penny journal to the shilling magazine, and from the shilling magazine to the thirty shillings volume.[107]

If the first part of the review has often been analysed, the second part is significant for the way in which it compares the sensation novel to Richardson's menagerie and its characters to exhibited creatures:

When Richardson, the showman, went about with his menagerie he had a big black baboon, whose habits were so filthy, and whose behaviour was so disgusting, that respectable people constantly remonstrated with him for exhibiting such an animal. Richardson's answer invariably was, 'Bless you, if it wasn't for that big black baboon I should be ruined; it attracts all the young girls in the country'. Now bigamy has been Miss Braddon's big black baboon, with which she has attracted all the young girls in the country. And now Mr. Wilkie Collins has set a big black baboon on his own account. His big black baboon is Miss Gwilt, a bigamist, thief, gaol-bird, forgeress, murderess, and suicide. This beats all Miss Braddon's big black baboons put together . . . But besides the big black baboon there are a number of small baboons and monkeys, for by no stretch of language can they be called human creatures. The most prominent are a hag, who paints and enamels women's faces, and a doctor, whose services, when we are first introduced to him, are apparently principally required by painted women. Lying, cheating, intriguing, and dreaming strange dreams are the characteristics of these animals.[108]

The significance of this passage is that the reviewer's comparison of the characters to exotic animals highlights key motifs of the narrative. Lydia Gwilt, as the novel's 'big black baboon', is joined in the novel by other 'animals': Mrs Oldershaw, the beautician based on Rachel Levison, and Dr Downward (alias Le Doux), the abortionist and quack psychiatrist referred to earlier. The review also alludes to prostitution and abortion, an indication of the novel's explicit references to the world of sexuality. The ape metaphors, together with the image of the menagerie, construct the sensation novel as a freak show displaying exotic creatures. In this way, images of poverty, corruption and immorality are joined by hints at foreignness and, perhaps, degeneration.

More significantly still, the review highlights the way in which Collins anchors the detective plot within a culture of exhibition which becomes central to the investigation. *Armadale* is set in 1851, at the time of the Great Exhibition in Hyde Park, and the characters even visit the exhibition. Throughout the novel, bodies are frequently on display, and many of them perform; from Lydia Gwilt, a born actress, displayed as a child by a travelling quack doctor 'as a living example of the excellence of his washes and hair-oils',[109] to characters who specialise in cosmetics, such as Mrs Oldershaw, or others who hide their identity or diseases under layers of make-up. The number of characters subjected to the medical gaze, moreover, constructs the novel as a vitrine of exhibited patients, not so unlike the reviewer's baboons. At the opening of the novel, Allan Armadale is dying of syphilis – the reference to this sexually transmitted disease strengthening even further the connections with Kahn's museum – and the character's body holds secrets which only the medical professional is able to 'penetrate' (p. 311), his gaze able to see through his patient's flesh:

He lay helpless on a mattress supported by a stretcher; his hair long and disordered under a black skull-cap; his eyes wide open, rolling to and fro ceaselessly anxious; the rest of his face as void of all expression of the character within him, and the thought within him, as if he had been dead. The leaden blank of his face met every question as to his age, his rank, his temper, and his looks which that face might once have answered, in impenetrable silence. Nothing spoke for him now but the shock that had struck him with the death-in-life of Paralysis. The doctor's eye questioned his lower limbs, and Death-in-life answered, *I am here*. The doctor's eye, rising attentively by way of his hands and arms, questioned upward and upward to the muscles around his mouth, and Death-in-Life answered, *I am coming*. (p. 13)

The focus on what lies inside, and holds the truth about, the body turns the latter into a territory awaiting investigation and anticipates the whole play upon poison on which the narrative hinges. Indeed, the stress on the 'doctor's eye' reveals the influence of pathological anatomy, which has substituted 'for a methodology of the visible a more complex reserve only in the passage to the inert, to the violence of the dissected corpse'.[110] Pathological anatomy was built on the premise that truth comes only at the point of the dissector's knife, which allowed the medical practitioner to penetrate beneath the visible surface, and thus 'to map the disease in the secret depths of the body'.[111] The rise of the medical gaze, as Michel Foucault argued, was accompanied by an estrangement from the patient's body. Both of these elements, characteristic of the development of medical practice and research in the eighteenth and nineteenth centuries, may be readily traced in Collins's novel: a gradual invasion of the patient's physical space, climaxing in autopsy, and a dehumanising objectification of the patient.

Collins's *Armadale* reworks the traditional Gothic plot. It opens with a father's confession which revisits the prototypical Gothic manuscript. The crimes of the past are revealed, thus foreshadowing that the sins of the fathers shall be visited upon the sons. Four characters bear the name of Allan Armadale. The villainess, Lydia Gwilt, a femme fatale whose beautiful looks and manners conceal her criminal propensities, marries Ozias Midwinter (alias Allan Armadale) before attempting to murder his rich namesake and pass for his widow. To do so, the novel plays upon poisons and alludes recurrently to the rise of medico-legal science and to the use of the post-mortem examination in criminal cases. The most significant poisoning case is Lydia Gwilt's murder of her first husband, as related in her trial, during which medical experts disagree as to the nature of the poison used.[112]

The poison plots soon conjure up scenes of post-mortem examinations and hint at anatomical dissection, the latter promising to reveal the truth beneath the layers of make-up. References to the human body dissected and exhibited appear as significant landmarks in the narrative. For instance, Dr Hawbury is accused by Ozias Midwinter (the son of the murderer) – whose name connects him with death and burial – of being unable to expand his point of view 'beyond the point of his dissecting-knife' (p. 143). We also learn that he keeps 'curious cases' at home, pickled specimens presumably, which feature at a turning point in the novel: it is because Allan Armadale visits Midwinter to see his collection that he borrows his boat and finds out how his father has been murdered. Likewise, Dr Le Doux, the abortionist-cum-quack psychiatrist, invites Lydia Gwilt to plot the murder of Allan Armadale. He takes her to his study, where the emblems of medical authority can be viewed on his shelves:

> The doctor's private snuggery was at the back of the house . . .
> Horrible objects in brass and leather and glass, twisted and turned as
> if they were sentient things writhing in agonies of pain, filled up one
> end of the room. A great book-case with glass doors extended over
> the whole of the opposite wall, and exhibited on its shelves long rows
> of glass jars, in which shapeless dead creatures of a dull white colour
> floated in yellow liquid. (p. 588)

By hinting at post-mortem examinations, an increasingly common feature of criminal cases in this period, the bottled creatures foreshadow the murder: Le Doux is a quack, who earlier in the novel is suspected of practising abortions and is thus linked with deviance. But more significantly, perhaps, the bottled specimens are dehumanised – neither human nor animal, in fact – an idea which is further emphasised by the animated laboratory apparatus, able to feel pain. The inversion recalls the objectification of patients, cut up, preserved and displayed in medical museums. However, the dehumanised specimens also partake of the Gothic thrill that Collins injects into his narrative, borrowing from contemporary medical research to underline the relativisation of the human. Indeed, Le Doux's creatures floating in preserving fluids represent the construction of humans as pieces of matter, thus prefiguring *fin-de-siècle* Gothic. Nameless and dehumanised, the creatures in jars, which appear just before the murder and the exchange of identity between the two namesakes, thus encapsulate the whole discourse on modern medicine's erasure of the human body and the suppression of volitional power, identity and humanity. However, because they are linked to a quack doctor's disciplinary mental home, Le Doux's bottled creatures, which may have been bought for decoration or may be the result of this charlatan's dissection of his innocent patients, nonetheless offer an ambiguous image of the icons of anatomical research. Oscillating as they do between the medical world and Victorian consumer culture, the exhibited remains constitute a subtle invitation to engage with medicine, its practice and its symbols, perhaps warning us not to act as uncritical consumers of morbid pathology.

It is not surprising in this context that the last part of Collins's novel, which takes place in Le Doux's medical establishment for nervous patients, should hinge upon allusions to autopsies. While Gwilt has so far used domestic poisons, inspired by contemporary criminal cases of female poisoners, the last part of the narrative associates their use with the medical field. Le Doux advises Gwilt to use his miraculous poison to dispose of Allan Armadale, indicating that its use would remain undetected when the body was subjected to the kind of post-mortem examination generally practised in cases of suspected poisoning,[113] as indeed had been the case following the death of Gwilt's first husband (p. 527):

Our Stout Friend by himself, is a most harmless and useful medicine. He is freely dispensed every day to tens of thousands of patients all over the civilized world. He has made no romantic appearances in courts of law; he has excited no breathless interest in novels; he has played no terrifying part on the stage. There he is, an innocent, inoffensive creature, who troubles nobody with the responsibility of locking him up! *But* bring him into contact with something else – introduce him to the acquaintance of a certain common mineral substance, of a universally accessible kind, broken into fragments; provide yourself with (say) six doses of our Stout Friend, and pour those doses consecutively on the fragments I have mentioned, at intervals of not less than five minutes. Quantities of little bubbles will rise at every pouring; collect the gas in those bubbles, and convey it into a closed chamber – and let Samson himself be in that closed chamber, our Stout Friend will kill him in half-an-hour! Will kill him slowly, without his seeing anything, without his smelling anything, without his feeling anything but sleepiness. Will kill him and tell the whole College of Surgeons nothing, if they examine him after death, but that he died of apoplexy or congestion of the lungs! What do you think of *that*, my dear lady, in the way of mystery and romance? Is our harmless Stout Friend as interesting *now* as if he rejoiced in the terrible popular fame of the Arsenic and the Strychnine which I keep locked up there? (p. 642)

Unlike arsenic or strychnine, therefore, Le Doux's 'Stout Friend' is capable of deceiving the anatomist's gaze. The motif of poison thus subtly introduces the world of dissection into the narrative, offering us an image of the body seen from the inside – a body opened and examined by medical professionals and subjected to the medical gaze. The word 'dissection' is never used, however, just as in the case of Gwilt's husband, where the phrase 'examination of the body' is employed instead (p. 530).[114]

'Our Stout Friend' works in tandem with the specimens exhibited in Le Doux's office, building up a Gothic web of meaning linked to anatomical culture. Despite Le Doux's claims that his sanatorium proposes modern and humane treatment for its inmates, his specimens evoke the large number of dissections performed on insane patients in both the eighteenth and nineteenth centuries. A well-documented case is that of the Frenchman Philippe Pinel (1745–1826), who conducted around 250 'openings' to prove the absence of lesions and justify the 'moral' treatment of his patients.[115] The attempts by Collins's near contemporaries Franz Joseph Gall (1758–1828), Johann Gaspar Spurzheim (1766–1832) and François-Joseph Victor Broussais (1772–1838) to discover the seats of various diseases[116] indicate how novels like *Armadale* found their source of inspiration in medical research and the development of mental science – a point which will be developed further in chapter 5.[117] Indeed, the character of Dr Le Doux is modelled, like Dr Sampson in Charles Reade's *Hard Cash* (1863), on William Harvey (1578–1657) and Edward Jenner

(1749–1823), both of whom made widespread use of dissection to discover, respectively, the circulation of blood and the vaccination against smallpox. Significantly, Le Doux claims that an autopsy would prove, not only that Allan Armadale was mad ('to assert that he exhibited symptoms of mental alienation after your marriage'), but also that his condition was incurable: 'I can certify his brain to have been affected by one of those mysterious disorders, eminently incurable, eminently fatal, in relation to which medical science is still in the dark' (p. 634).

When Gwilt eventually uses 'our Stout Friend' to poison Armadale, she realises that Armadale and Midwinter have changed rooms. She rescues Midwinter and then commits suicide by inhaling the toxic air. As Le Doux had predicted, the subsequent post-mortem fails to identify correctly the cause of death, and the conclusion that Gwilt died of apoplexy suggests that an autopsy has certainly been practised on the villainess's corpse. As this example shows, therefore, the introduction of drugs as a criminal weapon in narratives such as *Armadale* goes beyond mere references to celebrated cases of female poisoners. Poisons take readers into the world of dissection and anatomical research, showing the body shaped and modelled by beauty specialists through the looking glass. Opened up – both metaphorically and literally – to the gaze of doctors, the body, as anatomical object, participates in the construction of horror. However, it refuses to deliver all its secrets; the villain's poisons remain indetectable. Lydia Gwilt, whose smooth appearance never betrays her criminal nature, remains a sealed body, very much like a curiosity exhibited in a *Wunderkammer*, ultimately triggering both wonder and horror.

Looking at such sometimes marginal references to the world of anatomy and images of the dissected body reveals the corporeality of the body on which sensation fiction capitalised and which was denounced by critics on account of its 'morbid taste'. The sensation genre's stress on bodies subverted bourgeois literary taste, explaining why the 'surgical' novels were condemned, just as women were regularly forbidden entry to medical museums. The 'nakedness of truth', as Lady Blessington put it when she first entered the Specola museum in Florence and saw the anatomical Venuses and 'the disgusting details of the animal economy' on display,[118] were as shocking to the Victorians as popular fiction promising to uncover the secrets and bodies of the Victorian angels of the house. Thus, as these examples demonstrate, the Gothic was recurrently associated throughout the nineteenth century with objects representing the material culture of medicine. By framing Gothic victims as medical patients exhibited in medical museums, the genre followed contemporary scientific methods, illustrating a pervasive 'dissective' way of knowing, as John Pickstone has shown.[119] As dissection was gradually supplanted by medical experimentation at the end of the nineteenth century, however, the laboratory came to replace the dissecting room, a development reflected in R. L. Stevenson's *Strange Case of Dr Jekyll and Mr Hyde* (1886), inspired by John Hunter's Leicester Square house.[120] As late-Victorian Gothic suggested, indeed, the medical patient was no longer merely dissected and exhibited, but was now threatened with dissolution.

5

Death Misdiagnosed: Gothic Live Burials

໑

In February 1823, the *European Magazine* published an article entitled 'On Premature Interment'. The title was no doubt intended to be eye-catching, tantalising readers with the prospect of ghastly tales of live burials. In fact, the article dealt above all with the less sensational subject of the laws of burial in France and claimed that its people habitually buried their dead with an indecent haste that verged on the reckless:

> There are few persons ignorant that it is the unnatural custom of the French to inter twenty-four hours after the apparent decease. This practice, which is said to have had its origin in regard for the living by preventing the evil consequences of putrefaction, has excited horror in reflecting minds generally, and the deserved censure of many eminent medical men, who declare that the sanitary precaution has been carried to an extreme which outrages not only decency but humanity. That it should still exist is the best proof that can be offered of the obstinacy of the French government, or the ridiculous respect attached by the nation to a custom which sends many innocent victims prematurely to the grave, and serves to weaken the effect which scenes of death are calculated to produce upon the living. It is monstrous that the body of a parent or a child is to be dragged to the grave almost before it is cold, and with a people like the French such an indecent practice must tend to unhinge the secret ties of nature.[1]

The reviewer's portrait draws heavily upon national stereotypes, with the French seen as having 'unnatural', 'indecent' or 'monstrous' practices, whilst the British are depicted as taking good care of their people and their dead. The passage captures changing visions of the corpse and of death over the course of the eighteenth and nineteenth centuries, hinting at the sensibility of the eighteenth century ('the effect which scenes of death are calculated to produce upon the living'), while at the same time constructing the corpse as a scientific object. Revealingly, the contrast between the French and British ways of dealing with the human body after death is used here as a means of asserting British supremacy, especially in the scientific field. Thus, the article emphasises how the country's 'reflecting minds'[2] and medical professionals have been attempting to draw the attention of their neighbours across the Channel to the dangers inherent in burying people too soon after their apparent deaths.

The birth of modern medicine and the rise in the significance of anatomy, stressing as they did the importance of the 'artisanal skill of the brain-breaker' more than the 'scientific precision of the scales', as Michel Foucault put it, constructed death as 'an object and source of knowledge'.[3] The idea that the material body encapsulates the secrets of nature was also emphasised in literary works, as seen in Percy Bysshe Shelley's 'Alastor; or the Spirit of Solitude' (1815). This novel view of death transformed the image of the corpse. To cite Foucault again,

> gloomy respect had condemned it to putrefaction, to the dark work of destruction; in the boldness of the gesture that violated only to reveal, to bring to the light of day, the corpse became the brightest moment in the figures of truth. Knowledge spins where once larva was formed.[4]

Indeed, as the French anatomo-pathologist Marie François Xavier Bichat (1771–1802)[5] contended, 'knowledge of life [found] its origin in the destruction of life and in its extreme opposite'. Thus, in this conception it was above all 'at death that disease and life [spoke] their truth'.[6]

That 'anatomy reinvented not only notions of violence, but the very image of death itself',[7] as Richard Sugg puts it, is clear from the numerous medical works published in the course of the eighteenth and nineteenth centuries which attempted to distinguish real from apparent death, and to define the end of life clinically. Whilst in the mid-seventeenth century it had been widely believed that the patient's heartbeat and pulse were undisputable signs of life, in the next two centuries a vigorous and sometimes heated debate would rage about whether such evidence or rather other signs (like the onset of putrefaction) should be considered the most reliable indicators of death. The many reported cases of premature interment merely fed the flames of controversy. Indeed, throughout this period, fear of live burial was rife. Early works by Jacob B. Winslow (1669–1760) (*Morte incertae signa* (1740)) and Jean-Jacques Bruhier (1685–1756) (*Dissertation sur l'incertitude des signes de la mort* (1746–9)), who translated and rewrote Winslow's work, contributed to these fears. Bruhier collected 180 cases in which mistakes were made concerning the signs of death. These included fifty-two individuals interred alive, four whose bodies were cut open before death, and fifty-three who recovered from the ordeal of being shut up in their coffins.[8] Both Bruhier and Winslow underlined the uncertainty of the traditional signs of death and claimed that putrefaction offered the only reliable indicator. In France, at the Salpêtrière Hospital, medical professionals such as Antoine Louis (1723–92) had argued rather that rigor mortis or the transformation of the cornea after death were surer signs of death, preventing any risk of live burial, while a century later Eugène Bouchut's *Traité des signes de la mort* (1848) claimed that the invention of the stethoscope by Laënnec provided the medical practitioner with enhanced hearing and thus obviated the need to rely on signs of putrefaction.

Whilst Winslow advocated an exhaustive series of tests to prove death, ranging from tickling patients with a quill to rubbing their gums with garlic or pouring vinegar and pepper into their mouths, Bruhier was in favour of building so-called waiting mortuaries, supervised by watchmen, where corpses should be kept until the onset of putrefaction. Bruhier's book circulated throughout Europe and was translated into Italian in 1744, into English two years later and into Swedish in 1751. In France in 1787, physician François Thierry made proposals similar to Bruhier's to develop morgues for the recently deceased throughout the country, while in Austria in

1788 Johann Peter Frank (1745–1821) supported the building of communal dead-houses in every town. In the 1790s, Christoph Wilhelm Hufeland (1762–1836) was the first to draw up plans for a Weimar dead-house (*Leichenhaus*). Waiting mortuaries were subsequently established in many cities throughout the German states.[9]

The article from the *European Magazine* quoted at the beginning of this chapter is significant in the way it reveals the part played by medical periodicals, popular magazines and literature more generally in stoking fears about premature burial. Throughout the nineteenth century, many nervous affections were investigated, some of which mimicked the signs of death and led to medical misdiagnoses. Catalepsy, in particular, remained shrouded in mystery at the time, and cases of patients being buried alive were regularly reported both in the medical and popular literature of the day. Indeed, cataleptic patients, exhibiting as they did the signs of death, were sometimes buried alive or, for some luckier individuals, recovered their faculties just as they were about to be propelled to their untimely graves. As a consequence, many of the articles on catalepsy published in the nineteenth century were part of the larger literature on the signs of death and fears of premature burial that was disseminated during the period. Seen in this broader epistemological context, the study of catalepsy as revealed in this article throws valuable light on contemporary debates about the practice of clinical medicine and the circulation of medical knowledge in Europe, making it crucial to see beyond its simple denunciation of the French lack of 'decency' and 'humanity' in their habit of burying their dead too quickly. The article is based upon the testimony of a Doctor Macnab, an English physician residing in France, who tried to attract the attention of the French government to the need to change its country's laws on burials:

In every age and country history has furnished numerous instances of individuals, who, in apparent death, have been preserved by accidental causes from premature interment. The short period of twenty-four hours, allowed by the existing laws of France for the purpose of ascertaining the real or apparent death of individuals, is far too short. There are many cases in which the signs of apparent death are witnessed, and which cannot be determined for days after they have been manifested. I could enumerate diseases in which such signs are common.[10]

Several stories of people prematurely interred then follow, all of them cataleptic patients, one of the most famous being that of Lady Russell, 'well-known both in France and England', who remained in a cataleptic state for seven days and nights before recovering just as the parish bells were tolling for church.[11] Another case of catalepsy cited by Macnab is that of a young Parisian forced to marry a gentleman whilst betrothed to another. Her plight 'plunged [her] in a profound melancholy, which produced a lethargic affection, and in the end every appearance of death', ultimately leading her to be buried alive. However, her lover, knowing that she suffered from 'violent nervous attacks, which had produced for short periods the appearance of death', trusted he could resuscitate his love and actually succeeded in rescuing the young woman. The couple later 'exchanged vows of eternal constancy'.[12] The lover's 'romantic' idea, as the doctor underlines ('Romantic as the idea would seem to any but a lover'[13]), while once again in the author's eyes betraying the passionate character of the French, nonetheless enabled the young woman to be rescued. This idea is significant, because, as this chapter will demonstrate, medical professionals' reliance upon the Gothic imagination, and on romantic discourse more generally, enabled them to assert their authority on such mental affections as catalepsy, a stance which offers valuable insights into contemporary understandings of the clinical reality of death and its signs.

The case of the young Parisian was one of the 'Causes Célèbres' which captivated Paris. The lovers (Victorine Lafourcade and Julien Bossuet), after having escaped to England for some years, returned to France, where Victorine's husband recognised her and claimed her as his wife. Sensational as it may appear, this story of a melancholy young woman – apparently dead and buried, rescued by her sweet-heart from the grave, then faced with a trial for bigamy set in motion by her estranged husband – was frequently cited in both medical treatises on mental diseases and the signs of death and in popular journals. As we have seen, this was one of the cases of catalepsy, along with that of Lady Russell, cited in an article aimed primarily at asserting British medical authority. However, such cases were also inextricably bound to the Gothic imagination, especially since many of them seem to have been recorded 'on the Continent', notably in France. For the medical condition was not just a scientific mystery to most medical professionals in Britain and elsewhere; it also contained all the generic ingredients of the Gothic. The patient's helplessness, illustrated in stories of live burial where doctors surmised that the patients, though unconscious, remained aware of what was happening to them without being able to call for assistance, was a staple of Gothic fiction which sensationally rewrote in much more realistic terms older tales of imprisonment, particularly female imprisonment – since most victims of catalepsy seemed to be women. Moreover, the cruelty, monstrosity or indecency of the French, as underlined in the above example, ensured even more Gothic thrills, since British readers could safely witness and experience vicariously the barbarity of (Catholic) peoples situated on the other side of the Channel, who buried their dead alive.

A survey of medical journals published in France and Britain during the nineteenth century shows that the very same cases were described in medical journals, as for instance a case of 'spontaneous catalepsy' observed in Bologna in 1832, reported in the *Gazette médicale de Paris* and translated for the *Lancet* in February 1833.[14] Cases of catalepsy were also recorded in Ireland,[15] Italy,[16] Germany,[17] Denmark,[18] Austria[19] and even Cuba.[20] Monographs on the disease by both French[21] and British medical professionals were reviewed concurrently in journals on both sides of the Channel, such as the *Dictionnaire de Médecine* by Georget, mentioned in John Coldstream's 'Case of Catalepsy',[22] or Ernest-Charles Lasègue's 'Catalepsies partielles et passagères',[23] cited in Adolphe Wahltuch's *On Catalepsy: Read before the medical section of the Manchester Royal Institute* (1869).[24]

The detailed descriptions of cataleptic cases published in the medical literature from the early 1820s to the last decades of the nineteenth century often found their way into popular magazines, which capitalised on the sensational potential of such tales of medical misdiagnosis and live burial. Such articles stressed that cases of catalepsy were generally rare, especially in Britain, but were more frequently recorded in France or on the Continent. These remarks, however, often betrayed the way in which popularisers exploited the medical literature of the time, for in reality the geographical variation in the number of cases was often simply a function of differences in how catalepsy was defined.[25] This was the case for example in an article on catalepsy published in *Reynolds' Miscellany* at mid-century. It claimed that the mental condition was more likely to be found in countries whose inhabitants believed in the marvellous and the curious:

> It is a curious fact, that long protracted cases of catalepsy are not so uncommon in France as they are in England. Scarcely had the marvellous case at Nantes, which has been the theme of such much conversation and discussion terminated, when a new one presented itself in the department of the Aube [*sic*] . . . The marvel, as it may be supposed, excites the greatest curiosity, and individuals from all parts of the country, medical and non-medical, go to witness it.— *French paper.*[26]

Hence, because of the way in which the cases recurred in the medical literature on both sides of the Channel and throughout Europe more generally, and were then exploited by popular literature – like the 'celebrated case of Lady Russell',[27] the Parisian rescued by her passionate lover or the 'sexton and the lady's ring'[28] – these case histories frequently flirted with fiction.[29] Indeed, it was often difficult to establish the veritable facts of these cases, since the very same stories seemed to occur in different places in Europe in different centuries,[30] easily turning some of them into legends. In addition, while medical professionals believed that anger, grief, hatred or sudden terror produced cataleptic seizures,[31] thus preparing their readers for passionate or terrifying stories, their often embroidered descriptions of the patients' experiences when prematurely taken to their graves blurred further the boundaries between fact and fiction.[32] Not only would they regularly furnish what were in effect fabricated descriptions of the patients' imagined feelings, but, as we will see presently, some of the articles would also draw upon contemporary tales of terror.

Gothic catalepsy

Edgar Allan Poe's stories 'Berenice' (1835), 'The Fall of the House of Usher' (1839), 'The Premature Burial' (1844), 'The Cask of Amontillado' (1846) and even 'The Black Cat' (1843), along, to a lesser degree, with 'The Tell-Tale Heart' (1843), all draw upon the motif of live burial as a seminal Gothic trope. In 'The Premature Burial' (1844), the narrator argues that 'To be buried alive is, beyond question, the most terrific of these extremes which has ever fallen to the lot of mortality'.[33] He explains that cases of live burial are due to the difficulty of telling life from death, especially when the symptoms of disease mimic those of death:

> The boundaries which divide Life from Death are at best shadowy and vague. Who shall say where the one ends, and where the other begins? We know that there are diseases in which occur total cessations of all the apparent functions of vitality, and yet in which these cessations are merely suspensions, properly so called. They are only temporary pauses in the incomprehensible mechanism. A certain period elapses, and some unseen mysterious principle again sets in motion the magic pinions and the wizard wheels . . . [S]uch cases of suspended animation naturally give rise, now and then, to premature interments – apart from this consideration, we have the direct testimony of medical and ordinary experience, to prove that a vast number of such interments have actually taken place. I might refer at once, if necessary, to a hundred well-authenticated instances. (p. 271)

Poe's short story shows above all how, whether as a disease or a symptom, catalepsy had become by this point one of the clichéd traits of the helpless Gothic victim in the nineteenth-century tale of terror. In this way, terror marched hand in hand with the medical profession's inability to unravel the mysteries of apparent death and identify the causes of disease. Moreover, it is significant that medical knowledge is presented in the story as built upon empirical information from 'well-authenticated instances' which are pivotal to the medical realism of the tale of terror. Indeed, in the medical literature of the time as much as in Gothic fiction, medical knowledge results from the accumulation of case-based evidence, the sum of individual stories enabling the framing of symptoms and the making of the norm.[34] Hence, the series of actual cases cited in the narrative, from that of the wife of a Baltimore lawyer who 'baffled the skills of her physicians' ('The face assumed the usual pinched and sunken outline. The lips were of the usual pallor. The eyes were lustreless. There was no warmth. Pulsation had ceased' (p. 272)), to the French case of Victorine Lafourcade, cited earlier.[35] A case from Leipzig published in the *Chirurgical Journal* is also mentioned, as is the London case of Edward Stapleton whose body, stolen by body-snatchers, was resurrected by a galvanic experiment on the dissection table.[36] If the cases were probably borrowed from secondary sources, they all combine realistic descriptions (the symptoms are depicted in terms identical to those found in the medical literature of the time) and Romantic elements, as in the case of Victorine Lafourcade. These medical cases anticipate the story of the narrator, who himself suffers from catalepsy:

> For several years I had been subject to attacks of the singular disorder which physicians have agreed to term catalepsy, in default of a more definite title. Although both the immediate and the predisposing causes, and even the actual diagnosis of this disease, are still mysteries, its obvious and apparent character is sufficiently well understood. Its variations seem to be chiefly of degree. Sometimes the patient lies, for a day only, or even for a shorter period, in a species of exaggerated lethargy. He is senseless and externally motionless; but the pulsation of the heart is still faintly perceptible; some traces of warmth remain; a slight colour lingers within the centre of the cheek; and, upon application of a mirror to the lips, we can detect a torpid, unequal, and vacillating action of the lungs. Then, again, the duration of the trace is for weeks – even for months; while the closest scrutiny, and the most rigorous medical tests, fail to establish any material distinction between the state of the sufferer and what we conceive of absolute death. Very usually, he is saved from premature interment solely by the knowledge of his friends that he has been previously subject to catalepsy, by the consequent suspicion excited, and, above all, by the non-appearance of decay. (pp. 279–80)

The narrator's unconscious state ('exaggerated lethargy'), motionlessness and faintly perceptible heartbeat all match contemporary medical descriptions of catalepsy, all the more so as the narrator adds that his case 'differed in no important particular from those mentioned in medical books' (p. 280). Moreover, his mention of 'species' or 'variations' points to a nosological approach to the 'disorder' he is suffering from.

Poe's medical realism is characteristic of the nineteenth-century tale of terror, which radically differed from the eighteenth-century spectres and demons in the vein of Matthew Lewis's Gothic. In the story, the narrator has carefully arranged the family vault so that it may be opened from within; the space also admits air, and contains water and food. Above the coffin (which the narrator can also open from within) is a bell rope, which is to be fastened to one of the hands of the corpse. The arrangements are those typically found in nineteenth-century mortuaries, foregrounding therefore once again the narrative's verisimilitude – and the story's veracity. Yet, Poe quickly undermines the carefully constructed atmosphere of terror. As he feared, the narrator eventually discovers he has been entombed alive, but he finds himself buried in the earth in an ordinary coffin, and is therefore unable to escape or call for help. This, however, turns out to be merely a nightmare, which enables Poe to deflate the Gothic as the short story closes upon a comic note.

If comic, Poe's conclusion to 'The Premature Burial' nonetheless highlights how in 1844 the live-burial motif had become a hackneyed trope of the literature of terror.[37] Indeed, many of Poe's earlier short stories had already played with the motif. A case in point is 'Loss of Breath' (1832), which even more grotesquely parodies the clichés of the tale of terror: a character is believed dead once he becomes breathless; his body is sold to a surgeon who cuts off his ears and removes his viscera; he is also hanged (which he survives),[38] and eventually escapes from the public vault in which he has been interred. In both examples, however, Poe illuminates the significance of apparent death and cataleptic states in the nineteenth-century tale of terror.

Furthermore, as suggested, 'The Premature Burial' is notable for the way in which the narrative relies upon veritable case histories. For Meegan Kennedy, medical cases both 'produc[ed] subjectivity [and] construct[ed] the modern subject'.[39] Hence, their significance when they involved cataleptic patients, since they foregrounded a divided or fragmented subject that typically matched Gothic versions of the self. In fact, through its play with both literary and medical conventions, Poe's short story reveals a striking degree of cross-fertilisation between literature and medicine in the nineteenth century, with medical professionals frequently emphasising their patients' emotions and feelings in their case histories. According to the medical men of the period, catalepsy was linked above all with emotions, from anger and terror to extreme sorrow,[40] underlining thereby an increasingly psychological understanding of the disorder. The following medical article from 1835 exemplifies this trend:

> Gentlemen, it is much easier for you to imagine than it is for me to describe, what the feelings of this unhappy individual must have been on witnessing these awful preparations, and to contemplate the sudden transition from 'deep despair' to indescribable joy, which they experienced when her returning faculties enabled her to avert the horrors of a premature grave, by exclaiming in the frantic tone of triumphant exultation, 'I am not dead!'[41]

Another example from this period, from a work by physician John Elliotson, famous for advocating and practising mesmerism and phrenology at University College London (before being dismissed in 1838), revealingly compares the cataleptic patient with the character of Isabella in Thomas Southerne's play *The Fatal Marriage, or the Innocent Adultery* (1694, later known as *Isabella; Or, The Fatal Marriage*), an adaptation of Aphra Behn's *The History of the Nun; or, the Fair Vow-Breaker* (1689). Southerne's play was republished in the 1770s as a result of the rise of Gothic romances, following the publication of Walpole's *The Castle of Otranto* in 1764. Even if the literary character does not suffer from catalepsy, Isabella's nervousness serves here to illustrate the medical prose:

> Consciousness and perception are sometimes entirely destroyed; and sometimes only partially so. Frequently the person is not aware of her existence, or of what is going on around; – consciousness and perception being both absent. Dr. Gregory used to speak of the case of a lady, who had undergone great mental anguish. Her history, he

said, was like that of Isabella, in the tragedy of the 'Fatal Marriage'; and she was seized with catalepsy.[42]

Likewise, in a passage from an 1853 essay by the Scottish physician John Coldstream, the medical practitioner's definition of catalepsy is informed by literary references:

> Her statue-like immobility was most remarkable. It struck the beholder with a kind of awe, especially when found that, in no way, he could succeed in obtaining indications of either consciousness or attention. It has been well said that this strange state is 'a fearful blending of the conditions of life and death; presenting, so to speak, life in the aspect of death, and death in that of life'. It is especially with reference to this feature in the case of his 'thunder-struck' patient that the same author remarks:—'I protest I cannot conceive anything more dreadful'.[43]

Coldstream refers here to a fictional medical case history on catalepsy, taken from Samuel Warren's *Passages from the Diary of a Late Physician*, a series of short stories published two decades earlier in *Blackwood's Edinburgh Magazine*, which played upon mysterious or supernatural-looking diseases, as seen in chapter 3. Ironically, the stories mimicked so well the type of case histories published in the medical literature of the time that Warren's *Passages* prompted a great deal of negative comment from medical professionals for the way in which they appeared to reveal intimate details about the patients who featured in the stories. Critics condemned what they considered Warren's breach of medical confidentiality and made guesses as to the true identity of this medical man who dared publish his actual patients' cases.[44] A few weeks after the publication of Warren's first story in *Blackwood's*, an article was published in the *Lancet*,[45] to which Warren responded as follows:

> The Editor of Blackwood happily enough says, 'what periodical has sunk a shaft into this rich mine of incident and sentiment?' True; the reason has been, and is yet, I hope, to be found in the *honour* of our profession, and the determination of its members to *merit* the confidence of their patients, by continuing, in the language of Junius, 'the sole

depositary of their secrets, which shall perish with them'. If the writer of the papers in question, or the Editor of Blackwood, should see this letter, they are *implored* to consider its purport; and thus prevent the public from viewing their medical attendants with *distrust*, and withholding those confidential disclosures which are essential to the due performance of our professional duties. The very persons who would read such a series of articles as the 'Passages from the Diary of a Late Physician' promise to be, with intense interest, would be the first to act on the principle I have mentioned. (I, p. 103; emphasis in original)

Warren claimed that none of the patients described needed fear identification since, contrary to the practice in medical journals, he had changed their initials, and removed improper details from the narrative. The author even denounced medical publications such as the *Lancet*, the *Medical Gazette* and *Dr Reece's Journal* for failing to bear in mind that their journals were not only read by medical men:

I beg to ask the writer, who is so ready at starting the grave charge of a breach of professional confidence, what I do more, in publishing in your Magazine these papers of my late friend, with the most scrupulous concealment of everything which could possibly lead to undue disclosures, than is constantly done in the pages of the *Lancet* itself, as well as all the other professional journals, text-books, and treatises, which almost invariably append *real initials* – (I appeal to every medical man whether such is not the fact) – and other *indicia*, to the most painful, and, in many instances, revolting and offensive details? It may possibly be answered – as it really has been – that, in the latter case, the narratives meet only *professional eyes*. What! in the *Lancet*? in the *Medical Gazette*? in *Dr Reece's Journal*? Are these works to be found in the hands of professional men only? – I have but one other observation to make. Would the delicacy of patients be less shocked at finding the peculiar features of their physical maladies – a subject on which their feelings are morbidly irritable – exposed to every member, high and low, young and old, of our extensive profession – the theme of lectures – the subject of constant allusion and comment, from beneath the thin veil of 'Mrs J— M—t', &c. ; is this, I say, less likely to hurt their feelings, than seeing (as is improbable in nine cases out of ten of those who read these *Passages*) the *morale*, the *sentiment* of their case extracted, dressed in the shape of simple narrative, and challenging the sympathy and admiration of the public? (I, pp. 104–5; emphasis in original)

Warren's response suggests that medical prose, in contrast to his (much more edifying and 'a source of instruction and warning to all' (I, p. 105)), might be equivocal – or perhaps even pornographic in some cases. But Warren's remarks are also interesting for the way in which they depict medical and literary case histories as two types of narrative which potentially competed with one another. Warren's short stories were accused, for instance, of plagiarising a genuine medical case (Dr Henry Halford's), presented in an article published in the *London Medical Gazette* on 23 October 1830 (in which, interestingly, the author had resorted to the literary example of *Hamlet* to illustrate his medical case).[46] The debate on this subject, which rumbled on for several weeks, reveals not only the close relationship between the literary and medical fields, but also the commercial rivalry between them, just as between medical periodicals.[47] The publication of 'private circumstances . . . graphically detailed'[48] would ensure increased readership, and it is thus no coincidence that cases of cataleptic patients, especially when young and female, were considered likely to attract readers.

In 'The Thunder-Struck and the Boxer', Warren describes the case of a young woman suffering from catalepsy after being struck by thunder. Significantly, like most contemporary medical case histories, the story emphasises how mysterious the disorder is, and the tendency for contemporaries to confuse its symptoms with those of apoplexy, epilepsy and swooning (III, p. 25). The narrator explains the 'nosological anomaly' (III, p. 24) by referring to medical authorities in the field, ranging from Dr Cullen (known for his work on feigned catalepsy), and Dr Jacques Henri Désiré Petetin, one of the alleged discoverers of catalepsy, as suggested in his *Mémoire sur la découverte des phénomènes que présentent la catalepsie et le somnambulisme, symptômes de l'affection hystérique essentielle, avec des recherches sur la cause physique de ces phénomènes* (1787) and his *Électricité animale, prouvée par la découverte des phénomènes physiques et moraux de la Catalepsie hystérique, et de ses variétés; et par les bons effets de l'Électricité animale dans le traitement de ces maladies* (1808), to Dr John Jebb's *Select cases of the disorder commonly termed the paralysis of the lower extremities. To which is added, a case of catalepsy* (1783).[49] Although the story merely alludes to live burial through a dream (the doctor dreams that his patient lies in her coffin and is about to be interred alive), it relies on contemporary definitions and treatments of catalepsy: the patient is treated with mustard applications, ammonia, galvanism and later music, and the medical practitioner constantly wonders whether the patient is conscious of what is being said around her. Furthermore, the Gothic rhetoric of Warren's physician is particularly visible both in the multiple comparisons made between the young woman and a corpse – with references for example to her statue-like appearance and shroud-like dress – and in the way in which the medical practitioner experiences himself the very same symptoms of catalepsy as he looks at her. He thus becomes speechless, his lips rigid, before ultimately losing consciousness:

> It was Agnes! – She was in the attitude of stepping to the door, with both arms extended. Her hair was partly dishevelled. Her face seemed whiter than the white dress she wore. Her lips were of a livid hue. Her eyes, full of awful expression, were fixed with a petrifying stare on me. Oh, language fails me – utterly! – Those eyes have seldom since been absent from me when alone! I strove to speak – but could not utter a sound. My lips seemed rigid as those I looked at. The horrors of nightmare seemed upon me. My eyes at length closed; my head seemed turning round – and for a moment or two I lost all consciousness. I revived. *There* was the frightful thing still before me – nay, close to me! Though I looked at her, I never once thought of Agnes P—. It was the tremendous appearance – the ineffable terror gleaming from her eyes, that thus overcame me. I protest I cannot conceive any thing more dreadful! (III, pp. 9–10; emphasis in original)

In addition to the physician projecting himself on to his patient's experience of catalepsy and his dramatic rhetoric, the objectification of the cataleptic young woman, turned into a 'thing', highlights the association of catalepsy with automatism and contemporary developments in mental physiology. As seen in chapter 2, the figure of the automaton functioned as a potent symbol of woman's subjection to the forces of her body. Here, the character's lack of volition shapes her into the ideal Gothic victim of medical malpractice. This idea is strengthened, moreover, by the violent way in which the physician handles the patient to ensure that he is not faced with a case of feigned catalepsy (such as by thrusting an open blade into her eye, for instance, or pressing the blade of his knife upon the flesh at the root of her nail).

Warren's fictional medical case history is only one of the many Gothic tales of live burial published in the nineteenth century which had a profound influence on the medical literature of the period. Indeed, such fictional cases may have been as influential with medical professionals as the real case histories circulating in Europe at that time. An early example of the former is John Galt's 'The Buried Alive', mentioned in chapter 3, published anonymously in *Blackwood's Magazine* in 1821.[50] The tale relates the story of a young man who falls into a 'trance'.[51] His weakening physical strength coupled with continuing mental alertness matches all the symptoms of catalepsy:

One day towards the evening, the crisis took place. I was seized with a strange and indescribable quivering – a rushing sound was in my ears – I saw around my couch innumerable strange faces; they were bright and visionary, and without bodies. There was light and solemnity, and I tried to move but could not. For a short time a terrible confusion overwhelmed me, and, when it passed off, all my recollection returned with the most perfect distinctness, but the power of motion had departed. I heard the sound of weeping at my pillow, and the voice of the nurse say, 'He is dead'. I cannot describe what I felt at these words. I exerted my utmost power of volition to stir myself, but I could not move even an eyelid. After a short pause my friend drew near; and, sobbing and convulsed with grief, drew his hand over my face, and closed my eyes. The world was then darkened, but I would still hear, and feel, and suffer. (pp. 286–7)

Believed dead, he is then laid in a coffin after three days, when the smell of putrefaction is, it seems, noticed in the room:

When my eyes were closed, I heard by the attendants that my friend had left the room, and I soon after found the undertakers were

preparing to habit me in the garments of the grave. Their thoughtless-
ness was more awful than the grief of my friends. They laughed at
one another as they turned me from side to side, and treated what
they believed a corpse with the most appalling ribaldry.

When they had laid me out, these wretches retired, and the degrading
formality of affected mourning commenced. For three days a number
of friends called to see me. I heard them, in low accents, speak of
what I was; and more than one touched me with his finger. On the
third day some of them talked of the smell of corruption in the room.
(p. 287)

The uncaring handling of the corpse is a clichéd detail in Gothic
stories of live burial, in this case anticipating the arrival of body-
snatchers who rescue him from the tomb only to place him naked
on a table ready for an anatomical demonstration. The galvanic
experiment which is then performed on his 'corpse' allows him to
open one of his eyes, enabling him in turn to recognise some of
the students witnessing his dissection. Fortunately, the Frankensteinian
scene stops when the cataleptic patient recovers from his trance
at the moment when the demonstrator thrusts his knife into his
chest.

As in Warren's fictional case history, the association of the cataleptic
patient's powerlessness with his acute awareness of the events around
him[52] shapes him into a prototypical victim who may be handled
at will, an idea that flourished in many medical articles examining
trances, as we shall see, and which typified the parallel evolution
of the generic stereotypes of medical Gothic and Victorian medical
science. In the second half of the nineteenth century, moreover,
the clichéd figure of the cataleptic patient took several different
guises. Cataleptic, entranced, hypnotised or vampirised, such death-
in-life figures constantly suggested the failure of the 'corpse . . .
to signify as a coherent Gothic trope' – an idea, as Andrew Smith
has put it, 'bound up with the movement from sentimentality
to science'.[53] Indeed, as we shall see presently, by systematically
addressing the question of death through their cataleptic figures,
Gothic texts emphasised increasingly, especially in the last decades
of the century, that reading the corpse, the dead, or the undead
'constitute[d] a problem for both knowledge and scientific method'.[54]

Locating the soul: seizures, trances and death-like sleep

As suggested by the numerous articles published in Europe in the long nineteenth century, catalepsy was one of the trance-like states which fascinated both medical professionals and writers. As early as in Sarah Scudgell Wilkinson's *The Priory of St Clair; or Spectre of the Murdered Nun* (1811), chemically produced death-like sleep enabled Gothic writers to play with the signs of death and propose spectral characters whose behaviour reflected the medical debates of the time. G. W. M. Reynolds's *Mysteries of London*, which revolves around the figure of the resurrection-man, as seen in chapter 3, also features episodes related to cataleptic states which effectively revisit earlier Gothic spectral figures. In the following passage, the clichéd scene of the tale of terror involving body-snatchers, a surgeon and the 'resurrected' cataleptic patient is explained away by the term 'trance', which encapsulates all types of death-like states and serves to provide a rational explanation for the sensational event:

> 'Well, sir', returned the stranger, 'the plain truth is this:—An old man, without a name, took up his abode in a by-street some months ago. He was taken ill, and, to all appearance, died. He was buried. A surgeon fancied him as a subject, and hired me and a friend of mine to have him up again. We resurrectionized him, and took him in a cart last night to the surgeon's house. He was conveyed into the dissecting-room, and stretched on the table . . . My friend, who was left alone with the stiff 'un, was . . . alarmed when he suddenly felt the body stretch out its hand and catch hold of one of his?'
> 'Then Michael Martin was not dead?'. . .
> 'No – the old man is not dead . . . We went into the dissecting-room with a lamp, and there we found the light put out, and my comrade insensible on the floor. But what was more extraordinary still, we saw the corpse gasping for breath. '*He is not dead!*' cried the surgeon; and in a moment a lancet was stuck into his arm. The blood would not flow at first, but the surgeon chafed his temples and hands by turns; and in a few moments the blood trickled out pretty freely. Meanwhile I had recovered my companion, and explained to him the nature of the phenomenon that had taken place. When he heard the real truth, he was no longer alarmed, because he knew very well that people are often buried in a trance. In fact, one night, about

eighteen months ago, he and I went to Old Saint Pancras churchyard to get up a stiff 'un, and when we opened the coffin, we found
that the body had turned completely round on its face; it was, however,
stone dead when we got it up – and never shall I forget what a
countenance it had'. (I, pp. 944–5)

Catherine Crowe's 'The Monk's Story', included in *Light and
Darkness; or, Mysteries of Life* (1850), a collection of republished
stories, which Crowe claimed in her preface were based on fact, as
seen in chapter 4, is another case in point. As with Poe's or Warren's
fictional case histories, the difficulty in defining Crowe's stories as
fiction or non-fiction illuminates the strong links in this period
between medical literature, popular magazines and fiction. 'The
Monk's Story' relates the story of Charles Lisle, a British citizen,
who spends some time in the monasteries of southern France and
Spain and encounters a somnambulist monk who re-enacts at night
the frightful murder scene he witnessed as a child. The British
perspective on this French patient is telling. The monk's somnambulist
trance turns into a cataleptic state, leading him to be nearly buried
alive. The description of the monk, '[t]he colour of his great coarse
face [being] of an unnatural whiteness, and the rigid immobility of
his features favour[ing] the idea that the man was more dead than
alive',[55] once again associates the medical patient with a living-dead
creature that is barely human:

> If I forced myself to turn away my head for a moment, round it
> would come again, and there were his two great mysterious eyes
> upon me; and that stiff jaw, slowly and mechanically moving from
> side to side, as he ate his supper, like something acted on by a pendulum.
> (p. 310)

Tension and fear are triggered by the image of the automaton,
caught in a Gothic framework, since the main (British) character is
secluded in a monastery abroad. The association of catalepsy with
automatism, the epitome of terror, is in line with the medical
literature of the time,[56] the image of the machine challenging the
boundaries and nature of the self, and constructing the patient as a
creature driven merely by 'the tyranny of a bad organisation'.[57]

Indeed, as early as in the 1850s, the work of Victorian mental physiologists on the reflex actions of the brain revealed an interest in cerebral automatism. They drew parallels between various abnormal states of consciousness, finding links between somnambulism and epilepsy (nocturnal seizures being equivalent to epileptic fits), and looked for connections in multiple instances of double consciousness.[58] In so doing, they sought to probe the mysteries of the human brain – its 'uncharted territories', in Anne Stiles's terms.[59] Sleep, in particular, intrigued specialists in this field, with catalepsy and trances more generally increasingly considered as a type of artificial sleep. The interest in, and fascination with, trances and all types of suspended animation in the second half of the nineteenth century explains why catalepsy continued to inform realistic narratives[60] and Gothic fiction alike, even if by this period the figure of the entombed cataleptic patient was regarded as a dusty relic of the early nineteenth-century tale of terror.

In the 1880s and 1890s, more tales featuring live burial and drawing on catalepsy appeared, such as Emile Zola's *La Mort d'Olivier Bécaille* (1884) (*The Death of Olivier Bécaille*), in France, seen from the perspective of a cataleptic patient, buried alive, who describes his experience in the coffin. The surge in Gothic tales featuring live burials in the last decades of the nineteenth century on both sides of the Channel, like Maupassant's short story 'Le Tic' (1884) ('The Spasm'), or Charles Diguet's 'Le Doigt de la Morte' (1887)[61] ('The Dead Woman's Finger') in which a cataleptic woman buried alive recovers consciousness when the gravedigger cuts off her finger to steal her rings, or Wilkie Collins's cataleptic characters, suggests that premature interment continued to arouse anxieties that remained unassuaged at the end of the century. Indeed, the list of titles mentioned in the following 1895 article suggests, if anything, that concern about premature burial was stronger at that point than half a century before:

[W]e need not go to America for proofs of this terrible danger, inasmuch as cases are not infrequently reported in the daily and weekly press at home. Without going into distressing details, I find the following are the titles of recent cases from well-known journals:– 'Buried Alive', 'A Gruesome Narrative', 'Premature Burial', 'Mistaken for Dead', 'A Woman's Awful Experience', 'Almost Buried While

Alive', 'A Woman Buried Alive', 'Revivication After Burial', 'A Lady Nearly Buried Alive', 'Sounds from Another Coffin', 'The Dead Alive', 'Restored to Life in a Mortuary', etc.[62]

Williamson's review of Franz Hartmann's *Buried Alive: Examination into the Occult Causes of Apparent Death, Trance and Catalepsy* (1895),[63] like others published around the same period, was not unrelated to the development of (medical) discourses on cremation. As Mary Elizabeth Hotz explains, cremationists 'resurrected the worst of the horror stories from earlier in the century' so as to 'debunk the myth about the body resting peacefully in the grave'.[64]

As I have shown elsewhere, Wilkie Collins's novels span the second half of the nineteenth century and follow closely developments in Victorian medical science until the turn of the century.[65] His late-Victorian novels in particular echo the period's fear of medical misdiagnosis or malpractice, and reflect contemporary debates on death and death-like states. In the 1860s, sensation novels by Collins and his contemporaries played recurrently with metaphors of premature burial, combining the classical Gothic live burial with wrongful incarceration, often due to dubious medical theory and practice.[66] Indeed, switches of identity and the turning of life and death into mere figures of speech are so many tricks with which the sensation novel rewrites the Gothic, as illustrated by Laura Fairlie's fate in *The Woman in White* (1860). Collins's *The Moonstone* (1868) also typifies the period's interest in double consciousness and 'unconscious cerebration', as developed by William Carpenter in his *Principles of Mental Physiology with their applications to the training and discipline of the mind and the study of its morbid conditions* (1874).

However, some of Collins's later novels, while seemingly evoking an earlier tradition of cataleptic patients, were in fact deeply anchored in the contemporary debates around the signs of death referred to earlier in this chapter.[67] Both *Jezebel's Daughter* (1880) and *Heart and Science* (1883), for instance, revolve around death-like trances. In the former case, Collins even features a dead-house, where the corpse of a poisoned character (Mrs Wagner) is to remain for three nights in one of the cells designed to store corpses temporarily. Brass thimbles are placed on her fingers, each connected to a bell:

[T]he lofty cell [was] ventilated from the top, and warmed (like the Watchman's Chamber) by an apparatus under the flooring. In the middle of the cell was a stand, placed there to support the coffin. Above the stand a horizontal bar projected, which was fixed over the doorway. It was finished with a pulley, through which passed a long thin string hanging loosely downward at one end, and attached at the other to a small alarm-bell, placed over the door on the outer side – that is to say, on the side of the Watchman's Chamber.[68]

As Collins suggests in his dedicatory preface, the waiting mortuary found at the end of *Jezebel's Daughter* is in fact based upon the one which opened in Frankfurt in 1828, designed by architect Johann Michael Voit (1771–1846). Rebuilt and enlarged in 1848, it was still in use in the 1880s. The corpses had their hands and feet connected to a system of strings leading to an alarm bell. Ventilation and heating were provided, as well as the medical equipment needed in case of resuscitation.[69] Recalling Poe's 'Premature Burial', Mrs. Wagner's cold body and inaudible heartbeat construct her like a cataleptic patient, anticipating the character of Carmina in *Heart and Science*. The latter was published at a time when neurological science was developing and interest in cerebral localisation growing. A good illustration of these trends is the neurological experiments of David Ferrier. As we saw in chapter 3, his cerebral dissection of a live monkey led to virulent protests from anti-vivisectionists. The year 1876 alone was marked by the founding of the Physiological Society by London and Cambridge physiologists and by the Cruelty to Animals Act,[70] developments which illustrate how the exploration of the substance of the brain and the mapping of the cortex was both a fertile field of research and one regarded in some quarters as a 'hellish' abomination.[71]

In *Heart and Science*, Collins makes clear from the beginning of the novel that David Ferrier's experimental studies of cerebral localisation inform his narrative.[72] The physiologist was Professor of Forensic Medicine at King's College Hospital and Medical School, London. Between 1873 and 1874, he carried out both vivisections on live animals and post-mortem experiments on the patients of the Wakefield Lunatic Asylum, to which institution his laboratory was attached.[73] Ferrier was indebted to Hughlings Jackson (1835–

1911) for the latter's work on the motor functions of certain regions of the cerebral cortex; he also drew on Alexander Bain's view of the brain and mind (his conflation of associationism with sensory-motor physiology) and Herbert Spencer's evolutionary associationism. Ferrier's work offers a striking example of late-Victorian definitions of the mind and consciousness in essentially materialistic terms, a conception which left no room for the existence of the human soul.

As Carmina, the heroine of *Heart and Science*, is compelled to live with an aunt whose cruelty she must silently and patiently endure, she exhibits growing signs of nervous disease and hysteria. She gradually sinks into a form of morbid sensitivity. The description of her weak will is couched in the language of contemporary debates about cerebral localisation. Dr Benjulia, a physiologist who researches the mysteries of the brain and experiments on animals to perfect his knowledge of cerebral diseases, is attracted to the young woman's case when her nervous anxiety turns to 'partial catalepsy': [74] 'A ghastly stare, through half-closed eyes, showed death in life, blankly returning her look' (p. 250). Rigid and dumb, insensitive to touch, and sometimes drifting into 'partial unconsciousness' (p. 280), Carmina hovers between the animate and the inanimate. As a modernised ghost-like figure, her emotional, climactic convulsions resemble those of her Radcliffean forebears, a medical representation of the *Scheintod* or death trance. In the Victorian period, the effects of shock were believed to affect the nervous system,[75] and catalepsy in particular was thought to result from 'moral shocks'.[76] Framed by medical discourse, her 'death-struck look' (p. 269) and 'simulated paralysis' (p. 313) reflect the deathlike spells then seen as characteristic of certain hysterical disorders – for example, the 'lucid hysterical lethargy' distinguished by the French neurologist Gilles de la Tourette (1857–1904).[77] In such cases, the patient's pulse rate was observed to fall, the heartbeat became inaudible, and the patient grew pale, still and cold, often remaining in that state for several days and facing therefore the risk of live burial.[78]

With her symptoms of double consciousness, Carmina is the ideal test case for Benjulia, who invites the incompetent practitioner Mr Null to help treat his patient. Benjulia is thus able to witness the evolution of the disease as Carmina's condition goes from bad to worse:

The shock that had struck Carmina had produced complicated hysterical disturbance, which was now beginning to simulate paralysis. Benjulia's profound and practised observation detected a trifling inequality in the size of the pupils of the eyes, and a slightly unequal action on either side of the face – delicately presented in the eyelids, the nostrils, and the lips. Here was no common affection of the brain, which even Mr. Null could understand! Here, at last, was Benjulia's reward for sacrificing the precious hours which might otherwise have been employed in the laboratory! From that day, Carmina was destined to receive unknown honour: she was to take her place, along with the other animals, in his note-book of experiments. (p. 290)

Carmina's 'hysterical disturbance' and 'affection of the brain' illuminate how death-like states were increasingly examined in the context of the development of neurological science and the growing interest in cerebral localisation. Probing the limits between voluntary and reflex action, cataleptic patients, like other types of automatic behaviours or dual personalities, constituted a fragmented subject which matched Gothic representations of the modern self. Bound as they were to death, these revamped spectral or entranced figures could also serve to question knowledge of the afterlife. Tales such as Jules Lermina's 'La Deux Fois Morte' (1895) ('The Woman who Died Twice') also showed how catalepsy was associated with modern ways of defining the clinical reality of death. The story relates the story of a bereaved husband who manages to resurrect momentarily the soul of his deceased wife.[79] Yet, the tale uses Poe's 'The Fall of the House of Usher' (and Madeline Usher's disorder) as an intertext, in order to suggest that medical misdiagnosis is the only explanation to the mystery of the wife's resuscitation.[80] This indirect reference to catalepsy, if surprising (since the wife is dead), reveals how the mental affection was bound to a vision of death as an organic process, which may, therefore, be reversible.[81]

Lermina's presentation of death and life as decomposition–recomposition is typical of post-Darwinian constructions of mortality. As Thomas Richards has shown, Charles Darwin had argued that decay was 'the primordial constituent of life on earth'.[82] Consequently, Richards argues, reported cases of bodies which 'remained mysteriously immune to decay after death'[83] were much more likely to evoke horror in the last decades of the nineteenth century than decomposing corpses. Richards's analysis of Bram Stoker's *Dracula* (1897) is significant in this context, particularly his idea that 'the most terrifying moments' of the novel 'come when [Stoker's] characters view the undecomposed bodies of vampires'[84] – Dracula in his box, Lucy in her tomb or the three vampires in their Transylvanian crypt. As we shall see in the next section, Stoker uses the seminal Gothic trope of the vampire both to play with (and subvert) the corpse's spiritual status and question the biological reality of death. For Anne Stiles, Stoker's 'conflicted attitude towards science' may have resulted from 'the clash between his religious upbringing and his substantial scientific education'.[85] But Stoker's references to contemporary research on the brain also raise the issue of the relationship between life, death and the afterlife – an issue which often lay at the root of scientific discourses aimed at defining death.

Indeed, the force of uncertainties about the corpse's spiritual status and the biological reality of death undoubtedly help explain how the Gothic was able to capitalise so effectively upon tales of live burial and/or dead-alive characters. As shown in chapter 1, there was a widespread belief that while the soul left the body after death, it would nonetheless 'somehow be present in or near the body after death' and could 'remain hovering around the haunts of the living'.[86] The corpse's 'uncertain metaphysical nature',[87] and many of the practices and beliefs surrounding death, may have been related to contemporary Catholicism, as Ruth Richardson has argued, and may have been useful to the Gothic's anti-Catholic stance for this precise reason. Even if 'seen as heretical by the established Church at the time they were recorded', Richardson notes, these beliefs and practices 'depended upon two essentially Christian concepts: the vicarious location of sin, and the sacramental nature of an edible communion'.[88] Popular beliefs in the transitional status of the corpse in the period between death and burial were reflected 'in omens which presaged further deaths if a corpse's eyes refused to close, or if *rigor mortis* failed to set in' – beliefs which often suggested that the corpse 'possessed both sentience and some sort of spiritual power'.[89] Moreover, Andrew Smith's study of models of death and dying in Gothic texts has shown that both evolutionary theory and the scientific method shaped views of spirituality in the last decades of the nineteenth century, often with a view to combatting 'the "dissolutive" feelings of modern subjectivity'.[90] The idea that the dead might be 'in reality, alive in some other form'[91] lies at the root of Stoker's *Dracula*, the vampire functioning, in Smith's words, 'as an image of a living corpse that suggests that death is not quite the end'.[92] Hence, at the turn of the century, Stoker's vampires would become key motifs to map out anxieties related to the definition and meaning of the corpse and to explore the status and fate of the soul after death.

'She sleeps, and sleeps, and sleeps!': catalepsy and vampirism

In a series of articles published in *Blackwood's* in the 1840s entitled 'Letters on the Truths contained in Popular Superstitions', the anatomist Herbert Mayo (1796–1852) suggested that vampires may actually be but 'ordinary people that had been buried alive'.[93] According to Andrew Mangham, moreover, the fear of being buried alive, or *taphephobia*, emerged 'as a diagnostic label in the 1890s'.[94] The link between vampirism and taphephobia is particularly visible in the case of *Dracula*. As the plot mimics that of older Gothic romances, the vampire-hunt enables Stoker to probe the boundaries between sleep and death and rewrite vampirism as a search for the signs of death, a theme that resonated with contemporary debates on fears of premature burial.

The connection made by Mayo between vampirism and medical science is far from unexpected. Other celebrated medical case histories had already been linked to vampirism, such as that of Sergeant Bertrand, nicknamed 'The French Vampire', cited in an article published in the *Journal of Psychological Medicine and Mental Pathology* in July 1849. Medical cases were also used by both G. W. M. Reynolds and Catherine Crowe, and featured as well in Sabine Baring-Gould's *Book of Were-Wolves* (1865), which Stoker consulted when researching *Dracula*.[95] In Reynolds's *Mysteries of the Court of London*, the sequel to *Mysteries of London*, which ran from 1847 to 1856, the way in which the case history is cited suggests that psychiatric discourse was gradually superseding the

body-snatching tale, with the pathological discourse and morbid
body replacing the fear of the body-snatchers:

> 'Dreadful, indeed! . . . There never was such a thing known before:
> at least so the papers say. For, mark you – this is no affair in which
> resurrection-men are engaged – nor yet robbers. Body-snatchers
> don't leave the corpse behind them: – and the day's gone by when
> people were buried with rings on their fingers' . . .
> 'But I s'pose it's some Bedlamite that's broke loose and is amusing
> his-self in this uncommon style?'
> 'Or else it must be a cannibal', suggested another listener . . .
> 'It may be a madman – but this is not a cannibal', said Minks: 'for it
> don't appear that he has made a meal on the corpses. His delight
> seems to be to hack and hew them to pieces; and in all this there's
> what the papers call a fiendish revelry in the horrible pastime of
> exhuming and mutilating the dead'.[96]

Bram Stoker's creature was directly inspired by *The Vampyre*
(1819), written by English writer and physician John William
Polidori. However, late-Victorian research into mental physiology
and the growing interest in cerebral localisation were also major
influences. Polidori himself had been interested in somnambulism,
as his medical dissertation illustrates, and, as Anne Stiles has shown,
Stoker's vampires 'exhibit semi-conscious, trance-like behaviours
that owed much to late-Victorian interest in cerebral automatism
and unconscious cerebration'.[97] Moreover, Stoker's references to
contemporary Victorian physiologists, from David Ferrier and John
Scott Burdon-Sanderson (1828–1905) to Jean-Martin Charcot
(1825–93) and William Benjamin Carpenter (1813–85), evidence
his desire to present vampires as 'soulless machines governed solely
by physiological impulses'.[98]

Significantly, Stiles contends, Stoker also drew on older sources,
such as Robert Gray's *The Theory of Dreams* (1808), which examined
dreams, sleep and sleepwalking, and even quoted several case studies
of cataleptic patients.[99] Gray saw sleep as a 'suspension of the mental
as well as of the corporeal powers', and argued that during sleep
'the links of connection which subsist between the soul and body'
were loosened.[100] Seen as a 'sepulchre', sleep was thus defined as

the moment when the 'spirit' might be 'released' from its material prison.[101] The merging of such contrasting sources and references recalls Lermina's depiction of his character's experiment aimed at resurrecting the soul of his dead wife in 'La Deux Fois Morte' ('The Woman who Died Twice') – an experiment which conflated scientific and more metaphysical conceptions of the corpse. Stoker was also said to have been impressed by the opening of Elizabeth Siddal's coffin in 1869. Siddal – the wife of Dante Gabriel Rossetti, and Stoker's neighbour – had been found perfectly preserved seven years after her death, her hair having continued to grow so that it filled the coffin.[102]

Andrew Smith has shown how *Dracula* represents an example par excellence of late-nineteenth-century Gothic, shot through as it is with *fin-de-siècle* epistemological reflections on death. As a novel about 'the dead undead' – as its title suggests[103] – *Dracula* 'raises epistemic questions about how we gain knowledge about the dead'.[104] Indeed, for Smith, Dracula 'symbolises death'. The novel's investigation of death is thus carried out through decoding the vampire and understanding how 'death might not die'.[105] Building on both Smith's and Richards's arguments, it could be argued that *Dracula* is steeped in evolutionary discourses which emerge not only through depictions of the Count as a creature able to adapt to its environment, whose body and brain grow simultaneously,[106] or through the hints at degeneration which pepper the narrative ('he is of imperfectly formed mind', p. 296), but also through images of death, and of the reading of death, that are typical of the *fin-de-siècle* period.

Dracula hints repeatedly at Siddal's mysterious resistance to decay and her eternal sleep. The novel thus plays recurrently with the theme: characters wait for sleep, welcome sleep, deny sleep, fight sleep or lapse into sleep; they feel very sleepy, appear very sleepy, sleep a great deal or not at all; they forget they have fallen asleep, they oversleep or cannot be awoken; they refuse to admit they have fallen asleep, pretend to sleep, refuse to sleep or are asked to. When too agitated to sleep, furthermore, they take sedatives (chloral hydrate (p. 228), morphia (p. 119) or laudanum (p. 132)), while some look as if under the influence of opiates (p. 251). Sleep is 'happy' (p. 282), refreshing or uneasy; enjoyed or feared. In short, the whole vampire narrative revolves around sleep, as Dracula's victims are entranced or literally sleepwalk to their fates. Furthermore, the vampire himself finally threatens to escape his opponents through sleep. Sleep thus contributes to the uncanny atmosphere of the novel, which oscillates between the world of dreams and fairy tales and that of nightmares and Gothic creatures, as the characters wonder whether they are waking or dreaming, rub their eyes and pinch themselves. While *Dracula* does allude at times to the realm of fairy tales, referring to Charles Perrault's *Little Red Riding Hood* (p. 174) or Hans Christian Andersen's *The Ugly Duckling* (p. 295) to represent the vampire as a wolf-like creature able to take on multiple appearances and forms, the novel's play on lifelike death remains nevertheless firmly grounded in contemporary research on cerebral localisation.

At the beginning of the novel, as Jonathan Harker travels to Dracula's castle, the solicitor does not sleep well, believing his nightmares to result from the spicy local food or from a dog howling under his window. Although Harker is travelling away from the stresses of modern life, his senses are constantly stimulated in Transylvania: sounds, food and drink seem to enter his body, just like the vampires' musical laugh, their voices 'tingling' (p. 42) through the nerves of the young man. Everything around him involves him physically: the electric atmosphere of the coming storm, 'the heavy, oppressive sense of thunder' (p. 16), the mountains 'seem[ing] to come nearer . . . on each side' (p. 16). In addition, the characters he meets on his way seem entranced: 'Here and there was a peasant man or woman kneeling before a shrine, who did not even turn round as we approached, but seemed in the self-surrender of devotion to have neither eyes nor ears for the outer world' (p. 15). Harker's senses increasingly play tricks on him as he nears the castle: the coach rocks or flies, the coachman does not seem to obstruct the blue flame they are following, and Harker believes his eyes '[deceive] [him] straining through the darkness' (p. 19). In addition, he hears the sound of dogs howling, which 'seemed to come from all over the country, as far as the imagination could grasp it through the gloom of the night'. Indeed, he ends up convincing himself that he must have fallen asleep, until the castle suddenly looming up in front of him brings him back to his senses. Overstimulation leads to faintness or unconsciousness, it seems, the reader probably recalling

Dracula's first written welcome, in the shape of a letter, advising Harker to 'Sleep well' (p. 12). Harker's sleep deprivation during his journey is only the first stage of his experience of vampirism. As he stands outside Dracula's castle, time seems endless, and 'all seem[s] like a horrible nightmare' to him (p. 21). From the beginning, in fact, Harker's hallucinations and his mounting nervousness connect sleep (or the lack of it) with the character's nervous system, building up links between vampirism and mental disorder which will be developed throughout the narrative.

Furthermore, as soon as Harker enters Dracula's castle, the statue-like Count welcomes him and advises him not to sleep outside of his bedroom:

> Let me advise you, my dear young friend – nay, let me warn you with all seriousness, that should you leave these rooms you will not by any chance go to sleep in any other part of the castle. It is old, and has many memories, and there are bad dreams for those who sleep unwisely. Be warned! Should sleep now or ever overcome you, or be like to do, then haste to your own chamber or to these rooms, for your rest will then be safe. But if you be not careful in this respect, then— (p. 38)

Dracula's second reference to sleep is telling. Sleep is associated with rules not to be broken, as in a fairy tale, and Harker's nightmare reaches a climax when he falls asleep where he should not have. The Count's strictures link the figure of the Gothic villain to that of Bluebeard, and the latter's warning to his wife not to enter the secret chamber. Sleep in *Dracula* is thus defined as dangerous – even deadly – paving the way for the equation between sleep and death which marks the whole of the vampire narrative and Stoker's rewriting of the Sleeping Beauty myth. Of course, Harker ignores the Count's advice – indeed, he takes 'pleasure in disobeying it' (p. 41) – and, like a Gothic heroine, he lies helpless 'where of old ladies had sat and sung and lived sweet lives whilst their gentle breasts were sad for their menfolk away in the midst of remorseless wars' (p. 41). Harker also loses control over his body. Again resembling a prototypical Gothic heroine, he is held prisoner and has no control over the door of his bedroom. His 'mad' (p. 32) nervous system also takes on a life of its own, and ultimately becomes subjugated to Dracula's mesmerising powers. Eventually, suffering from a brain fever after his escape from the castle, Harker literally becomes Sleeping Beauty: he lies on a bed, sleeping most of the time, until his fiancée Mina joins him in Budapest and marries him just as he awakens (p. 100). Sleep is thus as much linked with the Gothic nightmare as with romance, linking vampirism with sexuality. Mina believes, indeed, that men and women should be allowed to see each other asleep before committing to each other (p. 87), and Dracula's first victim, Lucy Westenra, who symbolises feminine hypersensitivity and passivity as a sleepwalker, receives three propositions of marriage, all of which she would like to accept. But Lucy's desire, signalling the character's uncontrolled pursuit of pleasure,[107] is soon read as a mysterious illness – perhaps due to an abuse of her nerves.

Harker's experience in Transylvania, closing with his brain fever and his confinement to bed, launches a series of images of medical patients suffering from sleeping difficulties. Unlike Transylvania, the Western world – in the guise of *fin-de-siècle* England – is defined by technology: telegraphs and phonographs are used as modes of communication, while trains transport passengers at high speeds to various parts of the country or the world. This stressful modern urban existence which lurks in the shadows of the narrative may explain why sleep remains a recurrent source of anxiety in the part of the novel set in England. Opiates are prescribed to patients by physicians, and the declining health of Lucy Westenra, who suffers from sleepwalking fits, becomes a subject of medical interest. Ironically, in reality the characters' unbalanced nervous systems are related far less to modern technology than to the presence of a vampire. As Dracula reaches the British shores, Mina and Lucy become more and more nervous: Mina cannot sleep and Lucy is restless. The latter is looked after by Mina, who records in her diary all her friend's physical symptoms, from her 'anaemic look' to her breathing:

> Lucy seems to be growing weaker, whilst her mother's hours are numbering to a close. I do not understand Lucy's fading as she is doing. She eats well and sleeps well, and enjoys the fresh air; but all

the time the roses in her cheeks are fading, and she gets weaker and more languid day by day; at night I hear her gasping as if for air. (p. 92)

Lucy, who 'feels influences more acutely than other people do' (p. 85), is thus presented from the beginning as a medical patient. She fears she may be influenced by what she sees during the day and have nightmares, highlighting her hypersensitivity. The female character increasingly matches artistic representations of the consumptive woman, at a time when phthisis (or sometimes tuberculosis) was aestheticised in Victorian art.[108] As illustrated by Rossetti's representations of Elizabeth Siddal, whose uncannily preserved corpse, as we noted, may have influenced Stoker, the cult of invalidism and the cult of the dead woman worked in tandem throughout the period, and images of consumptive women oscillated between saintly emblems of womanhood and more sexually transgressive ones. Katherine Byrne's analysis of vampirism as pathology in *Dracula* is significant in this context. She argues that the mysteries of certain wasting diseases, like phthisis, and the difficulties encountered by medical practitioners in curing patients, could explain the rise of supernatural explanations of vampirism and the development of 'alternative' cures involving manipulations of the body/corpse, such as the removal of the heart.[109] As Lucy becomes an 'interesting' medical case, the doctors look for 'functional disturbance[s] or any malady that [they] know of' (p. 104), make 'diagnos[e]s' (p. 105), and beg to have a 'full opportunity of examination' (p. 104). But the novel also shows how, because she attracts medical interest, Lucy falls victim to medical experimentation. Unbeknown to her, a blood test is performed on her after she cuts her hand:

I could easily see that she is somewhat bloodless, but I could not see the usual anaemic signs, and by a chance I was actually able to test the quality of her blood, for in opening a window which was stiff a cord gave way, and she cut her hand slightly with broken glass. It was a slight matter in itself, but it gave me an evident chance, and I secured a few drops of the blood and have analysed them. The qualitative analysis gives a quite normal condition, and shows, I should infer, in itself a vigorous state of health. In other physical matters I was quite satisfied that there is no need for anxiety; but as there must be a cause somewhere, I have come to the conclusion that it must be something mental. (p. 105)

Dr Seward suspects 'something mental' and asks Professor Van Helsing, a specialist of 'obscure diseases' (p. 105), to examine the patient. This episode reveals how physical phenomena, like neurasthenia, or even hysteria, were gradually understood at the end of the nineteenth century through the workings of the nervous system. This idea connects once again vampirism with psychiatric discourse, paving the way for later parallels between Lucy and Seward's mental patient, Renfield. Indeed, Seward's interpretation of vampirism as a mental disease[110] allows Stoker to introduce significant allusions to contemporary research into mental physiology. As Seward's diagnosis suggests, Lucy's consumptive symptoms – the signs of vampirism – seem to result from her hypersensitivity or her sleep-walking fits, trance-like phases that typify hysterical manifestations. Moreover, because such unconscious states were believed to evince the sufferer's weak will, Lucy becomes the ideal medical patient, just as she is Dracula's ideal victim: naturally passive, she obeys and is even mesmerised by Dracula from a distance, following without question the vampire's will. The image of Lucy as Sleeping Beauty thus gradually comes to symbolise a state of double consciousness and to illustrate the 'complete subjection of the consciousness'.[111] Her weak will, as Mina observes, explains why Lucy yields every time: 'her will is thwarted in any physical way' (p. 84).[112]

However, after the vampire's bite, Lucy's bones show through her skin, and her pallor makes her look like 'a corpse after a prolonged illness' (p. 118): 'She was ghastly, chalkily pale; the red seemed to have gone even from her lips and gums, and the bones of her face stood out prominently; her breathing was painful to see or hear' (p. 112). This description of the vampirised female character recalls other contemporary mental disorders related to progressive physical decline, from chlorosis and dyspepsia to anorexia nervosa and hysteria. Just as Pip refuses to acknowledge the decaying body of Miss Havisham in *Great Expectations*, so the sight of Lucy's corpse-like appearance is unbearable to the medical professionals: the signs of decay undermine the reassuring image of wholeness represented by Sleeping Beauty's body eternally frozen in youth and evading death.

Revealingly, in order to cure her, the medical professionals – Dr Seward and Professor Van Helsing – first prescribe her an opiate. Indeed, ironically, part of the cure consists in turning Lucy into Sleeping Beauty before the blood transfusion, enabling thereby Lord Godalming to play the role of Prince Charming just before the medical experiment:

> The time seemed endless until sleep began to flicker in her eyelids. At last, however, the narcotic began to manifest its potency; and she fell into a deep sleep. When the Professor was satisfied he called Arthur into the room, and bade him strip off his coat. Then he added: 'You may take that one little kiss while I bring over the table. Friend John, help me!' So neither of us looked whilst he bent over her. (p. 114)

Both the opiate and the blood transfusion are closely related to contemporary concerns about the blurred boundary between sleep and death, and hint at experiments carried out by physiologists in this period.[113] The medicalisation of Sleeping Beauty (the sedative chloral hydrate is also defined by Seward as 'the modern Morpheus' (p. 97), turning the god of dreams into a chemical formula) highlights the tensions informing the image of woman's eternal sleep. Since the experiment aims at evading/avoiding decomposition, the male characters' attempts to assert medical control over the woman's body are also attempts to assert medical control over death. The cure thus illuminates the scientific exploration of death which runs through the novel, revealing in so doing the way in which Stoker partook of a 'culture [which] tried to make sense of the apparent permeability between the living and the dead'.[114] Ironically, however, by prolonging life, the cure emphasises even more the 'undecomposed bodies of vampires'[115] on which the novel's horror hinges.

Unsurprisingly, the vampire, 'an image of a living corpse that suggests that death is not quite the end',[116] pricks the interest of Dr Seward, whose research revolves around explorations of cerebral localisation. As suggested above, the novel establishes links between vampirism and research into mental disorders. Seward is an alienist familiar with Charcot's work, while Professor Van Helsing later hypnotises Mina, who sits 'stock still' (p. 271), as if dead. Mina's visual description of her feelings is telling: 'It is like death' (p. 272); 'I am deeper in death at this moment than if the weight of an earthly grave lay heavy upon me' (p. 288). Her words evoke the cataleptic patient's death-like state, as if she had also been entombed alive. As Mina's hypnotic trance intimates, therefore, the search for the vampire is also a medical quest to solve mysteries of mental physiology. Somnambulism and hypnosis were often equated in the second half of the nineteenth century. Indeed, the latter was often described as 'artificial somnambulism',[117] as the following article indicates:

> Both natural and artificial somnambulism are mere modifications of ordinary sleep, differing from it in proportion to a more or less intense activity of the nervous system, and consequently very often accompanied by cataleptic, hysterical, and other symptoms not usually present in this condition of the system . . . All the instances of particular seizures with which history or his own observation supplied him convinced Dr. Bertrand that artificial somnambulism, however produced, is but a species of ecstatic catalepsy – a rare disease, but one sufficiently well known for its characteristics to be clearly ascertained, and sometimes even assuming an epidemic form.[118]

In *Dracula*, the two female patients who are vampirised illustrate cases of abnormal states of consciousness, and it is revealing that they are treated with opiates and sedatives. Van Helsing's experiments hence recall contemporary attempts at interpreting types of sleep and pathological states, from lethargy to catalepsy,[119] and probe therefore the boundary between sleep and death.

Furthermore, from the very beginning of the novel, the figure of the vampire, who sleeps in coffins and ancient churchyards, enables Stoker to investigate Victorian definitions of the corpse and highlight anxieties related to the definition of death. Although the vampire is undead, when Harker discovers Dracula in his coffin, the ruined chapel, together with the 'sickly odour, the odour of old earth newly turned' (p. 50), which recur in the novel every time the characters look for Dracula and his coffins, construct the vampire as a corpse. Interestingly, the role of medical professionals in pronouncing death is stressed several times, as when a surgeon examines the corpse fastened to the helm of the schooner before placing it in a mortuary 'to await inquest' (p. 79) (that is, perhaps, to perform a post-mortem examination); or when Dr Seward and Van Helsing hastily fill in death certificates for Lucy and her mother so that they may be buried quickly and without further examination (p. 137). Yet, as Richards has underlined, if the creature is abject and the 'horrid thing' must be 'hid[den] . . . from [his] sight' (p. 54), this is, first and foremost, because it fails to resemble a corpse. Seeing that the Count's eyes are 'open and stony, but without the glassiness of death' (p. 50), Harker wonders whether he is 'dead or asleep' (p. 50), although the smell and the site (a former graveyard) hint at decomposition.[120]

The case is similar for Lucy's corpse. The narrative illuminates the work of undertakers, performing the last offices for the dead, who are concerned about the appearance of the corpse (they are relieved to see that Lucy's corpse will not shock the audience of the death-chamber). Yet, as a vampirised woman, Lucy appears first and foremost as an embalmed corpse, exemplifying arrested decomposition. Lying 'in all its death-beauty' (p. 190), her body blurs the boundary between life and death, turning the corpse into an object of the gaze. But, as already suggested, Lucy's corpse spurs Dr Seward and Professor Van Helsing into action. As soon as the young woman has been buried, they take on the role of pathologists (Dr Seward is later defined as 'a medico-jurist as well as scientist' (p. 215)), and decide to unscrew the coffin-lid and 'operate' on the corpse with their 'post-mortem knives' (p. 149), as if for an 'autopsy':

'Tomorrow, I want you to bring me, before night, a set of post-mortem knives'.
'Must we make an autopsy?' I asked.
'Yes, and no. I want to operate, but not as you think . . . Ah! you a surgeon, and so shocked! . . . when she is coffined ready for the next day, you and I shall come when all sleep. We shall unscrew the coffin-lid, and shall do our operation; and then replace all, so that none know, save we alone'. (p. 149)

The scene constructs the medical practitioners as body-snatchers, with Dr Seward pointing out the monstrosity of the deed and wondering about the benefit 'to science' or 'to human knowledge' (p. 149). Moreover, the idea that Lucy might have been 'buried alive' (p. 180) potently links vampirism with death-like medical states, such as catalepsy. This idea is in keeping with Mina's suggestion that Lucy's trance-like bouts of sleepwalking in her nightdress and her nightly encounter with the vampire may have induced a moral shock.[121] In addition, several stories of individuals buried alive punctuate the narrative, appearing as soon as Dracula arrives in England, as if to pave the way for Lucy's live burial. Thus, a reference to Whitby Abbey (p. 63) recalls Walter Scott's 'Marmion' (1808), in which the nun Constance de Beverley ends up walled up alive in the dungeon. Similarly, later in the narrative, Van Helsing attempts to explain vampirism through stories of entranced people buried alive and resurrected, such as that of the Indian fakir (p. 172).

These allusions to the kind of mental disorders that aroused medical interest in the second half of the nineteenth century explain why Lucy is seen as a significant case study, even – or above all – after her death. Tellingly, Seward and Van Helsing are compared to body-snatchers braving 'the perils of the law which [they] were incurring in [their] unhallowed work' (p. 178), a parallel reinforced when they later find the coffin empty and Van Helsing swears 'by all that [he] hold[s] sacred that [he has] not removed nor touched' the corpse (p. 185). From the beginning of the novel, moreover, Stoker's medical professionals are linked to anatomical practice. Van Helsing has a surgical case (p. 241); Dr Seward constantly plays with his lancet, nearly making Lucy scream (p. 58). Seward is even tempted to perform a vivisection on his patient Renfield, following in the footsteps of David Ferrier who, as we have seen, conducted autopsies on patients from the West Riding Lunatic Asylum. When involved in the vivisection of live animals, Ferrier rendered his subjects insensible by the use of chloroform,[122] just as Seward gives Renfield strong opiates:

> Men sneered at vivisection, and yet look at its results today! Why not advance science in its most difficult and vital aspect – the knowledge of the brain? Had I even the secret of one such mind – did I hold the key to the fancy of even one lunatic – I might advance my own branch of science to a pitch compared with which Burdon-Sanderson's

physiology or Ferrier's brain-knowledge would be as nothing. If only there were a sufficient cause! I must not think too much of this, or I may be tempted; a good cause might turn the scale with me, for may not I too be of an exceptional brain, congenitally? (p. 71)

The passage underlines the novel's obsession with research into mental physiology. Although the novel draws on *fin-de-siècle* criminal anthropology to define the vampire as a born criminal,[123] the framing of Dracula's 'child-brain' (p. 296) is preceded by Seward's observation of his patient in the lunatic asylum and his theorisation on 'unconscious cerebration' (p. 69), recalling how William Carpenter's research itself was influenced by Ferrier's experiments (the latter's 1873 vivisection experiments were included in an appendix to his *Principles of Mental Physiology*).[124]

Thus, Seward and Van Helsing's killing of Lucy-as-vampire, which involves first piercing her heart and then cutting off her head, enables the medical professionals to get closer 'to the heart' (p. 61) of the mysteries of death. Unable to win Lucy's hand, Seward eventually metaphorically possesses her heart. The body of the vampire, cut into pieces, grotesquely hints at anatomical practice and 'positive' medicine. The stake and headless corpse are the keys to the solution, it seems, in a novel which nevertheless constructs death as a shifting process – an elusive reality which cannot be grasped by signifiers, like the letters on the tombstones of Whitby's churchyard which '[fail] to recall the dead'[125] since the graves are empty. Thus, the body of the vampire in *Dracula* highlights the significance of the corpse and sensationalises the *fin-de-siècle* reading of the signs of death, suggesting that 'death is potentially knowable'.[126] The vampire, as a Gothic variation of the figure of the cataleptic patient, is ultimately but a new medical case history for medical professionals to record and study.

Epilogue: The Vanishing Corpse

❧

And after that, as his peculiar qualities allowed, he passed out of
human perceptions altogether, and he was neither heard, seen, nor
felt in Iping anymore. He vanished absolutely.[1]

We saw in chapter 5 that the mysteries of death and the baffling
phenomenon of the human corpse lay at the root of both anatomical
investigations and Gothic fiction in the period under study. Dissecting
the undead, as Dr Seward, Van Helsing and Harker demonstrate
when they cut through the vampire's flesh and plunge their knives
into its heart, ultimately makes the corpse vanish: Dracula's body
crumbles into dust and passes out of sight. By having the corpse
disappear in this way, Stoker's Gothic text sensationalises the growing
invisibility (and shifting significance) of the dead body at the turn
of the nineteenth and twentieth centuries.

Gothic Remains: Corpses, Terror and Anatomical Culture, 1764–1897
has argued that corpses – whether skeletons, artificial models, stolen
commodities, displayed specimens or undead bodies – participated
fully in the creation of the Gothic, a striking symbol of the horror
and of the broader significance of death in this period – from Ann
Radcliffe's iconic decomposing corpse to Stoker's un-decomposing
vampires. Moreover, *Gothic Remains* has also demonstrated how an
understanding of these now classic Gothic tropes is inextricably
bound up with the context from which they emerged. The traffic

between literature and medicine we have increasingly emphasised throughout the chapters, so as to illuminate the parallel evolution of the generic stereotypes of medical Gothic and Victorian medical science, the blurring of boundaries between tales of terror and medical case histories, as well as the Gothic aesthetic which informed medical writing during the same period, are so many examples of the cross-fertilisation of the medical and literary fields. It becomes, thus, no longer possible to regard the skeleton and its other accomplices in crime in Gothic texts as mere 'source[s] . . . of conceits',[2] in Mario Praz's words, or as baroque memento mori. Rather, these usual suspects need to be seen as realistic and scientific objects borrowed from the writers' everyday reality.

It follows, therefore, that as these objects became less central to medical education and practice, they tended to vanish from Gothic texts as well, especially around the turn of the twentieth century. As Kelly Hurley has shown, *fin-de-siècle* Gothic reflected anxieties about the nature of human identity – 'an anxiety generated by scientific discourses, biological and sociomedical'.[3] Hurley has underlined in particular the impact of the Darwinian evolutionary narrative on late-Victorian Gothic, notably T. H. Huxley's work on protoplasm, the effect of which was to radically undermine the 'solidity of the body'.[4] The idea that 'any transfiguration of form'[5] was within the realm of the possible informed the Gothic texts of the last decades of the nineteenth century and beyond, the genre reflecting 'human entrapment within the realm of matter'.[6] Hurley's stress on 'the gothicity of matter'[7] in *fin-de-siècle* Gothic parallels the 'distinct biological and anthropological cast' noted by Robert Mighall in works by Robert Louis Stevenson, Rider Haggard, Arthur Conan Doyle, Arthur Machen and Bram Stoker. All of this group, Mighall observes, belong to a 'new breed of Gothic fiction', interested in 'the bodies of savages, criminals, and degenerates'.[8] However, if Hurley's and Mighall's historicist approach to the Gothic[9] points to the role of evolutionary theory as a necessary backdrop to such new Gothic works, it has been suggested in this book that fresh insights may be gained by looking at the changes in the trajectory of the Gothic through a wider lens, one which includes aspects of the history of medicine, science and technology, as well as evolutionary theory.

As we saw in the introduction, the opening scene of Stevenson's *Strange Case of Dr Jekyll and Mr Hyde* (1886) hints at the dethroning of anatomy, for Dr Jekyll's laboratory is set up in the former dissecting rooms of a celebrated surgeon – most probably an allusion to John Hunter. A similar casting away of anatomical culture can be seen in a short story by C. R. T. Crosthwaite entitled 'Röntgen's Curse', published in 1896. The short story, informed by the invention of the X-ray by Wilhelm Röntgen (1845–1923) in 1895, relates the story of an ambitious scientist trained in chemistry and fascinated with Röntgen's discovery, who invents a drug that enables people to see as if with X-ray vision. Blind to the results of the experiment on his terrified dog, the scientist takes the drug himself so as to be able to 'see the working of the vital organs and their condition'.[10] However, the narrative shifts to the Gothic when the narrator realises he has himself become a skeleton:

> I began now to realise what I had done, and to feel that knowledge might be too perfect. Up to this time I had not paid much attention to anything beyond my table and my own hands and arms. Rising now from my chair, I saw that to my eyes I was a skeleton, with metal buttons and a watch and chain belonging to it in some mysterious way without touching it. I could see that my legs were nothing but bones without either clothes or flesh, although I was strangely conscious of the presence of both. It was a ghastly and sickening sight to look down at my legs and body and see the bare bones of my own skeleton, and watch the motions of the uncovered, or apparently uncovered, joints. (p. 476)

Crosthwaite's rewriting of Stevenson's 'double consciousness' or 'doubling of the personality'[11] as the narrator realises that he has become the Other – the skeleton, a figure of horror – is significant, both for the way in which it illustrates how the Gothic absorbs new technologies and for how it points to the end of anatomy as the supreme mode of access to knowledge. The characters encountered by the scientist, such as the 'eminent London physician' who looks like a 'grotesque collection of bones' (p. 480) turn the logic of the medical museum on its head, just as the scene mocks the conventions of the medical consultation:

About the man, as he was in the flesh, there was nothing absurd, but the skeleton, and especially the skull, had an air of priggish conceit that moved me to assault him. He felt my pulse again and examined me carefully with a stethoscope, took my temperature, looked at my tongue, and questioned me closely as to the state of my health. Then he began, evidently of a purpose, to discuss current events and every-day topics. It required all the self-control of which I was capable to look at him and keep my countenance while this was going on. The solemn movements of the physician-skeleton were sublimely burlesque. (p. 481)

While indeed 'burlesque', just like Stoker's dead undead, Cros-thwaite's skeleton is 'all the more dreadful *because* it [is] alive' (p. 478) (my emphasis). There is still room for an element of humour, however: when the narrator looks at his wife lying in bed, husband and wife both take fright, and the object of fear becomes impossible to locate – and thus to control:

There in her accustomed place beside me lay my wife's skeleton, as it were the skeleton of one who had died in her sleep long years ago and had been left to lie undisturbed. There it lay beside me, and I nearly touched the skull as I turned. I put out my hands to save my face from the hateful contact, when the arms began to move as if they would enfold me in their embrace. I could control my terror no longer. With the shriek of a madman I leapt from the bed. The skeleton rose with a start and tried to grasp me. I heard my wife's voice uttering a cry of fear. I tried to escape; my foot caught in something, and I fell heavily, and I remember no more. (p. 483)

The presentation of the skeleton in Crosthwaite's grotesque is very different from that favoured by earlier generations of anatomists, and thus stands in marked contrast with its portrayal in *Gothic Remains*. Crosthwaite's short story also shows how late-Victorian Gothic writing emphasised new ways of looking at, reading and knowing the human body. Similarly, in *The Strange Case of Dr Jekyll and Mr Hyde*, just as in H. G. Wells's *The Island of Dr Moreau* (1896) and *The Invisible Man* (1897), chemistry and experimentation – or vivisection – supplant anatomy and dissection. Wells's invisible man, whose nose rolls on the floor, is but 'a black cavity' (p. 167), identified more by the many bottles and test-tubes he carries than by his fragmented body: 'They were prepared for scars, disfigurement, tangible horrors, but *nothing!*' (p. 168).

Wells's characters, dissolving into thin air or able to take any shape, thereby challenging the taxonomy of species, Stevenson's parody of the medical case study,[12] or again Crosthwaite's grotesque, mocking as it does medical practitioners' attempts at seeing 'the working of the vital organs and their condition' (p. 470), all, in their different ways, denounce scientific research. Even more significantly, perhaps, each of these works also relinquishes the corpse as the essential 'object and source of knowledge'[13] and of anatomical culture more generally. In sharp contrast with these developments, we have seen in the preceding chapters of this book that the years between 1764 and 1897 (and especially between the 1790s and the 1890s) were marked above all by clinical realism. These were years when, in innumerable Gothic texts, writers borrowed from contemporary methods of analysis and representation to highlight the impossibility of communicating the reality of the fragmented – or dissected – self.

Maggie Kilgour argues that from the late nineteenth century onwards, 'the gothic dead have increasingly returned in fragmented forms that are not re-membered, like the mutilated corpse in W. W. Jacobs's classic short story, "The Monkey's Paw"' (1902).[14] This impossible re-membering haunts, indeed, the Gothic of the early twentieth century. A good example is W. F. Harvey's 'The Beast with Five Fingers' (1928), in which an embalmed hand lives a life of its own, an idea inspired by Maurice Renard's *The Hands of Orlac* (1920). No longer locked up in glass cases and exhibited in medical museums, these monstrous body parts effectively breathed new life and new agency into those voiceless and nameless 'remains' or 'materials' collected by inhumane anatomists. What was previously inanimate could now go bump in the night and strike back – with a vengeance. As for the body-snatchers who had for decades provided the anatomists with their raw materials, they could, perhaps, be laid to rest, at least for a few decades, peacefully awaiting their resurrection with later twentieth-century Gothic in the vein of

Patrick McGrath's fiction, for instance. In the meantime, the Gothic body – un-re-membered, but not unremembered – would be doing its own snatching.

Notes

❧

Introduction

1   Elisabeth Bronfen, *Over Her Dead Body: Death, Femininity and the Aesthetic* (Manchester: Manchester University Press, 1992).

2   Sharon Ruston, *Creating Romanticism: Case Studies in the Literature, Science and Medicine of the 1790s* (Basingstoke: Palgrave Macmillan, 2013), p. 2.

3   Ann Jessie Van Sant, *Eighteenth-Century Sensibility and the Novel. The Senses in Social Context* (Cambridge: Cambridge University Press, 1993), p. 12.

4   Karl Figlio, 'Theories of Perception and the Physiology of Mind in the Late Eighteenth Century', *History of Science*, 12 (1975), 177–212 (p. 177), quoted in Van Sant, *Eighteenth-Century Sensibility and the Novel*, p. 13.

5   G. J. Barker-Benfield, *The Culture of Sensibility: Sex and Society in Eighteenth-Century Britain* (Chicago and London: University of Chicago Press, 1996), pp. 20–2.

6   Ann Radcliffe, *The Mysteries of Udolpho* (1794) (Oxford: Oxford University Press, 1980), p. 15. All subsequent references are to this edition and will be given in the text.

7   Barker-Benfield, *The Culture of Sensibility*, p. 22.

8   Mrs Carver, *The Old Woman* (1800) (s.l.: Dodo Press, 2011), p. 9. All subsequent references are to this edition and will be given in the text.

9   Ann Radcliffe, *The Romance of the Forest* (1791) (Oxford: Oxford University Press, 2009), p. 5.

10 'She was one of those many on whom fortune had set a mark of persecution at a very early period' (p. 158); 'the innocence of that suffering angel' (p. 199); 'there is a long narrative produced by her sufferings' (p. 207).

11 Ingrid H. Tague, *Animal Companions: Pets and Social Change in Eighteenth-Century Britain* (University Park, PA: Pennsylvania State University Press, 2015), p. 192.

12 Van Sant, *Eighteenth-Century Sensibility and the Novel*, p. 56.

13 Van Sant, *Eighteenth-Century Sensibility and the Novel*, p. 59.

14 Van Sant, *Eighteenth-Century Sensibility and the Novel*, p. 59.

15 Anne C. Vila, *Enlightenment and Pathology* (Baltimore and London: John Hopkins University Press, 1998), p. 6.

16 Michel Foucault, *The History of Sexuality*, trans. Robert Hurley (New York: Pantheon Books, 1978), vol. I, p. 117, quoted in Robert Miles, *Gothic Writing, 1750–1820: A Genealogy*, 2nd edn (1993) (Manchester and New York: Manchester University Press, 2002), p. 20.

17 Miles, *Gothic Writing 1750–1820*, p. 2. Miles quotes here David Punter's reading of the Gothic in *The Literature of Terror. Vol. 1. The Gothic Tradition* (New York: Routledge, 1996).

18 Miles, *Gothic Writing 1750–1820*, p. 12.

19 Miles, *Gothic Writing 1750–1820*, p. 3.

20 Caroline McCraker-Flesher, *The Doctor Dissected: A Cultural Autopsy of the Burke and Hare Murders* (Oxford: Oxford University Press, 2012), p. 50.

21 Roy Porter, *Flesh in the Age of Reason: How the Enlightenment Transformed the Way We See Our Bodies and Souls* (London: Penguin, 2003), p. xiii.

22 I am following Miles's genealogy of Gothic writing here. Miles's Foucauldian approach to the Gothic posits that 'there cannot be a single, comprehensive genealogy, only genealogies'; Miles, *Gothic Writing 1750–1820*, p. 9.

23 Porter, *Flesh in the Age of Reason*, p. xiii.

24 Porter, *Flesh in the Age of Reason*, p. xv.

25 Porter, *Flesh in the Age of Reason*, p. xvi.

26 The Medical Act of 1858 created a single public Medical Register for all legally recognised practitioners. It then became illegal for those who were not on the register to claim to be medical practitioners, although they could still legally practise healing. See Roy Porter, *Disease, Medicine and Society in England, 1550–1860* (1987) (Cambridge: Cambridge University Press, 1999), pp. 47–8; and *Quacks: Fakers and Charlatans in English Medicine* (1989) (Stroud: Tempus, 2001).

27   Elizabeth T. Hurren, *Dying for Victorian Medicine: English Anatomy and Its Trade in the Dead Poor, c. 1834–1929* (Basingstoke: Palgrave Macmillan, 2012), p. 4.

28   Hurren, *Dying for Victorian Medicine*, p. 5.

29   Richard Sugg, *Murder After Death: Literature and Anatomy in Early Modern England* (Ithaca: Cornell University Press, 2007), p. 2.

30   Sugg, *Murder After Death*, p. 2.

31   Pickstone sees 'knowledge systems' as 'dominant paradigms' which influence ways of reading the world and its objects; John V. Pickstone, *Ways of Knowing: A New History of Science, Technology and Medicine* (2000) (Chicago: University of Chicago Press, 2001), pp. 42–3.

32   William Godwin, *The Enquirer: Reflections on Education, Manners, and Literature in a Series of Essays* (1797) (New York: Augustus M. Kelley, 1965), p. 49, quoted in Maggie Kilgour, *The Rise of the Gothic Novel* (New York and London: Routledge, 1995), p. 57.

33   Kilgour, *The Rise of the Gothic Novel*, p. 60.

34   Kilgour, *The Rise of the Gothic Novel*, p. 3.

35   Kilgour, *The Rise of the Gothic Novel*, pp. 10–11.

36   Kilgour, *The Rise of the Gothic Novel*, p. 12.

37   Michael Sappol, *A Traffic of Dead Bodies. Anatomy and Embodied Social Identity in Nineteenth-Century America* (2002) (Princeton and Oxford: Princeton University Press, 2004), p. 303.

38   As Ruth Richardson explains, although the Anatomy Act was much anticipated, it failed to prevent body-snatching, which remained widespread during the nineteenth century, especially as the largest medical collections were developing; Ruth Richardson, *Death, Dissection and the Destitute* (1987) (Chicago and London: University of Chicago Press, 2000), pp. 207–8.

39   Mario Praz, *The Romantic Agony* (1933) (London and New York: Oxford University Press, 1970), p. 38.

40   Erin O'Connor, *Raw Material: Producing Pathology in Victorian Culture* (Durham and London: Duke University Press, 2000), p. 13.

41   Andrew Smith, *Gothic Death, 1740–1914. A Literary History* (Manchester: Manchester University Press, 2016), p. 189.

42   Kilgour, *The Rise of the Gothic*, p. 5.

43   Kilgour, *The Rise of the Gothic*, p. 4.

1: The Skeleton in the Trunk

1   As will be seen, even if separated from the Company of Barbers, surgeons remained associated with the violence of the barber-surgeons

of the medieval period, because, unlike physicians, they performed operations and did not possess a very high social status. Whilst physicians were educated in universities or private medical schools, surgeons learned their trade through the less prestigious route of apprenticeship.

2   Physicians' canes contained aromatic preparations to protect themselves from contagion which, it was believed, propagated through miasmas.

3   Other anatomical atlases are also believed to have influenced Hogarth's work, such as the frontispiece of Pieter Paaw's *Succentarius anatomicus* (Leyde, 1617) which shows a dissection in an anatomical theatre. Characters standing to the right and left of the picture point their fingers in ways that are similar to James Field's and MacLaine's skeletons in *The Reward of Cruelty*. A bucket and skulls under the table also bear a striking resemblance to Hogarth's engraving. I owe Rafael Mandressi this reference.

4   Benjamin A. Rifkin, Michael J. Ackerman and Judith Folkenberg, *Human Anatomy: Depicting the Body from the Renaissance to Today* (London: Thames and Hudson, 2006), p. 69.

5   Ruth Richardson, *Death, Dissection and the Destitute* (1987) (Chicago and London: University of Chicago Press, 2000), p. 32.

6   Richardson, *Death, Dissection and the Destitute*, pp. 32–4.

7   As Maurice Lévy notes, between 1791 and 1820, fifty per cent of the publications of the Minerva Press were Gothic romances: 25 out of 51 in 1791–5; 48 out of 102 in 1796–1800; 35 out of 72 in 1801–5; 27 out of 74 in 1806–10; 13 out of 24 in 1811–15 and 15 out of 22 in 1816–20. Maurice Lévy, *Le Roman 'Gothique' anglais, 1764–1824* (Paris: Albin Michel, 1995), p. 469. These figures also illustrate the gradual decrease in the publication of Gothic romances and illuminate the period of high output between 1796 and 1800. As Dorothy Blakey underlines, the Minerva Press published more than 800 titles in all over a thirty-year period, many of them written anonymously by women (Regina Maria Roche, Mrs Eliza Parson, Mrs Mieke, Mrs Bennet or Dalton, etc.), and the Press was 'the chief purveyor of the circulating-library novel', which explains the growing popularity of Gothic novels. It was founded by William Lane and the name 'Minerva Press' was adopted in 1790. Romances only were published after 1790. Although the name Minerva Press no longer figured in the title page after 1820 (when Newman took over the business and developed children's books), the press remained in existence until the end of the nineteenth century. Dorothy Blakey, *The Minerva Press, 1790–1820* (London: Bibliographical Society at the University Press, Oxford, 1939 (for 1935)).

8   In the highly popular Victorian penny-dreadful *The Mysteries of London* (first series, 1844–6), however, George W. M. Reynolds uses both figures. Reynold's urban Gothic will be examined further in chapter 3.

9   Despite their moralising tone, many of Hogarth's works also reflect a growing anxiety in the mid-eighteenth century regarding medical practice and the increasing part played by anatomy in medical education. Many of Hogarth's prints deal with medical practitioners. He was one of the eighteenth-century artists, as Fiona Haslam points out, who contributed to disseminating pejorative images of doctors – a trend which Haslam sees, arguably perhaps, as a sign of 'a broad attack on the profession on behalf of the masses who were unable to speak for themselves and who welcomed such an attack on a profession that seemed to offer little consolation to them in their suffering'. Fiona Haslam, *From Hogarth to Rowlandson: Medicine in Art in Eighteenth-Century Britain* (Liverpool: Liverpool University Press, 1996), p. 13. The satirical stance of many eighteenth-century works of art, whether it may be seen, as Haslam contends, as 'an indication of what society feels is wrong with itself' or simply as a fashionable trend, nonetheless often targeted medical professionals and medical practice more generally (Haslam, *From Hogarth to Rowlandson*, p. 12). Hogarth's *Cunicularii, of the Wise Men of Godliman in Consultation* (1726), representing Mary Toft, the 'Rabbit Woman', and *The Company of Undertakers/A Consultation of Physicians* (1736), which combined portraits of orthodox medical practitioners and charlatans, both associated the medical profession with fraud and death. (It is believed, however, that Hogarth's *Cunicularii* was commissioned by a group of surgeons trying to denounce men midwives). Furthermore, as Haslam argues, Hogarth's freedom in artistic expression coincided with a period when '[m]embers of the medical profession came under increasing scrutiny', satire and caricature being recurrently used as 'weapons of controversy' (p. xv). Haslam's point is to use medical images – or images related to the medical profession – as a 'resource for historical study' so as to propose a social history of medicine that takes into account the iconography of the medical images produced in the eighteenth century. Following her attempt at using the arts to enrich the history of medicine, the intention here is to look at the Gothic writing of the period so as to provide, perhaps, a new understanding of medical history in which literature plays an active part, not simply in reflecting contemporary methods of knowing and investigating the body, but also in helping criticise and perhaps change contemporary ways of knowing.

10   As Andrew Cunningham recalls, even for anatomists, it '*felt* like a crime for an anatomist to dissect a fresh corpse' (emphasis in original).

Dissection was thus experienced as a transgressive act. Andrew Cunningham, *The Anatomist Anatomis'd: An Experimental Discipline in Enlightenment Europe* (Farnham: Ashgate, 2010), p. 226.

[11] Roy Porter, *Flesh in the Age of Reason: How the Enlightenment Transformed the Way We See our Bodies and Souls* (2003) (London: Penguin, 2004), p. xv.

[12] Robert Miles, *Gothic Writing, 1750–1820. A Genealogy* (1993) (Manchester and New York: Manchester University Press, 2002), p. 8.

[13] Ann Jessie Van Sant, *Eighteenth-Century Sensibility and the Novel: The Senses in Social Context* (Cambridge: Cambridge University Press, 1993), p. 56.

[14] The hanging of murderers at Tyburn provided entertainment for whole families. As Andrew Cunningham notes, when the gibbet was transferred to Newgate Prison in 1783, the struggles for the corpses of hanged men between families and surgeons became far less frequent, as the site ensured that opportunities for disorder be removed; Cunningham, *The Anatomist Anatomis'd*, p. 225.

[15] Van Sant, *Eighteenth-Century Sensibility and the Novel*, p. 56.

[16] Horace Walpole, *The Castle of Otranto*, in *Three Gothic Novels*, ed. Peter Fairclough (London: Penguin, 1986), pp. 37–148 (p. 52). All further references are to this edition and will be given parenthetically in the text.

[17] Lévy, *Le Roman 'Gothique' anglais, 1764–1824*, p. 396.

[18] Lévy, *Le Roman 'Gothique' anglais, 1764–1824*, p. 418. These latter cases, Lévy contends, are different from Reeve's skeleton in the trunk. The motif is isolated in the text rather than the plot woven around it. They testify nevertheless to Reeve's enduring success.

[19] As suggested in the previous note, the motif is sometimes used as a mere convention and is marginal to the development of the plot.

[20] Miles, *Gothic Writing, 1750–1820*, p. 2. Robert Miles draws on David Punter's *The Literature of Terror. Vol. 1. The Gothic Tradition* (New York: Routledge, 1996).

[21] Miles, *Gothic Writing, 1750–1820*, p. 2.

[22] Clara Reeve, *The Old English Baron: A Gothic Story; also The Castle of Otranto: A Gothic Story by Horace Walpole* (London: J. C. Nimmo and Bain, 1883), p. 11. All further references are to this edition and will be given parenthetically in the text.

[23] 'So probable, that any trial for murder at the Old Bailey would make a more interesting story', wrote Walpole in response to her novel. Letter, Horace Walpole to William Mason, 8 April 1778, Yale Edition, XXVIII, pp. 381–2; quoted in Lévy, *Le Roman 'Gothique' anglais, 1764–1824*, p. 176.

24 It is interesting to note here that they strip the body before burying it so as to avoid being charged with theft.

25 The role played by the trunk is emphasised by the case of Edmund's mother, who has also been buried in unconsecrated ground but in the earth, and does not return to haunt the castle.

26 Richardson explores the human corpse in popular death culture at the time of the Anatomy Act.

27 Richardson, *Death, Dissection and the Destitute*, p. 15.

28 Richardson, *Death, Dissection and the Destitute*, p. 15.

29 This latter point will be developed in chapter 3.

30 Richardson, *Death, Dissection and the Destitute*, p. 19.

31 Richard Sugg, *Murder After Death: Literature and Anatomy in Early Modern England* (Ithaca: Cornell University Press, 2007), p. 27.

32 We will see in chapter 3 that body-snatchers often tied the stolen corpses in this way before thrusting them into a sack.

33 Ann Radcliffe, *The Romance of the Forest* (1791) (Oxford: Oxford University Press, 2009), pp. 53–4. All further references are to this edition and will be given parenthetically in the text.

34 Many references to 'thrills' permeate the narrative, as in many other Gothic romances, especially Radcliffe's: 'A kind of pleasing dread thrilled her bosom' (p. 18); 'my blood now thrills as I repeat it' (p. 41), 'The idea thrilled her with horror' (p. 140), 'every nerve thrilled with horror' (p. 341), etc.

35 G. J. Barker-Benfield, *The Culture of Sensibility: Sex and Society in Eighteenth-Century Britain* (Chicago and London: University of Chicago Press, 1996), p. 22.

36 'Her features were bathed in tears, and she seemed to suffer the utmost distress' (p. 5); 'Her features, which were delicately beautiful, had gained from distress an expression of captivating sweetness' (p. 6). Adeline is not the only character marked by sensibility. Madame La Motte keeps crying and is often depicted with swollen eyes; Theodore is shown as 'suffer[ing] distress (p. 173) or suffering for Adeline's sake (p. 217); La Luc, 'ever sensible to the sufferings of others' (p. 258), is described with 'a tear strolling down his cheek' (p. 264), etc.

37 Adeline's heart is also 'chilled' (p. 175).

38 Van Sant, *Eighteenth-Century Sensibility and the Novel*, p. 59.

39 Women's capacity for healing is later developed through the character of Madame La Luc, La Luc's sister and Clara's aunt. Madame La Luc's room contains 'various medicines and botanical distillations, together with the apparatus for preparing them' (p. 248). She manages to rescue Adeline when she becomes delirious; she listens to the description of the case, examines her pulse and the quality of the air (p. 256), and makes

up a medicine. Her examination of the patient is more developed than the surgeon's or physician's, who simply 'examine' wounds (p. 199) or sometimes feel their patients' pulse (p. 202). She also ensures that Theodore leaves with 'a sufficient quantity of medicines' in his travelling trunk (p. 254). Not only does she treat fevers, but she also deals with cases usually reserved to surgeons: she heals Clara after her fall when there is no surgeon around, restoring her 'with the assistance of a balsam composed by herself' (p. 267), and she is even able to change her prescription when its 'restorative qualities' fail (p. 271), as when she swaps her balsam for 'an emollient fomentation' (p. 271) to cure Monsieur Verneuil's arm. Moreover, the narrative stresses recurrently the healing power of her medicines ('cordial of incomparable efficacy', her 'inestimable balsam' (p. 268)), contrasting even more with the other remedies.

40 This stress on the physician's humanity is important as Radcliffe's heroine seems to be investigating human nature through her ordeals: '"Is this human nature?" cried she. "Am I doomed to find every body deceitful?"' (p. 118). This remark in particular typifies how Radcliffe's Gothic romance reflects Enlightenment humanism, giving even more significance to the medical discourses and debates that pepper the narrative.

41 Van Sant, *Eighteenth-Century Sensibility and the Novel*, p. 59.

42 *The English Novel, 1770–1829: A Bibliographical Survey of Prose Fiction Published in the British Isles*, two vols (Oxford: Oxford University Press, 2000), item 1797: 33; quoted in Don Shelton, 'Sir Anthony Carlisle and Mrs Carver', *Romantic Textualities. Literature and Print Culture, 1780–1840*, 19 (Winter 2009), 54–69 (p. 54). Carlisle was appointed surgeon to Westminster Hospital in 1793. It is believed that he authored several Gothic novels for the Minerva Press (including *Elizabeth* (1797), *The Legacy* (1798) and *The Old Woman* (1800)), probably for financial reasons. He married in 1800 and was elected a Fellow of the Royal Society in 1804 before being appointed Professor of Anatomy at the Royal Academy in 1808. Shelton traces places and people in the novel which might match Carlisle's family history in his study of *The Horrors of Oakendale Abbey* and *The Old Woman*. Shelton arguably regards the medical details in *The Horrors of Oakendale Abbey* (such as the use of words like 'accoucheur', or the knowledge that corpses were stored hanging vertically) as well as the knowledge of resurrectionists as sufficient evidence to dismiss other potential authors, such as Carlisle's younger brother.

43 [Mrs Carver], *The Horrors of Oakendale Abbey* (1797) (s.l.: Zittaw Press, 2006). All further references are to this edition and will be given parenthetically in the text.

44 Other optical illusions are found throughout the narrative (p. 72).

45 Laura's reaction to the skeleton in the chest highlights her sensibility, however, in the same way as Adeline's when she reads her father's manuscript: 'The trunk stood exactly in the same place; she lifted up the lid, and the same ghastly skeleton presented itself to her view. She contemplated it with a mixture of horror and pity. "Ah!" says she, "would I could know what body enveloped these bones; perhaps thou are entitled to my tenderest regards". The idea that it might be the remains of the murdered, loved, Eugene, occurred to her sad memory, and the tears fell from her eyes in large drops upon the object which excited them' (p. 61).

46 References to fairy tales are frequent in Gothic novels and inform most canonical works, from Lewis's *The Monk* to Maturin's *Melmoth the Wanderer*.

47 As Maurice Lévy argues, the 'premature burial' motif is frequently detectable in many minor Gothic novels of the late eighteenth century, where the characters are entrapped in underground caverns, for instance. It appears moreover in Miss Showes's *The Restless Matron* (1799), published by the Minerva Press, where the heroine is buried alive by her husband, in Matthew Lewis's *The Monk* (1797), Joseph Fox's *Santa Maria; or the Mysterious Pregnancy* (1797) and Harriet Butler's *Count Eugenio; or, Fatal Errors. A Tale, Founded on Fact* (1807). Lévy, *Le Roman 'Gothique' anglais, 1764–1824*, pp. 413, 632. The motif will be further explored in chapter 5.

48 Shelton, 'Sir Anthony Carlisle and Mrs Carver', p. 62.

49 Charles Byrne's feet appear in the background of Sir Joshua Reynolds's 1786 portrait of John Hunter, however, less than four years after the giant's death, as an emblem of the surgeon's skill – and power.

50 The links between the Gothic and the piecing together of fragments and the making of (medical) collections will be further studied in chapters 2 and 4.

51 The motif recalls the animated statue in Lewis's *The Monk*, which uses human remains (the dried and shrivelled hand of the thief) to terrify the nuns in the convent. Both examples illuminate the potentially edifying role played by human remains in the Gothic.

52 [Anon.], *The Animated Skeleton* (1798) (Chicago: Valancourt Books, 2005), p. 103. All further references are to this edition and will be given parenthetically in the text.

53 Benjamin A. Rifkin, Michael J. Ackerman and Judith Folkenberg, *Human Anatomy: Depicting the Body from the Renaissance to Today* (London: Thames and Hudson, 2006), pp. 54–5. The year 1858 is another key date for Rifkin et al., one which saw the publication of

Henry Gray's *Anatomy Descriptive and Anatomical,* illustrated by H. V. Carter. This work, according to the authors, clearly marked 'the divorce between art and science' through its neutral illustrations which avoided any kind of stylistic distortion; Rifkin, Ackerman and Folkenberg, *Human Anatomy,* p. 67. Incidentally, 1858 is also the year when the Medical Act was passed, regulating the medical profession.

54   Anita Guerrini, 'Inside the Charnel House: The Display of Skeletons in Europe, 1500–1800', in Rina Knoeff and Robert Zwijnenberg (eds), *The Fate of Anatomical Collections* (Farnham, Burlington: Ashgate, 2015), pp. 93–109 (p. 97).

55   Guerrini, 'Inside the Charnel House', p. 100.

56   Guerrini, 'Inside the Charnel House', p. 94.

2: *Anatomical Models and the Gothic*

1   Wollstonecraft on embalmed corpses seen in Norway, quoted in Roy Porter, *Flesh in the Age of Reason: How the Enlightenment Transformed the Way We see Our Bodies and Souls* (London: Penguin, 2003), p. 220.

2   Marina Warner, *Phantasmagoria: Spirit Visions, Metaphors, and Media into the Twenty-First Century* (Oxford: Oxford University Press, 2006), p. 23.

3   Warner, *Phantasmagoria,* p. 23.

4   John V. Pickstone, *Ways of Knowing: A New History of Science, Technology and Medicine* (2000) (Chicago: University of Chicago Press, 2001), p. 63.

5   Pickstone, *Ways of Knowing,* pp. 63–4.

6   Walpole particularly distrusted humanity, writing to Henry Seymour Conway in 1784 that 'our race in general is pestilently bad and malevolent'; Walpole to Henry Seymour Conway, 28 November 1784, 39: 428, quoted in Ingrid H. Tague, *Animal Companions: Pets and Social Change in Eighteenth-Century Britain* (University Park, PA: Pennsylvania State University Press, 2015), p. 219.

7   Pickstone, *Ways of Knowing,* pp. 42–3.

8   Introduction to Ann Radcliffe, *The Romance of the Forest* (1791), ed. Chloe Chard (Oxford: Oxford University Press, 2009), p. xiii.

9   As Paul Westover contends, however, the Grand Tour, as a means of reviving the classics and raising the dead (especially through contemplating ruins, battlegrounds or churchyards), was also a way of engaging with the dead; Paul Westover, *Necromanticism: Travelling to Meet the Dead, 1750–1860* (Basingstoke: Palgrave Macmillan, 2012), p. 39.

10 Emily Brontë, *Wuthering Heights* (1847) (London: Penguin, 2003), p. 57.
11 'The Prince is currently setting up a cabinet of natural history, the individual parts of which seemed to me quite comprehensive. It will be possible to reach the cabinet from the Pitti Palace. So the Prince will be able to walk from there to the famous gallery' ('Le prince forme actuellement un cabinet d'histoire naturelle dont toutes les parties de détail m'ont paru bien remplies . . . On fera de ce cabinet une communication au Palais Pitti. Alors le prince, de là, pourra aller jusqu'à la fameuse galerie'); D. A. F. Sade, *Voyage d'Italie* (1775–6), in *Œuvres complètes* (Paris: Tchou, 1965), pp. 147–8, quoted in Michel Lemire, *Artistes et Mortels* (Paris: Chabaud, 1990), pp. 40–1. All translations are mine.
12 'Dans une de ces armoires on voit un sépulcre rempli d'une infinité de cadavres, dans chacun desquels on peut observer les différentes gradations de la dissolution, depuis le cadavre du jour jusqu'à celui que les vers ont totalement dévoré. Cette idée bizarre est l'ouvrage d'un Sicilien nommé Zummo. Tout est exécuté en cire et colorié au naturel. L'impression est si forte que les sens paraissent s'avertir mutuellement. On porte naturellement la main au nez sans s'en apercevoir en considérant cet horrible détail, qu'il est difficile d'examiner sans être rappelé aux sinistres idées de la destruction et par conséquent à celle, plus consolante, du Créateur. Près de cette armoire, il en est une dans le même genre, représentant un sépulcre de presbytère, où les mêmes gradations de dissolution s'observent à peu près. On y remarque surtout un malheureux, nu, apportant un cadavre qu'il jette avec les autres, et qui, suffoqué lui-même par l'odeur et le spectacle, tombe à la renverse et meurt comme les autres. Ce groupe est d'une vérité effrayante'; D. A. F. Sade, *Voyage d'Italie* (1775–6), in *Œuvres complètes* (Paris: Tchou, 1965), pp. 150–3.
13 Putrefying bodies, festering with maggots, are found time and again in Matthew Lewis's *The Monk* (1797) and in his collection, *Tales of Wonder* (1801), anticipating Victor Frankenstein's description of the 'grave-worms crawling in the folds of the flannel' in his nightmare (Mary Shelley, *Frankenstein; or the Modern Prometheus* (1831) (London: Penguin, 2003), p. 59).
14 Warner, *Phantasmagoria*, p. 31.
15 'On peut y voir un sépulcre empli de cadavres à divers stades de putréfaction, de l'instant de la mort jusqu'à la destruction totale de l'individu. Cette œuvre sombre a été exécutée en cire colorée imitant si bien le naturel que la nature ne saurait être plus expressive ni plus vraie. L'impression est si forte face à ce chef-d'œuvre que les sens

semblent se donner l'alarme l'un l'autre: sans le vouloir, on porte sa main à son nez. Mon imagination cruelle s'est délectée de ce spectacle. A combien d'êtres, ma méchanceté a-t-elle fait éprouver ces degrés épouvantables? . . . Non loin de là, se trouve un autre sépulcre de pestiférés où l'on observe les mêmes degrés de putréfaction ; on y voit surtout un malheureux entièrement nu qui porte un cadavre pour le jeter avec les autres et qui, lui-même suffoqué par la puanteur, tombe à la renverse et meurt; ce groupe est d'une vérité effrayante' (D. A. F. Sade, *Histoire de Juliette ou les prospérités du vice*, in *Œuvres complètes* (Paris: Cercle du livre précieux, 1963), vol. 8, p. 23). A similar passage may also be found in *The 120 Days of Sodom*, written in 1785, where the female character is taken to a wax cabinet; D. A. F. Sade, *Les Cent-vingt Journées de Sodome*, in *Œuvres complètes* (Paris: J. J. Pauvert, 1986), vol. 1, p. 393.

16 Lemire, *Artistes et Mortels*, p. 74.

17 *Daily Courant*, 5421 (7 March 1719).

18 *Daily Journal*, 2487 (27 December 1728); *Daily Journal*, 2508 (21 January 1729).

19 However, in 1728 the notice made explicit that a 'Gentlewoman [would] attend the Ladies' who wished to look at the exhibits, whilst Sargent's lectures in contrast seemed intended exclusively for the gentlemen willing to know more about anatomy.

20 It may be difficult to say for certain that such recommendations to keep women away from anatomical knowledge and/or anatomical waxworks was a mere sign of Georgian prudishness, for women's practical role as healers at home and their knowledge of birthing was coming to be dismissed as unscientific at the time when eighteenth-century scientists turned to study women's reproductive functions and to define gynaecology and obstetrics as a male medical profession. The responses to anatomical collections and female audiences must therefore also be related to the growing exclusion of female midwives and the control of male medical practitioners. Indeed, the reception and fate of some collections were partly related to their link with medical figures who became associated with fringe medicine, as will be developed in chapter 4.

21 We will see in chapter 4 how in the second half of the nineteenth century medical discourse increasingly revolved around syphilis and gonorrhoea (and dealt therefore more with deviant sexuality) rather than around gynaecology and obstetrics.

22 This passage from a pamphlet on the state of matrimony exemplifies strikingly the connection between waxworks and (female) sexuality: ''Tis a deplorable Truth, that our young Ladies, a great many of them

at least, are wiser, and more knowing in the Arts of Coquetry, Galantry, and other Matters relating to the Difference of Sexes, &c. before they come to be Twenty, than our Great-Grandmothers were all their Lives. Thanks to our Plays, Songs, Poems, and more Conversation, for that; unless you will allow the late Anatomical Wax-Works with the Explainers of them, to have a great Share in teaching them such useful Knowledge. I really wonder some of our breeding Women did not bring forth Children, cut and mangled after the same Manner, unless such Births are meer Fables. Perhaps they are grown so familiar with such Speculations, that now they make no impression on them. However, I believe our Women would be full as good Breeders, and our Young Men as proper for the Propagation of their Species, without such vast Knowledge of the Parts belonging to it'; Philogamus, *The Present State of Matrimony: Or, The Real Cause of Conjugal Infidelity and Unhappy Marriages. In a Letter to a Friend. With some Reflections on the State of Matrimony among the Antient Greeks and Romans; and a View of their manner of Educating their young Ladies, compared with the Modern Practice* (London: John Hawkins, 1739), pp. 25–6.

23 See JoEllen DeLucia, 'Transnational Aesthetics in Ann Radcliffe's *A Journey Made in the Summer of 1794 . . .* (1795)', in Dale Townshend and Angela Wright (eds), *Ann Radcliffe, Romanticism and the Gothic* (Cambridge: Cambridge University Press, 2014), pp. 135–50; Maurice Lévy, *Le Roman 'gothique' anglais, 1764–1824* (Paris: Albin Michel, 1995), p. 232.

24 Clara Frances McIntyre, *Ann Radcliffe in Relation to her Time*, Yale Studies in English, 62 (New Haven: Yale University Press; London: Humphrey Milfort, Oxford University Press, 1920), p. 58. Maurice Lévy mentions as well Radcliffe's use of travel books, such as Piozzi's; Lévy, *Le Roman 'gothique' anglais*, p. 254.

25 J. M. S. Tompkins, 'Ramond de Carbonnières, Grosley and Mrs Radcliffe', *Review of English Studies*, 5/19 (July 1929), 294–301. See pp. 299–300 for the mention of the wax image.

26 P. J. Grosley, *New Observations on Italy and its Inhabitants, written in French by two Swedish Gentlemen*, trans. Thomas Nugent, L.L.D. (London: Davis and C. Reymers, 1769), p. 205.

27 Ann Radcliffe, *The Mysteries of Udolpho* (1794) (Oxford and New York: Oxford University Press, 1980), p. 662.

28 On Anna Morandi Manzolini's waxworks see Rebecca Messbarger, *The Lady Anatomist: The Life and Works of Anna Morandi Manzolini* (Chicago: University of Chicago Press, 2010); Rebecca Messbarger, 'Waxing Poetic: Anna Morandi Manzolini's anatomical sculptures', *Configurations*, 9 (2001), 65–97; and Claudia Pancino, 'Questioni di

genere nell'anatomia plastica del Settecento bolognese', *Studi tanatologici*, 2/2 (2006), 317–32.

[29] Grosley, *New Observations on Italy and its Inhabitants*, pp. 129–30.

[30] Victoria Carroll, 'Natural History on Display: The Collection of Charles Waterton', in Aileen Fyfe and Bernard Lightman (eds), *Science in the Marketplace: Nineteenth-Century Sites and Experiences* (Chicago and London: University of Chicago Press, 2007), pp. 271–300 (p. 275).

[31] 'We dined at Servoz, a little village, where there are lead and copper mines, and where we saw a cabinet of natural curiosities, like those of Keswick and Bethgelert', 'There is a cabinet of *Histoire Naturelle* at Chamouni, just as at Keswisk, Matlock and Clifton'; Percy Bysshe Shelley, *History of A Six Weeks' Tour through a part of France, Switzerland, Germany, and Holland: with letters descriptive of a sail round the Lake of Geneva and of the Glaciers of Chamouni* (London: T. Hookham, Jun. and C. and J. Ollier, 1817), pp. 149, 170.

[32] Many public anatomical museums which opened in the nineteenth century also closed their doors before the end of the century, such as Dr Kahn's in London. This point will be developed further in chapter 4.

[33] Shelley, *History of A Six Weeks' Tour*, p. 171.

[34] Shelley, *History of A Six Weeks' Tour*, p. 171.

[35] 'We saw in this cabinet some chamois' horns, and the horns of an exceedingly rare animal called the bouquetin, which inhabits the desarts [*sic*] of snow to the south of Mont Blanc: it is an animal of the stag kind; its horns weigh at least twenty-seven English pounds. It is inconceivable how so small an animal could support so inordinate a weight. The horns are of a very peculiar conformation, being broad, massy, and pointed at the ends, and surrounded with a number of rings, which are supposed to afford an indication of its age: there were seventeen rings on the largest of these horns'; Shelley, *History of A Six Weeks' Tour*, pp. 149–50.

[36] Mary Shelley, *Frankenstein; or, the modern Prometheus* (1831), in *Three Gothic Novels*, ed. Peter Fairclough (London: Penguin, 1986), p. 430. All further references are to this edition and will be given parenthetically in the text.

[37] See also E. and J. de Goncourt, *L'Italie d'hier. Notes de voyages, 1855–65* (Paris: Charpentier and Fasquelle, 1894), pp. 140–1.

[38] Anne Williams, '"Mummy possest": Sadism and Sensibility in *Frankenstein*', in *Frankenstein's Dream. Romantic Circles Praxis Series* (2003). Available at *www.rc.umd.edu/praxis/frankenstein/williams.williams.html*. Accessed on 28 June 2015.

[39] 'Je voudrais pouvoir décrire le cabinet d'histoire naturelle, que, depuis dix ans, le grand duc s'occupe d'enrichir, et M. Fontana d'arranger

. . . Il est impossible de rendre l'élégance des appartements, l'ordre, la distribution; . . . Les armoires de ce cabinet représentent les cases de la mémoire de M. Fontana, remplie d'histoire naturelle'; Charles Dupaty, 'à Florence', *Lettres sur l'Italie en 1785*, Lettre XXVI, 2nd edn (Tours: Ad Mame et Cie., 1843), p. 63.

40 'Musée d'histoire naturelle. – Quel plaisir doit avoir un anatomiste en entrant dans le Musée! Rien ne m'a paru plus propre, plus net, plus instructif. Ces signes sont disposés de manière à donner sans efforts des idées nettes. La salle des accouchements me semble fort supérieure à celle de Bologne et de Vienne. Je me souviens avec plaisir de la visite que je fis à l'Académie Joséphine et à cette salle with lady A.

Je vois avec le plaisir des yeux d'un ignorant les muscles et les nerfs, qui sont exprimés très nettement . . . J'ai vu ici le premier squelette qui m'ait paru beau. On sent de quel genre de beauté est susceptible un squelette . . . Il est à gauche en entrant dans les salles de préparations en cire, dans une belle cage de verre' ; Stendhal, *Journal 1810–1811*, vol. 4 (Paris: Le Divan, 1937), pp. 340–1.

41 RCS Board of Curators 2 July 1813, quoted in Samuel J. M. M. Alberti, 'The Organic Museum: The Hunterian and other Collections at the Royal College of Surgeons in England', in Samuel J. M. M. Alberti and Elizabeth Hallam (eds), *Medical Museums: Past, Present, Future* (London: Royal College of Surgeons, 2013), pp. 17–29 (p. 20).

42 Samuel J. M. M. Alberti, 'The Museum Affect: Visiting Collections of Anatomy and Natural History', in Aileen Fyfe and Bernard Lightman (eds), *Science in the Marketplace: Nineteenth-Century Sites and Experiences* (Chicago and London: University of Chicago Press, 2007), pp. 371–403 (p. 390).

43 In particular, Forsyth noted that the mysteries of the human body on display were not unrelated to sexual reproduction: 'I was struck by the immensity of this collection, which occupies fourteen rooms . . . This awful region, which should be sacred to men of science, is open to all. Nay, the very apartment where the gravid uterus and its processes lie unveiled, is a favourite lounge of the ladies, who criticise aloud all the mysteries of sex'; Joseph Forsyth, *Remarks on Antiquities, Arts and Letters, During an Excursion in Italy in the Years 1802 and 1803* (1813), 4th edn (London: John Murray, 1835), pp. 33–4.

44 P. R. Feldman and D. Scott-Kilvert (eds), *The Journals of Mary Shelley*, 2 vols (Oxford: Clarendon Press, 1987), vol. 1, p. 257.

45 Feldman and Scott-Kilvert, *The Journals of Mary Shelley*, p. 306, quoted in Tim Marshall, *Murdering to Dissect: Grave-Robbing, Frankenstein and the Anatomy Literature* (Manchester: Manchester University Press, 1995), p. 68.

[46] Joseph Forsyth, *Remarks on Antiquities, Arts and Letters, During an Excursion in Italy in the Years 1802 and 1803* (1813), 2nd edn (Geneva: Ledouble, 1820), pp. 46–9.

[47] Forsyth was not the first critic to view the modeller as a modern Prometheus. Patience Wright (1725–86), an American wax modeller who settled in London in the 1770s, had also been nicknamed 'The Promethean Modeller'. She was particularly known for her model of King George III.

[48] See Charles Dupaty, 'à Florence', *Lettres sur l'Italie en 1785*, Lettre XXVI, p. 63.

[49] Alberti, 'The Museum Affect', pp. 390–1.

[50] Laurence Talairach-Vielmas, '"I have bottled babes unborn": The Gothic, Medical Collections and Nineteenth-Century Culture', special issue on 'Medical Gothic', ed. Sara Wasson, *Gothic Studies*, 17/1 (2015), 28–42.

[51] Stefani Englestein, *Anxious Anatomy: The Conception of the Human Form in Literary and Naturalist Discourse* (New York: State University of New York Press, 2008), p. 183.

[52] William Wordsworth, 'Residence in London', in *The Prelude*, ed. Stephen Gill, *The Oxford Authors: William Wordsworth* (1805) (Oxford and New York: Oxford University Press, 1990), pp. 375–590, ll. 680–95.

[53] Thomas Frost, *The Old Showmen and the Old London Fairs*, 2nd edn (London: Tinsley Brothers, 1875), p. 305.

[54] As Thomas Frost relates in *The Old Showmen and the Old London Fairs* (1875), the world of the fair was a carnivalesque realm which civic authorities attempted to control – or even suppress. In 1840, the complete abolition of the fair was proposed. Bartholomew Fair was eventually limited to three days, with theatrical booths forbidden and restricted to just a few stalls in 1849; John Timbs, *Curiosities of London* (London: David Bogue, 1855), p. 31.

[55] George Brewer, *The Witch of Ravenworth* (1808), ed. Allen Grove (Chicago: Valancourt Books, 2006), p. 102. All further references are to this edition and will be given parenthetically in the text.

[56] Cartoons and drawings representing the work of surgeons, such as Thomas Rowlandson's 'The Persevering Surgeon' (n.d.), which depicts an anatomist dissecting a female cadaver, placed emphasis on the medical professional's phallic scalpel raised just above the female corpse, one hand close to her breast and a smile on his face. See Fiona Haslam, *From Hogarth to Rowlandson: Medicine in Art in Eighteenth-Century Britain* (Liverpool: Liverpool University Press, 1996), pp. 282–3.

[57] Marguerite Countess of Blessington, *The Idler in Italy* (Paris: Galignani, 1839), p. 215.

58 Joseph Forsyth, *Remarks on Antiquities, Arts and Letters, During an Excursion in Italy in the Years 1802 and 1803* (1813), 4th edn (London: John Murray, 1835), pp. 33–4.

59 Renato G. Mazzolini, 'Plastic Anatomies and Artificial Dissections', in Soraya de Chadarevian and Nick Hopwood (eds), *Models: The Third Dimension of Science* (Stanford: Stanford University Press, 2004), pp. 43–70 (p. 54).

60 Francesco de Ceglia, 'Rotten Corpses, a Disembowelled Woman, a Flayed Man. Images of the Body from the End of the 17th to the Beginning of the 19th Century. Florentine Wax Models in the First-Hand Accounts of Visitors', *Perspectives on Science*, 14/4 (2006), 417–56 (p. 439). Francesco de Ceglia mentions that in France Denis Diderot used the anatomical models of Marie-Catherine Biheron (1719–95) to prepare his daughter for matrimony.

61 Anna Maerker, 'Anatomy and Public Enlightenment: The Florentine Museo "La Specola"', in Alberti and Hallam (eds), *Medical Museums*, pp. 88–101 (p. 99).

62 See Matthew Craske, '"Unwholesome" and "pornographic": A Re-assessment of the Place of Rackstrow's Museum in the Story of Eighteenth-century Anatomical Collection and Exhibition', *Journal of the History of Collections*, 23/1 (2011), 75–99 (p. 84); and Laurence Talairach-Vielmas, '"In all its Hideous and Appalling Nakedness and Truth": The Reception of some Anatomical Collections in Georgian and Victorian England', *Medicina nei Secoli, Journal of History of Medicine*, 27/2 (2015), 553–74.

63 Andrew T. Chamberlain and Michael Marker Pearson (eds), *Earthly Remains: The History and Science of Preserved Human Bodies* (London: British Museum Press, 2001), p. 7.

64 Warner, *Phantasmagoria*, p. 15.

65 Warner, *Phantasmagoria*, p. 54.

66 Lemire, *Artistes et Mortels*, p. 74.

67 Warner, *Phantasmagoria*, p. 37. Curtius also exhibited Vaucanson's automata at the Salon de Cire, while natural specimens, such as giants or freaks, were displayed at the Caverne des Grands Voleurs. Lemire, *Artistes et Mortels*, p. 88.

68 Victor Gatrell notes that 'a Londoner growing up in the 1780s could by 1840 have attended some four hundred execution days outside Newgate alone'; Victor A. C. Gatrell, *The Hanging Tree: Execution and the English People 1770–1868* (Oxford: Oxford University Press, 1994), p. 32. I wish to thank Neil Davie for suggesting this reference.

69 This was the case of the Red Barn Murder with William Corder, who had killed his fiancée Maria Martin; Pamela Pilbeam, *Madame Tussaud*

and the History of Waxworks (London and New York: Hambledon and London, 2003), pp. 101–2. The portraits of the famous body-snatchers Burke and Hare may also be mentioned here. Burke was modelled by Tussaud during the trial; Tussaud's sons completed Hare and a cast of Burke's head was done three hours after the execution; Pauline Chapman, *Madame Tussaud's Chamber of Horrors: Two Hundred Years of Crime* (London: Constable, 1984), pp. 43–6.

70 John Carey, *The Violent Effigy: A Study of Dickens' Imagination* (London: Faber and Faber, 2008), pp. 80–104.

71 Pilbeam, *Madame Tussaud and the History of Waxworks*, p. 159.

72 Clara Reeve, *The Old English Baron: A Gothic Story; also The Castle of Otranto: A Gothic Story by Horace Walpole* (London: J. C. Nimmo and Bain, 1883), p. 63.

73 [Anon.], *The Animated Skeleton* (1798) (Chicago: Valancourt Books, 2005), p. 41.

74 See, for instance, Charles Dickens, 'History in Wax', *Household Words*, 9 (18 February 1854), 17–20.

75 Mrs Salmon (1650–1740) exhibited at Bartholomew and Southwark fairs before she settled in Fleet Street; Mrs Clark took over Mrs Salmon's show when she died. Dickens refers to Mrs Clark in *David Copperfield* (1850).

76 Pilbeam, *Madame Tussaud and the History of Waxworks*, pp. 11–13.

77 Frost, *The Old Showmen and the Old London Fairs*, p. 310.

78 Charles Dickens, *The Old Curiosity Shop* (1840–1) (Ware: Wordsworth Classics, 1995), p. 64. All further references are to this edition and will be given parenthetically in the text.

79 See note 54 above.

80 The reference to old giants who are kept in caravans and are waited upon by dwarfs because they become weak upon their legs may be an allusion to the Irish giant Patrick O'Brien, who exhibited himself at Bartholomew Fair but found it difficult to maintain an upright position; Frost, *The Old Showmen and the Old London Fairs*, p. 196.

81 The association of Jarley's waxes with death is also manifest when Nell sees a resemblance between the dwarf and the 'death-like faces' of the waxes (p. 184), turning the waxworks into sinister artworks.

82 Charles Dickens, *Great Expectations* (1861) (Oxford: Oxford University Press, 1994), p. 3. All further references are to this edition and will be given parenthetically in the text.

83 Dickens owned a copy of *The Dance of Death* (1833) by F. Douce, which included engravings by Hans Holbein, hence the haunting quality of the skeletons depicted in many of his novels; Mary Elizabeth

Hotz, *Literary Remains: Representations of Death and Burial in Victorian England* (New York: State University of New York, 2009), p. 188.

84 Tussaud's sumptuous costumes, symbolising her support for the monarchy, were also criticised. In an 1846 cartoon, *Punch* satirised Tussaud's advertisements by depicting paupers as exhibited specimens. The cartoon mocked the snobbish tone of Tussaud's advertising, promising middle-class ladies and gentlemen an insight into the social conditions of the British population at the time of the famine in Ireland and of widespread poverty in England.

85 Pilbeam, *Madame Tussaud and the History of Waxworks*, pp. 137–9.

86 Let us add here, however, that Tussaud's was careful never to include anatomical models in the exhibition in order to make sure that it would not be confused with fairground exhibitions, and because the institution was wary of the Obscene Publications Act of 1857. The impact of the act on public anatomical museums will be developed in chapter 4.

87 The model had been made by Curtius (Marie Grosholz's, later Tussaud's, 'uncle'), and inherited by Madame Tussaud after his death in 1794.

88 Giuliana Bruno, *Atlas of Emotion: Journeys in Art, Architecture and Film* (London: Verso, 2002), p. 149.

89 Bruno, *Atlas of Emotion*, p. 147.

90 Pilbeam, *Madame Tussaud and the History of Waxworks*, p. 113.

91 [George Dodd], 'Dolls', *Household Words*, 7/168 (11 June 1853), 352–6 (p. 353).

92 [Dodd], 'Dolls', p. 353.

93 [Dodd], 'Dolls', p. 354.

94 [Dodd], 'Dolls', p. 355.

95 Nineteenth-century study of automatism will be further examined in chapter 5 in relation to the development of mental physiology.

96 Bram Dijkstra, *Idols of Perversity: Fantasies of Feminine Evil in Fin-de-Siècle Culture* (Oxford: Oxford University Press, 1986), p. 62.

97 Elisabeth Bronfen, *Over Her Dead Body: Death, Femininity and the Aesthetic* (Manchester: Manchester University Press, 1992).

98 Bronfen, *Over Her Dead Body*, p. 5.

99 Significantly perhaps, Tickler, which Pip's sister uses to beat him, is described as a 'wax-ended piece of cane' (p. 9).

100 Human hair and teeth were used by wax modellers like Curtius and Tussaud.

101 Bruno, *Atlas of Emotion*, p. 149.

3: Body-snatching

1 David Pae, *Mary Paterson; Or, the Fatal Error. A Story of the Burke and Hare Murders* (London: Fred. Farrah, 1866), pp. 34–5.

2 Megan Coyer, *Literature, Medicine and the Nineteenth-Century Periodical Press: Blackwood's Edinburgh Magazine, 1817–1858* (Edinburgh: Edinburgh University Press, 2017), p. 49.

3 [Anon.], 'Charge against a surgeon for the removal of a dead body for anatomical purposes', *The Lancet*, 2 (20 October 1855), 377.

4 For more on late eighteenth-century caricaturists and medical pratice see Fiona Haslam, *From Hogarth to Rowlandson: Medicine in Art in Eighteenth-Century Britain* (Liverpool: Liverpool University Press, 1996).

5 On this point, see in particular Andrew Cunningham, *The Anatomist Anatomis'd: An Experimental Discipline in Enlightenment Europe* (Farnham: Ashgate, 2010). See also Samuel Richardson's description: 'As soon as the poor creatures were half-dead, I was much surprised before such a number of peace-officers, to see the populace fall to hauling and pulling the carcasses with so much earnestness, as to occasion several warm encounters, and broken heads. These were the friends of the persons executed . . . and some persons sent by private surgeons to obtain bodies for dissection. The contests between these were fierce and bloody, and frightful to look at'; Samuel Richardson, *Familiar Letters of Important Occasions* (1740) (1928 edn), p. 219, quoted in Peter Linebaugh, 'The Tyburn Riot Against the Surgeons', in *Albion's Fatal Tree: Crime and Society in Eighteenth-Century England* (London: Allen Lane, 1975), pp. 65–117 (p. 81).

6 As Ruth Richardson explains, private anatomy schools generally provided supplementary tuition in anatomy to students studying surgery at the hospital schools, since the latter failed to provide proper surgical training. Apothecaries who could not afford the hospital teaching fees also trained there; Ruth Richardson, *Death, Dissection and the Destitute* (1987) (Chicago and London: University of Chicago Press, 2000), p. 40.

7 Cunningham, *The Anatomist Anatomis'd*, p. 227.

8 Cunningham, *The Anatomist Anatomis'd*, p. 230.

9 Richardson, *Death, Dissection and the Destitute*, p. 52.

10 Joshua Naples was active as a body-snatcher from 1811 to 1832 and supplied all the main schools of anatomy in London. When the Anatomy Act made his activity superfluous, Naples became a 'servant' in the dissecting room at St Thomas' Hospital; Richardson, *Death, Dissection and the Destitute*, pp. 40, 61. Among the names of famous anatomists which appear in his diary are those of Abernethy, Brookes and Bell;

James Blake Bailey, *The Diary of a Resurrectionist, 1811–12, to which are Added an Account of the Resurrection Men in London and a Short History of the Passing of the Anatomy Act* (London: Swan Sonnenschein and Co., 1896).

[11] Richardson, *Death, Dissection and the Destitute*; Tim Marshall, *Murdering to Dissect: Grave-Robbing, Frankenstein and the Anatomy Literature* (Manchester: Manchester University Press, 1995).

[12] Richardson, *Death, Dissection and the Destitute*, p. 54.

[13] See *The Trial of William Burke and Helen M'Dougal before the High Court of Judiciary at Edinburgh on Wednesday, December 24. 1828 for the Murder of Margery Campbell, or Docherty taken in shorthand by Mr. John Macnee* (Edinburgh: Robert Buchanan, William Hunter, John Stevenson; London: Balwick and Cradock, 1828), preface.

[14] See, for instance, a 1747 article: 'The affair which lately happened to the vaults at St Andrew's, Hobourne . . . [the] body was taken away by the sexton, the very night of its interment, and sold to a surgeon'; *Gentleman's Magazine* (24 October 1747), 487, quoted in Haslam, *From Hogarth to Rowlandson*, p. 280; or a 1762 case: 'A man going to take up a load of dung in St George's fields, found at the dunghill the bodies of a woman and eight children, cut and mangled in a shocking manner, the handywork probably, of some young anatomist, who deserves a rigorous punishment for his carelessness and indiscretion'; *Gentleman's Magazine* (14 July 1762), 340.

[15] Richardson mentions several cases where the police needed to escort the body-snatchers to the magistrate to avoid attacks by the mob; Richardson, *Death, Dissection and the Destitute*, pp. 85–90.

[16] William Hunter, *Two introductory lectures, Delivered by Dr. William Hunter, to his Last Course of Anatomical Lectures, at his Theatre in Windmill Street: as they were left Corrected for the Press by himself. To which are Added, Some Papers Relating to Dr. Hunter's Intended Plan, for Establishing a Museum in London, for the Improvement of Anatomy, Surgery, and Physic* (London: printed by order of the Trustees, for J. Johnson, 1784), pp. 108–9, quoted in Cunningham, *The Anatomist Anatomis'd*, p. 231.

[17] *Commons Journal*, 22/4 (1828), 260, quoted in Richardson, *Death, Dissection and the Destitute*, p. 101.

[18] Richardson, *Death, Dissection and the Destitute*, p. 101.

[19] John Abernethy, *Hunterian Oration* (London: s.n., 1819); Thomas Southwood Smith, 'The Use of the Dead to the Living', *The Westminster Review*, 2 (1824), 59–97, reprinted in Thomas Southwood Smith, *The Use of the Dead to the Living* (Albany: Websters and Skinners, 1827).

[20] Abernethy, *Hunterian Oration*, p. 108.

[21] Abernethy, *Hunterian Oration*, p. 159.

22 Southwood Smith, *The Use of the Dead to the Living*, p. 8.
23 George Mac Gregor, *The History of Burke and Hare, and of the Resurrectionist Times* (Glasgow and London: Thomas D. Morison; Hamilton, Adams and Co., 1884), p. 14.
24 The Gothic romances published by the Minerva Press often allude to the increasing construction of the human body as a commodity. Coffins are frequently empty or do not contain the right bodies, teeth are stolen from cadavers, etc. as in *The Old Woman* (1800) and in George Brewer's *The Witch of Ravensworth* (1808).
25 Robert Southey, 'A Surgeon's Warning', in *The Poetical Works of Robert Southey, Complete in One Volume* (1796) (Paris: A. and W. Galignagni, 1829), p. 664.
26 John V. Pickstone, *Ways of Knowing: A New History of Science, Technology and Medicine* (2000) (Chicago: University of Chicago Press, 2001), p. 43.
27 *The Complete Poetical Works of Percy Bysshe Shelley*, ed. Thomas Hutchinson (Humphrey Milord: Oxford University Press, 1914), pp. 14–31 (p. 16, ll. 23–9).
28 Mary Shelley, *Frankenstein; or the Modern Prometheus* (London: Penguin, 2003), p. 39. All further references are to this edition and will be given parenthetically in the text.
29 Sharon Ruston however identifies links between Frankenstein and Abernethy, notably his vitalist notions; Sharon Ruston, *Creating Romanticism: Case Studies in the Literature, Science and Medicine of the 1790s* (Basingstoke: Palgrave Macmillan, 2013), p. 126.
30 Marshall, *Murdering to Dissect*, p. 13.
31 This is the point that Marshall makes in his book, *Murdering to Dissect.*
32 Anatomists and surgeons were seen as the 'suspected accomplice[s] or encourager[s]', as in this 1829 article published in *Blackwood's Edinburgh Magazine* on Dr Knox's involvement in the Burke and Hare case: 'Dr Knox . . . stands', the writer argues, 'in that of the suspected accomplice or encourager of unparalleled murders'; [Anon] 'Noctes Ambrosianae', *Blackwood's Edinburgh Magazine*, 25 (1829), 371–400 (p. 388).
33 Anne K. Mellor, *Mary Shelley: Her Life, Her Fiction, Her Monsters* (1988) (London: Routledge, 1989), p. 105. Shelley may have heard about the experiment through John William Polidori (1795–1821), who was Lord Byron's personal physician and travelling companion and who had studied medicine at Edinburgh (Mellor, *Mary Shelley*, p. 107).
34 John Galt, 'The Buried Alive', *Blackwood's Edinburgh Magazine*, 10 (1821), 262–4.
35 The difference between real life and fictional narratives was not always easy to assert. For example, Galt's short story was republished in journals as an actual medical case. See 'Case of John McIntire, Miraculous

Circumstances. Being a full and particular account of John MacIntire, who was buried alive, in Edinburgh, on the 15th day of April, 1824, while in a trance, and who was taken up by the resurrection-men, and sold to the doctors to be dissected, with a full account of the many strange and wonderful things which he saw and felt while he was in that state, the whole being taken from his own words' (Gateshead: Stephenson, Printer, 1824). The article reproduces most of Galt's text verbatim.

36 Coyer, *Literature, Medicine and the Nineteenth-Century Periodical Press*, p. 37.

37 Coyer, *Literature, Medicine and the Nineteenth-Century Periodical Press*, p. 43.

38 Coyer, *Literature, Medicine and the Nineteenth-Century Periodical Press*, pp. 47–8. Coyer draws on Meegan Kennedy's description of the rise of a clinical realist (and objective) discourse in medical case histories and a rejection of earlier 'curious', exotic, sentimental, sensational or Gothic styles in medical writing; Meegan Kennedy, *Revising the Clinic: Vision and Representation in Victorian Medical Narrative and the Novel* (Columbus: Ohio State University, 2010).

39 It is important to note here, however, that Coyer only refers to realist novels, from Martineau's *Deerbrook* (1839) to Trollope's *Dr Thorne* (1858) and George Eliot's *Middlemarch* (1871).

40 [Anon.], 'On the Pleasures of Body-Snatching', *Monthly Magazine*, 3/16 (April 1827), 355–65. All further references are to this edition and will be given parenthetically in the text.

41 The process is identical in Mary Shelley's *Frankenstein*, where the collected body parts remind us that at the time they were much more marketable for resurrectionists than complete corpses, while the literary motif of the blason used in the creation scene simultaneously erases the material substance of the creature's body; see the description of the creature (p. 58), quoted in chapter 4. For the market of body parts, see, for instance, the frequent references to 'extremities' in Bailey, *The Diary of a Resurrectionist*, pp. 155, 162, 163, ff.

42 As seen in chapter 2, anatomical wax models were often represented as sleeping female bodies, especially the models from the Bologna and Florentine schools. Wax modellers such as Joseph Towne (1806–79), working for Guy's Hospital in nineteenth-century London, proposed more ghastly reproductions of corpses.

43 Sir Edward Bruce Hamley, 'A Recent Confession of an Opium-Eater', *Blackwood's Edinburgh Magazine*, 80/494 (December 1856), 629–36 (p. 634). All further references are to this edition and will be given parenthetically in the text.

44 Like the tales of terror which made the fame of *Blackwood's Edinburgh Magazine*, De Quincey's 'Confessions of an English Opium-Eater', although published in the *London Magazine* in 1821, was originally intended for *Blackwood's*; Coyer, *Literature, Medicine and the Nineteenth-Century Periodical Press*, p. 37.

45 Samuel Warren, *Passages from the Diary of a Late Physician*, 3 vols, 5th edn (Edinburgh: William Blackwood and Sons; London: T. Cadell, 1838). All further references are to this edition and will be given parenthetically in the text.

46 Samuel Warren, 'Grave Doings', in *Passages from the Diary of a Late Physician*, vol. 1, pp. 321–38.

47 This may be a hint at the Burke and Hare case: Burke was first lodged in Hare's house, in a cellar with a donkey belonging to Hare.

48 We will return to this point in the following chapter, proposing different conclusions, however.

49 Ruth Richardson, *The Making of Mr. Gray's Anatomy. Bodies, Books, Fortune, Fame* (Oxford: Oxford University Press, 2008), p. 122.

50 George W. M. Reynolds, *The Mysteries of London* (Kansas City: Valancourt Books, 2013), I, p. 7. All further references are to this edition and will be given parenthetically in the text.

51 The commodification of cadavers is also evident in the frequent use of the word 'thing' at the time, as a euphemism or code to talk about corpses. Examples may be found in *The Diary of a Resurrectionist*, which records the body-snatching activity of Joshua Naples, active from 1811 to 1832. The mention of body parts (from 'extremeties' to teeth ('canines')) indicates as well that body parts were valuable, especially for those who could not afford the price of a whole body; Bailey, *The Diary of a Resurrectionist*. Similarly, on the literary stage, the word appears in David Pae's *Mary Paterson; or, The Fatal Error. A Story of the Burke and Hare Murders*, as in the example quoted at the beginning of this chapter.

52 Plentiful details are given concerning the process of decomposition throughout the novel, from the 'body bugs' which come out of the corpse to the smelly 'fatty fluid' and gas produced by the putrefying cadaver (I, pp. 912–14).

53 Michael Sappol, *A Traffic of Dead Bodies: Anatomy and Embodied Social Identity in Nineteenth-Century America* (2002) (Princeton and Oxford: Princeton University 2004), p. 235.

54 'A dreadful convulsion appeared to pass through the murderer's frame; and for nearly a minute his hands moved nervously up and down. Perhaps during those fifty seconds, the horrors of his dream were realised, *and he felt the blood rushing with the fury of a torrent and with a*

heat of molten lead up into his brain; perhaps his eyes shot sparks of fire; and in his ears was a loud droning sound, like the moan of the ocean on a winter's night! . . . But the convulsive movement of the hands soon ceased, and the murderer hung a lifeless corpse' (I, p. 279, emphasis in original).

55 'I would not for the world that the family of the deceased should learn that this tomb has been violated. Suspicions would immediately fall upon me; for it would be remembered how earnestly I desired to open the body, and how resolutely my request was refused' (I, p. 348).

56 As Jean-Jacques Lecercle contends, the story is probably situated around the period 1792–9; Jean-Jacques Lecercle, *Frankenstein: Mythe et Philosophie* (Paris: PUF, 1988), p. 55.

57 Chris Baldick, *In Frankenstein's Shadow: Myth, Monstrosity, and Nineteeth-Century Writing* (1987) (Oxford: Clarendon Press, 1996), p. 18.

58 Edmund Burke, *The Works of the Right Honourable Edmund Burke*, 12 vols (London: John C. Nimmo, 1887), vol. 4, p. 459.

59 Burke, *The Works of the Right Honourable Edmund Burke*, vol. 5, p. 175.

60 Abbé Barruel, *Memoirs Illustrating the History of Jacobinism*, trans. R. Clifford (London, 1798), iii, p. 414, quoted in Lee Sterrenburb, 'Mary Shelley's Monster: Politics and Psyche in *Frankenstein*', in George Levine and U. C. Knoepflmacher (eds), *The Endurance of 'Frankenstein'* (Berkeley: University of California Press, 1979), pp. 143–71 (p. 156).

61 Whether or not linked to the medical field, the issue of the objecti-fication and commodification of human remains also permeates *Bleak House* (1853) and *Our Mutual Friend* (1865). Dickens's denunciation of the commodification of human remains will be further developed in chapter 4.

62 Charles Dickens, 'A Great Day for the Doctors', *Household Words*, 32/2 (9 November 1850), 137–9 (p. 139).

63 Dickens, 'A Great Day for the Doctors', p. 139.

64 Charles Dickens, 'Use and Abuse of the Dead', *Household Words*, 17 (3 April 1858), 361–5 (p. 361).

65 Dickens, 'Use and Abuse of the Dead', p. 361.

66 Dickens, 'Use and Abuse of the Dead', pp. 361–2.

67 Charles Dickens, *A Tale of Two Cities* (1859) (Oxford: Oxford University Press, 2008), p. 53. All further references are to this edition and will be given parenthetically in the text.

68 Changing the viewpoint of body-snatching, as has been seen, was a frequent means of stressing horror. In 1832, an article published in *Fraser's Magazine* reversed the viewpoint on Burke and Hare's actions, presenting them as philanthropists eager to save humanity from un-trained medical practitioners: 'Be that as it may, the sapient law-officers of Edinburgh, in their great wisdom, thought fit to arrest Mr Burke

on the charge of MURDER! Such were the bigotry and ignorance of these individuals, that they actually had him dragged from his own house, and thrown, as a felon, into the public jail! Nor did their folly and injustice stop here; for they arrested his wife and Mrs Hare upon the same preposterous charge; and, to put a climax to their iniquity, they even seized upon the person of Mr Hare himself, and threw him into prison! The whole party, including the great founder of the system, were charged with committing *murder*, at a time, too, when their whole energies were devoted to save the human race, by promoting surgery and anatomy! Yes; these individuals, whose minds were unweariedly directed to protect their countrymen from *murders* at the hands of ignorant physicians and surgeons, and whose efforts have already, doubtless, had this effect to a considerable extent, were charged with being themselves guilty of *murder!*'; [Anon.], 'The Philosophy of Burking', *Fraser's Magazine*, 5/25 (February 1832), 52–65 (p. 58).

69   Dickens owned *The French Revolution*; Chris Baldick, *In Frankenstein's Shadow: Myth, Monstrosity, and Nineteenth-Century Writing* (Oxford: Clarendon Press, 1987), p. 106.

70   *The Works of Thomas Carlyle*, Centenary Edition, 30 vols (London, 1896–9), I, p. 172, quoted in Baldick, *In Frankenstein's Shadow*, p. 105.

71   See *The Pickwick Papers*, ch. 48: 'Here's a wenerable old lady a lying' on the carpet waitin' for dissection, or galwanism, or some other rewivin' and scientific inwention'; Charles Dickens, *The Pickwick Papers* (1837) (Ware: Wordsworth Classics, 1993), p. 676. Galvanism is also mentioned in *Our Mutual Friend* (vol. 1, ch. 10), *David Copperfield* (ch. 35) and *Nicholas Nickleby* (ch. 56); Baldick, *In Frankenstein's Shadow*, pp. 107–8.

72   David Pae, *Mary Paterson; or, The Fatal Error. A Story of the Burke and Hare Murders* (London: Fred. Farrah, 1866), p. 390. All further references are to this edition and will be given parenthetically in the text.

73   Robert Louis Stevenson, 'The Body-Snatcher' (1884), in *The Story of a Lie: And Other Tales* (Boston: Herbert B. Turner and Co., 1904), pp. 237–76 (p. 250). All subsequent references are to this edition and will be given parenthetically in the text.

74   *The Animated Skeleton* (1798) is an example, but optical illusions were commonplace, notably in Gothic romances published by the Minerva Press.

75   The notion of 'first phase' as a Gothic literary period is borrowed from Robert Mighall, *A Geography of Victorian Gothic Fiction: Mapping History's Nightmares* (Oxford: Oxford University Press, 1999), p. 130. Throughout this study, I term as 'Gothic novels' or 'Gothic romances' only novels published during the first wave of the Gothic, namely 1764–1824.

76   Mighall, *A Geography of Victorian Gothic Fiction*, p. 130.

4: *The Medical Museum*

1   Thomas Hood, 'Mary's Ghost: A Pathetic Ballad' (1827), in *The Complete Poetical Works of Thomas Hood*, ed. Walter Jerrold (London: Henry Frowde, 1906), p. 77.

2   Alberti's work builds on the earlier research of scholars such as Elizabeth Wanning Harries, *The Unfinished Manner: Essays on the Fragment in the Late-Eighteenth Century* (Charlottesville and London: University Press of Virginia, 1994); Linda Nochlin, *The Body in Pieces: The Fragment as a Metaphor of Modernity* (London: Thames and Hudson, 1994); and D. A. Hillman and Carla Mazzio (eds), *The Body in Parts: Fantasies of Corporeality in Early Modern Europe* (New York and London: Routledge, 1997). All explore the impact and significance of human fragments.

3   Samuel J. M. Alberti, *Morbid Curiosities: Medical Museums in Nineteenth-Century Britain* (Oxford: Oxford University Press, 2011), p. 73.

4   Mary Shelley, *Frankenstein; or the Modern Prometheus* (1831) (London: Penguin, 2003), p. 58. All subsequent references are from this edition and will be given parenthetically in the text.

5   The first records of the Patagonian giants (around 15 feet tall) may be traced to the Portugese explorer Ferdinand Magellan's voyage of 1519–22. The legend was revived in the eighteenth century, when the expedition of John Byron (Lord Byron's grandfather) on *HMS Dolphin* (1764–6) came across beings of a much smaller size (9 feet tall, revised to 6 feet 6 inches in a later accout of 1773), probably the Tehuelche people. These discoveries discredited earlier European accounts of a race of giants. Considering Mary Shelley's relationship with Lord Byron, it is likely that that she heard about the legend directly from him.

6   Paul Youngquist, *Monstrosities: Bodies and British Romanticism* (Minneapolis and London: University of Minnesota Press, 2003), pp. 54–5.

7   S. T. Asma, *On Monsters* (Oxford: Oxford University Press, 2009), p. 155, quoted in Sharon Ruston, *Creating Romanticism: Case Studies in the Literature, Science and Medicine of the 1790s* (Basingstoke: Palgrave Macmillan, 2013), p. 121.

8   Ruston, *Creating Romanticism*, p. 121.

9   Ruston, *Creating Romanticism*, p. 121; Ruston is rephrasing Youngquist, *Monstrosities*, p. 9.

10 Youngquist, *Monstrosities*, p. 28.

11 Russell C. Maulitz, *Morbid Appearances: The Anatomy of Pathology in the Early Nineteenth Century* (Cambridge: Cambridge University Press, 1987), p. 37.

12 Maulitz, *Morbid Appearances*, p. 110.

13 Alberti, *Morbid Curiosities*, p. 6.
14 Richard Sugg, *Murder after Death: Literature and Anatomy in Early Modern England* (Cornell: Cornell University Press, 2007), p. 218. As Daston and Park argue, '[i]n the middle decades of the seventeenth century, title pages of works in natural history and natural philosophy began to address themselves to "the curious" or "the ingenious" of Europe. These terms defined a new community of inquirers primarily by sensibility and object, and only secondarily by university training or social status'. As seen in chapter 1, this emphasis on the link between knowledge and sensibility is highly relevant in Radcliffean Gothic novels where heroines often fight their maids' love of the marvellous, thus confirming Barbauld and Aikin's view of terror as part and parcel of the Enlightenment enterprise. As Daston and Park add, indeed, '[t]he "curious" or "ingenious" constitued themselves as a self-declared, cosmopolitan elite . . . which was the immediate ancestor of the Republic of Letters of the Enlightenment'; Lorraine Daston and Katharine Park, *Wonders and the Order of Nature, 1150–1750* (New York: Zone Books, 2001), p. 218.
15 John Aikin and Anna Letitia Barbauld, 'On the Pleasure Derived from Objects of Terror', in *Miscellaneous pieces, in prose* (Belfast: James Magee, 1774), pp. 57–65 (p. 59).
16 Aikin and Barbauld, 'On the Pleasure Derived from Objects of Terror', p. 57.
17 Peter Brooks, *Body Work: Objects of Desire in Modern Narrative* (Cambridge, MA: Harvard University Press, 1993), pp. 18–19.
18 Brooks, *Body Work*, p. 19.
19 [Anon.], 'Anatomical Studies – Mrs Sexton', *Punch, or the London Charivari*, 31 (13 September 1856), 108.
20 John Frederick Knox, *The Anatomist's Instructor, and Museum Companion: Being Practical Directions for the Formation and Subsequent Management of Anatomical Museums* (Edinburgh, Black, 1836), p. vi. Emphasis in original.
21 As A. W. Bates explains, anatomy teachers were expected to own a museum worth more than £500 in the 1820s in order to be recognised by the College of Surgeons; A. W. Bates, '"Indecent and Demoralising Representations": Public Anatomy Museums in mid-Victorian England', *Medical History*, 52 (2008), 1–22 (p. 5). Bates cites Adrian Desmond, *The Politics of Evolution: Morphology, Medicine, and Reform in Radical London* (Chicago: University of Chicago Press, 1989), pp. 162–3.
22 Kahn's Museum, open only to men in the first instance, began to admit women two months later; Bates, 'Indecent and Demoralising Representations', p. 10.

23 Bates, 'Indecent and Demoralising Representations', p. 11.
24 Knox, *The Anatomist's Instructor, and Museum Companion*, p. 131.
25 Francesco de Ceglia, 'Rotten Corpses, a Disembowelled Woman, a Flayed Man. Images of the Body from the End of the 17th to the Beginning of the 19th Century', *Perspectives on Science*, 14/4 (Winter 2006), 417–56 (p. 430). Francesco de Ceglia cites Geoffrey Gorer, *Death, Grief and Mourning in Contemporary Britain* (London: Cresset Press, 1965).
26 Pamela Pilbeam, *Madame Tussaud and the History of Waxworks* (London and New York: Hambledon, 2003), p. 16.
27 [Anon.], 'Dr. Kahn's Anatomical Museum', *Medical Times: Journal of Medical Science, Literature, Criticism, and News*, new series, 2 (4 January–28 June 1851), 496.
28 [Anon.], 'Dr. Kahn's Anatomical Museum', *The Lancet*, 1 (1851), 474.
29 [Anon.], 'Dr. Kahn's Anatomical Museum', *The Lancet*, 1 (17 June 1854), 654.
30 [Anon.], 'Dr. Kahn's Anatomical Museum', *The Lancet*, 1 (24 June 1854), 684.
31 [Anon.], 'Dr. Kahn's Anatomical Museum', *The Lancet*, 1 (1 July 1854), 700.
32 [Anon.], 'Pater Familias, A Visitor, and Others', *The Lancet*, 2 (8 July 1854), 22.
33 [Anon.], 'Dr. Kahn's Anatomical Museum', *The Lancet*, 2 (15 August 1857), 175.
34 [Anon.], 'Dr. Kahn's Anatomical Museum', *The Lancet*, 2 (28 November 1857), 558.
35 A. W. Bates, 'Dr Kahn's Museum: Obscene Anatomy in Victorian London', *Journal of the Royal Society of Medicine*, 99 (December 2006), 618–24 (p. 620).
36 After the Apothecaries Act of 1815, which specified that qualified apothecaries should be in possession of a licence issued by the Society of Apothecaries (involving courses, practical experience, and examination), general practitioners continued to complain about unfair competition from unqualified druggists and quacks. Eventually, the Medical Act of 1858 created a single public register for all legally recognised practitioners. It then became illegal for those who were not on the Medical Register to claim to be medical practitioners, although they could still legally practise healing. See Roy Porter, *Disease, Medicine and Society in England, 1550–1860* (1987) (Cambridge: Cambridge University Press, 1999), pp. 47–8.
37 See chapter 2.
38 Bates, 'Indecent and Demoralising Representations', p. 8.

39   Bates, 'Dr Kahn's Museum: Obscene Anatomy in Victorian London',
      p. 621.

40   Bates, 'Dr Kahn's Museum: Obscene Anatomy in Victorian London',
      p. 621.

41   Alison Smith, *The Victorian Nude: Sexuality, Morality and Art* (Manchester:
      Manchester University Press, 1996), p. 62.

42   In the 1850s, books such as William Acton's *Prostitution, Considered in
      its Moral, Social and Sanitary Aspects* (1857), or *The Night Side of London*
      (1857), by James Ewing Ritchie, denounced the prostitute as the
      epitome of vice and condemned the ostentatious/deviant female body
      as a source of depravity.

43   Smith, *The Victorian Nude*, p. 50.

44   The broadside was printed in May 1711; *The Trial of William Burke
      and Helen M'Dougal before the High Court of Judiciary at Edinburgh on
      Wednesday, December 24. 1828 for the Murder of Margery Campbell, or
      Docherty taken in shorthand by Mr. John Macnee* (Edinburgh: Robert
      Buchanan, William Hunter, John Stevenson; London: Balwick and
      Cradock, 1828), pp. xi–xii.

45   Samuel Warren, 'Grave Doings', in *Passages from the Diary of a Late
      Physician*, 3 vols, 5th edn (Edinburgh: William Blackwood and Sons;
      London: T. Cadell, 1838), vol. 1, pp. 321–38 (p. 338). All further refer-
      ences are to this edition and will be given parenthetically in the text.

46   Meegan Kennedy, 'The Ghost in the Clinic: Gothic Medicine and
      Curious Fiction in Samuel Warren's *Diary of a Late Physician*', *Victorian
      Literature and Culture*, 32/2 (2004), 327–51 (p. 332).

47   'My gentle reader – start not at learning that I have been, in my time,
      a resurrectionist. Let not this appalling word, this humiliating con-
      fession, conjure up in your fancy a throng of vampire-like images and
      associations, or earn your Physician's dismissal from your hearts and
      hearths' (I, p. 321).

48   James Blake Bailey, *The Diary of a Resurrectionist, 1811–12, to which
      are Added an Account of the Resurrection Men in London and a Short History
      of the Passing of the Anatomy Act* (London: Swan Sonnenschein and
      Co., 1896), pp. 15–16.

49   Its first Edinburgh edition was in 1832; Megan Coyer, *Literature,
      Medicine and the Nineteenth-Century Periodical Press: Blackwood's Edinburgh
      Magazine, 1817–1858* (Edinburgh: Edinburgh University Press, 2017),
      p. 124.

50   Charles Dickens, *Oliver Twist; or, the Parish Boy's Progress* (Paris: Baudry's
      European Library, 1839), p. 76.

51   Silas Weir Mitchell, 'The Case of George Dedlow', *The Atlantic* (July
      1866). Available at: *www.theatlantic.com/magazine/archive/1866/07/*

the-case-of-george-dedlow/308771. Accessed on 1 March 2017. All further references are to this on-line edition. I wish to thank Maria Parrino for suggesting this reference to me.

52 On hauntings and mental science, see Julian Wolfreys, *Victorian Haunting: Spectrality, Gothic, the Uncanny and Literature* (Basingstoke: Palgrave Macmillan, 2002); Christine Berthin, *Gothic Hauntings: Melancholy Crypts and Textual Ghosts* (Basingstoke: Palgrave Macmillan, 2010); Hilary Grimes, *The Late Victorian Gothic: Mental Science, the Uncanny and Scenes of Writing* (Farnham: Ashgate, 2011).

53 Kelly Hurley, *The Gothic Body: Sexuality, Materialism and Degeneration at the Fin de Siècle* (1996) (Cambridge: Cambridge University Press, 2004), p. 5.

54 Daston and Park, *Wonders and the Order of Nature*, p. 14.

55 Daston and Park, *Wonders and the Order of Nature*, p. 145.

56 Daston and Park, *Wonders and the Order of Nature*, p. 146.

57 Daston and Park, *Wonders and the Order of Nature*, p. 267.

58 Daston and Park, *Wonders and the Order of Nature*, p. 217.

59 Daston and Park, *Wonders and the Order of Nature*, p. 172.

60 Daston and Park, *Wonders and the Order of Nature*, p. 329.

61 Daston and Park, *Wonders and the Order of Nature*, p. 15.

62 Daston and Park, *Wonders and the Order of Nature*, p. 110.

63 Caroline McCracker-Flesher, *The Doctor Dissected: A Cultural Autopsy of the Burke and Hare Murders* (Oxford: Oxford University Press, 2012), p. 50.

64 Fiona Haslam, *From Hogarth to Rowlandson: Medicine in Art in Eighteenth-Century Britain* (Liverpool: Liverpool University Press, 1996), p. 108.

65 Haslam adds that stuffed crocodiles or alligators had been used from the seventeenth century in many Dutch genre paintings as symbols of quackery because of their resemblance to the salamander, 'a creature accredited in alchemic theory with the *elixir vitae* and believed to live in fire'; Haslam, *From Hogarth to Rowlandson*, p. 112.

66 Haslam, *From Hogarth to Rowlandson*, p. 111.

67 Charles Dickens, *The Lamplighter* (London: Chapman and Hall, Ltd; New York: Charles Scribner's Sons, 1905). Available at: *www.gutenberg. org/files/927/927-h/927-h.htm*. Accessed on 5 July 2018. All references are to this edition and will be given parenthetically in the text.

68 David Pae, *Mary Paterson; Or, the Fatal Error. A Story of the Burke and Hare Murders* (London: Fred. Farrah, 1866), p. 208.

69 Catherine Crowe, *Light and Darkness; or, Mysteries of Life* (London: Henry Colburn, 1850), III, p. 98. All subsequent references are taken from this edition.

70 George Eliot, *Middlemarch* (1871) (London: Penguin, 1985), p. 498.

71 [Anon.], [Review of *The Monk*], *Monthly Review*, 2nd series, 23 (1797), 453, quoted in Michael Gamer, *Romanticism and the Gothic: Genre, Reception, and Canon Formation* (Cambridge: Cambridge University Press, 2000), p. 79.

72 Gamer, *Romanticism and the Gothic*, p. 79.

73 Gamer, *Romanticism and the Gothic*, p. 80.

74 See Laurence Talairach-Vielmas, *Wilkie Collins, Medicine and the Gothic* (Cardiff: University of Wales Press, 2009), and 'Du cadavre en putréfaction au corps enterré vivant: Le rôle du corps mort chez Wilkie Collins', in Anne Carol and Isabelle Renaudet (eds), *La Mort à l'œuvre: Usages et représentations du cadavre dans l'art* (Aix-en-Provence: Publications de l'Université de Provence, 2013), pp. 137–53.

75 Pamela K. Gilbert, *Disease, Desire, and the Body in Victorian Women's Popular Novels* (Cambridge: Cambridge University Press, 1997), p. 93.

76 [Anon.], [Sensation Novels], *Nation* (17 September 1868), 235.

77 Charles Dickens, 'The Uncommercial Traveller', *All the Year Round* (16 May 1863), 276–80 (p. 277).

78 Dickens, 'The Uncommercial Traveller', p. 278.

79 Knox, *The Anatomist's Instructor, and Museum Companion*, p. 131.

80 Leslie Stephen, 'The Decay of Murder', *Cornhill Magazine*, 20 (December 1869), 722–33 (p. 722).

81 Stephen, 'The Decay of Murder', p. 722.

82 [Anon.], 'The Popular Novels of the Year', *Fraser's*, 68 (August 1863), 253–69 (p. 262).

83 [H. F. Chorley], [Review of *Armadale*], *The Athenaeum* (2 June 1866), 732–3 (p. 733).

84 [Anon.], [Review of *Poor Miss Finch*], *Nation*, 14 (7 March 1872), 158–9 (pp. 158–9).

85 [Anon.], [Review of *The Moonstone*], *Spectator*, 61 (25 July 1868), 881–2 (pp. 881–2).

86 [Anon.], 'Novels of the Day: Their Writers and Readers', *Fraser's*, 62 (August 1860), 205–17 (p. 210).

87 Frances Power Cobbe, 'The Morals of Literature', *Fraser's*, 70 (July 1864), 124–33 (p. 124).

88 Cobbe, 'The Morals of Literature', p. 124.

89 Cobbe, 'The Morals of Literature', p. 125.

90 Cobbe, 'The Morals of Literature', p. 130.

91 Cobbe, 'The Morals of Literature', p. 131.

92 E. S. Dallas, '*Lady Audley's Secret*', *The Times* (18 November 1862), 8 (p. 8).

93 [Anon.], [Review of *Armadale*], *Saturday Review*, 21 (16 June 1866), 726–7 (p. 726–7).
94 [Anon.], [Review of *Jezebel's Daughter*], *Spectator*, 53 (15 May 1880), 627–8 (pp. 627–8).
95 [Anon.], [Review of *Poor Miss Finch*], *Saturday Review*, 33 (2 March 1872), 282–3 (pp. 282–3).
96 [E. D. Cook], [Review of *Heart and Science*], *Athenaeum* (28 April 1883), 538–9 (p. 538).
97 J. L. Stewart, 'Wilkie Collins as a Novelist', *Rose-Belford's Canadian Monthly and National Review*, 1 (November 1878), 586–601; quoted in Norman Page, *Wilkie Collins: The Critical Heritage* (London: Routledge, 1974), pp. 226–7.
98 Brooks, *Body Work*, p.65.
99 Lawrence Rothfield, *Vital Signs: Medical Realism in Nineteenth-Century Fiction* (Princeton: Princeton University Press, 1992), p. xiii.
100 Rothfield, *Vital Signs*, pp. 5, 7.
101 Rothfield, *Vital Signs*, p. 95.
102 Rothfield, *Vital Signs*, p. 95.
103 Mary Elizabeth Braddon was well read and travelled extensively throughout her life, fuelling her fiction with manifold influences. She could read and write French, had a subscription to the French circulating library Rolandi in London, read French journals, such as the *Revue des Deux Mondes*, and loved French literature, from Balzac and Zola to Flaubert, Maupassant and Dumas. Balzac was a particular influence in her novels, such as *Birds of Prey* (1867) and its sequel, *Charlotte's Inheritance* (1868), in which a poisoner reads Balzac. Her 1891 novel, *Gerard*, was also based upon Balzac's *La Peau de Chagrin*. Her novels of the 1880s were more significantly marked by the influence of French naturalism. The recurrent theme of alcohol and the figures of drunkards, as in *The Cloven Foot* (1879) or *The Golden Calf* (1883), illustrate Braddon's reliance on naturalistic themes and motifs. Shifting from Balzac and Flaubert (as exemplified by *The Doctor's Wife* (1864), a reworking of Flaubert's *Madame Bovary*), to Zola-esque characters, Braddon followed the literary trends of her day, adapting French characters to English society and often featuring degenerate English gentlemen.
104 See, for instance, [Anon.], '"The Most Shameful Sight in the World": An Impudent Quack', *The Tomahawk* (22 February 1868), 81.
105 See, for example, the following passage from an article relating the case of a French tailor who decapitated his wife: 'His brother stated that he was in the habit of going to Dr Kahn's Museum, and studying the arteries about the neck and throat, and especially familiarising himself with the position of the jugular vein', quoted in Kate Summerscale,

The Suspicions of Mr Whicher (2008) (London, Berlin and New York: Bloomsbury, 2009), p. 106.

106   Gilbert, *Disease, Desire, and the Body in Victorian Women's Popular Novels*, p. 4.

107   [Anon.], 'Belles Lettres', *Westminster Review*, 86 (October 1866), 268–80 (p. 269).

108   [Anon.], 'Belles Lettres', pp. 269–70.

109   Wilkie Collins, *Armadale* (1866) (London: Penguin Classics, 1995), p. 520. All further references are to this edition and will be given parenthetically in the text.

110   Michel Foucault, *The Birth of the Clinic: An Archaeology of Medical Perception* (1973), trans. A. M. Sheridan (London: Routledge, 2000), p. 159.

111   Foucault, *The Birth of the Clinic*, p. 136.

112   The issue of the familiarity of murderers with poisons was raised in an article published in the *Cornhill Magazine* the year before the start of serialisation: [Anon.], 'The Medical Evidence of Crime', *Cornhill Magazine*, 7 (January–June 1863), 338–48.

113   From the thirteenth century, autopsies were ordered in legal proceedings when death from poison was suspected; Stanley Joel Reiser, *Medicine and the Reign of Technology* (1978) (Cambridge: Cambridge University Press, 1981), p. 11.

114   As Elizabeth Hurren explains, the word 'dissection' long remained concealed behind that of 'anatomical examination'; Elizabeth T. Hurren, *Dying for Victorian Medicine: English Anatomy and Its Trade in the Dead Poor, c.1834–1929* (Basingstoke: Palgrave Macmillan, 2012), p. 28.

115   Pinel would eventually discover lesions, leading him to believe some of his patients were incurable; Jan Goldstein, *Console and Classify: The French Psychiatric Profession in the Nineteenth Century* (1987) (Chicago and London: University of Chicago Press, 2001), p. 90.

116   See F. J. Gall and G. Spurzheim, *Anatomie et physiologie du système nerveux en général et du cerveau en particulier*, vol. 2 (Paris: F. Schoell, 1812) and F.-V.-J Broussais, *De l'irritation et de la folie* (Bruxelles: Librairie Polymathique, 1828).

117   As Anne Stiles contends, experiments in neurological science 'began in earnest in 1861, when Broca linked the third frontal convolution of the left brain hemisphere to linguistic ability', the very same period which saw the rise of sensation fiction; Anne Stiles, *Popular Fiction and Brain Science in the Late Nineteenth Century* (Cambridge: Cambridge University Press, 2012), p. 2.

118   Marguerite Countess of Blessington, *The Idler in Italy* (Paris: Galignani, 1839), p. 215.

[119] John V. Pickstone, *Ways of Knowing. A New History of Science, Technology and Medicine* (2000) (Chicago: University of Chicago Press, 2001), pp. 106–17.

[120] See the description of Dr Jekyll's laboratory: 'Mr Utterson . . . was carried . . . to the building which was indifferently known as the laboratory or the dissecting-room. The doctor had bought the house from the heirs of a celebrated surgeon; and his own tastes being rather chemical than anatomical, had changed the destination of the block at the bottom of the garden'; Robert Louis Stevenson, 'The Strange Case of Dr Jekyll and Mr Hyde' (1886), in *Dr Jekyll and Mr Hyde, The Merry Men and Other Stories* (Ware: Wordsworth Classics, 1993), pp. 3–62 (p. 22).

5: Gothic Live Burials

[1] [Anon.], 'On Premature Interment', *European Magazine and London Review*, 83 (December 1822–July 1823), 124–7 (p. 124).

[2] [Anon.], 'On Premature Interment', p. 124.

[3] Michel Foucault, *The Birth of the Clinic: An Archaeology of Medical Perception* (1973), trans. A. M. Sheridan (London: Routledge, 2000), pp. xiii, 125.

[4] Foucault, *The Birth of the Clinic*, p. 125.

[5] See chapter 4 for the role that Bichat played in the development of pathological anatomy.

[6] Foucault, *The Birth of the Clinic*, p. 146.

[7] Richard Sugg, *Murder After Death: Literature and Anatomy in Early Modern England* (Ithaca: Cornell University Press, 2007), p. 13.

[8] James Bower Harrison, *The Medical Aspects of Death, and the Medical Aspects of the Human Mind* (London: Longman, Brown, Green and Longmans, 1852), p. 8.

[9] See Jan Bondeson, *Buried Alive: The Terrifying History of Our Most Primal Fear* (2001) (New York: Norton, 2002), pp. 53, 55, 60, 81–92.

[10] [Anon.], 'On Premature Interment', p. 125.

[11] [Anon.], 'On Premature Interment', p. 125.

[12] [Anon.], 'On Premature Interment', p. 126.

[13] [Anon.], 'On Premature Interment', p. 127.

[14] 'Magnétisme animal: Cas extraordinaire de catalepsie d'abord naturelle, puis reproduite artificiellement; observé à Bologne . . .', *Gazette médicale de Paris: journal de médecine et des sciences accessoires*, 2/1 (1833), 106; 'Wonderful Case of Catalepsy: Case of Spontaneous Catalepsy, &c.,

Observed at Bologna by M. M. Carini and J. Visconti, and by M. Mazzacorati', *The Lancet*, 19/494 (16 February 1833), 663–5. French journals like the *Annales médico-psychologiques*, the *Bulletin général de thérapeutique médicale et chirurgicale* and the *Union médicale* regularly published articles from the *Medical Times*, the *Journal of Mental Science* or the *London Medical Gazette*, as did the *Archives générales de médecine*, in which articles from the *Lancet* could also be found.

15   Andrew Ellis, Esq., 'Clinical Lecture on a Case of Catalepsy, occurring in the Jervis-Street Hospital, Dublin', *The Lancet*, 2 (2 May 1835), 129–34.

16   'Magnétisme animal: Cas extraordinaire de catalepsie d'abord naturelle, puis reproduite artificiellement; observé à Bologne . . .', *Gazette médicale de Paris: journal de médecine et des sciences accessoires*, 2/1 (1833), 106; 'Wonderful Case of Catalepsy: Case of Spontaneous Catalepsy, &c., Observed at Bologna by M. M. Carini and J. Visconti, and by M. Mazzacorati', *The Lancet*, 19/494 (16 February 1833), 663–5; 'Injection d'une solution de tartre stibié dans les veines dans un cas de catalepsie', *Bulletin général de thérapeutique médicale et chirurgicale*, 10 (1836), 103–4; 'Catalepsie (Emploi avantageux du valérianate de zinc dans la)', *Bulletin général de thérapeutique médicale et chirurgicale*, 40 (1851), 472.

17   'Premature Interment', *Chambers's Edinburgh Journal* (4 May 1839), 115.

18   'Catalepsie qui a duré 8 ans, guérie par le vomissement d'un ver, par le docteur Hubertz (à Aalbug)', *Gazette médicale de Paris: journal de médecine et des sciences accessoires*, 3/2 (6 February 1847), 111.

19   'De la catalepsie', *Archives générales de médecine*, 5/10 (1857), 206–21.

20   'Prolonged catalepsy in a soldier', *The Lancet* (22 August 1883), 354.

21   See, for instance, Timothée Puel's monograph, which recorded 150 European cases of catalepsy; Timothée Puel, *De la catalepsie* (Paris: J.-B. Baillière, 1856).

22   John Coldstream, 'Case of Catalepsy', *Edinburgh Medical and Surgical Journal*, 81 (July 1854), 477–91.

23   Ernest-Charles Lasègue, 'Catalepsies partielles et passagères', *Archives Générales de Médecine* (Juillet 1865), 385–402.

24   Adolphe Wahltuch, *On Catalepsy: Read before the medical section of the Manchester Royal Institute* (London: John Churchill and Sons, 1869), p. 6.

25   See Martin H. Lynch, 'Case of Catalepsy Ushering in Mania during Pregnancy, with remarks', *The Lancet*, 31/804 (26 January 1839), 641–4.

26   'Catalepsy', *Reynolds's Miscellany* (10 November 1849), 248.

27 Ellis, 'Clinical Lecture on a Case of Catalepsy', p. 129.
28 [Anon.], 'Premature Interment', *Chambers's Edinburgh Journal* (4 May 1839), 115; W. J. Gordon, 'Trance', *The Leisure Hour* (June 1887), 393–5.
29 Ellis, 'Clinical Lecture on a Case of Catalepsy', p. 129; [Anon.], 'Premature Interment', p. 115.
30 See [Anon.], 'Premature Interment', p. 115. In France, Timothée Puel's record of 150 cases in Europe in 1856 was an attempt at providing a clear register for these stories; Puel, *De la catalepsie*.
31 John Eberle, *A Treatise on the Practice of Medicine* (Philadelphia: John Grigg, 1831), vol. 2, p. 70.
32 See Anne Carol's book on medical professionals and death. Carol explains that in France in the first half of the nineteenth century medical professionals in particular played upon such fictional descriptions in order to encourage the government to alter the laws regarding burial. She argues that medical professionals' descriptions of premature burials due to medical misdiagnosis oscillated between Gothic narrative and popular fiction, using a stereotypical set of actions whereby the patient recovered in the grave, starting with fits of panic and madness and ending with codified gestures, such as scratching and biting (out of despair or hunger). It is important to underline here that Carol's study does not focus on the medical literature related to catalepsy: the French medical literature on catalepsy we have examined never provided such gruesome and sensational details. However, as Carol explains, the rise of live burial stories in medical literature led to the publication of fictions that capitalised on the selling potential of such tales, such as A. Debay's *Les Vivants enterrés et les morts ressuscités, considérations physiologiques sur les morts apparentes et les inhumations précipitées* (1846) and Hyacinthe Le Guern's *Rosoline, ou les Mystères de la tombe, recueil historique d'événements nécessitant qu'on prenne des précautions pour bien constater l'intervalle qui peut s'écouler entre la mort imparfaite et la mort absolue* (1834). As a result, Carol adds, medical professionals complained about the lack of seriousness of such publications, and often denounced them as mere legends; Anne Carol, *Les Médecins et la mort, XIXᵉ-XXᵉ siècle* (s.l.: Aubier, 2004), pp. 151–5. Their protest, Carol explains, concealed in fact their wish to assert their unique authority over knowledge about death, paradoxically suggesting that the sensational rhetoric of French medical literature on the signs of death ensured its scientific value; Carol, *Les Médecins et la mort*, p. 161.
33 Edgar Allan Poe, 'The Premature Burial', in *Tales of Mystery and Imagination* (Ware: Wordsworth, 1993), pp. 270–88 (p. 271). All further references are to this edition and will be given parenthetically in the text.

³⁴ As seen in chapter 4, the collection of pathological cases was illustrated by the growth of medical collections over the course of the eighteenth and nineteenth centuries, which emblematised the normative function of pathological anatomy.

³⁵ As J. Gerard Kennedy contends, Poe probably read this case in *The Casket*, 2 (September 1827), 340–2; *Poe: A Critical Biography*, in J. Gerard Kennedy, 'Poe and Magazine Writing of Premature Burial', *Studies in the American Renaissance* (1977), 165–78 (p. 177 n.10).

³⁶ As Andrew Mangham argues, the case of Stapleton is most certainly a fictional one, perhaps directly inspired by John Galt's 'The Buried Alive' (1821). Thus, Poe blurs even more the frontiers between fiction and reality; Andrew Mangham, 'Buried Alive: The Gothic Awakening of Taphephobia', *Journal of Literature and Science*, 3/1 (2010), 10–22 (p. 15). Galt's tale will be analysed in the second part of this chapter.

³⁷ Robert Morrison and Chris Baldick's collection of tales of terror from *Blackwood's Magazine*, published by Oxford University Press (1995), contains many other illustrations of tales playing upon the live-burial motif, even if not related to a medical condition.

³⁸ The short story had certainly been inspired by Henry Thomson's 'Le Revenant', anonymously published in *Blackwood's Magazine* in April 1827. The story may also have inspired Dickens's 'The Black Veil' (1836), as seen in chapter 3, and *Oliver Twist* (1839).

³⁹ Meegan Kennedy, *Revising the Clinic: Vision and Representation in Victorian Medical Narrative and the Novel* (Columbus: Ohio State University, 2010), p. 26.

⁴⁰ Catalepsy would increasingly be associated with shocks over the course of the nineteenth century, especially 'moral shocks', as explained below.

⁴¹ Ellis, 'Clinical Lecture on a Case of Catalepsy', p. 129.

⁴² John Elliotson, *The Principles and Practices of Medicine: Founded on the most extensive experience in public hospitals and private practice; and developed in a course of lectures, delivered at University College London* (London: Joseph Butler, 1839), p. 545.

⁴³ Coldstream, 'Case of Catalepsy', p. 483.

⁴⁴ [Anon.], 'The Physician's Diary, in Blackwood', *The London Medical Gazette* (23 Oct. 1830), 118–19 (p. 119).

⁴⁵ [Anon.], 'Blackwood's Magazine v. the Secrets of the Medical Profession', *The Lancet*, 14/365 (28 August 1830), 878–9.

⁴⁶ [Anon.], 'The Physician's Diary, in Blackwood', p. 119.

⁴⁷ This idea is confirmed by the fact that the article from the *London Medical Gazette* proceeds to denounce the *Lancet* for having deleted all reference to the *London Medical Gazette* in their reply: 'By the way, we were very much amused in observing the manner in which the

fear of this journal influences the proceedings of a worthy contemporary even on the most trifling occasions. The writer in Blackwood speaks of what was done by the 'Lancet or the Medical Gazette'. The Editor of the former, in quoting the passage, omits altogether the name of the latter journal, and inserts only that of his own!!'; [Anon.], 'The Physician's Diary, in Blackwood', p. 119.

48 [Anon.], 'The Physician's Diary, in Blackwood', p. 119.

49 As Alexandra Bacopoulos-Viau observes, drawing on the work of Régine Plas (Régine Plas, *Naissance d'une science humaine: la psychologie. Les psychologues et 'le merveilleux psychique'* (Rennes: Presses Universitaires de Rennes, 2000)), Petetin emphasised the supernatural in particular in order to explain catalepsy, whilst moving away from theories then current on mesmerism; Alexandra Bacopoulos-Viau, 'La Danse des corps figés. Catalepsie et imaginaire medical au XIXe siècle', *Revue d'histoire du XIXe siècle*, 44/1 (2012), 165–84 (p. 169). Warren's mention of Petetin (and one of his patients exhibiting a transfer of the senses to the pit of the stomach and the fingers and toes) is therefore all the more significant in his Gothic clinical case histories.

50 It is noteworthy that an early 1831–2 edition of Warren's collection of fictional medical cases, published under the title of *Affecting Scenes: Being Passages from the Diary of a Physician*, included John Galt's 'The Buried Alive'.

51 John Galt, 'The Buried Alive', *The Provost and other tales* (Edinburgh and London: Blackwood and Sons), vol. 4, pp. 286–90 (p. 290). All further references are to this edition and will be given parenthetically in the text.

52 Ellis, 'Clinical Lecture on a Case of Catalepsy', p. 129.

53 Andrew Smith, *Gothic Death, 1740–1914. A Literary History* (Manchester: Manchester University Press, 2016), p. 4.

54 Smith, *Gothic Death, 1740–1914*, p. 164.

55 Catherine Crowe, 'The Monk's Story', in *Light and Darkness; or, Mysteries of Life* (London: Henry Colburn, 1850), vol. 2, pp. 305–20; vol. 3, pp. 1–21, 310. All further references are to this edition and will be given parenthetically in the text.

56 This idea would be particularly underlined in the medical literature of the last decades of the nineteenth century: 'The distinctive feature of catalepsy is automatism, so that the mind is manipulated with the same ease as the limbs. The somnambulist, on the other hand, has strong personality, aversions and preferences'; [Anon.], 'Science', *Westminster Review* (January 1888), 242–8 (p. 244).

57 Henry Maudsley, *Body and Mind: An Inquiry into Their Connection and Mutual Influence, Specially in Reference to Mental Disorders* (London:

Macmillan, 1870), p. 43. See also this passage from an 1890 article, which describes an experiment aimed at inducing catalepsy, and associates catalepsy with brain localisation ('certain special departments of the brain'), a point which we will develop later in this chapter: 'We open the eyelids, we cause a flashing light to penetrate right into his eyes; the light passes into his brain, and proceeds to cause special kinds of activity and to illuminate certain special departments of the brain. A new condition is now produced, the condition of catalepsy . . . A man in this cataleptic condition ceases to be a man, and becomes a machine, and a machine which, when set in motion, develops extra-ordinary force'; [Anon.], 'The Miracles of Hypnotism', *Review of Reviews* (June 1890), 486.

58   See, for instance, Henry Maudsley's *The Pathology of Mind* (1857) (New York: D. Appleton and Co., 1880), ch. 2, pp. 50–82. On Maudsley, see Trevor Turner, 'Henry Maudsley: Psychiatrist, Philosopher and Entrepreneur', in W. F. Bynum et al. (eds), *The Anatomy of Madness: Essays in the History of Psychiatry* (London: Routledge, 1988), vol. 3, pp. 151–89. I owe this reference to Neil Davie.

59   Anne Stiles, *Popular Fiction and Brain Science in the Late Nineteenth Century* (Cambridge: Cambridge University Press, 2012), p. 13.

60   George Eliot's *Silas Marner* (1861), and a few years later Jules Barbey d'Aurevilly's *Un Prêtre marié* (1865) (*A Married Priest*) in France, used catalepsy as a narrative plot device, albeit without hints at fears of premature interment.

61   Jean Frollo in 'Outre-Tombe', *Le Petit Parisien* (12 January 1887), mentions the case of a servant in Toulouse who cut off his mistress's finger to steal her jewels and woke her from her cataleptic trance. This cause célèbre is probably the story which influenced Maupassant and Diguet, although no date is given and several versions of the same story seemed to have been circulating throughout the nineteenth century.

62   Jas R. Williamson, 'Hypnotic Trance and Premature Burial', *The Speaker* (21 September 1895), 315–16 (p. 316).

63   Franz Hartmann, *Buried Alive: Examination into the Occult Causes of Apparent Death, Trance and Catalepsy* (Boston: s.n., 1895).

64   Mary Elizabeth Hotz, *Literary Remains: Representations of Death and Burial in Victorian England* (New York: State University of New York Press, 2009), pp. 142–3. See also W. R. J., 'Cremation and Premature Burial', *British Architect* (20 May 1896), 201.

65   Laurence Talairach-Vielmas, *Wilkie Collins, Medicine and the Gothic* (Cardiff: University of Wales Press, 2009). This section summarises parts of chapter 6.

66   When literal cases of live burial are evoked in sensation novels, they tend to remain confined to the recesses of the text – to the world of dreams and imagination. For instance, in M. E. Braddon's *Lady Audley's Secret* as serialised in the *Sixpenny Magazine*, the amateur detective Robert Audley sees the grave of Lucy Talboys (alias the bigamous Lady Audley) open and the eponymous heroine gaily trip out of her grave (*Sixpenny Magazine*, 3 (1862), 65). There, the theme of the 'living dead' serves to dramatise the detective's suspicions concerning his aunt's identity, in a dream in which the female criminal is reborn out of putrefying matter.

67   As I have suggested in *Wilkie Collins, Medicine and the Gothic*, Collins may have read James Bower Harrison's *The Medical Aspects of Death* (1852), which dealt with the signs of death and recorded cases simulating death. Illustrating his argument with many anecdotes, Harrison made explicit the difficulties encountered by professionals when interpreting the indications of death, especially in cases of catalepsy – though these, he claimed, should not deceive the people 'familiar with the appearances of a corpse'; James Bower Harrison, *The Medical Aspects of Death, and the Medical Aspects of the Human Mind* (London: Longman, Brown, Green and Longmans, 1852), p. 13.

68   Wilkie Collins, *Jezebel's Daughter* (1880) (Stroud: Alan Sutton, 1995), p. 197.

69   Bondeson, *Buried Alive*, pp. 100, 105.

70   See Laura Otis, 'Howled out of the Country: Wilkie Collins and H. G. Wells Retry David Ferrier', in Anne Stiles (ed.), *Neurology and Literature, 1860–1920* (Basingstoke: Palgrave, 2007), pp. 27–51 (p. 33). A very large number of articles were published in professional and lay journals denouncing cruelty to animals. See, for instance, [Anon.], 'Cruelty to Animals', *The Cornhill Magazine*, 170 (February 1874), 213–26 (p. 218).

71   Professor Jevons, 'Cruelty to Animals – A Study in Sociology', *The Fortnightly Review*, 19 (January–June 1876), 671–84 (p. 674).

72   Collins even quotes a sentence from Ferrier's *The Localisation of Cerebral Disease*: 'We cannot even be sure whether many of the changes discovered are the cause or the result of the disease, or whether the two are the conjoint result of a common cause'; David Ferrier, *The Localisation of Cerebral Disease, being the Gulstonian Lectures of the Royal College of Physicians for 1878* (London: Smith, Elder and Co., 1878), p. 6.

73   Valerie Pedlar, 'Experimentation or Exploitation? The Investigations of David Ferrier, Dr. Benjulia and Dr. Seward', *Interdisciplinary Science Reviews*, 28/3 (September 2003), 169–74 (p. 169).

74 Wilkie Collins, *Heart and Science* (1883) (Stroud: Alan Sutton, 1994), p. 255. All further references are to this edition and will be given parenthetically in the text.

75 See Harrison, *The Medical Aspects of Death*, p. 51: 'the effects of *shock* are much more numerous and interesting than might at first be imagined. At least, impressions on the nervous system, analogous in their nature, play an important part in the fatal termination of many diseases'.

76 'A disease which is closely allied to the abnormal states described, holding an intermediate place between them and epilepsy, is catalepsy. The person who is subject to cataleptic attacks falls suddenly into a state of seeming unconsciousness, but does not fall down . . . To all appearance he is little more than a half-animated statue while the paroxysm lasts. He seems partially or completely insensible to external impressions, and when his arm or any part of the body is put unto a certain position that position is retained for an indefinite time, or until he comes to himself again. The pulse is usually more feeble and the respiration more slow than in the natural state. The fit may last for a few minutes only, or for a few hours, occasionally for a yet longer period, and when it is over there is no memory of what has happened during it. No particular mental state, voluntary or involuntary, seems to have anything to do with the induction of the cataleptic state, although it is probably enough that a moral shock might be the occasion of an attack'; Maudsley, *The Pathology of Mind*, p. 74. In some medical articles, lethargy is defined as the first stage when a patient is hypnotised, followed by catalepsy; see [Anon.], 'The Miracles of Hypnotism', p. 486.

77 Gilles de la Tourette worked with Charcot at the Salpêtrière from 1884; his experiments often sought to prove that murders could be provoked by hypnotic suggestion. See Gilles de la Tourette, *L'Hypnotisme et les états analogues du point de vue médico-légal* (Paris: Plon, 1887).

78 See Bondeson, *Buried Alive*, p. 251.

79 Using ether, the husband reconstructs past thoughts or images of his wife as particles of matter, hence he resuscitates her by casting out of his body millions of molecules. I am aligning here the woman's etheric body, inspired by late nineteenth-century occultism and esoteric philosophies (Theosophy), with her soul, since Lermina rewrites the ghost story as a *fin-de-siècle* 'spirit' story, from the Latin *spiritus*, meaning breath.

80 Medical practitioners are, indeed, more associated with death than with resuscitation, throughout the narrative. At the end of the short story, the best Parisian physician is called to put an end to the husband's flow of memories, thus burying the resurrected wife for ever.

81 This is similar in Charles Dickens's 'The Black Veil', where a mother has her hanged son's body stolen by body-snatchers and brought to a surgeon for reanimation. The mother defines, indeed, death, as 'life . . . passing away', as if flowing through the body before leaving it, and therefore not as a series of signs but rather primarily as an organic and physical process, unlike the medical practitioner, who is constructed as a sign reader throughout the short story; Charles Dickens, 'The Black Veil' (1836) (London: Hodder and Stoughton, 2000), p. 22.

82 Thomas Richards, *The Imperial Archive: Knowledge and the Fantasy of Empire* (London and New York: Verso, 1993), p. 60.

83 Richards, *The Imperial Archive*, p. 61.

84 Richards, *The Imperial Archive*, p. 61.

85 Stiles, *Popular Fiction and Brain Science in the Late Nineteenth Century*, p. 56.

86 Ruth Richardson, *Death, Dissection and the Destitute* (1987) (Chicago and London: University of Chicago Press, 2000), p. 16. Hence the rise of discourses around the afterlife which accompanied the popularisation of cremation. For Mary Elizabeth Hotz, by 'banish[ing] decay through incineration', cremation could thus 'undermine faith in the resurrection of the body'; Hotz, *Literary Remains*, pp. 37, 142.

87 Richardson, *Death, Dissection and the Destitute*, p. 16.

88 Richardson, *Death, Dissection and the Destitute*, p. 8.

89 Richardson, *Death, Dissection and the Destitute*, p. 15.

90 Smith, *Gothic Death, 1740–1914*, p. 171. See in particular his analysis of Henry Drummond's *Natural Law in the Spiritual World* (1883) and Frederic W. H. Myers, *Human Personality and Its Survival of Bodily Death* (1907), pp. 138–63.

91 Smith, *Gothic Death, 1740–1914*, p. 185.

92 Smith, *Gothic Death, 1740–1914*, p. 189.

93 Herbert Mayo ['MacDavus'], 'Letters on the Truth contained in Popular Superstitions: Vampirism', *Blackwood's Edinburgh Magazine*, 61 (1847), 432–40, quoted in Mangham, 'Buried Alive', p. 17.

94 Mangham, 'Buried Alive', p. 11.

95 Robert Mighall, *A Geography of Victorian Gothic Fiction: Mapping History's Nightmares* (Oxford: Oxford University Press, 1999), p. 221.

96 G. W. M. Reynolds, *The Mysteries of the Court of London*, first series, new edn (London: John Dicks, n.d.), vol. 2, pp. 116–17, quoted in Mighall, *A Geography of Victorian Gothic Fiction*, p. 218. As Robert Mighall explains, 'Reynolds's version of Bertrand, which appeared shortly after the accounts found in the medical press, restores all the Gothic status that "The Vampire's" encounter with clinical science may have diminished'; Mighall, *A Geography of Victorian Gothic Fiction*, p. 217.

97 Stiles, *Popular Fiction and Brain Science in the Late Nineteenth Century*, p. 6.

98 Stiles, *Popular Fiction and Brain Science in the Late Nineteenth Century*, p. 6.

99 Stiles, *Popular Fiction and Brain Science in the Late Nineteenth Century*, p. 59.

100 John Gray, *The Theory of Dreams, in Which an Inquiry is Made into the Powers and Faculties of the Human Mind, as They are Illustrated in the Most Remarkable Dreams in Sacred and Profane History* (London: F. C. and J. Rivington, 1808), vol. 2, p. 29.

101 Gray, *The Theory of Dreams*, vol. 2, p. 73.

102 Katherine Byrne, *Tuberculosis and the Victorian Literary Imagination* (Cambridge: Cambridge University Press, 2011), p. 131.

103 The full title of the novel is *Dracula; or, the Dead Undead*; Andrew Smith, *Gothic Literature* (2007) (Edinburgh: Edinburgh University Press, 2013), p. 114.

104 Smith, *Gothic Death, 1740–1914*, p. 185.

105 Smith, *Gothic Death, 1740–1914*, pp. 187–8.

106 Bram Stoker, *Dracula* (1897), ed. Nina Auerbach and David S. Skal (New York and London: Norton and Company, 1997), p. 278. All further references are to this edition and will be given parenthetically in the text.

107 This is typical of the turn of the century, leading to much medical concern. The novel shows the female characters entertaining themselves and going to concerts, and refers several times to women's appetites: Mina even mentions once that she and Lucy 'should have shocked the "New Woman" with [their] appetites' (p. 86).

108 See for instance Herman Moest's *The Fate of Beauty* (1898) or John Collier's *The Death of Albine* (c.1895). On Victorian art and representations of feminine mortality, see Bram Dijkstra, *Idols of Perversity: Fantasies of Feminine Evil in Fin-de-Siècle Culture* (Oxford: Oxford University Press, 1986), pp. 50–63.

109 Byrne, *Tuberculosis and the Victorian Literary Imagination*, p. 130. Drawing upon Lawlor's analysis of the novel (Clark Lawlor, *Consumption and Literature: The Making of the Romantic Disease* (Basingstoke: Palgrave, 2006), p. 188), Byrne contends as well that *Dracula* may have been influenced by medical discoveries related to contagious diseases such as Robert Koch's identification of the agents of tuberculosis.

110 Some critics have read *Dracula*'s obsession with contamination as related to the fear of syphilis, and read the mark of the Sacred Wafer on Mina's forehead as a lesion. See Elaine Showalter, 'Syphilis, Sexuality and the fiction of the *Fin de Siècle*', in Ruth Bernard Yeazell (ed.), *Sex, Politics*

Notes

and *Science in the Nineteenth Century* (Baltimore: John Hopkins University Press, 1986), pp. 88–115 (p. 99), quoted in Byrne, *Tuberculosis and the Victorian Literary Imagination*, p. 130.

111 William Carpenter, *Principles of Mental Physiology with Their Applications to the Training and Discipline of the Mind and the Study of Its Morbid Conditions*, 4th edn (New York: D. Appleton and Co., 1889), p. 591.

112 As Jane Wood has pointed out, beneath the cultural given of woman's patience and endurance lay widespread confusion as to the actual meaning of the female will. Signifying simultaneously both wilfulness and volition, will was a key term to naturalise and enforce woman's powerless position. Caught within this physiological discourse, the supposed weakness of the female inevitably placed women alongside animals and half-wits on the evolutionary scale. Hence the parallel between Lucy and Renfield in the novel, both having their head cut off or their skull broken, both becoming the victims as much of Dracula as of the medical professionals (ironically, Renfield also plays the role of Sleeping Beauty, as he pretends to sleep to escape the asylum, wearing a white nightgown, just like Lucy). Jane Wood, *Passion and Pathology in Victorian Fiction* (Oxford: Oxford University Press, 2001), p. 45.

113 See Anne Carol's study of physiological experiments carried out on guillotined heads, for instance, and how transfusion gradually replaced electricity to reanimate the heads; Carol, *Les Médecins et la mort*.

114 Smith, *Gothic Death, 1740–1914*, p. 189.

115 Richards, *The Imperial Archive*, p. 61.

116 Smith, *Gothic Death, 1740–1914*, p. 189.

117 Maudsley, *The Pathology of Mind*, p. 60.

118 [Anon.], 'Somnambulism', *Saturday Review* (18 August 1860), 202–3 (p. 202).

119 See A. Watterville, 'Sleep and its Counterfeits', *Fortnightly Review* (May 1887), 732–42: 'it is difficult to draw a line between normal and abnormal sleep; the physiological condition merges by insensible degrees into all kinds of pathological states, known as lethargy, trance, stupor, coma. Through the usual phenomena of dreaming, we pass likewise into those of nightmare, somnambulism, hypnotism, ecstasy, and the like' (p. 732).

120 Smith also notes how the Count's association with death is sustained throughout the novel, from the smell which characterises the vampire to Van Helsing, who believes that 'all of the dead that he can come nigh to are for him to command' (p. 209), or Swales's death, which is believed to have involved a visual encounter with Death ('Perhaps he had seen Death with his dying eyes' (p. 85)); Smith, *Gothic Death, 1740–1914*, p. 188.

259

121 The links between catalepsy and hysteria are reinforced when the vampire finally dies, writhing like one of Charcot's hysterics.

122 Carpenter, *Principles of Mental Physiology*, pp. 709–10.

123 The characters refer to the theories expounded by Cesare Lombroso in his book, *Criminal Man* (1876). Lombroso's theories, notably that of the 'born criminal', first became known to British readers when French and German translations of *Criminal Man* became available in the late 1880s. His ideas received further exposure following the publication of Max Nordau's *Degeneration* (1893). See Neil Davie, 'Lombroso and the "Men of Real Science": British Reactions, 1886–1918', in Paul Knepper and P. J. Ystehede (eds), *The Cesare Lombroso Handbook* (London: Routledge, 2013), pp. 342–60.

124 Carpenter, *Principles of Mental Physiology*, pp. 709–22.

125 Smith, *Gothic Death, 1740–1914*, p. 187.

126 Smith, *Gothic Death, 1740–1914*, p. 195.

6: Epilogue

1 H. G. Wells, *The Invisible Man*, in *Six Novels* (San Diego: Canterbury Classics, 2012), pp. 145–247 (p. 185). All further references are to this edition and will be given in the text.

2 Mario Praz, *The Romantic Agony* (1933) (London and New York: Oxford University Press, 1970), p. xxi.

3 Kelly Hurley, *The Gothic Body: Sexuality, Materialism and Degeneration at the Fin de Siècle* (1996) (Cambridge: Cambridge University Press, 2004), p. 5.

4 Hurley, *The Gothic Body*, p. 32.

5 Hurley, *The Gothic Body*, p. 6.

6 Hurley, *The Gothic Body*, p. 34.

7 Hurley, *The Gothic Body*, p. 33.

8 Robert Mighall, *A Geography of Victorian Gothic Fiction: Mapping History's Nightmares* (Oxford: Oxford University Press, 1999), p. xxiii.

9 Hurley analyses however the increasing stress on the physical and physiological, rather than on the psychological, which Mighall sees as characteristic of the 'somatic' character of late-Victorian Gothic fiction (Mighall, *A Geography of Victorian Gothic Fiction*, p. 130).

10 C. R. T. Crosthwaite, 'Röntgen's Curse', *Longman's Magazine*, 28 (1896), 469–84 (p. 470). All subsequent references are to this edition and will be given parenthetically in the text.

11 Caroline MacCracker-Flesher reads Dr Jekyll as a double of Dr Knox; Caroline McCraker-Flesher, *The Doctor Dissected: A Cultural Autopsy*

of the Burke and Hare Murders (Oxford: Oxford University Press, 2012), pp. 101–17. Anne Stiles traces connections with the Bordeaux physician Eugène Azam, who published a series of cases in the *Revue Scientifique* in the late 1870s. These included the case of Félida X., suffering from 'double consciousness' or 'doubling of the personality', as well as that of Sergeant F., a soldier in the Franco-Prussian War whose left cerebral hemisphere had been damaged by a gunshot wound and who suffered in addition from dual personality. Both cases were mentioned by Victorian scientists and popularisers and related by the periodicals of the time; Anne Stiles, *Popular Fiction and Brain Science in the Late Nineteenth Century* (Cambridge: Cambridge University Press, 2012), pp. 28–9.

[12]   As Anne Stiles puts it, Stevenson 'parodies the form of the case study in order to reveal the weaknesses of late-Victorian scientific narrative, specifically, how the linearity and emotional detachment of medical case studies obscures the baroque complexity of mental pathology'; Stiles, *Popular Fiction and Brain Science in the Late Nineteenth Century*, p. 30.

[13]   Michel Foucault, *The Birth of the Clinic: An Archeology of Medical Perception* (1973), trans. A. M. Sheridan (London: Routledge 2000), p. 125.

[14]   Maggie Kilgour, *The Rise of the Gothic Novel* (New York and London: Routledge, 1995), p. 31.

Select Bibliography

༄

Primary sources

Abernethy, John, *Hunterian Oration* (London: s.n., 1819).

Acton, William, *Prostitution, Considered in its Moral, Social and Sanitary Aspects* (s.l.: s.n., 1857).

Aikin, John and Anna Letitia Barbauld, 'On the Pleasure Derived from Objects of Terror', in *Miscellaneous pieces, in prose* (Belfast: James Magee, 1774), pp. 57–65.

[Anon.], 'Anatomical Studies – Mrs Sexton', *Punch, or the London Charivari*, 31 (13 September 1856), 108.

[Anon.], *The Animated Skeleton* (1798) (Chicago: Valancourt Books, 2005).

[Anon.], 'Belles Lettres', *Westminster Review*, 86 (October 1866), 268–80.

[Anon.], 'Blackwood's Magazine v. the Secrets of the Medical Profession', *The Lancet*, 14/365 (28 August 1830), 878–9.

[Anon.], 'Case of John McIntire, Miraculous Circumstances. Being a full and particular account of John Macintire, who was buried alive, in Edinburgh, on the 15th day of April, 1824, while in a trance, and who was taken up by the resurrection-men, and sold to the doctors to be dissected, with a full account of the many strange and wonderful things which he saw and felt while he was in that state, the whole being taken from his own words' (Gateshead: Stephenson, Printer, 1824).

[Anon.], 'Catalepsie (Emploi avantageux du valérianate de zinc dans la)', *Bulletin général de thérapeutique médicale et chirurgicale*, 40 (1851), 472.

[Anon.], 'Catalepsie qui a duré 8 ans, guérie par le vomissement d'un ver, par le docteur Hubertz (à Aalbug)', *Gazette médicale de Paris: journal de médecine et des sciences accessoires*, 3/2 (6 February 1847), 111.

[Anon.], 'Catalepsy', *Reynolds's Miscellany* (10 November 1849), 248.

[Anon.], 'Charge against a surgeon for the removal of a dead body for anatomical purposes', *The Lancet*, 2 (20 October 1855), 377.

[Anon.], 'Cruelty to Animals', *The Cornhill Magazine*, 170 (February 1874), 213–26.

[Anon.], 'De la catalepsie', *Archives générales de médecine*, 5/10 (1857), 206–21.

[Anon.], 'Dr. Kahn's Anatomical Museum', *Medical Times: Journal of Medical Science, Literature, Criticism, and News*, new series, 2 (4 January–28 June 1851), 496.

[Anon.], 'Dr. Kahn's Anatomical Museum', *The Lancet*, 1 (1851), 474.

[Anon.], 'Dr. Kahn's Anatomical Museum', *The Lancet*, 1 (17 June 1854), 654.

[Anon.], 'Dr. Kahn's Anatomical Museum', *The Lancet*, 1 (24 June 1854), 684.

[Anon.], 'Dr. Kahn's Anatomical Museum', *The Lancet*, 1 (1 July 1854), 700.

[Anon.], 'Dr. Kahn's Anatomical Museum', *The Lancet*, 2 (15 August 1857), 175.

[Anon.], 'Dr. Kahn's Anatomical Museum', *The Lancet*, 2 (28 November 1857), 558.

[Anon.], 'Injection d'une solution de tartre stibié dans les veines dans un cas de catalepsie', *Bulletin général de thérapeutique médicale et chirurgicale*, 10 (1836), 103–4.

[Anon.], 'Magnétisme animal: Cas extraordinaire de catalepsie d'abord naturelle, puis reproduite artificiellement; observé à Bologne . . .', *Gazette médicale de Paris: journal de médecine et des sciences accessoires*, 2/1 (1833), 106.

[Anon.], 'The Medical Evidence of Crime', *Cornhill Magazine*, 7 (January–June 1863), 338–48.

[Anon.], 'The Miracles of Hypnotism', *Review of Reviews* (June 1890), 486.

[Anon.], *Mort Castle. A Gothic Story* (London: Printed for the Author, 1798).

[Anon.], '"The Most Shameful Sight in the World": An Impudent Quack', *The Tomahawk* (22 February 1868), 81.

[Anon.], 'Noctes Ambrosianae', *Blackwood's Edinburgh Magazine*, 25 (1829), 371–400.

[Anon.], 'Novels of the Day: Their Writers and Readers', *Fraser's Magazine*, 62 (August 1860), 205–17.

[Anon.], 'On Premature Interment', *The European Magazine and London Review*, 83 (December 1822–July 1823), 124–7.

[Anon.], 'On the Pleasures of Body-Snatching', *Monthly Magazine*, 3/16 (April 1827), 355–65.

[Anon.], 'Pater Familias, A Visitor, and Others', *The Lancet*, 2 (8 July 1854), 22.

[Anon.], 'The Philosophy of Burking', *Fraser's Magazine*, 5/25 (February 1832), 52–65.

[Anon.], 'The Physician's Diary, in Blackwood', *The London Medical Gazette* (23 October 1830), 118–19.

[Anon.], 'The Popular Novels of the Year', *Fraser's Magazine*, 68 (August 1863), 253–69.

[Anon.], 'Premature Interment', *Chambers's Edinburgh Journal* (4 May 1839), 115.

[Anon.], 'Prolonged catalepsy in a soldier', *The Lancet* (22 August 1883), 354.

[Anon.], [Review of Wilkie Collins's *Armadale*], *Saturday Review*, 21 (16 June 1866), 726–7.

[Anon.], [Review of *Jezebel's Daughter*], *Spectator*, 53 (15 May 1880), 627–8.

[Anon.], [Review of Wilkie Collins's *Poor Miss Finch*], *Nation*, 14 (7 March 1872), 158–9.

[Anon.], [Review of Wilkie Collins's *The Moonstone*], *Spectator*, 61 (25 July 1868), 881–2.

[Anon.], [Review of Matthew Lewis's *The Monk*], *Monthly Review*, 2nd series, 23 (1797), 453.

[Anon.], 'Science', *Westminster Review* (January 1888), 242–8.

[Anon.], [Sensation Novels], *Nation* (17 September 1868), 235.

[Anon.], 'Somnambulism', *Saturday Review* (18 August 1860), 202–3.

[Anon.], *The Spirit of Turretville; or, the Mysterious Resemblance* (London: R. Dutton, 1800).

[Anon.], *The Trial of William Burke and Helen M'Dougal before the High Court of Judiciary at Edinburgh on Wednesday, December 24. 1828 for the Murder of Margery Campbell, or Docherty taken in shorthand by Mr. John Macnee* (Edinburgh: Robert Buchanan, William Hunter, John Stevenson; London: Balwick and Cradock, 1828).

[Anon.], 'Wonderful Case of Catalepsy: Case of Spontaneous Catalepsy, &c., Observed at Bologna by MM. Carini and J. Visconti, and by M. Mazzacorati', *The Lancet*, 19/494 (16 February 1833), 663–5.

Aurevilly, Jules Barbey d', *Un Prêtre marié* (1865) (Paris: Garnier-Flammarion, 1993).

Bailey, James Blake, *The Diary of a Resurrectionist, 1811–12, to which are Added an Account of the Resurrection Men in London and a Short History of the Passing of the Anatomy Act* (London: Swan Sonnenschein and Co., 1896).

Baring-Gould, Sabine, The *Book of Were-Wolves: being an account of a terrible superstition* (London: Smith, Elder and Co., 1865).

Behn, Aphra, *The History of the Nun; or, the Fair Vow-Breaker* (London: A. Baskerville, 1689).

Blessington, Marguerite Countess of, *The Idler in Italy* (Paris: Galignani, 1839).

Bouchut, Eugène, *Traité des signes de la mort* (1848) (Paris: J.-B. Baillière, 1849).

Braddon, Mary Elizabeth, *Birds of Prey* (London: Ward, Lock and Tyler, 1867).

Braddon, Mary Elizabeth, *Charlotte's Inheritance* (London: Ward, Lock and Tyler, 1868).

Braddon, Mary Elizabeth, *The Cloven Foot* (London: s.n., 1879).

Braddon, Mary Elizabeth, *The Doctor's Wife* (1864) (Oxford: Oxford University Press, 1998).

Braddon, Mary Elizabeth, *The Golden Calf* (London: J. and R. Maxwell, 1883).

Braddon, Mary Elizabeth, *Lady Audley's Secret* (1862) (Oxford: Oxford University Press, 1991).

Brewer, George, *The Witch of Ravenworth* (1808), ed. Allen Grove (Chicago: Valancourt Books, 2006).

Brontë, Emily, *Wuthering Heights* (1847) (London: Penguin, 2003).

Broussais, F.-V.-J., *De l'irritation et de la folie* (Bruxelles: Librairie Polymathique, 1828).

Burke, Edmund, *The Works of the Right Honourable Edmund Burke*, 12 vols (London: John C. Nimmo, 1887).

Burton, Robert, *Anatomy of Melancholy* (1621) (Oxford: Henry Cripps, 1651).

[Butler, Harriet], *Count Eugenio; or, Fatal Errors. A Tale, Founded on Fact* (London: J. F. Hughes, 1807).

Butler, Samuel, *Hudibras* (1725–6) (London: D. Midwinter, 1732).

Carlyle, Thomas, *The French Revolution* (London: James Fraser, 1837).

Carlyle, Thomas, *The Works of Thomas Carlyle*, Centenary Edition, 30 vols (London: s.n., 1896–9).

Carpenter, William, *Principles of Mental Physiology with Their Applications to the Training and Discipline of the Mind and the Study of Its Morbid Conditions*, 4th edn (New York: D. Appleton and Co., 1889).

Select Bibliography

[Carver, Mrs], *The Horrors of Oakendale Abbey* (1797) (s.l.: Zittaw Press, 2006).

[Carver, Mrs], *The Old Woman* (1800) (s.l.: Dodo Press, 2011).

[Chorley, H. F.], [Review of *Armadale*], *The Athenaeum* (2 June 1866), 732–3.

Cobbe, Frances Power, 'The Morals of Literature', *Fraser's*, 70 (July 1864), 124–33.

Coldstream, John, 'Case of Catalepsy', *Edinburgh Medical and Surgical Journal*, 81 (July 1854), 477–91.

Collins, Wilkie, *After Dark* (Leipzig: Bernhard Tauchnitz, 1856).

Collins, Wilkie, *Armadale* (1866), ed. John Sutherland (London: Penguin Classics, 1995).

Collins, Wilkie, *Basil* (1852) (Oxford: Oxford University Press, 1990).

Collins, Wilkie, *The Complete Shorter Fiction*, ed. Julian Thompson (London: Robinson, 1995).

Collins, Wilkie, *The Haunted Hotel: A Story of Modern Venice* (1879) (Stroud: Alan Sutton, 1994).

Collins, Wilkie, *Heart and Science* (1883), ed. Steve Farmer (Toronto: Broadview Press, 1997).

Collins, Wilkie, *Heart and Science* (1883) (Stroud: Alan Sutton, 1994).

Collins, Wilkie, *Jezebel's Daughter* (1880) (Stroud: Alan Sutton, 1995).

Collins, Wilkie, *The Legacy of Cain* (1888) (Stroud: Alan Sutton, 1993).

Collins, Wilkie, *Mad Monkton and Other Stories*, ed. Norman Page (Oxford: Oxford University Press, 1994).

Collins, Wilkie, *The Moonstone* (1868) (London: Penguin, 1986).

Collins, Wilkie, 'The Unknown Public', *Household Words*, 18 (21 August 1858), 217–22.

Collins, Wilkie, *The Woman in White* (1860) (Stroud: Alan Sutton, 1992).

[Cook, E. D.], [Review of Wilkie Collins's *Heart and Science*], *Athenaeum* (28 April 1883), 538–9.

Crosthwaite, C. R. T., 'Röntgen's Curse', *Longman's Magazine*, 28 (1896), 469–84.

Crowe, Catherine, *Light and Darkness; or, Mysteries of Life* (London: Henry Colburn, 1850).

Crowe, Catherine, *The Night Side of Nature; or, Ghosts and Ghost Seers* (London: T. C. Newby, 1848).

Cullen, Stephen, *The Castle of Inchvally; A Tale* (1796) (London: J. S. Pratt, 1844).

Cullen, Stephen, *The Haunted Priory; or, the Fortunes of the House of Rayo* (London: J. Bell, 1794).

267

Curties, T. J. Horsley, *Ancient Records; Or, the Abbey of Saint Oswythe. A Romance, etc.* (London: William Lane, 1801).

Dallas, E. S., '*Lady Audley's Secret*', *The Times* (18 November 1862), 8.

Debay, A., *Les Vivants enterrés et les morts ressuscités, considérations physiologiques sur les morts apparentes et les inhumations précipitées* (Paris: Moquet, 1846).

Dickens, Charles, 'A Great Day for the Doctors', *Household Words*, 32/2 (9 November 1850), 137–9.

Dickens, Charles, *Barnaby Rudge* (1841) (London: Penguin, 1998).

Dickens, Charles, *The Black Veil* (1836) (London: Hodder and Stoughton, 2000).

Dickens, Charles, *Bleak House* (1853) (Oxford: Oxford University Press, 2008).

Dickens, Charles, *David Copperfield* (1850) (Oxford: Oxford University Press, 2000).

Dickens, Charles, *Great Expectations* (1861) (Oxford: Oxford University Press, 1994).

Dickens, Charles, 'History in Wax', *Household Words*, 9 (18 February 1854), 17–20.

Dickens, Charles, *The Lamplighter* (London: Chapman and Hall, Ltd; New York: Charles Scribner's Sons, 1905).

Dickens, Charles, *Martin Chuzzlewit* (1844) (Ware: Wordsworth Classics, 1994).

Dickens, Charles, *Our Mutual Friend* (1865) (Oxford: Oxford University Press, 2008).

Dickens, Charles, *Nicholas Nickleby* (1839) (London: Penguin, 1994).

Dickens, Charles, *Oliver Twist; or, the Parish Boy's Progress* (Paris: Baudry's European Library, 1839).

Dickens, Charles, *The Pickwick Papers* (1837) (Ware: Wordsworth Classics, 1993).

Dickens, Charles, *A Tale of Two Cities* (1859) (Oxford: Oxford University Press, 2008).

Dickens, Charles, 'The Uncommercial Traveller', *All the Year Round* (16 May 1863), 276–80.

Dickens, Charles, 'Use and Abuse of the Dead', *Household Words*, 17 (3 April 1858), 361–5.

Diguet, Charles, 'Le Doigt de la Morte' (1887), in *Petit Musée des Horreurs: Nouvelles Fantastiques, Cruelles et Macabres*, ed. Nathalie Prince (Paris: Robert Laffont, 2008), pp. 100–7.

Dupaty, Charles, *Lettres sur l'Italie en 1785*, 2nd edn (Tours: Ad Mame et Cie., 1843).

[Dodd, George], 'Dolls', *Household Words*, 7/168 (11 June 1853), 352–6.

Drummond, Henry, *Natural Law in the Spiritual World* (London: Hodder and Stoughton, 1884).

Eberle, John, *A Treatise on the Practice of Medicine* (Philadelphia: John Grigg, 1831).

Eliot, George, *Middlemarch* (1871) (London: Penguin, 1985).

Eliot, George, *Silas Marner* (1861) (Stroud: Alan Sutton, 1991).

Elliotson, John, *The Principles and Practices of Medicine: Founded on the most extensive experience in public hospitals and private practice; and developed in a course of lectures, delivered at University College London* (London: Joseph Butler, 1839).

Ellis, Andrew Esq., 'Clinical Lecture on a Case of Catalepsy, occuring in the Jervis-Street Hospital, Dublin', *The Lancet*, 2 (2 May 1835), 129–34.

Ferrier, David, *The Localisation of Cerebral Disease, being the Gulstonian Lectures of the Royal College of Physicians for 1878* (London: Smith, Elder and Co., 1878).

Forsyth, Joseph, *Remarks on Antiquities, Arts and Letters, During an Excursion in Italy in the Years 1802 and 1803* (1813), 4th edn (London: John Murray, 1835).

Forsyth, Joseph, *Remarks on Antiquities, Arts and Letters, During an Excursion in Italy in the Years 1802 and 1803* (1813), 2nd edn (Geneva: Ledouble, 1820).

Fox, Joseph, *Santa Maria; or the Mysterious Pregnancy. A Romance* (London: s.n., 1797).

Frost, Thomas, *The Old Showmen and the Old London Fairs*, 2nd edn (London: Tinsley Brothers, 1875).

Gall, F. J. and G. Spurzheim, *Anatomie et physiologie du système nerveux en général et du cerveau en particulier*, vol. 2 (Paris: F. Schoell, 1812).

Galt, John, 'The Buried Alive', *Blackwood's Edinburgh Magazine*, 10 (1821), 262–4.

Galt, John, 'The Buried Alive', in *The Provost and Other Tales* (Edinburgh and London: Blackwood and Sons, 1842), vol. 4, pp. 286–90.

Garth, Samuel, *The Dispensary. A Poem . . .* (Dublin: George Risk, 1730).

Godwin, William, *Things as They Are; or The Adventures of Caleb William* (1794) (London: Penguin, 2005).

Godwin, William, *The Enquirer: Reflections on Education, Manners, and Literature in a Series of Essays* (1797) (New York: Augustus M. Kelley, 1965).

Goncourt, E. and J. de, *L'Italie d'hier. Notes de voyages, 1855–1865* (Paris: Charpentier and Fasquelle, 1894).

Gordon, W. J., 'Trance', *The Leisure Hour* (June 1887), 393–5.

Gray, Henry, *Anatomy, Descriptive and Surgical* (London: s.n., 1875).

Gray, John, *The Theory of Dreams, in Which an Inquiry is Made into the Powers and Faculties of the Human Mind, as They are Illustrated in the Most Remarkable Dreams in Sacred and Profane History* (London: F. C. and J. Rivington, 1808).

Green, Thomas, *Extracts from the Diary of a Lover of Literature* (Ipswich: s.n., 1810).

Grosley, P. J., *New Observations on Italy and its Inhabitants, written in French by two Swedish Gentlemen*, trans. Thomas Nugent, L.L.D. (London: Davis and C. Reymers, 1769).

H. I., *The Phantom of the Cloister; or, the Mysterious Manuscript* (London: Minerva Press, 1795).

Hamley, Sir Edward Bruce, 'A Recent Confession of an Opium-Eater', *Blackwood's Edinburgh Magazine*, 80/494 (December 1856), 629–36.

Harrison, James Bower, *The Medical Aspects of Death, and the Medical Aspects of the Human Mind* (London: Longman, Brown, Green, and Longmans, 1852).

Hartmann, Franz, *Buried Alive: Examination into the Occult Causes of Apparent Death, Trance and Catalepsy* (Boston: s.n., 1895).

Hood, Thomas, *The Complete Poetical Works of Thomas Hood*, ed. Walter Jerrold (London: Henry Frowde, 1906).

Hunter, William, *Two introductory lectures, Delivered by Dr. William Hunter, to his Last Course of Anatomical Lectures, at his Theatre in Windmill Street: as they were left Corrected for the Press by himself. To which are Added, Some Papers Relating to Dr. Hunter's Intended Plan, for Establishing a Museum in London, for the Improvement of Anatomy, Surgery, and Physic* (London: Printed by order of the Trustees, for J. Johnson, 1784).

J. W. R., 'Cremation and Premature Burial', *British Architect* (20 May 1896), 201.

Jebb, John, *Select cases of the disorder commonly termed the paralysis of the lower extremities. To which is added, a case of catalepsy* (London: s.n., 1783).

Jevons, Pr., 'Cruelty to Animals – A Study in Sociology', *The Fortnightly Review*, 19 (January–June 1876), 671–84.

Johnson, Samuel, *A Journey to the Western Islands of Scotland* (Dublin: J. Williams, 1775).

Knox, John Frederick, *The Anatomist's Instructor, and Museum Companion: Being Practical Directions for the Formation and Subsequent Management of Anatomical Museums* (Edinburgh: Black, 1836).

Lasègue, Ernest-Charles, 'Catalepsies Partielles et Passagères', *Archives Générales de Médecine* (Juillet 1865), 385–402.

Le Guern, Hyacinthe, *Rosoline, ou les Mystères de la tombe, recueil historique d'événements nécessitant qu'on prenne des précautions pour bien constater l'intervalle qui peut s'écouler entre la mort imparfaite et la mort absolue* (Paris: s.n., 1834).

Lermina, Jules, 'La Deux Fois Morte' (1895), in *Petit Musée des Horreurs: Nouvelles Fantastiques, Cruelles et Macabres*, ed. Nathalie Prince (Paris: Robert Laffont, 2008), pp. 679–716.

[Lewis, M. G., et al.], *Tales of Terror and Wonder*, ed. Henry Morley (1887) (s.l.: Routledge, 1889).

Lewis, Matthew, *The Monk* (1797) (Oxford: Oxford University Press, 1980).

Lewis, Matthew (ed.), *Tales of Wonder* (s.l.: Bulmer, 1801).

Lynch, Martin H., 'Case of Catalepsy Ushering in Mania during Pregnancy, with remarks', *The Lancet*, 31/804 (26 January 1839), 641–4.

Mac Gregor, George, *The History of Burke and Hare, and of the Resurrectionist Times* (Glasgow and London: Thomas D. Morison; Hamilton, Adams and Co., 1884).

Maturin, Charles Robert, *Melmoth the Wanderer* (1820) (London: Penguin, 2011).

Maudsley, Henry, *Body and Mind: An Inquiry into Their Connection and Mutual Influence, Specially in Reference to Mental Disorders* (London: Macmillan, 1870).

Maudsley, Henry, *The Pathology of Mind* (1857) (New York: D. Appleton and Co., 1880).

Maupassant, Guy de, 'Le Tic' (1884), in *Contes fantastiques complets*, ed. Anne Richter (Verviers: Gérard et Cie, 1973), pp. 193–9.

Mayo, Herbert ['MacDavus'], 'Letters on the Truth contained in Popular Superstitions: Vampirism', *Blackwood's Edinburgh Magazine*, 61 (1847), 432–40.

Morrison, Robert and Chris Baldick (eds), *Tales of Terror from Blackwood's Magazine* (Oxford: Oxford University Press, 1995).

Myers, W. H. Frederic, *Human Personality and Its Survival of Bodily Death* (London: Longmans, 1907).

Nordau, Max Simon, *Degeneration* (1893), trans. from the 2nd edn (s.l.: William Heinemann, 1896).

Pae, David, *Mary Paterson; Or, the Fatal Error. A Story of the Burke and Hare Murders* (London: Fred. Farrah, 1866).

Palmer, John, *The Haunted Cavern; A Caledonian Tale* (London: s.n., 1796).

Petetin, Jacques Henri Désiré, *Électricité animale, prouvée par la découverte des phénomènes physiques et moraux de la Catalepsie hystérique, et de ses variétés; et par les bons effets de l'Électricité animale dans le traitement de ces maladies* (Paris: Brunot-Labbé, 1808).

Petetin, Jacques Henri Désiré, *Mémoire sur la découverte des phénomènes que présentent la catalepsie et le somnambulisme, symptômes de l'affection hystérique essentielle, avec des recherches sur la cause physique de ces phénomènes* (s.l.: s.n., 1787).

Philogamus, *The Present State of Matrimony: Or, The Real Cause of Conjugal Infidelity and Unhappy Marriages. In a Letter to a Friend. With some Reflections on the State of Matrimony among the Antient Greeks and Romans; and a View of their manner of Educating their young Ladies, compared with the Modern Practice* (London: John Hawkins, 1739).

Piozzi, Hester Lynch, *Observations and Reflections Made in the Course of a Journey through France, Italy and Germany*, ed. Herbert Barrows (Ann Arbor: University of Michigan Press, 1967).

Poe, Edgar Allan, *Tales of Mystery and Imagination* (Ware: Wordsworth, 1993).

Polidori, John William et al., *The Vampyre, and Other Tales of the Macabre*, ed. Robert Morrison and Chris Baldick (Oxford University Press, 1998).

Proby, William Charles, *Spirit of the Castle. A Romance* (London: Crosby and Letterman, 1800).

Puel, Timothée, *De la catalepsie* (Paris: J.-B. Baillière, 1856).

Quincey, Thomas de, *Confessions of an English Opium-Eater* (1821) (Oxford: Oxford University Press, 1998).

Radcliffe, Ann, *A Journey Made in the Summer of 1794, through Holland and the Western Frontier of Germany, with a Return down the Rhine: To which are added Observations during a Tour of the Lakes of Lancashire, Westmoreland and Cumberland* (London: G. G. and J. Robinson, 1795).

Radcliffe, Ann, *The Mysteries of Udolpho* (1794) (Oxford: Oxford University Press, 1980).

Radcliffe, Ann, *The Romance of the Forest* (1791), ed. Chloe Chard (Oxford: Oxford University Press, 2009).

Radcliffe, Ann, *A Sicilian Romance* (1790), ed. Devendra P. Varma (New York: Arno Press, 1972).

Ramond, Louis-François de Carbonnières, *Observations faites dans les Pyrénées, pour servir de suite à des observations sur les Alpes, insérées dans une traduction des lettres de W. Coxe, sur la Suisse* (Paris: s.n., 1789).

Reade, Charles, *Hard Cash. A Matter-of-Fact Romance* (London: s.n., 1863).

Reeve, Clara, *The Old English Baron: A Gothic Story; also The Castle of Otranto: A Gothic Story by Horace Walpole* (London: J. C. Nimmo and Bain, 1883).

Reynolds, George William MacArthur, *Faust: A Romance of the Secret Tribunals* (1845–6) (London: J. Dicks, 1883).

Reynolds, George William MacArthur, *The Mysteries of the Court of London* (1848–56), new edn (London: John Dicks, n.d).

Reynolds, George William MacArthur, *The Mysteries of London* (1845) (Kansas City: Valancourt Books, 2013).

Reynolds, George William MacArthur, *The Necromancer* (1852) (London: J. Dicks, 1884).

Reynolds, George William MacArthur, *Wagner, the Wehr-Wolf* (1846–47), ed. Dick Collins (Ware: Wordsworth Editions, 2006).

Richardson, Samuel, *Clarissa; or, the History of a Young Lady* (1747–48) (London: Penguin, 2011).

Ritchie, James Ewing, *The Night Side of London*, 2nd edn (London: s.n., (1857) 1858).

Sade, D. A. F., *Les Cent-vingt Journées de Sodome*, in *Œuvres complètes* (Paris: J. J. Pauvert, 1986), vol. 1.

Sade, D. A. F., *Histoire de Juliette ou les prospérités du vice*, in *Œuvres complètes* (Paris: Cercle du livre précieux, 1963), vol. 8.

Sade, D. A. F., *Justine; or Good Conduct Well-Chastized* (1791) (Paris: Olympia Press, 1954).

Sade, D. A. F., *The Story of Juliette; or Vice Amply Rewarded* (1801) (Paris: Olympia Press, 1958–61).

Sade, D. A. F., *Voyage d'Italie* (1775–6), in *Œuvres complètes* (Paris: Tchou, 1965).

Shelley, Mary, *Frankenstein; or the Modern Prometheus* (1831) (London: Penguin, 2003).

Shelley, Mary, *Frankenstein; or the Modern Prometheus* (1831), in *Three Gothic Novels*, ed. Peter Fairclough (London: Penguin, 1986).

Shelley, Percy Bysshe, *Alastor; Or, the Spirit of Solitude: and Other Poems* (London: Baldwin, Cradock and Joy; Carpenter and Son, 1816).

Shelley, Percy Bysshe, *History of A Six Weeks' Tour through a part of France, Switzerland, Germany, and Holland: with letters descriptive of a sail round the Lake of Geneva and of the Glaciers of Chamouni* (London: T. Hookham, Jun. and C. and J. Ollier, 1817).

Southerne, Thomas, *Isabella; Or, The Fatal Marriage. A Play. Alter'd from Southern. At it is now performing at the Theatre-Royal in Drury-Lane* (London: J. and R. Tonson, 1758).

Southey, Robert, *The Poetical Works of Robert Southey, Complete in One Volume* (Paris: A. and W. Galignagni, 1829).

Smith, Thomas Southwood, 'The Use of the Dead to the Living', *The Westminster Review*, 2 (1824), 59–97.

Stendhal, *Journal 1810–1811* (Paris: Le Divan, 1937).

Stephen, Leslie, 'The Decay of Murder', *The Cornhill Magazine*, 20 (December 1869), 722–33.

Stevenson, Robert Louis, 'The Body-Snatcher' (1884), in *The Story of a Lie: And Other Tales* (Boston: Herbert B. Turner and Co., 1904), pp. 237–76.

Stevenson, Robert Louis, 'The Strange Case of Dr Jekyll and Mr Hyde' (1886), in *Dr Jekyll and Mr Hyde, The Merry Men and Other Stories* (Ware: Wordsworth Classics, 1993), pp. 3–62.

Stewart, J. L., 'Wilkie Collins as a Novelist', *Rose-Belford's Canadian Monthly and National Review*, 1 (November 1878), 586–601.

Stoker, Bram, *Dracula* (1897), ed. Nina Auerbach and David S. Skal (New York and London: Norton and Co., 1997).

[Thomson, Henry], 'Le Revenant', *Blackwood's Edinburgh Magazine*, 23/124 (April 1827), 409–16.

Timbs, John, *Curiosities of London* (London: David Bogue, 1855).

Tourette, Gilles de la, *L'Hypnotisme et les états analogues du point de vue médico-légal* (Paris: Plon, 1887).

Wahltuch, Adolphe, *On Catalepsy: Read before the medical section of the Manchester Royal Institute* (London: John Churchill and Sons, 1869).

Walpole, Horace, *The Castle of Otranto*, in *Three Gothic Novels*, ed. Peter Fairclough (London: Penguin, 1986).

Warren, Samuel, *Passages from the Diary of a Late Physician*, 3 vols, 5th edn (Edinburgh: William Blackwood and Sons; London: T. Cadell, 1838).

Watterville, A., 'Sleep and its Counterfeits', *Fortnightly Review* (May 1887), 732–42.

Wells, H. G., *The Invisible Man* (1897), in *Six Novels* (San Diego: Canterbury Classics, 2012), pp. 145–247.

Wilkinson, Sarah Scudgell, *The Priory of St Clair; or Spectre of the Murdered Nun* (London: R. Harrild, 1811).

Williamson, Jas R., 'Hypnotic Trance and Premature Burial', *The Speaker* (21 September 1895), 315–16.

Winslow, Jacobus Benignus, *Dissertation sur l'incertitude des signes de la mort et l'abus des enterrements précipités*, ed. and trans. Jean-Jacques Bruhier d'Ablaincourt (Paris: s.n., 1742).

Winslow, Jacobus Benignus, *The Uncertainty of the Signs of Death, and the danger of precipitate interments and dissection* (London: M. Cooper, 1746).

Wordsworth, William, *The Prelude* (1805), *The Oxford Authors: William Wordsworth*, ed. Stephen Gill (Oxford and New York: Oxford University Press, 1990), pp. 375–590.

Zola, Emile, *La Mort d'Olivier Bécaille* (1884) (Paris: Librio, 2004).

Secondary sources

Alberti, Samuel J. M., *Morbid Curiosities: Medical Museums in Nineteenth-Century Britain* (Oxford: Oxford University Press, 2011).

Alberti, Samuel J. M., 'The Museum Affect: Visiting Collections of Anatomy and Natural History', in Aileen Fyfe and Bernard Lightman (eds), *Science in the Marketplace: Nineteenth-Century Sites and Experiences* (Chicago and London: University of Chicago Press, 2007), pp. 371–403.

Alberti, Samuel J. M., 'The Organic Museum: The Hunterian and other Collections at the Royal College of Surgeons in England', in Samuel J. M. M. Alberti and Elizabeth Hallam (eds), *Medical Museums: Past, Present, Future* (London: Royal College of Surgeons, 2013), pp. 17–29.

Asma, S. T., *On Monsters* (Oxford: Oxford University Press, 2009).

Bacopoulos-Viau, Alexandra, 'La Danse des corps figés. Catalepsie et imaginaire médical au XIXᵉ siècle', *Revue d'histoire du XIXᵉ siècle*, 44/1 (2012), 165–84.

Baldick, Chris, *In Frankenstein's Shadow: Myth, Monstrosity, and Nineteenth-Century Writing* (1987) (Oxford: Clarendon Press, 1996).

Barker-Benfield, G. J., *The Culture of Sensibility: Sex and Society in Eighteenth-Century Britain* (Chicago and London: University of Chicago Press, 1996).

Bates, A. W., 'Dr Kahn's Museum: Obscene Anatomy in Victorian London', *Journal of the Royal Society of Medicine*, 99 (December 2006), 618–24.

Bates, A. W., '"Indecent and Demoralising Representations": Public Anatomy Museums in Mid-Victorian England', *Medical History*, 52 (2008), 1–22.

Berthin, Christine, *Gothic Hauntings: Melancholy Crypts and Textual Ghosts* (Basingstoke: Palgrave Macmillan, 2010).

Blakey, Dorothy, *The Minerva Press, 1790–1820* (London: The Bibliographical Society at the University Press, Oxford, 1939 (for 1935)).

Bondeson, Jan, *Buried Alive: The Terrifying History of Our Most Primal Fear* (2001) (New York: Norton, 2002).

Bronfen, Elisabeth, *Over Her Dead Body: Death, Femininity and the Aesthetic* (Manchester: Manchester University Press, 1992).

Brooks, Peter, *Body Work: Objects of Desire in Modern Narrative* (Cambridge, MA: Harvard University Press, 1993).

Bruno, Giuliana, *Atlas of Emotion: Journeys in Art, Architecture and Film* (London: Verso, 2002).

Bynum, W. F., *Science and the Practice of Medicine in the Nineteenth Century* (Cambridge: Cambridge University Press, 1994).

Byrne, Katherine, *Tuberculosis and the Victorian Literary Imagination* (Cambridge: Cambridge University Press, 2011).

Carey, John, *The Violent Effigy: A Study of Dickens' Imagination* (London: Faber and Faber, 2008).

Carol, Anne, *Les Médecins et la mort, XIXe-XXe siècle* (s.l.: Aubier, 2004).

Carroll, Victoria, 'Natural History on Display: The Collection of Charles Waterton', in Aileen Fyfe and Bernard Lightman (eds), *Science in the Marketplace: Nineteenth-Century Sites and Experiences* (Chicago and London: University of Chicago Press, 2007), pp. 271–300.

Ceglia, Francesco de, 'Rotten Corpses, a Disembowelled Woman, a Flayed Man. Images of the Body from the End of the 17th to the Beginning of the 19th Century. Florentine Wax Models in the First-Hand Accounts of Visitors', *Perspectives on Science*, 14/4 (2006), 417–56.

Chamberlain, Andrew T. and Michael Marker Pearson (eds), *Earthly Remains: The History and Science of Preserved Human Bodies* (London: British Museum Press, 2001).

Chapman, Pauline, *Madame Tussaud's Chamber of Horrors: Two Hundred Years of Crime* (London: Constable, 1984).

Coyer, Megan, *Literature, Medicine and the Nineteenth-Century Periodical Press: Blackwood's Edinburgh Magazine, 1817–1858* (Edinburgh: Edinburgh University Press, 2017).

Craske, Matthew, '"Unwholesome" and "pornographic": A Reassessment of the Place of Rackstrow's Museum in the Story of Eighteenth-century Anatomical Collection and Exhibition', *Journal of the History of Collections*, 23/1 (2011), 75–99.

Cunningham, Andrew, *The Anatomist Anatomis'd: An Experimental Discipline in Enlightenment Europe* (Farnham: Ashgate, 2010).

Daston, Lorraine and Katharine Park, *Wonders and the Order of Nature, 1150–1750* (New York: Zone Books, 2001).

Davie, Neil, 'Lombroso and the "Men of Real Science": British Reactions, 1886–1918', in Paul Knepper and P. J. Ystehede (eds), *The Cesare Lombroso Handbook* (London: Routledge, 2013), pp. 342–60.

DeLucia, JoEllen, 'Transnational Aesthetics in Ann Radcliffe's *A Journey Made in the Summer of 1794* [. . .] (1795)', in Dale Townshend and Angela Wright (eds), *Ann Radcliffe, Romanticism and the Gothic* (Cambridge: Cambridge University Press, 2014), pp. 135–50.

Desmond, Adrian, *The Politics of Evolution: Morphology, Medicine, and Reform in Radical London* (Chicago: University of Chicago Press, 1989).

Dijkstra, Bram, *Idols of Perversity: Fantasies of Feminine Evil in Fin-de-Siècle Culture* (Oxford: Oxford University Press, 1986).

Englestein, Stefani, *Anxious Anatomy: The Conception of the Human Form in Literary and Naturalist Discourse* (New York: State University of New York Press, 2008).

Feldman, P. R. and D. Scott-Kilvert (eds), *The Journals of Mary Shelley*, 2 vols (Oxford: Clarendon Press, 1987).

Figlio, Karl, 'Theories of Perception and the Physiology of Mind in the Late Eighteenth Century', *History of Science*, 12 (1975), 177–212.

Foucault, Michel, *The Birth of the Clinic: An Archaeology of Medical Perception* (1973), trans. A. M. Sheridan (London: Routledge, 2000).

Gamer, Michael, *Romanticism and the Gothic: Genre, Reception, and Canon Formation* (Cambridge: Cambridge University Press, 2000).

Gatrell, Victor A. C., *The Hanging Tree: Execution and the English People 1770–1868* (Oxford: Oxford University Press, 1994).

Gilbert, Pamela K., *Disease, Desire, and the Body in Victorian Women's Popular Novels* (Cambridge: Cambridge University Press, 1997).

Goldstein, Jan, *Console and Classify: The French Psychiatric Profession in the Nineteenth Century* (1987) (Chicago and London: University of Chicago Press, 2001).

Gorer, Geoffrey, *Death, Grief and Mourning in Contemporary Britain* (London: Cresset Press, 1965).

Grimes, Hilary, *The Late Victorian Gothic: Mental Science, the Uncanny and Scenes of Writing* (Farnham: Ashgate, 2011).

Guerrini, Anita, 'Inside the Charnel House: The Display of Skeletons in Europe, 1500–1800', in Rina Knoeff and Robert Zwijnenberg (eds), *The Fate of Anatomical Collections* (Farnham, Burlington: Ashgate, 2015), pp. 93–109.

Harries, Elizabeth Wanning, *The Unfinished Manner: Essays on the Fragment in the Late-Eighteenth Century* (Charlottesville and London: University Press of Virginia, 1994).

Haslam, Fiona, *From Hogarth to Rowlandson: Medicine in Art in Eighteenth-Century Britain* (Liverpool: Liverpool University Press, 1996).

Hillman, D. A. and Carla Mazzio (eds), *The Body in Parts: Fantasies of Corporeality in Early Modern Europe* (New York and London: Routledge, 1997).

Hotz, Mary Elizabeth, *Literary Remains: Representations of Death and Burial in Victorian England* (New York: State University of New York, 2009).

Hurley, Kelly, *The Gothic Body: Sexuality, Materialism and Degeneration at the Fin de Siècle* (1996) (Cambridge: Cambridge University Press, 2004).

Hurren, Elizabeth T., *Dying for Victorian Medicine: English Anatomy and Its Trade in the Dead Poor, c.1834–1929* (Basingstoke: Palgrave Macmillan, 2012).

Kennedy, J. Gerard, 'Poe and Magazine Writing of Premature Burial', *Studies in the American Renaissance* (1977), 165–78.

Kennedy, Meegan, 'The Ghost in the Clinic: Gothic Medicine and Curious Fiction in Samuel Warren's *Diary of a Late Physician*', *Victorian Literature and Culture*, 32/2 (2004), 327–51.

Kennedy, Meegan, *Revising the Clinic: Vision and Representation in Victorian Medical Narrative and the Novel* (Columbus: Ohio State University, 2010).

Kilgour, Maggie, *The Rise of the Gothic Novel* (New York and London: Routledge, 1995).

Lawlor, Clark, *Consumption and Literature: The Making of the Romantic Disease* (Basingstoke: Palgrave, 2006).

Lecercle, Jean-Jacques, *Frankenstein: Mythe et Philosophie* (Paris: PUF, 1988).

Lemire, Michel, *Artistes et Mortels* (Paris: Chabaud, 1990).

Lévy, Maurice, *Le Roman 'Gothique' anglais, 1764–1824* (Paris: Albin Michel, 1995).

Linebaugh, Peter, *Albion's Fatal Tree: Crime and Society in Eighteenth-Century England* (London: Allen Lane, 1975).

Levine, George and U. C. Knoepflmacher (eds), *The Endurance of 'Frankenstein'* (Berkeley: University of California Press, 1979).

Mangham, Andrew, 'Buried Alive: The Gothic Awakening of Taphephobia', *Journal of Literature and Science*, 3/1 (2010), 10–22.

McCraker-Flesher, Caroline, *The Doctor Dissected: A Cultural Autopsy of the Burke and Hare Murders* (Oxford: Oxford University Press, 2012).

Mazzolini, Renato G., 'Plastic Anatomies and Artificial Dissections', in Soraya de Chadarevian and Nick Hopwood (eds), *Models: The Third Dimension of Science* (Stanford: Stanford University Press, 2004), pp. 43–70.

McIntyre, Clara Frances, *Ann Radcliffe in Relation to her Time, Yale Studies in English*, 62 (New Haven: Yale University Press; London: Humphrey Milfort, Oxford University Press), 1920.

Marshall, Tim, *Murdering to Dissect: Grave-Robbing,* Frankenstein *and the Anatomy Literature* (Manchester: Manchester University Press, 1995).

Maerker, Anna, 'Anatomy and Public Enlightenment: The Florentine Museo "La Specola"', in Samuel J. M. M. Alberti and Elizabeth Hallam (eds), *Medical Museums: Past, Present, Future* (London: Royal College of Surgeons, 2013), pp. 88–101.

Maulitz, Russell C., *Morbid Appearances: The Anatomy of Pathology in the Early Nineteenth Century* (Cambridge: Cambridge University Press, 1987).

Mellor, Anne K., *Mary Shelley: Her Life, Her Fiction, Her Monsters* (1988) (London: Routledge, 1989).

Messbarger, Rebecca, *The Lady Anatomist: The Life and Works of Anna Morandi Manzolini* (Chicago: University of Chicago Press, 2010).

Messbarger, Rebecca, 'Waxing Poetic: Anna Morandi Manzolini's anatomical sculptures', *Configurations,* 9 (2001), 65–97.

Miles, Robert, *Gothic Writing, 1750–1820: A Genealogy* (1993), 2nd edn (Manchester and New York: Manchester University Press, 2002).

Nochlin, Linda, *The Body in Pieces: The Fragment as a Metaphor of Modernity* (London: Thames and Hudson, 1994).

O'Connor, Erin, *Raw Material: Producing Pathology in Victorian Culture* (Durham and London: Duke University Press, 2000).

Otis, Laura, 'Howled out of the Country: Wilkie Collins and H. G. Wells Retry David Ferrier', in Anne Stiles (ed.), *Neurology and Literature, 1860–1920* (Basingstoke: Palgrave, 2007), pp. 27–51.

Page, Norman, *Wilkie Collins: The Critical Heritage* (London: Routledge, 1974).

Pancino, Claudia, 'Questioni di genere nell'anatomia plastica del Settecento bolognese', *Studi tanatologici,* 2/2 (2006), 317–32.

Pedlar, Valerie, 'Experimentation or Exploitation? The Investigations of David Ferrier, Dr. Benjulia and Dr. Seward', *Interdisciplinary Science Reviews,* 28/3 (September 2003), 169–74.

Pickstone, John V., *Ways of Knowing: A New History of Science, Technology and Medicine* (2000) (Chicago: University of Chicago Press, 2001).

Pilbeam, Pamela, *Madame Tussaud and the History of Waxworks* (London and New York: Hambledon and London, 2003).

Plas, Régine, *Naissance d'une science humaine: la psychologie. Les psychologues et 'le merveilleux psychique'* (Rennes: Presses Universitaires de Rennes, 2000).

Porter, Roy, *Bodies Politic: Disease, Death and Doctors in Britain, 1650–1900* (London: Reaktion Books, 2001).

Porter, Roy, *Disease, Medicine and Society in England, 1550–1860* (1987) (Cambridge: Cambridge University Press, 1999).

Porter, Roy, *Flesh in the Age of Reason: How the Enlightenment Transformed the Way We See Our Bodies and Souls* (London: Penguin, 2003).

Porter, Roy, *Quacks: Fakers and Charlatans in English Medicine* (1989) (Stroud: Tempus, 2001).

Praz, Mario, *The Romantic Agony* (1933) (London and New York: Oxford University Press, 1970).

Punter, David, *The Literature of Terror. Vol. 1. The Gothic Tradition* (New York: Routledge, 1996).

Reiser, Stanley Joel, *Medicine and the Reign of Technology* (1978) (Cambridge: Cambridge University Press, 1981).

Richards, Thomas, *The Imperial Archive: Knowledge and the Fantasy of Empire* (London and New York: Verso, 1993).

Richardson, Ruth, *Death, Dissection and the Destitute* (1987) (Chicago and London: University of Chicago Press, 2000).

Richardson, Ruth, *The Making of Mr. Gray's Anatomy. Bodies, Books, Fortune, Fame* (Oxford: Oxford University Press, 2008).

Rifkin, Benjamin A., Michael J. Ackerman and Judith Folkenberg, *Human Anatomy: Depicting the Body from the Renaissance to Today* (London: Thames and Hudson, 2006).

Rothfield, Lawrence, *Vital Signs: Medical Realism in Nineteenth-Century Fiction* (Princeton: Princeton University Press, 1992).

Ruston, Sharon, *Creating Romanticism: Case Studies in the Literature, Science and Medicine of the 1790s* (Basingstoke: Palgrave Macmillan, 2013).

Ruston, Sharon, *Shelley and Vitality* (2005) (Houndmills and New York: Palgrave Macmillan, 2012).

Sappol, Michael, *A Traffic of Dead Bodies. Anatomy and Embodied Social Identity in Nineteenth-Century America* (2002) (Princeton and Oxford: Princeton University Press, 2004).

Shelton, Don, 'Sir Anthony Carlisle and Mrs Carver', *Romantic Textualities. Literature and Print Culture, 1780–1840*, 19 (Winter 2009), 54–69.

Showalter, Elaine, 'Syphilis, Sexuality and the fiction of the *Fin de Siècle*', in Ruth Bernard Yeazell (ed.), *Sex, Politics and Science in the Nineteenth Century* (Baltimore: John Hopkins University Press, 1986), pp. 88–115.

Smith, Alison, *The Victorian Nude: Sexuality, Morality and Art* (Manchester: Manchester University Press, 1996).

Smith, Andrew, *Gothic Death, 1740–1914. A Literary History* (Manchester: Manchester University Press, 2016).

Sparks, Tabitha, *The Doctor in the Victorian Novel: Family Practices* (Farnham and Burlington: Ashgate, 2009).

Stiles, Anne, *Popular Fiction and Brain Science in the Late Nineteenth Century* (Cambridge: Cambridge University Press, 2012).

Sugg, Richard, *Murder After Death: Literature and Anatomy in Early Modern England* (Ithaca: Cornell University Press, 2007).

Summerscale, Kate, *The Suspicions of Mr Whicher* (2008) (London, Berlin, New York: Bloomsbury, 2009).

Tague, Ingrid H., *Animal Companions: Pets and Social Change in Eighteenth-Century Britain* (University Park, PA: Pennsylvania State University Press, 2015).

Talairach-Vielmas, Laurence, 'Du cadavre en putréfaction au corps enterré vivant: Le rôle du corps mort chez Wilkie Collins', in Anne Carol and Isabelle Renaudet (eds), *La Mort à l'œuvre: Usages et représentations du cadavre dans l'art* (Aix-en-Provence: Publications de l'Université de Provence, 2013), pp. 137–53.

Talairach-Vielmas, Laurence, '"I have bottled babes unborn": The Gothic, Medical Collections and Nineteenth-Century Culture', in 'Gothic and Medical Humanities', ed. Sara Wasson, a special edition of *Gothic Studies*, 17/1 (2015), 28–42.

Talairach-Vielmas, Laurence, '"In all its Hideous and Appalling Nakedness and Truth": The Reception of some Anatomical Collections in Georgian and Victorian England', *Medicina nei Secoli, Journal of History of Medicine*, 27/2 (2015), 553–74.

Talairach-Vielmas, Laurence, *Wilkie Collins, Medicine and the Gothic* (Cardiff: University of Wales Press, 2009).

Todd, Dennis, *Imagining Monsters: Miscreations of the Self in Eighteenth-century England* (Chicago and London: University of Chicago Press, 1995).

Tompkins, J. M. S., 'Ramond de Carbonnières, Grosley and Mrs Radcliffe', *Review of English Studies*, 5/19 (July 1929), 294–301.

Turner, Trevor, 'Henry Maudsley: Psychiatrist, Philosopher and Entrepreneur', in W. F. Bynum et al. (eds), *The Anatomy of Madness: Essays in the History of Psychiatry*, vol. 3 (London: Routledge, 1988), pp. 151–89.

Van Sant, Ann Jessie, *Eighteenth-Century Sensibility and the Novel. The Senses in Social Context* (Cambridge: Cambridge University Press, 1993).

Vila, Anne C., *Enlightenment and Pathology* (Baltimore and London: John Hopkins University Press, 1998).

Warner, Marina, *Phantasmagoria: Spirit Visions, Metaphors, and Media into the Twenty-First Century* (Oxford: Oxford University Press, 2006).

Westover, Paul, *Necromanticism: Travelling to Meet the Dead, 1750–1860* (Basingstoke: Palgrave Macmillan, 2012).

Williams, Anne, '"Mummy possest": Sadism and Sensibility in *Frankenstein*', in *Frankenstein's Dream. Romantic Circles Praxis Series* (2003). Available at *www.rc.umd.edu/praxis/frankenstein/williams/williams.html*. Accessed on 28 June 2015.

Wolfreys, Julian, *Victorian Haunting: Spectrality, Gothic, the Uncanny and Literature* (Basingstoke: Palgrave Macmillan, 2002).

Wood, Jane *Passion and Pathology in Victorian Fiction* (Oxford: Oxford University Press, 2001).

Youngquist, Paul, *Monstrosities: Bodies and British Romanticism* (Minneapolis and London: University of Minnesota Press, 2003).

Index

∾

Index

Index

Index

Specola museum 50, 52, 61–4,
    68–9, 169, 237 n. 42
Spencer, Herbert 193
Spirit of the Castle, The 21
*Spirit of Turretville or the Mysterious
    Resemblance, The* 21
Spurzheim, Johann Gaspar 168
Stapleton, Edward (case of) 179,
    252 n. 36
Stendhal 61–2
Stevenson, Robert Louis 6, 11,
    130–1, 170, 210, 211, 213,
    261 n. 12
  'The Body-Snatcher' 11, 130–1
  *Strange Case of Dr Jekyll and
    Mr Hyde* 6, 131, 170, 211,
    212
Stoker, Bram 6, 12, 131, 195–208,
    209, 210, 212
Dracula 12, 131, 195–208, 209
suspended animation 178, 190
  see also catalepsy; sleepwalking;
    somnambulism
Sylvester, Mrs 77
syphilis 141, 144, 164, 226 n. 21,
    258 n. 110

taphephobia 196
Thierry, François 173
Thomson, Henry 252 n. 38
Thornton, Abraham 77
Tourette, Gilles de la 193, 256 n. 77
Tussaud, Madame 76, 78, 80, 81,
    82–3
Towne, Joseph 50, 54, 237 n. 42
Trollope, Anthony 237 n. 39
tuberculosis 202, 258 n. 109
Tyburn 19, 95, 126, 220 n. 14

unconscious cerebration 191, 197,
    208

Val-de-Grâce (military hospital)
    140
vampirism 196–208
Vesalius, Andreas 5, 16–17, 18,
    94, 119
  De humani corporis fabrica 16–17
vivisection 4, 130, 192, 207, 208,
    213
Voit, Johann Michael 192

Wahltuch, Adolphe 176
Wakefield Lunatic Asylum 192
Walpole, Horace 3, 8, 17, 18, 21,
    23, 25, 27, 31, 35, 39, 46,
    50, 55, 97, 136, 181
  The Castle of Otranto 3, 8, 17,
    18, 20–1, 22, 27, 35, 39, 97,
    181
Warren, Samuel 12, 106–9,
    146–8, 182–6, 187, 189
  *Passages from the Diary of a Late
    Physician* 106–9, 146–8,
    182–6
Wells, H. G. 6, 212–13
  The Invisible Man 6, 212–13
  The Island of Dr Moreau 212
Whytt, Robert 4
Wilkinson, Sarah Scudgell 188
Williams, Thomas 95, 112
  see also Bishop, John; Italian
    Boy (case of)
Winslow, Jacob B. 173
Wollstonecraft, Mary 49
Wordsworth, William 67
Wright, Patience 77, 230 n. 47

X-rays 6, 211

Zola, Emile 190, 247 n. 103
Zummo, Gaetano Giulio 52, 54,
    61, 63–4